Friendship and the Political

Kierkegaard, Nietzsche, Schmitt

Graham M. Smith

imprint-academic.com

Copyright © Graham M. Smith, 2011

The moral rights of the author have been asserted.
No part of this publication may be reproduced in any form
without permission, except for the quotation of brief passages
in criticism and discussion.

Published in the UK by
Imprint Academic, PO Box 200, Exeter EX5 5YX, UK
Published in the USA by
Imprint Academic, Philosophy Documentation Center
PO Box 7147, Charlottesville, VA 22906-7147, USA

ISBN 9781845402464

A CIP catalogue record for this book is available from the
British Library and US Library of Congress

Contents

Acknowledgements	v
Introduction	vii
Chapter One: Relocating Friendship	1

Part I: The Foundations of Friendship

Chapter Two: *Plato*	19
Chapter Three: *Aristotle*	45

Part II: Three Modern Transformations

Chapter Four: *Kierkegaard*	79
Chapter Five: *Nietzsche*	129
Chapter Six: *Schmitt*	187
Chapter Seven: Friendship and the Political	225
Bibliography	241
Index	253

Acknowledgements

I suspect that most books are ultimately the product of more than one mind. An author of a book on friendship should perhaps be more aware of this than most—nevertheless, such an author must accept sole responsibility for what has been produced. My own interest in friendship as a *political* idea began two decades ago. It is clear that it shall occupy me for a good time to come. As a result, there are countless people—both professional and personal—who have shaped my thinking and supported my endeavours. Some, however, have made a particular contribution that I would like to explicitly recognise here. I have been fortunate enough to have benefitted from the conversation of Felix Berenskotter, Oleg Kharkhordin, Andrea Oelsner, Evgeny Roshchin, Sibyl Schwarzenbach, Gabriella Slomp, Antoine Vion, and Evert van der Zweerde. Several people were generous enough to give their time to read and comment on earlier versions of chapters. Thomas Wolstenholme and Alison Stone offered comments on the chapters on Kierkegaard and Nietzsche, respectively. I am also grateful to Andrew W. Neal whose comments on a previous version of the chapter on Schmitt encouraged me to revise and clarify my own thinking. Andrew has engaged and challenged me in conversation on this (and related) topics for over a decade now. In this respect I am also grateful for the insight obtained from numerous conversations with Adam David Morton, who continues to be a critical but open-minded interlocutor. I am happy to recognize my debt to them both. Patrick Bishop, Alan Metcalfe, and Steven Dempster have also supported me with the encouragement at well-timed moments. Anthony Freeman of Imprint Academic also deserves my gratitude. He has shown patience to an author who has not always been as punctual as he might.

Two people have been a continuing source of companionship in my journey into friendship and the political. Preston King introduced me to this topic, and continues to provide insight concerning the significance of this topic and its many questions. A British Council grant enabled me to spend some time visiting Heather Devere in New Zealand where many productive conversations took place during the early stages of writing. Heather was not only generous enough to read and comment on the entire manuscript, she has also been an invaluable source of encouragement during the process of its composition. Finally, I would like to recognise the contribution that my wife Sarah has made to the production of this book. She has often given up her time so as I can make use of my own. Without her support, encouragement, and understanding this volume would never have been written at all. In recognition of this I would like to dedicate this book to our children Henry and Julian — because I know that will make Sarah happiest of all.

Introduction

Friendship was once considered indispensable to an understanding the political and to the practice of politics. Contemporary thinkers would tend to assume that this pairing is inimical. This change is in need of both explanation and analysis. It is also an outlook which is in need of re-evaluation. This book understands friendship as being a means to conceptualise the bonds between person and person. As such, it works towards the conclusion that friendship is indispensable to the analysis of the political. For without an understanding and analysis of what draws and binds persons together there can be no analysis of that which is structured around it. Friendship tends to point to the horizontal, the shared and the open. The dominant analysis of modernity tends to point to the vertical, limited and closed. Here the stress has too often been to foreground the individual at the expense of other concerns. The living sinews that connect person to person and make politics an activity have sometimes been ignored. Instead, the individual has been used as an atomistic starting point, and the tropes of power and liberty are seen as being in the possession of the individual both over and from others. Whilst there has been some benefit to such an analysis, we gain little if we mistake this part for the whole. For devoid of its connection to the other dimensions of the political, and *in the extreme case,* such an analysis is hardly political at all. In contrast, here the political is taken to indicate a concern—however minimally—with the shared relations and experience of persons. Such persons are taken to be both valuable and to be the creators of value. Friendship is thus indispensable to the political because just as friendship is understood to denote the bonds between person and person, the political is understood to denote a concern with the *shared* world of order and value. This shared world rests upon and is shaped by the bonds of friendship. How this is configured—and what is emphasised and why—is an open question.

This book offers an exploration of this link between friendship and the political. It is an attempt to begin to open this question by showing some of the resources that are available for such a theorisation. It is also a first step towards such a theorisation. **Chapter One** attempts to **relocate friendship** as a theoretical and political concern. It offers an account of how friendship is now generally thought to be separated from our understanding of the political. Here one specific kind of friendship (a personal friendship based in affection and particularity) has come to stand for our understanding of *all* friendship. However, this instance does not exhaust the varieties of friendship. Nor does it exhaust the possibilities that a general analysis offers. This chapter goes on to explore the challenges of any theorisation of the idea of friendship. Taken as a concern with the bonds between person and person, friendship is found to denote a variety of associated relations. This chapter also highlights the kinds of analytical work that friendship is being asked to perform: the identification of what holds persons together, the forms that this can take, how it can be sustained, how this contributes to our political life, and the contribution that this can make to a normative evaluation of political order.

In **Part I** (The Foundations of Friendship) attention is focused on two thinkers who might be considered to be foundational for thinking about friendship and the political: Plato and Aristotle. Of course, these are not the only two thinkers who could be considered in such a role, but they are perhaps the best known and most influential. These two thinkers are also significant insofar as they offer two contrasting patterns for friendship. **Chapter Two** takes up the thought of **Plato** where friendship sees individuals drawn to the good through each other. In Plato's thought there is only one true form of friendship, and other forms of friendship are really striving towards this or stages on the way towards it. This form of friendship is seen to act as the complement to justice. It structures the true political form binding difference harmoniously into unity. Friendship's work is not only to educate the individual friends, but for them to leave a legacy of justice and harmony for others. **Chapter Three** takes up the thought of **Aristotle.** In contrast to Plato, Aristotle recognises a variety of friendships ranging from relations between citizens, to relations in the family, to relations between those seeking to cultivate virtue. These all aim at some good, but not all friendships aim at the good in the fullest sense. Aristotle recognises that friendship does not need to be complete to be of value, and that it can have differing and limited aims. Aristotle's account sees concord playing a specific role in binding the members of a city, but he recognises that this is—in most cases—a friendship of utility. This analysis opens a space for understanding political forms which are less than perfect. Nevertheless, for Aristotle friendship in its most complete form is connected to both equality and a genuine concern for the other. Ultimately, friendship is claimed to be more desirable and more necessary than justice.

Part II (Three Modern Transformations) looks at friendship in the thought of three modern thinkers: Kierkegaard, Nietzsche, and Schmitt. Unlike many in modernity each of these thinkers has something quite explicit to say about friendship, and the bonds between person and person play a significant role in their thought. Thus, each of these thinkers attempts to rethink the basic human bonds which are denoted by friendship—although each in their own particular way. Each thinker also shows us some of the tensions and challenges to friendship in modernity, not least the increasing hold of the idea of the individual (for Kierkegaard and Nietzsche) and the nation-state (for Schmitt), the thinning of social and cultural fabric, and the view of the political (and the forms of politics) that this engenders.

Chapter Four looks at the case of **Kierkegaard**. Kierkegaard's distinctive contribution is to recast discussions about human bonding in a theistic context. For Kierkegaard how the self relates to others is a crucial question. Kierkegaard views humans as spiritual beings, and he casts the human self in a three-fold relation. All selves must relate to God and in so doing are able to properly relate to both self and others. Kierkegaard's thought thus challenges presentations of human bonding which displace this relationship and attempt to substitute it with purely human relations. For Kierkegaard, friendship (in the guise of the forms of ethical friendship proposed by the Ancients and romantic love) is a part of this pattern. Ultimately these forms of friendship are a misrelation as they base human bonding on the purely human aspects of self and the instability of human emotions. Kierkegaard finds that human friendship offers no moral task. Although a person might seek a friend, it is a matter of fortune whether they find one. Furthermore, Kierkegaard finds the reciprocity that characterises friendship a sign of selfishness. Reciprocity sees an individual offer love for only as long as it continues to be returned. Indeed, Kierkegaard suspects that the desire for the return of love is the motivation for offering love in the first place. In contrast to this Kierkegaard advocates a form of bonding that can be considered to be a kind of spiritual friendship: the neighbour. Kierkegaard urges individuals to recognise themselves as spiritual beings and to relate themselves to God. In so doing they come to recognise the commandment to love their neighbour, and thus relate to all others as spiritual equals. Kierkegaard thus sets a high demand on human sociality, a demand which might not be possible in this world.

Nietzsche is the subject of **Chapter Five**. Contrary to what is sometimes assumed about Nietzsche's views, in his thought he both entertains and finds a space for friendship—at least for some. Nietzsche reconnects friendship to the task of Philosophy. In his middle period the role of friendship tends to be one of mutual self-discovery. The right kind of friendship can be a useful aid in understanding the relationship between self, others, and the world. Furthermore, during this period it appears that shared endeavours are possible. Indeed, Nietzsche dreamed of a circle of philosophically minded friends to be realised as a part of his own life. *Thus Spoke Zarathustra* sees a shift in Nietzsche's thinking (although perhaps not his dreaming). The drama of the journey of the protagonist of this book can be seen a quest for a kind of friendship—a quest that ends in failure for Zarathustra who ends by promoting not a sharing of the self, but a radical form of self-overcoming. Now friends serve each other by becoming hard, and friendship itself is a dependency which must be overcome. Nietzsche's earlier and more suggestive hopes for friendship are thus seen to be eclipsed by his later commitment to the sovereign individual.

Chapter Six sees friendship developed in the thought of **Schmitt**. The jurist can be considered to be both an unavoidable and problematic contributor to our understanding of friendship. Schmitt must come to our attention as he is one of the few thinkers in modernity to tackle friendship. Moreover, he not only promotes friendship as a *public* category, but also places it at the very centre of his account of the political. However, any theorist who wishes to employ or draw from Schmitt's account in their own reconstruction of friendship must beware. First, it is not possible to take Schmitt's thought at face-value. Rather than offer his reader a detailed account of friendship, Schmitt deploys a 'friend-enemy' distinction as a tool of polemicisation. Moreover, it is a device which not only weaves conflict into political groups, but which structures other 'non-political' concerns in such a way that they can intensify into conflict. Second, Schmitt's thought sees friendship as a part of a wider structure which privileges an authoritarian nation-state. As such, friendship quickly becomes shaped by homogeneity, unity, and the subsuming of the individual into the group. As a result, Schmitt never escapes the notion that friends entail enemies, and that peace and equality with some entails inequality and violence to others. The danger of Schmitt's account is that it reinforces the very structures of power that friendship promises to disrupt. Indeed, we can even say that it takes them to the extreme. Schmitt is thus useful insofar as he can show what happens to friendship in modernity—but his own account provides not a template, but a picture of friendship askew.

The book concludes with a speculative essay in **Chapter Seven** which suggests a point of departure for a **contemporary theorisation of friendship and the political**. Here the view that friendship and the political are coterminous is defended. This essay builds on the space opened by Chapter One and begins to fill in some of the possible features of this terrain. It is argued that friendship and the political are aspects of the same concern: a concern which sees self and others as centres of value in a shared world. As such, tyranny is seen to be an outside limit to friendship and the political as it closes down this shared world. Friendship and the political are then explored through three dimensions: identity, holding, and possibility. The aim is to produce not only an account of friendship and the political, but to show how such an account can be used to evaluate and promote the best forms of politics. Here these forms of politics are said to acknowledge that self and others are bound together in a shared world, and that such a world is characterised by not only plural values but plural ways of bonding.

This book is a thus a contribution towards the project of understanding friendship. In so doing it must recognise its own limitations. In particular, two need special mention. First, no particular space has not been set aside here for a discussion of gender. Nor has space been set aside to address the contribution of Derrida. This is not because these tasks are unimportant. It is simply that the first of these tasks would require its own volume, and the second would require more groundwork than even this volume provides. It is hoped that what is presented here will be of value nonetheless, and a contribution to the conversation which is now taking place on the numerous aspects and themes that friendship raises. In this respect it is also recognised that this volume focuses on just one aspect of this conversation (the political) although it spans beyond what might be traditionally thought of as the boundaries of that concern. This can only be expected. Friendship is a project which is seeing increasing interest from scholars across disciplinary boundaries. This is both inevitable and welcome as friendship is not something that can ever be understood and captured by a single discipline. Friendship is varied and ubiquitous. It is seen in all cultures, in all times, and in all places. All people strive for friendship, and no one would choose to be without it. It is a fundamental human experience. Friendship is simply inescapable.

Chapter One
Relocating Friendship

FRIENDSHIP is a way of conceptualising the bonds between person and person. These bonds are conceived of as a nexus forming the framework of human life. As such, friendship reflects the encounter between self and others. Friendship points to reciprocity, combination, cohesion, mutuality, and affinity. Yet it is also capable of accommodating difference, plurality, and even disagreement. It might be more or less voluntary, more or less focused on equality, more or less comprehensive and encompassing. It will have a combination of ethical and affective elements, placing obligations and commitments on its participants. Friendship is about belonging and connecting. It is something shared. Taken *politically*, its dimensions and characteristics are as real and as binding as the ties and affects of hierarchy, power, authority, and sovereignty. However, whereas these ties can be understood as vertical threads, the threads of friendship *tend* to run horizontally. These horizontal bonds of mutual concern provide motivation for justice and action. They are fundamental in apprehending, ordering, and giving significance to the shared world of self and others. Understood in this way friendship is indispensable to political thought. From this perspective the political is a particular response to being human and the reality of others. Friendship is a *vital* component of the political attempt to respond to and resolve the question of order and value in a world of self and others.

Despite these claims, in modernity there has been a separation of friendship from the political. At the level of practice the separation is pursued as being highly desirable at the sharp-end of politics as instanced in numerous Western democracies. It should be noted that, insofar as a separation of friendship and politics is thought desirable, a much more *personal* conception of friendship is often being employed here than the more generic concept outlined above. Nevertheless, too much friendship is thought to be a particularly repugnant symptom of a diseased democracy. Simultaneously, at the level of political thought little attention is given to friendship by contemporary thinkers, and by and large the tradition and practice of political thought in modernity has abandoned an overt focus on friendship. When modern thinkers turn their minds in this direction they do so from non-political perspectives. The prejudice is that there is something at best unsavoury and at worst fairly repellent about the association of friendship and the political. In terms of justice, liberty and the use of power, friendship seems to run counter to the demands of impartiality and universalism. The fear is that friendship equates to nepotism, favouritism, and fiefdoms, and that these all diminish the transparency of the state and its institutions. In terms of friendship's role in political analysis there are two sets of objections. First, friendship seems to suggest the 'pre-modern' either in terms of a way of theorising what literally came before modernity as historical fact (e.g. tribalism, the polis, feudalism, small-scale community), or as a way of theorising the kind of politics that modernity has cast asunder. Second, any reintroduction of friendship to the political would be seen as a dangerous step towards a closed politics based on personal loyalty, dependency, and emotion. After all, isn't friendship irrational and arbitrary both in its foundations (the human heart) and in its display (of favourites, clients, flatterers, and cronies of all descriptions)? All of these things are to be overcome — in modernity at least.[1] It is argued that what *should* characterise politics and the theorisation of the political is a concern with the themes of power (and its restraint), equality, the public-private divide, and the rights, freedoms and liberty of the individual. All of this tends to be filtered through the ideas of sovereignty, the state, the rule of law, and procedural justice. To most modern minds, friendship would seem to serve little purpose other than identifying what the political is not, and what politics should not become.

This sketch — suggestive rather than substantiated — is assumed to be familiar. It reflects the standard analysis of friendship in relation to the political in modernity. Yet, widespread as this perspective and these conclusions are, things have not always been thus. Insofar as modern political thinkers tend to marginalise and disparage friendship, their thought stands in sharp contrast to the thought and concerns of their predecessors and especially the Greco-Roman thinkers. In Greco-Roman thought not only was friendship a concern for the major figures, it was also theorised in an overtly political way. Friendship allowed the

---

[1] For representatives of this view see: Ferdinand Tönnies, *Community and Civil Society [Gemeinschaft und Gesellschaft]*, Jose Harris and Margaret Hollis trans. (Cambridge: Cambridge University Press, 2001 [1887]); Georg Simmel, 'The Web of Group-Affiliations', in Everett C Hughes (ed.), *Conflict and The Web of Group-Affiliations*.

Greco-Roman thinkers to identify and connect a wide-range of bonds from the immediate family, to the familial, to the pleasurable, to the useful, to the virtuous. Importantly, just as there is a standard disassociation between friendship and the political in the thought of modern figures, for the Greco-Romans there was a standard connection between friendship and the political. This perspective viewed friendship as a crucial component in understanding both the theory and practice of politics, justice, social cohesion, the good society, and the life of the polis.

There is a clear disjuncture between the Ancient analysis and that of the Moderns. It is a disjuncture which stands in need of both explanation and evaluation. Has modernity lost something in overcoming friendship? What are the consequences for political thought in allowing friendship to fall into neglect? Has friendship really gone away, or is it simply hidden and obscured from view? When contrasted to the pre-modern (in both its Greco-Roman and Christian guises) modern thought clearly has a new dimension: that of the significance of the individual. However, it gains this only by sacrificing something equally as worthwhile: a focus on friendship. A reversal of fortunes is not here suggested. Instead reincorporation and reconciliation is proposed. It is easily recognised that the resources of pre-modernity are not necessarily well-suited to theorisation in modernity. The assumptions of the various pre-modern modes of thought (not least the tendency to view the world as having some kind of moral unity, a single purpose to human existence, and a connection between politics and hierarchy based in community) are at odds with some of the inescapable features of the contemporary world (moral and cultural pluralism, the loss of *telos*, and the inclination towards equality, liberty, and individuality). So, there is no suggestion here of importing (wholesale) the ideas and institutions of the pre-modern analysis into the environs of contemporary political thought. Instead, by observing how friendship operated there we can gain insights into both the work that it did in that context and suggestions as to the work it could do in the contemporary context. This is not to disregard the modern approach, but to redevelop a forgotten dimension.

Friendship and commonsense

This enquiry, then, is an endeavour in political thought. As such it incorporates aspects of both the history of ideas *and* themes and methods associated with analysis in political philosophy. In addition, it should be noted that such an enquiry is likely to draw from resources beyond those traditionally associated with political thought.[2] The central task here is to provide an account of the relationship between friendship and the political. Two related questions are thus pursued. The first concerns resources and examples. What role has friendship played in the thought of those who *have* theorised it (and especially those few in modernity who have turned their minds in this direction)? Of special interest here is the thought of Kierkegaard, Nietzsche, and Schmitt. As such these thinkers give us not only resources with which to start to think this through in a contemporary setting, but their thought also gives us important clues as to the fate of friendship in modernity when it is theorised 'against the grain'. This gives rise to the second set of questions: What space is now available for the theorisation of friendship and the political, what might such a theorisation look like, and what is to be gained? In response to these questions the basic framework advanced here is that friendship is a way of conceptualising the bonds between person and person reflecting the encounter between self and other. Such bonds are (to a greater or lesser extent) characterised by mutual ethical and affective concern. Friendship, then, addresses one of the basic questions of the political: How can we understand what binds us together, and how does this binding help to structure politics?

This programme is not without its difficulties. One set of difficulties revolve around objections to the construction of friendship offered so far. Another set of problems are raised by a focus on method and revolve around the possibility of defining and tracing friendship in previous systems of thought. As a preliminary to the endeavour as a whole, it is desirable to anticipate and respond to some of the possible objections.

One set of objections might be that here 'friendship' is being employed in a somewhat peculiar way. It might be said that the definition of friendship offered here is all very well, but it is far from its everyday or ordinary use. This line of argument can concede that it is true that the understanding of friendship here captures *some* of what is usually to be understood by the idea: friendship is a mutual concern for

---

[2] Lovejoy argues for this kind of approach explaining that ideas are unlikely to be confined to a single 'province', AO Lovejoy, 'The Study of the History of Ideas', in Preston King (ed.), *The History of Ideas: An Introduction to Method*, p. 189. Indeed, Lovejoy is generally keen to stress the idea that 'ideas' are not confined to disciplinary boundaries, Lovejoy, 'The Study of the History of Ideas', pp. 189, 191, 195; AO Lovejoy, *Essays in the History of Ideas* (Baltimore: The Johns Hopkins Press, 1948), pp. 2, 7. This is an argument that strikes the mind as being intuitively right, but it should also be recognised that it does not imply that it is impossible to narrow a focus for a specific purpose. Indeed, the very operation of identifying and pursuing an idea already presupposes this.

another, and it is based around ethical and affective considerations. However, what the ordinary meaning of 'friendship' seems to point to is that whilst the term denotes a relationship which is widespread and commonplace, the relationships themselves are characterised by individuality and uniqueness. Here friendship is assumed to be something personal, displaying privacy, intimacy, openness to the other, and reciprocated support. Although stability is expected in friendship it remains a freely chosen relationship that can be terminated at any time and for any reason—or for no reason at all. Friendships have no contract, no preconditions, and no clear rules. Ultimately it might be concluded that friendship is best described as being ubiquitous but ineffable. In other words, whilst it cannot be said exactly what friendship is, we 'know it when we see it'.

It is not being suggested that this view of friendship is wrong—at least not in the context in which it is being employed. Whether it is how actual individuals experience their relationships is another matter.[3] What is significant about this view for the present concern is that it fuses together two assumptions that need to be considered as being answers to separate questions. The first of these is whether the account of friendship presented above (the 'personal friendship' account) is *in fact* the only accepted account of friendship. The second question is indicated by the claims of the supposed ineffability of friendship. Here the implication is that the only sensible response to the question 'What is friendship?' is to admit that (valuable though it is) friendship is a profound mystery whose contours and shape quite simply cannot be defined.

These are pertinent questions given the scope of the endeavour pursued here. The contemporary account of 'personal friendship' is clearly not absurd, nor is its prejudice of separating friendship from politics and the political. Moreover, the starting assumption here that the term 'friendship' has come to mean 'personal friendship' is

---

[3] For discussion of this issue see Graham Little, *Friendship: Being Ourselves with Others* (Melbourne: Scribe Publications, 1993), pp. 2-3; Ray Pahl, *On Friendship* (Oxford: Polity Press, 2000), pp. 9, 39ff. For a summary of how friendship is connected to class, gender, and age see Stephanie Garrett, 'Friendship and the Social Order', in Roy Porter and Sylvana Tomaselli (eds.), *The Dialectics of Friendship*. For an account of how men and women have different expectations of friendship, but do not necessarily conform to these expectations see Karen Walker, 'Men, Women, and Friendship: What They Say, What They Do', *Gender and Society* 8(2), 1994. Here 'notions that women share intimate feelings whereas men share activities in their friendships are more accurately viewed as cultural ideologies than as observable gender differences in behaviour', and (contrary to common assumptions) 'working-class men appeared to have more intimate friendships than professional men and women' Walker, 'Men, Women, and Friendship: What They Say, What They Do', pp. 246, 261.

obviously initially plausible. What is to be gained by now attempting to redefine 'friendship' and to press it into the service of political thought? It might be feared that rather than benefiting our understanding of the political it is likely to bring about a good deal of confusion and vexatiousness. The sibling concern of attempting to 'define' friendship in the first place might also seem to carry some weight. This might be especially true if the point about the superiority of the 'personal friendship' usage is accepted. If friendships are both unique and multifarious, the task of defining them even in the most general terms is going to be extremely taxing. If the point is taken further, and the ineffability of 'friendship' is accepted, then the task becomes impossible. How, then, is it possible to weigh and respond to these concerns?

First let us reconsider these 'personal friendship' arguments in more detail. As has been said already, it is not being disputed that this account of friendship is the one that is *usually* intended when the term is employed in everyday language. However, it is important not to simply accept this at face value. A less hasty consideration of the everyday use of 'friendship' will begin to cast doubt on the surety of this initial assertion. It is certainly true that friendship is a term which is employed to mean something along the lines of a an intimate relationship based on reciprocated concern. However, this relationship seems to admit a host of degrees and variation.[4] It is this variety, and the unexamined assumption as to what friendship means, which quickly opens this view of friendship to some standard problems and puzzles. These problems help to shed light on why we should be reluctant to accept the privileging of the 'personal friendship' account. This is especially the case where this view is taken to *exclude* the possibility of alternative accounts and usage. Thus, it is not being suggested that these puzzles and problems cannot be resolved—many thinkers have made attempts to do so. What *is* being suggested is that attempts at resolution expose the complexity and variety hidden by the commonsense view.

We do not need to stray from ordinary language or usage to recognise some of these problems and questions (although they have *significant* philosophical implications). One set of problems are focused on the basis of the bond between the friends. One view would seem to imply that the friends are friends merely for the sake of each other. It

---

[4] For a further discussion of these points see Mark Vernon, *The Philosophy of Friendship* (Basingstoke and New York: Palgrave MacMillan, 2005); Pahl, *On Friendship*; Little, *Friendship*; Sandra Bell and Simon Coleman, 'The Anthropology of Friendship: Enduring Themes and Future Possibilities', in Sandra Bell and Simon Coleman (eds.), *The Anthropology of Friendship*, pp. 9-29.

would seem to be a small concession to say that the friends are attracted to each other on grounds of character and personality. After all, on this account friendship is a personal relation, and not a formal and general relation within a system (such as teacher-pupil, buyer-seller, parent-child). However, if this is the case then questions can be raised as to how much 'change' the relationship can endure. Do friends stop being friends because the character or personality of one of the friends changes? This is a common conundrum: if a friend takes up objectionable pursuits, opinions, or habits, should the friendship be broken-off? Is it possible to remain friends with Dr Jekyll when he is increasingly manifesting as Mr Hyde?[5] Can our friends do us wrong? Either way difficulties arise for the 'personal friendship' view. If it is the case that a friendship can be broken off for these reasons, then it casts doubt on whether the friend is really attracted to the other person *for the sake of the other*, or whether the attraction is to a set of characteristics or behaviours. If it is not the case that friendships should be broken off for these reasons, then it becomes less clear as to what sustains that particular friendship. If the relationship is simply impervious to changes in character, personality, and lifestyle, then it would seem to imply that there was nothing special about that *particular* bond—the friends could have paired up with just anybody. This seems to leave friendship in the zone of accident and caprice, and undermines what is usually thought to be one of its most valuable aspects: that there is something both special and valuable in the charter or person of the friend.[6]

Other questions also arise. How far does friendship 'map on to' other relations such as kinship and those of civil society?[7] Can parents be the friends of their children? Can siblings be friends—and are they friends because they are related or in addition to it? Do siblings choose to be friends—is choice essential to friendship? If so, when does it happen? A further question is generated by the relationship of marriage. Are marriage partners the closest of friends, or not really 'friends' at all? Does love count as friendship? The question is complicated by the legal status of the union, the expectations of tradition and society, and the introduction of a sexual element to the relationship. Indeed, sexuality and gender pose all sorts of problems (and even dilemmas) for the notion of friendship. Not merely is the question raised about the features of *friendships* between the pairings of

---

[5] Cf. Robert Paine, 'Friendship: The Hazards of an Ideal Relationship', in Sandra Bell and Simon Coleman (eds.), *The Anthropology of Friendship*, pp. 44-46.
[6] Robert R Bell, *Worlds of Friendship* (London: Sage Publications, 1981), pp. 23-26.
[7] Julian Pitt-Rivers, 'The Kith and the Kin', in Jack Goody (ed.), *The Character of Kinship*; Bell and Coleman, 'The Anthropology of Friendship', pp. 7-8.

men-men, men-women, women-women, but this matrix is further complicated by considerations of *sexuality*: homo-homo, homo-hetero, hetero-hetero.[8] To take just one example, the question as to whether (heterosexual) men and women can ever be *'just* good friends' is well-known in social life, and the subject of countless plays, films, poems, books, and TV soaps. This picture is also complicated by questions that are raised when friendship 'maps on to' elements of civil society. For example, are workmates and colleagues 'friends'? What about business partners, or those who trade with each other? What distinguishes people pursuing common interests (sports clubs, churches, trades unions, political parties, late-night revellers imbibing in a public house) from true friends? Is sharing an activity necessary *and* sufficient for friendship? Must there be an element of affection? What more needs to be in place? Can people who do not share activities together be friends? Are friendships really possible over vast distances and tracts of time? Can friendship *merely* be based around utility and pleasure? Indeed, how can we distinguish friends from people who are merely useful, amiable, and take an interest in us?

The commonsense view needs to address these issues if it is to be recommended as a part of analysis—as would any account of friendship. This is not the end of the trouble. This view is strained further when we start to think about other uses of 'friendship' and more marginal cases. It can be observed that 'friendship' is not only applied to relationships between *two adults* who appear to have some equality. This raises more questions. What are the numerical limits to friendship—how many more than two is allowed? Need there only be one—can a person to be a friend to their own self? Is friendship confined to the world of adults? Can children have friendships? Can friendships exist between people of differing ages? What about persons of different status (classes, wealth, education, experience)?[9] In addition, it is not merely 'people' who ordinary language applies friendship to. Can we have friendships with animals? Can countries, states, and nations be friends?[10] Can we be a friend of an abstract idea such as truth or justice? It is not uncommon to say that someone is a friend of democracy, or freedom, or even humanity.

---

[8] Elke Bruckner and Karin Knaup, 'Women's and Men's Friendships in Comparative Perspective', *European Sociological Review* 9(3), 1993; Walker, 'Men, Women, and Friendship: What They Say, What They Do'.

[9] Garrett, 'Friendship and the Social Order', pp. 132-136; Robert Paine, 'In Search of Friendship: An Exploratory Analysis in 'Middle-Class' Culture', *Man* 4(4), 1969.

[10] Ninian Smart, 'Friendship and Enmity among Nations', in Leroy S Rouner (ed.), *The Changing Face of Friendship*.

In short, although the contemporary 'commonsense' view appears to be initially attractive it hides a host of questions and ambiguities even within its own context. Here the term 'friendship' has been used in its ordinary sense in the English speaking West, but already it is clear that it is standing for a variety of ideas about friendship: sometimes complementary, sometimes in competition. However, an additional observation casts further relief on these assumptions. Not only is the 'personal friendship' view challenged by an examination of contemporary usage, it is also thrown into perspective when compared and contrasted to both contemporary cultural variations, *and* historical depth. It is clear that the idea of friendship is subject to considerable cultural variation and is not restricted to Western notions and practices.[11] Moreover, the term and idea have had a much wider compass in European history. Here it should be noted that the 'personal friendship' view (insofar as it can be assumed to represent a set of core ideas) is not the only view and construction of the idea in previous eras. Nor has this personal account necessarily been the most highly celebrated. Indeed, some systems of thought would view the contemporary focus as somewhat misguided, if not inferior. From this perspective the rise of the 'personal friendship' view is especially modern, and perhaps even peculiarly contemporary.[12]

One response, then, to the view that we should simply accept the contemporary 'personal friendship' view is to say that this is not an exceptionally coherent account; and that this would be to ignore a larger and longer tradition. However, it could still be asked why anyone should be especially concerned about all of this. The answer to this depends entirely on the purpose and level of analysis. It is not suggested that in day-to-day circumstances the 'personal friendship' account is especially defective. However, why should this account be allowed to restrict accounts outside of its remit? What is being proposed here is *not* that the ordinary account be changed, but that the plane of analysis is. Everyday assumptions are not necessarily conducive to identifying and addressing the concerns of the political.

---

[11] Bhikhu Parekh, 'An Indian View of Friendship', in Leroy S Rouner (ed.), *The Changing Face of Friendship*; Claudia Barcellos Rezende, 'Building Affinity through Friendship', in Sandra Bell and Simon Coleman (eds.), *The Anthropology of Friendship*; James G Carrier, 'People Who Can Be Friends: Selves and Social Relationships', in Sandra Bell and Simon Coleman (eds.), *The Anthropology of Friendship*; Alan Smart, 'Expressions of Interest: Friendship and *guanxi* in Chinese Societies', in Sandra Bell and Simon Coleman (eds.), *The Anthropology of Friendship*; Mario I Aguilar, 'Localized Kin and Globalized Friends: Religious Modernity and the 'Educated Self' in East Africa', in Sandra Bell and Simon Coleman (eds.), *The Anthropology of Friendship*.

[12] Carrier, 'People Who Can Be Friends: Selves and Social Relationships', p. 23ff.

Thinking about the political is a different kind of operation to day-to-day discourse. The political generates its own language and context. As such, language and ideas are being employed and developed in a specific and specialised way. Ordinary language is fine for ordinary use. However, when we enter the realm of political thought we are concerned about language in a more exacting way, and rightly so. We are also concerned to develop and use a vocabulary which helps us to both pose questions and attempt to answer them. 'Friendship' is a potential part of this. By drawing attention to the wider and longer use of the idea of friendship—a longer and wider tradition that connects friendship *directly* to political thought—the door is opened for a reconnection to that tradition and a redeployment of its resources. This is a perfectly legitimate endeavour within political thought. The sphere would be moribund without both recourse to the past and the right to develop and redeploy its vocabulary and ideas to confront changing circumstances and concerns.

So, whilst there is nothing especially wrong with contemporary accounts and use of 'personal friendship', from the point of view of someone engaged in political thought this account is somewhat unsatisfying. Not only is this account discovered to be somewhat amorphous, it also fails to recognise the longer and richer tradition which ties friendship to political thought. Political thought has its own tasks and its own language. Here it is examining the connection between friendship and the political. Ordinary language can be a starting place for such a task—but ultimately it must give way to a language that is more adapted to context.

Defining friendship

Having considered the relationship between the ordinary 'personal friendship' account and the 'political' account being developed here, it is now possible to identify and address a second set of questions. The stress on the variety and even ambiguity of friendship might be thought troubling, and now the whole the issue of the definition of 'friendship' must be addressed. An initial account of 'friendship' has already been suggested: the bonds between person and person. It has also been suggested that these bonds are characterised by mutual concern and that obligations and expectations are held by the participants. However, questions can be raised about this attempt. Central here is the question of the activity of defining itself. Is it possible to offer a definition of a phenomenon like friendship at all? If it is possible to define 'friendship' then this quickly leads to other worries. One is that the any definition will be too narrow to be of any real use. Here the worry is that 'friendship' would apply to so few instances that friendship is practically defined out of existence. Additionally, such a definition might leave some things outside its boundaries that we would expect to find within them. What language would we use for such remaindered phenomena? The second worry is the converse of the first. Here the fear is that friendship will be defined so loosely as to encompass too broad a range of phenomena. Here the problem is that by encompassing so much the term loses its analytical focus. It points to very little by pointing to so much. Additionally, we might be concerned about finding things in this category which we would expect to find beyond its scope.[13]

In order to address the questions relating to the analytic use of 'friendship' it is necessary to consider the process of 'defining' itself. When the issue is unpacked it quickly becomes clear that any 'final' definition — or definite definition — is seemingly impossible. There are two main reasons for this. The first is that such a demand would presuppose that the thing defined is objective, static, and can be related directly to our language. This comes close to what has been termed the 'correspondence theory' of reality.[14] This theory holds that there is an objective world 'out there' which can be accurately captured and represented by language. To see more clearly we must speak more clearly: and we speak more clearly by making what we say and think correspond more accurately and directly to an objective reality which is independent of our purposes and intentions. However, it seems that concepts about human interactions and human values are unlikely to meet these requirements. The second reason that definitions are likely to fail is that *all* language rests on the further use of language to derive its meaning. Language doesn't go all the way down to foundations; on the contrary, every word supports and is supported by every other word. In this sense, language can be likened to the well-used simile of sailors attempting to rebuild their ship whilst it is at sea.[15] The ship is created and recreated with each joist supporting a few others, with no single joist being foundational. In addition, there is no central authority and the process is endlessly dynamic. Here the issue would seem to be that *any* definition is itself subject to clarification (and further

---

[13] These questions also impinge on the problems of the methodology of the History of Ideas in general. On these issues see RG Collingwood, *An Autobiography* (Middlesex, England: Penguin Books, 1939), p. 44; George Boas, *The History of Ideas: An Introduction* (New York: Charles Scribner's Sons, 1969), p. 36; Preston King, *Thinking Past a Problem: Essays on the History of Ideas* (London: Frank Cass, 2000), p. 62.

[14] Richard Rorty, *Philosophy and the Mirror of Nature* (Princeton, New Jersey: Princeton University Press, 1979); Ibid., *Philosophy and Social Hope* (London: Penguin Books, 1999), pp. 23-46.

[15] The origin of the metaphor is attributed to Otto Neurath.

definition) and thus defining falls into infinite and pointless regress. If this were the case then not only does this spell the end of any attempt to theorise friendship is also signals the end of any attempts to theorise *per se*.

The way to avoid this conclusion is to re-approach the notion of defining itself—but from a different direction. It should be noted that defining isn't simply something that just happens; defining happens for particular reasons or purposes, and that these reasons and purposes are located in given contexts.[16] A definition is a kind of clarification; but it is not an attempt at a correspondence with an objective (or pre-existing and independent) reality. A definition is a kind of clarification that helps us to navigate and to act in a given world. In this sense it is more akin to a rule of thumb or a symbol on a map than an iron law or a photographic reproduction. Most of the time we do not seek formal definitions—definitions are only sought as a means of clarification, or as guidance, when our understanding breaks-down or comes to an halt. In political thought we often find ourselves unable to proceed. We may be uncertain as to where we are, or where we are going. Definitions are a necessary part of establishing our bearings. Definitions are thus produced for particular reasons and in particular contexts. The political theorist *is not* necessarily attempting to offer the first and last word on a given term or concept. Instead, the political theorist is attempting to delineate a terrain or concern from the vast mass of things which they (and others) might be interested in.[17] They are doing so to point out a direction for themselves and to signal this direction to others. The theorist of 'democracy' is not attempting to create a perfect demarcation of the term where all dispute and query about whether something is or is not a democracy is ended once and for all. On the contrary, they are attempting to bring into relief a set of relations, practices, institutions, and values that they find significant and wish to draw others' attention to. That definitions are not *exact*, and that they have blurred edges is neither here-nor-there. As Wittgenstein comments, it does not seriously affect their use.[18] The purpose here is to

---

[16] Ludwig Wittgenstein, *Philosophical Investigations*, GEM Anscombe trans. (Oxford: Basil Blackwell, 1953), section 87; King, *Thinking Past a Problem*, p. 66; Boas, *The History of Ideas*, p. 25.

[17] It is not necessary here to comment on *why* a person might take an interest in *this* rather than *that*. Indeed, it might not even be possible—it might be the case that we have to accept 'interest' as one of the fundamental facts about ourselves that can neither be anticipated more explained. In any case, for the present argument all that is needed is an acceptance that people do, in fact, find some things more interesting than others (and that some people are so minded to communicate that interest to others).

[18] Wittgenstein, *Philosophical Investigations*, section 79.

help us to focus and to look in a particular direction and in a particular way. In terms of political theory the task is not to try to get beyond all perspective, but to find ways of assuming the perspectives of others.[19] This can only be achieved if we accept that there must be horizons and that we are capable of pointing things out.

So, the question here is not can a term be defined without ambiguity or an idea identified completely. It is conceded that such a task is not possible in relation to the world of human affairs. Rather, the question here is what purpose is being served in defining a term, and in what context. These questions can produce *satisfactory* answers, and also point to a much more modest enterprise. The answers are described here as satisfactory because they have the limited aim of allowing the enquirer to proceed. They aim at the practical outcome of focus not a complete or universal definition. In defining 'friendship' the aim is to identify a concern with a set of relations. This will allow us to begin to compare and contrast them with other kinds of relations. In particular it will enable to show us how friendship can help to better understand and theorise the political, and (by implication) other terms in our political lexicon.[20] Of course, it is conceded that there will be overlap with some other terms and some peculiar cases. However, this does not jeopardise the potential usefulness of the term. It only means that it cannot achieve the impossible or be used outside of the context that motivates and supports its purpose.[21] 'Friendship' and the idea of friendship are not excluded from this conclusion.

Reconnecting friendship and the political

The previous discussion has addressed some initial concerns about defining 'friendship' in a political way. In so doing not only has it cleared the ground for what is to follow, it has also begun to illuminate some of the more general contours of the enquiry. One key issue that has been addressed is the fear that any *political* use of friendship would bend the ordinary account beyond all recognition. To this it was answered that the 'ordinary' account does not, in fact, stand for all accounts. No doubt it is privileged in ordinary language and for practical purposes. However, not only does ordinary language indicate a variety of uses for 'friendship', but the 'personal' account is also historically and contextually bound. Moreover, when it is examined the ordinary account is found to be far from unified and it masks a host of

---

[19] For a discussion of this see Graham M Smith, 'Through A Glass, Darkly: The Vision and Visions of Political Theory', *British Journal of Politics and International Relations* 11(2), 2009.
[20] Lovejoy, *Essays in the History of Ideas*, p. 9.
[21] Wittgenstein, *Philosophical Investigations*, sections 132, 133.

ambiguities and questions. Thus, the assumption that there is *an* ordinary account is somewhat misleading as there are multiple competing accounts of friendship subsumed in this common usage.

This observation and line of argument led to a second set of issues focusing in the problems with attempts to produce definitions. Here there were concerns that 'friendship' could not be adequately defined (as indicated by the defence of the political reading of friendship). Without some form of definition friendship would remain somewhat amorphous and opaque. Such an entity would not seem to be a likely candidate to be of assistance in argument and analysis. In addition, without identity the task of tracing the notion in the history of political thought seems condemned to certain failure. However, these particular questions relating to friendship are, in fact, a subset of a wider set of questions relating to the idea and practice of defining *per se*. The fate of friendship is tied to the fate of this wider genus. In addressing this second set of concerns it was useful to draw on the ideas derived from Wittgenstein. Here it was conceded that *final* definitions were impossible. However, this concession does not mean that the enterprise is useless. Instead, this concession was coupled with the insight that the significant point about definition is not to create a hermetically sealed category of things *in the abstract*, but to enable the definer to achieve particular purposes. As such, we should not expect definitions to be perfect, but merely useful. The purpose of any definition is to guide thought and argument, and any definition exists only as a part of a wider context. This helps to alleviate anxiety about peculiar and marginal cases. Such cases only emerge when definitions are conjured in the abstract.

In approaching the second set of questions in this manner a further elaboration of the answer to the first set is also generated. Here the personal account of friendship can be seen to be addressing a specific focus on intimate relations. In effect, the personal account of friendship is a way of identifying a set of relations which can be differentiated from the other relations in modern society, where these other relations are said to exclude certain emotions, transactions, and accounts of the self. As such, the 'personal' view of friendship is the product of a certain time and culture. It is also the product of a certain way of theorising that time and culture. However, it can be seen to be only one branch of a much wider cluster of relations that may fall under the rubric of 'friendship'. All such relations share similarities. They are distinguished not by any objective criteria in the sense that they map on to reality, but by the perspectives and problems of the questioner. In this sense all definitions are a piece of theory, and all theories are the result of perspectives.

Understood in this way, not only is there nothing especially objectionable in seeking a political account of friendship, but we can also better understand the purpose of doing so. What is being sought here is the theorisation of a group of ideas, ideals, and phenomena that are connected to the investigation of the connective bonds between person and person as they manifest in the political sphere. Although there is some variation between the form of these bonds, such bonds are indicative both of expectation and obligation. They are connected to the recognition of value in self and others. As such the bonds have been identified in a variety of ways as successive generations and cultures have attempted to place 'friendship' within their systems of thought. Sometimes this has included a direct theorisation within political thought; sometimes friendship has been theorised elsewhere. In any event, in terms of Western political thought friendship has come to take on a wide variety of forms: *eros*, *philia*, *agape*, amity, dynasty, citizenship, concord, loyalty, community, solidarity, neighbourliness, fraternity, compatriotism, and comradeship. Each of these terms can be viewed as a way of conceptualising the bonds between person and person, and then locating the structuring effects and consequences of these within the forms of politics. Thus the question can be asked as to whether these ideas and ideals are mapped on to kinship, family, and ancestry; touched by hierarchy, power, and even subordination; overlap with the economic, spiritual, or cultural; veer towards innovation or tradition; or admit more of less equality, more or less liberty. They could be characterised as oppressive, conservative, reforming, or revolutionary. However, this question is secondary to the purposes of definition here. The variety and the detail threaten to turn the eye from the essential. What is significant for this analysis is that each of these relations and their conceptual apparatus share the key features of friendship understood politically. That definition of friendship is a specific response generated by questions about the bonds between person and person in relation to order and value. As such friendship is to be considered coterminous with the political.

PART I

The Foundations of Friendship

Chapter Two

Plato

PLATO is rightly considered to be a central figure of Western political thought, speaking to subsequent generations through his influential *Republic*. It is in this book that Plato has Socrates conjure an ideal polis. As is well known, here there is a clear distinction between those who are suited to rule and those who are not. It is Socrates' argument that only those who have had a vision of the form of the good are suited to rulership. Far from creating a self-serving elite, it is this vision of the good that enables the rulers to frame just laws that will achieve harmony. Indeed, for Socrates such a state of affairs is the very epitome of a good society. However, what has perhaps received less attention is the role that friendship plays in developing and maintaining a harmonious polity. This concern (developed primarily through *eros* but also through *philia*)[22] reveals not only a unity within Plato's thought, it

---

[22] Although not synonyms, both of these terms denote a concern with friendship understood as the bonds between person and person. There is a wide commentary on these terms. The usual assumption is that Aristotle's use of *philia* is an explicit alternative to Plato's use of *eros*. For a discussion of this see Michael Pakaluk, ed., *Other Selves: Philosophers on Friendship* (Indianapolis: Hackett, 1991), p. 28; AW Price, *Love and Friendship in Plato and Aristotle* (Oxford: Clarendon Press, 1989), p. 1. Clearly the terms denote a distinction, and some have argued that they are incompatible. For an exponent of this view see David Konstan, *Friendship in the Classical World* (Cambridge: Cambridge University Press, 1997), pp. 38-39. In *eros* there is an asymmetry between the lover and the beloved. In contrast, *philia* points to symmetrical relations being the norm. In addition, there is concern to separate *philia* (as 'friendship' meaning a freely chosen and personal relationship) from both *eros* and relations of kin. See Konstan, *Friendship in the Classical World*, pp. 53-56. However, Trevor J Saunders takes the view that whilst there can be a distinction 'It is, however, impossible to put *philia* in one semantic compartment and *eros* in another: some instances of *eros* may manifest elements of *philia* and vice versa'. See Saunders in Plato, *Lysis*, p. 119. Things become even more complicated when the terms later come under the influence of Christianity. For a discussion of this see Cyril C Richardson, 'Love: Greek and Christian', *The Journal of Religion* 23(3), 1943. Irving Singer's book also remains indispensable in this regard: Irving Singer, *The Nature of Love: Plato to Luther*, 2 ed., 3 vols., vol. 1 (Chicago and London: The University of Chicago Press, 1984). What is crucial

also shows that there is a strand of enquiry which links the notions of friendship, education, and the good. To anticipate what is to come: friendship is both the starting point for philosophy and the activity of seeking the good itself. Education through the bonds created by eros is the means by which we come to love the good in the correct way. When these elements are in place, the result is harmony within and between individuals, both on the personal and political scale.

In order to pursue this connection this discussion will select and focus on three key dialogues: *Lysis*, the *Symposium*, and the *Republic*.[23] In so doing the connection between the early concern with friendship (in *Lysis*) and Plato's later political thought (in the *Republic*) will be made.[24] For although much has been made of Socrates' account of justice in this later work, it should also be observed that this account of justice rests upon the recognition that what binds people together is not mere command or advantage, but a shared desire for the good. Whilst the ability to actually gaze upon the good is limited to a very small number, it is the common enterprise to attempt to attain the good. The desire to do so binds people together, both as individuals and in wider associations. In the early dialogue *Lysis* the theme of friendship is first discussed. Although this dialogue ends in apparent failure, it is important—a careful reading shows it to not only explore the central themes of friendship, but also to demonstrate the link between friendship, education, and the good life. In the second stage comment is

---

here is that the kind of *concern* that is treated in both Plato and Aristotle (and by *eros* and *philia*) is the same: the bonds between person and person. The contrast is found in the foundation, nature, and extent of this bond, and whether all friendship points in the same direction to achieve the same thing (Plato) or whether there are various forms of friendship with differing aims (Aristotle). For a full review of these terms and the literature surrounding them see Heather Devere, 'Reviving Greco-Roman Friendship: A Bibliographical Review', in Preston King and Heather Devere (eds.), *The Challenge to Friendship in Modernity*.

[23] Other dialogues could be added to this list, notably *Pheadrus*. This dialogue repeats some of the themes of both *Lysis* and the *Symposium* but casts them in a different way. On the links between these dialogues see GMA Grube, *Plato's Thought* (London: Hackett, 1935); Price, *Love and Friendship in Plato and Aristotle;* Gerasimos Santas, *Plato and Freud: Two Theories of Love* (Oxford: Blackwell, 1988); Gregory Vlastos, *Platonic Studies* (Princeton: Princeton University Press, 1973).

[24] For previous (and more extensive) treatments of these connections please consult Werner Jaeger, *Paideia: The Ideals of Greek Culture*, Gilbert Highet trans., 3 vols., vol. 2 (Oxford: Basil Blackwell, 1957). Jaeger pays special attention to the connection of *Lysis*, the *Symposium*, and *Phaedrus* arguing how in these dialogues 'the Socratic concept of *philia*, affection, is raised to the metaphysical plane', Jaeger, *Paideia: The Ideals of Greek Culture*, p. 57. Seung's study also makes this connection (although focusing on the *Phaedo* rather than *Phaedrus*) in his chapter entitled 'The Bond of Love and Friendship' which leads him directly onto his next topic 'Birth of the *Republic*', see TK Seung, *Plato Rediscovered: Human Value and Social Order* (Maryland, USA: Rowman and Littlefield, 1996).

made on the *Symposium*. In this piece a more positive account of the relationship between beauty and the good is made. Here friendship becomes both educative and creative. Far from merely being an inward-looking phenomenon, friendship is seen to be a universal binding force leading to harmony and justice and a concern with not only immediate others, but posterity. Thus, friendship leads us not merely to pursue the good for ourselves, but to reproduce that good in others. It is through an appreciation of the role that friendship plays in these pieces that reveals how we can begin to understand the more general connection between *eros* and the political in Plato's wider thought. In Plato's thought *eros* plays a role in both the foundation and aim of politics. In the *Republic* the role that friendship takes is to bind the polity.[25] It can be understood to have a connection to the previous dialogues through the notions of 'harmony' and 'education' and it provides the binding and motivating force for the actions of the citizens who not only attempt to live just lives in a just society, but are also attempting to perpetuate this forever.

Lysis: The aporia of friendship

The contours of the concern with friendship are first sketched in a cautious and somewhat inconclusive way in the early dialogue *Lysis*. In this dialogue—which is as complex as it is short[26]—Socrates is motivated to consider the nature of friendship through a series of related themes. Within the dialogue there are three main sets of friendships.[27] With each set the relationships become increasingly complex. First there is the friendship between Lysis himself and Menexenos. This is characterised by its unreflective (or unanalysed) nature and its equality.[28] The second set of friendships exist between the boys and their lovers. These form the pairings of Hippothales and Lysis, and Ctesippus and Menexenos. Here there is inequality between the lover and his beloved registering in terms of age, supposed wisdom, and accomplishment. There is also a difference in the approaches of the lovers: Hippothales being portrayed as fawning over Lysis and yet remaining hidden during Socrates' dialogue with the boys; whereas Ctesippus is portrayed as being more direct (and scornful of Hippothales' approach) and is active in leading the boys

---

[25] It is interesting to note that Plato is not the only thinker to connect *eros* and the political, this is also a theme in Zeno's thought. See Geroge Boys-Stones, 'Eros in Government: Zeno and the Virtuous City', *The Classical Quarterly* 48(1), 1998.
[26] Seung, *Plato Rediscovered*, p. 35.
[27] Paul Friedländer, *Plato: The Dialogues 2*, Hans Meyerhoff trans. (London: Routledge and Kegan Paul, 1965), p. 94.
[28] Plato, *Lysis*, 207b-d, 212.

into discussion with Socrates.²⁹ Finally, there is the friendship between Socrates and both boys (and, in a slightly less pronounced way, between Socrates and Hippothales and Ctesippus too). Here the relationship is characterised by the pedagogical role of Socrates both as an educator of the boys (on the question of friendship and the question of our ignorance and desire for the good), and of their lovers (on how they should treat their beloved if they truly love them).³⁰ This third set of friendships is also characterised by philosophical activity as Socrates' manner with the boys and the way that the enquiry is conducted is just as important as what is actually said.³¹ These friendships map on to the friendships which are examined in the conversation itself. In this way there is a clear tension in the dialogue between that which is existing in the very lives of the protagonists and the difficulties of conjuring this into a conceptual framework. This creates a cluster of aporia which Socrates summarises in his ironic comment at the end of the dialogue where his final parting comment is that:

> Lysis and Menexenus, we've now made utter fools of ourselves, an old man like me and you, since these people will go away and say that we think that we're friends of one another — for I consider myself one of your number — though we were not as yet able to find out precisely what a friend is.³²

The themes of the dialogue itself revolve around intersecting questions which approach the topic of friendship from differing perspectives. In reading the dialogue we get the sense that the conversation is circling the topic and practice of friendship catching glimpses of it from various approaches, but never being able to break the motion of the orbit to settle on a definition. The themes of the dialogue are never dealt with conclusively, and the termination point of each approach seems to be incompatible with the end-points of alternative approaches. Despite this it is still possible to identify some overarching themes. The central question of the dialogue is what is the nature of friendship? This if further subdivided by two planes of concern: (1) *How* do people become friends?³³ And (2) *Why* do people become friends?³⁴ These two primary questions are addressed through

---

²⁹ Plato, *Lysis*, 204-206 and 206-207b (respectively).
³⁰ Plato, *Lysis*, 206c and 210e.
³¹ Cf. Friedländer, *Plato: The Dialogues 2*, pp. 93-94; James M Rhodes, 'Platonic *Philia* and Political Order', in John von Heyking and Richard Avramenko (eds.), *Friendship and Politics: Essays in Political Thought*.
³² Plato, *Lysis*, 223b.
³³ Plato, *Lysis*, 212a.
³⁴ Plato, *Lysis*, 214ff.

intersecting discussions of the following five themes: (a) Whether there is a connection between friendship and 'being useful and good'; (b) Whether friendship has to be reciprocal, and if not then whether it is the lover or the loved who is truly said to be 'the friend'; (c) Whether similarity or dissimilarity draws the friends together; (d) Whether friendship has a 'first principle' that is its final cause; (e) Whether friendship is the result of sufficiency, deficiency, and the connection to this with 'belonging'.[35]

As has been claimed, these questions seem simply to lead to impasse and contradiction. For example, on the question of *who* is the friend (the one who loves, or the one who is loved, or those who share reciprocated love) it seems as if none of the options are acceptable.[36] The first two options present different sides of the same difficulty. It doesn't seem at all correct to claim that the *lover is the friend* if that love is not recognised or returned (or returned with animosity).[37] Conversely, the *person who is loved* does seem to be a friend unless they return the love.[38] This doesn't sound possible. The final option is rejected as if *reciprocation* is central then it would not be possible to 'love' wine or wisdom.[39] Thus, it would appear that neither the lover, nor the loved, nor those who love mutually can be called friends. This conclusion is hardly acceptable as this would mean that friendship is impossible—an unacceptable conclusion which is contradicted by the very friendship of those who have reached it!

Despite the apparent aporia in the dialogue, *Lysis* has more to offer than simple paradox and impasse. Indeed, Socrates' closing comments would seem to suggest that there is more to this than meets the eye, and that things haven't yet been brought to their conclusion. This is why his closing comments should be considered partly ironic. Whilst they might be true for Lysis himself (who cannot overcome his immaturity and selfishness), they might not be true for the potential of Menexenos. Additionally, they feign Socrates' intellectual defeat whilst also indicating the possibility of resolution. In respect to *Lysis* as a whole, from the perspective of our current concern three things are of particular significance. The first is so obvious that it is likely to be overlooked: that *Lysis* is a *dialogue* on friendship. In some ways this should not be considered peculiar. As has already been suggested,

---

[35] Plato, *Lysis*, e.g. 210c-d and 214e, 212a-b, 214a and 215d, 219c-d, and 221 (respectively).
[36] Plato, *Lysis*, 123c.
[37] Plato, *Lysis*, 212b-d.
[38] Plato, *Lysis*, 212e-213c.
[39] Plato, *Lysis*, 212d-e. The implication here is that it is possible to love both wine and wisdom, and that these can be our friends.

friendship was a standard theme for the Ancient mind. It finds expression not only in Plato, but in many other great minds such as Pythagoras, Aristotle, and later Seneca, Cicero, and Plutarch. However, this dialogue does highlight the peculiarities of the modern approach to this theme. In modernity the approach would find different problems with friendship, invariably reducing it to a purely personal relationship based on sentiment rather than a question about the attraction of men to each other based around the themes of affinity and the good.

The second and third points to note concern the connections in the dialogue itself. In the dialogue the possibility is raised that friendship could form the basis of bonds between good men. The thought here is that good men might be naturally attracted to each other. Although this thought is discounted (forming part of the puzzlement about what is attracted to what) a reformulated version of it is to reappear in later discussions. In particular, it will be argued that all men are attracted to the good (indeed, it is later revealed that the good is a kind of 'first beloved' to which all men are attracted in their particular attractions).[40] This is one of the lessons of the *Symposium* and it is the foundation of the *Republic*. In this sense the element of desire which is present in friendship (and illustrated by the attitudes and actions of the lovers towards their beloved in *Lysis*) will be seen not merely to be the passion of two individuals for each other, but of a more general striving to identify and attain the good. Thus, friendship is an attraction based on this search for the good: the attachment to the *particular* points to a yearning for the *universal*.

Finally, it is also of significance that this dialogue connects the themes of friendship and education. Indeed, these themes are tightly connected in the person of Socrates himself. In the explicit discussion Socrates is educating the boys (and anyone else willing to listen) on friendship. However, on a more dramatic level two things are in play. First, Socrates is also educating the lovers of the boys about their responsibilities in respect to developing the most noble parts of their characters. A part of the love that the older men should have for the boys is to educate them in such a way as to improve their characters. In so doing, they also improve themselves (and do not appear 'ridiculous' and harmful to themselves as Hippothales is accused of doing). The second point is perhaps more fundamental. It is Socrates' own friendship for the boys that leads him into dialogue with them. Throughout the dialogue the beauty and attractiveness of the boys is stressed. Indeed, it is this which seems to pique Socrates' interest. However (and as we shall see) this is not mere physical attraction, it is a

---

[40] Jaeger, *Paideia: The Ideals of Greek Culture*, p. 175.

response to the possibility that the boys can engage in the friendship of philosophy. What Socrates sees in the boys is not just physical beauty, but the possibility that they might also have beautiful souls.[41] Socrates — as friend and educator — wishes to be the midwife to this progeny. Thus, education is connected to birth and production.[42] It is the effort of one person to help another to deliver the good within them.

The *Symposium*: In praise of Eros

If we understand *Lysis* as a dialogue in which the questions of friendship are initially identified and explored, we might be inclined to consider the *Symposium* as being both a more mature and more definitive responses to those initial questions and themes. In this dialogue Plato has Socrates revisit the questions of *Lysis* and to not only consider them in more detail and at more length, but to link them to wider themes in his philosophy. Furthermore, dramatically this dialogue see Socrates move away from his role in the shepherding of young and immature minds to the direct engagement with the minds of his peers (and his own relationship as a lover). To be sure, there is still something of the teacher about the Socrates of this dialogue, but he is also revealed to be the student of others. Moreover, he is shown to be practising philosophy at a deeper and more fulfilling level. Thus, if Socrates' purpose in *Lysis* was to prepare the ground of his charges' minds and to awaken them to the seeds of philosophy, in this later dialogue we can view him as further nurturing and harvesting the fruits of both philosophy and friendship.

The dialogue itself appears to present no particular difficulties in the way that *Lysis* does — although the piece is dramatic.[43] Ostensibly it is easier to discern Socrates' position, and clearly he is not challenging the other characters in such an obvious way as he does in the earlier dialogue. Plato contrives to animate a discussion of *eros* amongst several companions of Socrates placing a speech praising *eros* in the mouth of each. Staged as a competition, the successive speeches highlight aspects of *eros* until the tournament culminates with Socrates' account of the teaching of the priestess Diotima on the mysteries of *eros* and the tumultuous arrival of Alcibiades. Yet, the *Symposium* offers challenges of its own. From the start there is a double ambiguity concerning the *authority* of what is said.[44] The first of these ambiguities

---

[41] Jaeger, *Paideia: The Ideals of Greek Culture*, p. 196.
[42] Cf. Rhodes, 'Platonic *Philia* and Political Order', pp. 25-26.
[43] See Henry G Wolz, 'Philosophy as Drama: An Approach to the Symposium', *Philosophy and Phenomenological Research* 30(3), 1970.
[44] Indeed, it could even be said that there is a triple ambiguity as the whole affair is narrated not by one who was present, but by Apollodorus (who is described by

concerns the speeches themselves: are we to assume that they are superseded by that of Socrates? The drama of the piece would seem to indicate that each speaker is attempting to 'out perform' the others.[45] The issue is further complicated by the fact that—apart from a brief exchange between Socrates and Agathon—the speeches are left as virtually self-contained performances. Although the speeches form a succession, and although the drama would seem to *imply* improvement, this is never established as either being achieved nor (from Plato's authorial viewpoint) intended. The second ambiguity concerns the status of what Socrates himself has to say. Whereas all the other speakers are clearly advancing views in their own person, Socrates uses the occasion to relate the teaching of the priestess Diotima.[46] It is therefore not at all clear as to how far we are supposed to identify Diotima with Socrates (and, indeed, with Plato).

Without wishing to underplay these interpretive difficulties, it is perhaps fair to say that the *Symposium* goes some of the way towards allowing us to establish a view of friendship which is attributable to Plato's Socrates. The format of the contest of the symposium prevents Socrates engaging directly in conversation with his companions about their speeches. Indeed, when Socrates initially attempts some conversation with Agathon before Agathon's speech he is playfully admonished by Phaedrus.[47] Nevertheless, Socrates does not simply contradict or dismiss the claims of the other speakers when it is his turn, nor does he offer any form of direct refutation. It would have been perfectly possible for Plato to have portrayed Socrates as having done so despite the restrictions placed on Socrates by the context of the symposium. After all, some of the other speakers do take issue with each other (notably Phaedrus and Agathon disagree as to whether Eros is the oldest or youngest of the gods).[48] Moreover, not only does

---

his listener as a friend of Socrates) and in any case Appollodorus makes it clear that not only was he not present at the symposium, but that it was also many years ago. Plato, *The Symposium*, 172.

[45] Plato, *Symposium*, section 194a.

[46] There is much discussion of the significance of Socrates having learnt about *eros* from Diotima, and his retelling of this knowledge with reference to her. It should be noted that (other than the flute-players who are dismissed) Diotima is the only female presence in the *Symposium*. In addition, the kinds of *eros* that have been praised previously have tended to focus on the union of two men. For a sample of some of the literature on this topic see Luce Irigaray, 'Sorcerer Love: A Reading of Plato's *Symposium*, Diotima's Speech', *Hypatia* 3(3), 1989; Harry Neumann, 'Diotima's Concept of Love', *The American Journal of Philology* 86(1), 1965; Arlene W Saxonhouse, 'Eros and the Female in Greek Political Thought: An Interpretation of Plato's Symposium', *Political Theory* 12(1), 1984.

[47] Plato, *Symposium*, 194d.

[48] Plato, *Symposium*, 195b-c.

Socrates not criticise the claims of his companions, he actually takes-up some of their themes in his own speech. In so doing the characters in the *Symposium* repeat and endorse positions raised by the questions of *Lysis*. It is possible to view the speeches as forming a complex whole.[49] The speakers themselves are not only engaged in a common enterprise, but they also explicitly endorse and commend what each other have to say and their skill in saying it.[50] Thus the speeches of the *Symposium* form the threads in a complexly spun fabric—but on a frame which was first used for the fabric of *Lysis*.

Despite the interwoven structure of the speeches several clusters of concern can be identified. Here three (or possibly four) pairings are considered.[51] The first is that of Phaedrus and Pausanias. Their speeches focus on the connection between *eros* and the theme of right conduct and developing an ethical character. The second pairing is that of Eryximachus and Aristophanes. Their speeches connect *eros* to the themes of harmony and wholeness. The third pairing is that of Agathon and Socrates. Here the initial theme is on the connection between *eros* the beautiful and the good. However, what Agathon holds as an opinion Socrates gives philosophical foundations. Socrates then repeats the account of *eros* offered by Diotima. In so doing he casts the previous speeches into a new light where their claims and themes can be evaluated against the foundation of knowledge. Again, Socrates takes the role of a kind of midwife to the soul, in this case helping the truth to emerge from the intoxicated confusion of the speeches. The final (possible) pairing occurs when the drunken Alcibiades arrives. His arrival allows a demonstration of eros in action, and for the reader to judge. In his speech he implicitly reveals how far Socrates has ascended on Diotima's account of love. Thus, Socrates and Alcibiades can be considered paired as a kind of illustration of the most genuine *eros*: Alcibiades sees and desires the wisdom within the ugly Socrates, and Socrates is drawn to this attractive young man not physically, but because he perceives the want of a potentially beautiful soul.

The circle of speeches

The speeches begin with the first two speakers (Phaedrus and Pausanias) stressing the connection between *eros* and developing an

---

[49] Paul Friedländer, *Plato: The Dialogues 3*, Hans Meyerhoff trans. (London: Routledge and Kegan Paul, 1969), p. 27.
[50] Plato, *Symposium*, 195b.
[51] For an alternative way of clustering the speeches see Christopher Gill's 'Introduction' to *The Symposium*. Gill places the speeches of Phaedrus, Pausanias and Eryximachus together, followed by the speeches by the comic and tragic perspectives offered by Aristophanes and Agathon.

ethical character and the virtues. It is Phaedrus' claim that *eros* provides us with a sense of pride and shame.[52] This connects back to *Lysis* as there one of Socrates' chief tasks is to demonstrate to the love-sick Hippothales that this should be the purpose of his love for the somewhat arrogant and conceited Lysis (who therefore fails to display proper pride or shame). Pausanias' speech reinforces this. Initially Pausanias makes a distinction between two kinds of love: a vulgar love of the body (directed at both women and boys), and a heavenly form directed at boys but focused on the mind. In contrast to those practising the vulgar form of love whose 'sole aim is to get what they want [without caring] whether they do this rightly or not',[53] heavenly love 'is a source of great value to the city and to individuals, because it forces the lover to pay attention to his own virtue and the boyfriend to do the same'.[54] In both speeches love is connected to the attainment of virtues. Moreover, these virtues have wider social and political benefits.

Eryximachus[55] and Aristophanes[56] are the next to speak. In their speeches the themes of deficiency, wholeness, and harmony are developed. Again, in so doing the speeches re-open questions raised in *Lysis*. The first (a) concerns the misguided line of thought advanced by Lysis that friends are attracted to one who is both 'useful and good' (albeit that Lysis confuses the true basis for this—*phronesis*—with the more instrumental and utilitarian notion of *episteme*).[57] The second (b) are the questions of what is attracted to what. In some sense this is perhaps more significant as (unlike the mistaken line of argument offered by Lysis) it begins to get to grips with what friendship is, rather than what it is not. In *Lysis* three propositions were advanced: (i) that like is attracted to like; (ii) that unlike is attracted to unlike (i.e. opposites attract). Finally, the question is shifted into the language of ethics which results in (iii) that which is neither good nor bad is attracted to the good. Whereas these questions lead to aporia in *Lysis* they are resolved in a more definitive way through their being taken up in the more comprehensive settings of these two speeches.

---

[52] Plato, *Symposium*, 178d.
[53] Plato, *Symposium*, 181b.
[54] Plato, *Symposium*, 185b.
[55] For a more detailed and sympathetic treatment of the role of Eryximachus see Ludwig Edelstein, 'The Role of Eryximachus in Plato's *Symposium*', *Transactions and Proceedings of the American Philological Association* 76(1), 1945.
[56] For a treatment of Aristophanes' role in the *Symposium* which links it to his wider view of *eros* and politics see Paul W Ludwig, 'Politics and Eros in Aristophanes' Speech: *Symposium* 191E-192A and the Comedies', *The American Journal of Philology* 117(4), 1996.
[57] Plato, *Lysis*, 210d. See also Rhodes, 'Platonic *Philia* and Political Order', p. 30.

In terms of the first set of questions (i.e. [a] the question of the connection between friendship, being useful, and being good), these are re-approached most clearly in the speech of the doctor Eryximachus. Although there is a degree of self-importance (and perhaps even vanity) in the manner of his delivery and his focus on medicine ('to give pride of place to this form of expertise'),[58] he goes on to begin to show how we must unpick the mistakes of Lysis. In particular, the doctor doesn't simply use his knowledge to satisfy *any* desire within the body, but only the good ones.[59] As Eryximachus proclaims:

> Pausanias just said that it's right to gratify good people but wrong to gratify self-indulgent ones. It's the same with the body: in the case of each body, it is right to gratify the good parts and you should do this... but it's wrong to gratify the bad and diseased parts and you should deprive them of satisfaction if you're going to be an expert doctor.[60]

Thus, friends are both useful and good; but not without discrimination. Indeed, it is discrimination that shows them to be useful and good.[61] For Eryximachus, however, this attending to 'good love' is achieved through a sense of balance or harmony. The first thing to note about this use of harmony is an unstated assumption: that wholeness and harmony are good. That this is a commonplace of Greek thought (and not limited to Plato) can be seen in numerous thinkers (Aristotle also works on this assumption) and can be traced back to a Pythagorean influence in philosophy.[62] It is this sense of harmony both in terms of a unity and a balance of plural elements that come to characterise (and differentiate) the respective political pronouncements of Plato and Aristotle. As we shall see, in the *Republic* friendship, harmony, and the good are intimately linked. In that account friendship is the desire for the good in ourselves and others, and the city is animated by this desire and held together insofar as it is fulfilled. In the *Symposium* harmony is brought into the dialogue by a consideration of the question of what is attracted to what. This forms the second set of questions and can be seen as an echo of the concern in *Lysis* with whether similar or dissimilar persons are attracted to each other.[63] Here it is reflected in the speeches not only of Eryximachus (who is trying to achieve harmony within the body), but also that of

---

[58] Plato, *Symposium*, 186b.
[59] Plato, *Symposium*, 186b-c.
[60] Plato, *Symposium*, 186c.
[61] Plato, *Symposium*, 186c-d. See also 187e where the issue of pleasure from the wrong type of love leads to 'self-indulgence'.
[62] See Hutter, *Politics as Friendship*, pp. 48ff.
[63] Plato, *Lysis*, 214a and 215d.

Aristophanes. Here the dramatist's myth points to the normativity of reuniting the two parts of a human being as being a good thing. Indeed, in this respect it is perhaps significant to note that the separation of the original humans has come about as a result of their own wickedness in attempting to supplant the gods. The separation is a result of man's immoral behaviour (presumably his impiety towards Zeus in particular).

The second thing to note is that the nature of harmony and wholeness raises similar questions concerning whether like is attracted to like, or whether opposites attract. These questions are re-calibrated in Eryximachus' speech. This is set again in the context of the overall question of doing the right thing and obeying the right kind of love. Thus, whilst initially it might seem that like wishes for like—health for health, and disease for disease—it would be wrong to gratify the latter and not the former. Moreover, it is clear from this (and Eryximachus' other examples) that even the right form of love should not become excessive. The aim is to combine potentially opposing elements to create a coherent whole. The thought which seems to lie behind this is that coherence is connected to stability, and excess (even excessive 'goodness') creates an instability, is disharmonious, and so must be considered 'bad'.[64] Thus, what at first appears to be a question about attraction and gratification is transformed into a question of achieving the right sort of harmony from diverse (or at least differing) elements. Aristophanes' speech addresses this question in a more direct way— but again a new approach is taken. For in Aristophanes' myth it is not only that like is drawn to like, but that the same is drawn to the same. In other words, after human beings were split they did not search for those who were similar to their 'missing' half, but that self-same half that once belonged to a whole. In contrast to the harmony of opposites (or at least difference) as set out by Eryximachus, Aristophanes' conclusion is that harmony is achieved only by being reunited with the same. We can only presume that if this is achieved then desire would cease.

Although these pictures are somewhat different there are clear similarities in theme and ambition, and there is a line of thought which would draw them closer together. Whilst there is a sense in which in Aristophanes' tale we are divided from and looking for *ourselves* (i.e.

---

[64] It is interesting to note, in this respect, the connection between this mode of thinking and the Ancient practice of ostracism. The ostracised was considered to have displayed some extreme trait (either negative or positive) which meant that they could no longer be folded into the community and threatened disharmony. See Richard Kraut, *Aristotle: Political Philosophy* (Oxford: Oxford University Press, 2002), pp. 272, 399n.

the same thing that we have lost) there are some important notes and limitations to this *strict* reading of the myth. The first thing to note is that whilst the other half of us is a part of us (and irreplaceable with any other *similar* half) it is not the case that all the halves are, in fact, identical. That is to say, whilst the other half of us is *uniquely us* it does not mean that the two halves are an identical pair. One way to think of this is to imagine if Zeus' further warning to humans were to be carried out and we were divided again—the left-hand side of ourselves would seek the right-hand side. However, although the sides belong together (and are in this sense halves) they are not identical. At best they are reflections of each other (and, in fact, the left and right-hand side of human beings do tend to differ rather than being exact mirrorings of each other). In Aristophanes' tale this is further complicated in the first (actual) division of the person as we are told that originally there were three sexes, male, females, and hermaphrodites. Thus, at least in one of the cases the divided humans are seeking something that is their own, but cannot be identical to what they are: the opposite sex. This observation serves to lessen the force of the claim that in this tale we are merely seeking replicas of ourselves to achieve wholeness, and to strengthen the idea that (at least in some of the cases) that we are seeking wholeness through finding our other *complementary* halves. The halves are not identical, but share identity. If this is the case then the idea of the harmony and balancing of opposites begins to creep back in.

The last two speakers are Agathon and Socrates. The speeches of these men are directly linked as not only does Socrates' speech accept and build on some of the suggestions that Agathon makes, but the speeches are linked through two brief conversations. In a sense, then, Agathon and Socrates are paired together in a closer engagement and interaction than the other speakers. Socrates is working with Agathon to find what is true in his speech. These brief conversations reflect the edifying purpose of *eros* that Socrates is about to explain. Indeed, he is acting as a teacher to Agathon in the same way as Diotima has acted as a teacher to him. Ultimately, though, it is *eros* itself which is drawing the men closer to the good.

Agathon begins his speech by criticising the previous speakers.[65] Specifically, he accuses them of '[congratulating] human beings on the good things that come to them from the god' rather than praising the god himself.[66] Agathon's first claim about *Eros* is later revealed by Socrates to have been along the right lines (although Agathon himself

---

[65] Plato, *Symposium*, 194e.
[66] Plato, *Symposium*, 194e.

admits that he didn't know what he was he talking about).[67] Nevertheless, the crucial claim is that of all the gods Eros 'is the happiest, because he is the most beautiful and the best'.[68] This is elaborated in two ways. Eros is the most beautiful because he is young and sensitive. Agathon thus opposes what Phaedrus has said. After this, and with some rather dubious reasoning,[69] the god's virtues are listed and illustrated: justice, moderation, courage, and wisdom. Of these wisdom has special significance because it leads to the gods acquiring skills and their peaceful organisation. Agathon ends with kind of 'prose-poem' in lavish praise of the god.[70]

As has been noted, there is conversation between Socrates and Agathon both before and after his speech. Before his speech Socrates has enough time to wheedle out of Agathon that he considers the crowd that he had previously been addressing to be 'unintelligent'.[71] Yet, Socrates points out that those present were in that crowd. After the speech Socrates has Agathon admit that he didn't know what he was talking about. However, it should be remembered that Agathon's speech at the symposium was greeted by the others with 'shouts of admiration'.[72] What is the meaning of this? It would seem to indicate that there is general confusion amongst those present as to the truth about *eros*. However, as Socrates is about to demonstrate, although those present might not have knowledge, their ignorance isn't complete. They have all touched upon some aspect of the truth. It is Socrates' task to provide a foundation of knowledge for those opinions. In so doing he is attracted to his friends and they to him as they seek knowledge. Socrates also manages something else in this conversation. Whereas the previous speakers had maintained the connection between *eros* and Eros (that is to say human love or desire and the god), Socrates craftily shifts the terrain to focus on *eros* as human desire.[73] Indeed, Eros is revealed to be neither god nor mortal, but a 'daemon' residing in-between.

In his own speech Socrates presents the teaching of Diotima. Before doing so he makes the connection between *eros*, the beautiful, and the good concrete. Through questioning Agathon he establishes that: (1) Love is *of* something; (2) that it is of something that a person *needs*; (3)

---

[67] Plato, *Symposium*, 201b.
[68] Plato, *Symposium*, 195a.
[69] Gill in Plato, *Symposium*, p. xxvi.
[70] Plato, *Symposium*, 197d-e. The description of the end of the speech as a 'prose-poem' is Gill's, p. xxv.
[71] Plato, *Symposium*, 194b.
[72] Plato, *Symposium*, 198a.
[73] Wolz, 'Philosophy as Drama: An Approach to the Symposium', p. 339.

Love needs beauty (but does not have it); and (4) Good things are beautiful.[74] In relating the teaching of Diotima Socrates establishes that (whilst not ugly) *eros* cannot be beautiful for that is what he desires. *Eros* therefore connects humans with the gods. However, given that beauty and the good have been established as virtual synonyms by Socrates, the real desire of *eros* is the good itself. Possession of the good makes a person happy (and there can be no further discussion about that).[75] Furthermore, this wish is common to everyone. However, Socrates-Diotima go even further. The object of love is not beauty but reproduction as this brings mortals closer to immortality.[76] Thus, two kinds of 'pregnancy' are revealed. A physical kind which produces a kind of immortality through children, and a pregnancy of the mind which produces 'wisdom and other kinds of virtues'.[77] Importantly, Diotima makes the connection between this second kind of pregnancy and its 'finest type of wisdom... that connected with the organisation of cities and households, which is called moderation and justice'.[78] *Eros*, then, is not simply to be considered to have personal affects, it is also a desire to achieve immortality through political acts.

The end of the teaching demonstrates how *eros* leads to the form of Beauty itself (which is also supposed to be a vision of the form of the Good). The striving for this vision is also what underpins the *Republic*. However, here Socrates reports Diotima's teaching of the stages that such a journey must take. In each stage the lover overcomes a limitation and adopts a wider and more abstract focus. This process must be begun when a man is young.[79] This explains Socrates' attraction to youths as they are most well-placed to begin such a journey. First the lover is drawn to beautiful bodies, then just one body with whom 'beautiful discourses' are produced (thus *eros* is already producing something of the mind). Next he must recognise that beauty resides not just in one body, but in all bodies. This causes his passion to relax. Having overcome his physical urges, he then moves on to valuing the beauty of the mind over that of the body. In this stage the lover will see the beauty in 'practices and laws'. From this he is led upwards to beauty in general. Gazing upon this 'great sea of knowledge' the lover will 'give birth; through knowledge to magnificent discourses and ideas'. Finally, he catches sight of knowledge itself.[80]

---

[74] Plato, *Symposium*, 199c-201c. cf. Friedländer, *Plato: The Dialogues 3*, pp. 23-24.
[75] Plato, *Symposium*, 205a.
[76] Plato, *Symposium*, 206c-e.
[77] Plato, *Symposium*, 208e-209e.
[78] Plato, *Symposium*, 209a.
[79] Plato, *Symposium*, 210a.
[80] Plato, *Symposium*, 210a-212a.

Before concluding something must be said about Alcibiades' arrival. The youth arrives drunk and disrupts the symposium. However, here we see *eros* in action. Alcibiades' arrival provides a demonstration of Socrates' skill as a lover. In his speech he implicitly reveals how far Socrates has ascended on Diotima's account of love. Alcabiades, half-praising, half-accusing, claims that Socrates is a satyr.[81] Yet, Socrates is revealed to have 'scorned' Alcibiades'good looks by declining to sleep with him. As a result of this Alcibiades claims to admire Socrates. Here *eros* brings the pair together, but much depends on what lies within the soul of Alcibiades. Thus, Socrates and Alcibiades can be considered paired as a kind of illustration of the most genuine *eros*: Alcibiades sees and desires the wisdom within the ugly Socrates, and Socrates is drawn to this attractive young man not physically, but because he perceives the needs of a potentially beautiful soul.

In this dialogue, then, the features of *eros* are sketched-out and then developed. It can be seen that the dialogue uses themes from *Lysis*. However, unlike the earlier dialogue these themes are resolved. Importantly the issue of whether like is drawn to like, or whether opposites attract, is addressed not only the by the participants, but by Socrates himself. The simple dichotomy between sameness and difference is broken by Socrates. Now we are drawn towards beauty, knowledge, and the good not because we either possess them or are characterised by their opposites. We are drawn towards them because that is what we lack.

Important, too, is the imagery that links education with birth and reproduction. Now the lover is not simply attracted to the beloved, but has a specific task to perform: to bring out what is beautiful in the other. In this way the relationship is given both an educative and an ethical status. Eros works not simply to bring people together to reproduce physically, but also to bring beautiful and lasting things into the world. Most crucial of all (for our current perspective) is the idea that *eros* can have not only person but social consequences. It is in this dialogue that two connections are made. The first is to bring *eros* and the good together and to establish that all people desire the good. Thus, there is a common desire running through all human life. Second, the connection is made between *eros* and immortality. Immortality is considered good, and reproduction is one way of achieving this. Thus *eros* explains both physical desire (and the possible sacrifice involved in this) and also the desire to reproduce the good in law and politics. Thus, the *Symposium* lays the foundations to see the bonds created by

---

[81] Plato, *Symposium*, 216c.

eros to move from the individual to society, and from the particular to the general. This also sets the scene for the *Republic*.

The *Republic*: Friendship as brotherhood and harmony

The *Republic* is perhaps the best known of Plato's Socratic dialogues — at least to those concerned with political thought. Despite this in some ways it is one of the least deserving pieces to be called a true dialogue, nor is the relationship between its political conclusions and Plato's wider philosophy (and Socrates' method) necessarily appreciated. This is especially true in relation to our present concern: friendship. As has been seen from the dialogues that have been reviewed thus far, for Plato's Socrates there is a link between friendship, education, and the good. Friendship has been shown to be both the grounds for the first engagement with philosophy and for education in philosophical method (in *Lysis*) as well as capable of extension beyond the realm of individuals. Indeed, in the *Symposium eros* is seen to reach a higher stage if initial desire is turned towards higher forms of beauty and the good. For the good to be apprehended individuals must cultivate the desire for knowledge through the educative effects of genuine friendship. It should also be noted that in the *Symposium* the beloved and his lover are improved and gain from this relationship. The beloved is inculcated in virtue and has the good parts of his character brought to fruition. For his part the lover creates a lasting legacy by reproducing the good and the desire for the good.

The account in the *Symposium* has also shown how a personal concern or attachment can lead to a more generalised concern with the good. As such it is an ethical and social task to be encouraged in both oneself and others. The friendship of Socrates acts as a model for this task. In the *Republic* attention turns from the individual to the community. In so doing, the implications for friendship in the dialogues examined so far are drawn out and writ large. However, friendship is also significantly transformed.[82] Now desire (even correctly targeted desire) must be kept under strict control by rationality.[83] Whilst relations within the ideal city are said to be friendly and harmonious, Plato moves away from the notions of a personal friendship and sexuality that underpinned the educative relationships in the former dialogues. Now stress is placed on the more

---

[82] Gerasimos Santas, 'Plato's Theory of Eros in the Symposium: Abstract', *Nous* 13(1), 1979, pp. 71, 74.

[83] Cf. Neumann, 'Diotima's Concept of Love'. Neumann identifies a shift from the position of the *Symposium* where 'all *eros* is by nature aimed at the good' to that of the *Republic* where reason and spiritedness are needed least 'the lover [be] driven blindly as beasts are', p. 54.

formalised attachments of family, and especially brothers. In so doing Plato introduces an additional dimension for modelling the bonds between person and person. The bonds of an acquired status are supplemented with those of a structural one.

Ostensibly the *Republic* is an enquiry into the nature of justice. Indeed, this is the motivating concern at the outset and its pursuit prompts Thrasymachus' outburst and challenge to Socrates.[84] Unlike the *Symposium* here Socrates takes direct responsibility for his views as Plato puts an explicit doctrine concerning justice in the mouth of Socrates: 'that in our state one man [is] to do one job, the job he [is] naturally suited for'.[85] This is a conclusion which is repeated at 441e where 'each of us will be just and perform his proper function only if each part of him is performing its proper function'. In order for this external manifestation of justice to be achieved a corresponding internal justice must also exist whereby the parts of a person are performing their correct and appropriate functions. It is this doctrine of the correct functions of parts which is mirrored both within the individual and throughout the ideal polis. When individuals achieve internal harmony then there is harmony in that polis. Injustice is the consequence of the failure to achieve such harmony or self-control and leads to faction and strife at both a personal and political level.[86] Such harmony consists of reason controlling appetite and spirit.[87]

It is notable that the notion of friendship is tied-up in two of the earlier formulations of justice, although both are interpretations of a maxim attributed to Simonides and later to Homer. In the first formulation Polemarchus claims that '[Simonides'] thought is that one friend owes it as a due to another to do him good, not harm'.[88] This basic formulation is maintained and extended through the conversation of Polemarchus and Socrates until it reaches the formulation of 'justice is to help your friends and harm your enemies' offered (in exasperation) by Polemarchus.[89] It is important to note that in the book as a whole Socrates does not move away from this basic formulation, but he does transform it in three ways. First he questions what it means to be a friend.[90] The conclusion of this enquiry is that it is the good man who is truly the friend.[91] The second modification is to the idea of

---

[84] Plato, *The Republic*, 336c-d.
[85] Plato, *The Republic*, 433a.
[86] Plato, *The Republic*, 352a-b.
[87] Cf. Plato, *Phaedrus and Letters VII and VIII*, 246-250 and 253-254.
[88] Plato, *The Republic*, 332a.
[89] Plato, *The Republic*, 334b.
[90] Plato, *The Republic*, 334c.
[91] Plato, *The Republic*, 335a.

justice as giving a person his due which was tangled up with friendship in an earlier part of the dialogue.[92] In respect to this, Socrates moves away from the restorative connotations first implied by this statement (i.e. that the friend restores to the other something that they have taken from them), and supplants it with a more positive notion of providing an addition. Thus, in helping our friends we are not simply returning to them what is theirs, but positively benefiting them in some way. The final modification sees Socrates dissolve the second part of the formulation concerning the injunction to 'harm enemies'. It is easy to see how this follows from the previous two moves. First, Socrates has argued that only those who seek the good can be friends (and it is in this sense that the friends wish goods for each other). Good men will not seek to make another unjust (for this clearly does not seek the good).[93] Thus, the good man (who is also the true friend) will not seek to harm his enemy, but will instead attempt to correct him.[94] Helping friends is therefore rescued from its limited concern with a closed circle and basis in attendant hostility to a concern with helping ourselves and others to approach the good.[95] Giving each person his due is not (primarily) a principle of distribution or restoration in the sense of economic or legal justice. It is an instruction to attend to that part of the person that we all (should) share: the desire for the good.

In the *Republic*, then, we do not see the abandonment of Plato's concern with friendship but its fulfilment. Indeed, in this sense the *Republic* can be seen as the complement and completion of the account of friendship that Plato has Socrates develop elsewhere. It could be said that the previous accounts (such as those in the *Symposium*) were predominantly focused on individuals, whereas the employment of friendship in the *Republic* is focused on the wider relations of community. Although there is some truth to this, it is to miss the deeper lesson and significance of the relationship between the accounts as a whole. In the former accounts Socrates focuses on individuals and moves outwards. In the latter Socrates uses the wider community to make us look inward. In fact, both accounts are ultimately focused on the same relationship: that of the soul with beauty as an expression of the good, and the role of another in helping us towards this. Beauty plays a central role because (for the Greek mind) beauty was synonymous with harmony. It is only when we know the good that we

---

[92] Plato, *The Republic*, 332a-b. This was first supported by Polemarchus at 331d.
[93] Plato, *The Republic*, 335c.
[94] Plato, *The Republic*, 335e. This is also in line with what Socrates famously concludes in *Gorgias* between 476a2 – 481b5.
[95] Richard Kraut, 'Egoism, Love, and Political Office in Plato', *The Philosophical Review* 82(3), 1973, pp. 336 and 339-40.

can see the harmony in our own soul and live harmoniously with others recognising our affinity to the good in them.[96] A correct view of the good and beauty also transforms the lower stages and forms of attraction and existence (indeed, this must be why Socrates is considered a great lover despite his reported ugliness). Thus, harmony in the soul, harmony between individuals, and harmony in the city all follow from each other.

In making the connection between the individual and the city Socrates is doing something more than drawing an analogy. If this were all that he was doing then the connection would be debatable at best. To understand what he is actually doing calls for a refocusing. For Socrates' move to connect the individual to the city is not simply to show one 'writ large' but to show what is *common* to them both. Socrates is not simply showing us a comparison based on size, but pointing to the continuation of a particular quality: the relationship between the soul and the good. This relationship continues *across* individuals and *across* the parts of the city. All citizens have an immortal soul, and the soul of each citizen seeks the good. As the good is unitary and singular, ultimately what is sought is the *same* for each citizen. The good, however, is not limited. Indeed, not only can it be possessed by all worthy citizens, its possession brings harmony.[97] Thus, there is truly an identity and unity of interests and desires. This identity cannot be the mere accident of living together. It is not simply that the citizens all happen to face the same difficulties, or realise that common action is the best way to realise their several ends. Instead, there is a truly shared identity as the citizens (insofar as they are capable of striving for the good) all desire the same shared way of life. Socrates stresses that in the ideal city there will be no distinction between 'mine' and 'thine' overcoming the tension between private and public interest.[98] This tension is only really a feature of corrupt cities where there is no common goal directed at life governed by the good.[99]

Within the city, as within an individual, there is a connection between attraction to the good and harmony. The possession of the

---

[96] Horst Hutter, *Politics as Friendship: The Origins of Classical Notions of Politics in the Theory and Practice of Friendship* (Ontario: Wilfrid Laurier University Press, 1978), p. 97.

[97] On the issue of harmony in the *Republic* see Gregory Vlastos, 'Justice and Psychic Harmony in the *Republic*', *The Journal of Philosophy* LXVI(16), 1969; Julius Moravcsik, 'Inner Harmony and the Human Ideal in *Republic IV* and *IX*', *The Journal of Ethics* 5(1), 2001. See too Singer, *The Nature of Love: Plato to Luther*, p. 75.

[98] Plato, *The Republic*, 462-465.

[99] Gerald M Mara, 'Politics and Action in Plato's *Republic*', *The Western Political Quarterly* 36(4), 1983, pp. 604, 612.

good is the foundation for harmony itself. A truly good person does not find themselves in conflict—nor would a truly good community. However, as Socrates is only too well aware, there are many pitfalls to the attainment of the good. Two are central. The first is the very excess of passion itself. Although it is appropriate to be drawn towards the good, this desire can take perverted forms and even become ensnared on the 'lower' levels of its ascent. This is precisely what happens when a lover confuses his love for the good with his desire to possess the physical beauty of his beloved.[100] The second snare is that of never having the philosophical flame properly kindled in the first place. Here the problem is less one of an excess but a deficit of passion. In the *Republic* Socrates is keen to focus not only on the regulation of the conditions for the polis as a whole, but special attention is also paid to the nurturing and education of the young.

In the previous dialogues we have seen the awareness of these pitfalls played out in Socrates' concern to inculcate the philosophical drive in the young (via *Lysis*), and later to show the path to the good via the friendship and love between individuals (via the *Symposium*). In the *Republic* this concern is echoed and reproduced for the city as a whole. It can be conceded that the arrangements that Socrates proposes for the instruction of the citizens as a whole are deeply paternalistic. Indeed, the focus on myths might be considered to be little more than indoctrination. However, for the Guardians Socrates proposes an education that can truly be described as edifying. For Socrates, true education is not simply the reproduction of regimented knowledge, but the kindling and feeding of the flame of desire that draws individuals towards the good. Without this flame, without this desire, there can be no city. This desire has to be carefully and properly controlled. Thus, in contrast to the lower forms of love, the educated man falls in love with the harmony of beauty. Unlike the lower and mistaken forms of love

---

[100] This helps to explain what might be taken to be Plato's ambivalence concerning homosexuality. Whilst in the *Symposium* he has Socrates promote some forms of homosexuality, in *The Laws* Plato's Athenian 'outlaws' homosexuality outright (although the detail of the text would seem to point to the conclusion that Plato only has male homosexuality consciously in mind). This edict is also closely connected to pronouncements on the importance on 'self-control'. Plato, *The Laws*, Trevor J Sanders trans. (London: Penguin Books, 2004), pp. 838a-839d and 839e-841a respectively. In the city the concern is with reproduction. Reproduction has two aspects. First the physical (flesh and blood) reproduction of citizens and what is needed to live. Second, the reproduction of harmony and justice (and homosexuality might be a part of this). However, for the second to occur citizens must be harmoniously engaged in the first. This can only be achieved if they appreciate that their own welfare is connected to that of others. Indeed, in the family (which becomes one of the motifs of the *Republic*) reproduction in both senses is immediately understood.

this is not excessive, but is disciplined and self-controlled. As Socrates claims 'to love rightly is to love what is orderly and beautiful in an educated and disciplined way'.[101] To love in this way lovers must not indulge in 'frenzy and excess' including sexual relations. The city must have laws to promote the right kind of love, and to discourage the wrong kind. For it is only by doing so that the good can reproduce itself in every new generation. The laws direct men to love in the right way.[102] This is especially the case with the young. As the relationships in *Lysis* have indicated (and as the problematic Alcibiades illustrates), if the philosophical flame is to be kindled, young minds need to come into relationship with those of good character. This is repeated in a formalised way in the *Republic*.[103]

However, Socrates seems to be aware that this truly philosophical friendship is unlikely to be attainable by the vast majority of citizens in the ideal city. Indeed, it would seem that philosophical relationships are reserved for the very few.[104] Nevertheless, citizens are still motivated by their desire for the good however dimly they are aware of this, and however poorly they understand this desire.[105] This partly explains that the recourse Socrates has to myth in the *Republic* (such as the foundational myth concerning the metals the gods put into the citizens' natures, or the myth of Er at the end of the book)[106] is a pictorial way of representing the truth, a way that also strikes persons in an immediately emotional and evocative way.[107] It might be for these reasons that Socrates uses the imagery of the family to describe and promote the relations between the citizens. Families are motivated by a common good (or should be) where each member plays their individual part. In so doing they achieve harmony, and come to understand the role that each plays in promoting the interests of the others. It is this motif that Socrates stresses when he is talking of the relationship between the Guardians and the ordinary citizens, and when he discusses how ordinary citizens will view each other. Thus,

---

[101] Plato, *The Republic*, 403a.
[102] Kraut, 'Egoism, Love, and Political Office in Plato', p. 331.
[103] Plato, *The Republic*, 409a.
[104] Hutter describes the guardians as 'philoi', see Hutter, *Politics as Friendship*, p. 99. This is also implicit in the teaching of Diotima where the ascension is shown to be both difficult and limit to the few.
[105] Cf. Mara who comments that 'the difference between philosophers and non-philosophers would appear to be more continuous than dichotomous. The philosopher's concern with identifying and educating lovers of wisdom is precisely why he cannot deal *only* with potential philosophers.' Mara, 'Politics and Action in Plato's *Republic*', p. 613.
[106] Plato, *The Republic*, 415ff., and 614ff. respectively.
[107] Plato, *The Republic*, 518c.

the ordering formalities of the family are used to promote a form of civic friendship which is underpinned by the principles and practices of true friendship: edification and the desire for the good. Whereas the relations between ordinary citizens might remain somewhat formal, they need not be devoid of affection; and whereas the Guardians must seem at times remote from their charges, they are driven by a correctly controlled passion which brings them into deep unity with their charges, seeking what is good in and for them.

What we see in the *Republic* is the erotic friendship of the dialogues such as the *Symposium* transformed into the basic drive that animates the city and its relations. In fact, it is the love of the good which enables individual citizens to work in harmony with each other, and to see how their ends are connected beyond the confines of any one body or any one life.[108] If there were no such desire, the mere 'dictates' of Socrates' formal definition of justice would not seem sufficient. Indeed, the *Republic* would recommend to its readers the totalitarian dystopia that some have attributed to its pages. What saves the *Republic* from this fate is that its value is not that it is a blueprint for an ideal society, but that it is actually concerned to relate to us a striking truth about human beings: that we are at our best when we strive for the good, and that this striving has both an individual and communal dimension—indeed, the striving holds the two together in harmony. Thus, just as *eros* is the first step towards philosophy and an apprehension of the good, so too is it the animating force that breathes life into the city, and which transforms it from a collection of parts to a living organism.

Plato: Friendship and political ideals

Plato's account of friendship will be the source of inspiration for some. For others, it will leave a sense of doubt and concern. This is understandable as what is most attractive about Plato's account is also what could become the most dangerous. Plato's idealism helps to generate this ambivalence. It is one thing to have Socrates educate the youth of Athens, but how will the *daemon* of *eros* which he has provoked be controlled in a world where there may not be a Socrates to guide and instruct. What new and terrible objects might it find to pursue? Furthermore, in presenting Socrates' account of the path of friendship towards the Good and its generation of benefits for politics Plato cuts his interlocutors off from the vicissitude of the world. In the *Symposium* the intoxicated Alcabiades appears as a warning of that world. In the *Republic* the proto-realist Thrasymachus plays a similar role. Both of these characters remind us that in the world outside of the

---

[108] Plato, *The Republic*, 462ff.

pages of philosophy there are many who are governed by the desire for power. Can friendship—even the beautiful friendship of the ugly Socrates—ever successfully check this urge?

This is not the only question which haunts Plato's account. Taken as a form of bonding, *eros* might raise a concern in our minds as to how well it understands and accommodates the individuality and particularity of persons. Again, Plato's focus on the other world rather than on the inconvenient facts of this one heightens this doubt. Whilst the idea of *eros* might commonly denote something passionate and even sexual, we see in Plato's thought that (rightly understood and correctly channelled) this desire can be controlled. Indeed, in transcending desire for a particular other and then for particularity itself, *eros* can find its true beloved in an ecstatic vision of the Form of the Good. In promising such a vision of a true and eternal world Plato's thought casts doubt on the importance of the lovers themselves. What is special or significant about *this particular* person? How must we respond to the challenges thrown-up by the other person who is living in a world of change? Of course, Plato does not have Socrates deny that friends and lovers must care for each other in some tangible way. Indeed, we would expect this to be the case. However, the fact that it is not his focus underscores the worry. Although we might presume that such a relationship could entail care for the particular other (perhaps as Socrates demonstrates in his own life), it is the abstract form of the Good which remains the real source of concern and attention. In a sense lovers must see through each other to have a chance of seeing the true focus of *eros*—and seeing through another is not necessarily seeing them at all.

This leaves a second question: what are we to make of all those relationships which don't live up to Plato's exacting standards? Plato is surely right to have Socrates and his interlocutors identify that there is a difference between loving in a decent and deviant way. Loving in the wrong way shows the dangerous and corrupting side of human bonding. Just as loving in the right way fosters and brings forth virtue and understanding, loving in the wrong way inculcates vice and confusion. Virtue and vice are shown to be reproduced socially, not only in the relationships of particular individuals, but also in the relationships which form and support the polis itself. Yet clearly the vast majority of relationships are not going to be of a philosophical kind, although they might well be decent enough. Indeed, it is far from clear that even Socrates himself has achieved the dizzy heights of the ascent described by Diotima. There is a sense, then, in which the ideal of friendship in Plato's thought is precisely that: an ideal. Perhaps it could be said that the ideal rescues other bonds from the mundane. The ideal shines light on to these relationships to show what is valuable within them. This value must be recognised and drawn out. However, in shining its light in this way, Plato's thought also casts shadow on much which is necessary but not ideal. It is interesting to note that in his ideal city Plato has Socrates leave all of the practical tasks to the ordinary folk. They do not share in the higher friendship of the Guardians, and the repeated metaphor that Socrates is made to employ is that of a family. Thus, whilst the Guardians share in the true friendship and aim at philosophical reproduction, the secondary form of friendship and physical reproduction is left to the less philosophically able. Although the republic is supposed to be ruled for the benefit of all, it sometimes appears that ultimately it is *justified* by the opportunity that it gives the Guardians to witness the Forms. Does one form of friendship support the other? How do the two intersect?

Politically Plato's account of friendship is the model for the kind of fraternity, camaraderie, and solidarity associated with both centralised states and revolutionary movements. Of course, the former is often the unwitting result of the latter. The kind of friendship that Plato promotes (both the ideal friendship of those engaged in philosophy and the fraternal friendship of the ordinary folk) promotes unity rather than pluralism. Ultimately the Good is singular, and there is only one correct way to order the soul of a person and the city. Combined with the educative aspects of *eros* and *philia* Plato can be viewed as the precursor to the tradition which sees small but dedicated groups attempt to transform whole societies. Such groups tend to be tight-knit. The bonds of such groups are not simply based around their affection for each other as individuals. Whilst this is undoubtedly important, the crucial bond is that which is generated by the passion and zeal for the revolutionary idea itself. Such groups view themselves not as usurpers, but as the genuine carriers of the truth. Their role is to educate the masses who will probably never fully grasp the ideal. The masses are to be guided towards the ideal. Here we now see the weaker bonds of public fraternity that Plato describes in the *Republic*. Here, too, we see societies where harmony is achieved by each person playing their part. The parts add up to a unified whole. However, here playing one's part tends to come to mean knowing one's place—and staying there.

What we see prefigured in Plato's thought, then, are the contours that shape the revolutionary and centralist thought of both the left and right. Prefigured too are the kinds of friendships that are needed to support these positions: the passion of *eros* with its idealistic focus, and the fraternal and disciplined relations of ordinary citizens engaged in everyday tasks. Here too we find instances of the desire to shape society around a single unifying idea, and to see all the bonds of society work towards that idea. The idea hovers over society and becomes the goal of the friends as leaders. Yet it is also seen in potential in the souls of ordinary people. Here passion is directed away from the personal and into the political. Yet this is only one outcome of Plato's account of friendship. It need not be the only outcome. Despite the obvious danger there is still something attractive in Plato's account. It shows that people can both have a commitment to the good, and wish to see that good realised for themselves and for others. This is a useful corrective to the view that politics cannot achieve anything greater than preventing evil. It shows that friendship need not undermine the aims of the political. Indeed, Plato's thought shows that friendship is conducive to its aims. Seen from another direction, Plato's thought also shows that it is only those regimes which stray from a focus on truth and the Good that need fear friendship. The relationship produces bad citizens for such regimes as it reproduces the desire for justice for self and other, and fosters the virtues needed to achieve it. Therefore, Plato's thought suggests that friendship is essential to the very fabric of the political. Without friendship—the right kind of friendship—we are doomed to allow justice to perish. Most of all, Plato's view of friendship shows us the possibility of a politics where persons are concerned about searching for the good together and are willing to view the achievements of others as their own. This aspect of Plato's account still holds the power to inspire.

Chapter Three

Aristotle

ARISTOTLE has cast the most enduring spell on our thinking about friendship and the political. It is perhaps not an exaggeration to say that every subsequent account of friendship that has found a place in the canon draws something from Aristotle. Even contemporary thinkers find Aristotle's account enchanting in both senses of that word. For whilst Aristotle's account is widely appreciated for its elegance and sophistication, it also acts as a lure from which contemporary thinkers find it difficult to move away despite the obvious dangers that it represents. Once glimpsed it is seemingly impossible to think outside of Aristotle's categories, his gift seemingly both intuitive and true. It is Aristotle's account (rather than Plato's) that seems to speak most clearly to our everyday and somewhat mundane concerns; and it is Aristotle's account (rather than Plato's) that seems to offer the best hope of understanding and appreciating the myriad of communities and relationships in which we find ourselves. Nevertheless, Aristotle draws on Plato's themes and questions, and in some ways Aristotle's thought can be seen to be a partial response to the problems first raised by Plato's Socrates.[109]

Given these observations it is perhaps not surprising that those concerned with making the connection between friendship and the political have also been influenced by Aristotle. Indeed the account of friendship that Aristotle offers in the *Nicomachean Ethics* has become a virtual standard for theorising friendship and the political. This is no mere coincidence as not only does the *Nicomachean Ethics* offer us one of the most original accounts of friendship *per se*, it also offers us an explicit connection between friendship and the political. The *Nicomachean Ethics* contains political themes and it is addressed to those likely to be engaged in politics. With this in mind it is best considered as the sibling of the *Politics* and the two books should be understood

---

[109] Price, *Love and Friendship in Plato and Aristotle*, pp. 1-14.

together.[110] From the perspective of those thinking about friendship and the political four features of Aristotle's account make it especially illuminating. First, Aristotle's account is simultaneously philosophical and practical. It is a philosophy of both the ideal and the mundane. Thus, whilst Aristotle clearly has a vision of the 'best' or 'complete' friendship, he also takes time to analyse the relative merits and dynamics of the less complete and more common forms of friendship. Indeed, these vastly outnumber the ideal type which remains both somewhat rare and reified. What Aristotle highlights is the extensive role that friendship plays across all relations within the polis, and he explores the basis, potential, and value of those relationships. Second, Aristotle links friendship and justice as basic features of all community (*koinonia*). This link is important as it develops the suggestion that there are a whole variety of friendships with differing purposes and standards of conduct and evaluation. Moreover, it raises the question of the primacy of friendship over justice especially in justice's 'legalised' forms. Famously Aristotle claims that legislators are more concerned to foster friendship than justice as the former dispenses with the need for the latter.[111]

Third, Aristotle develops the connection between friendship and equality (and this is linked to the issues surrounding justice). It is sometimes thought that in friendship it is the friends themselves who have to be equal. Aristotle shows that it is, in fact, an equality of reciprocity within the relationship which is both desirable and should be sought after. In this sense, friendship is a relationship of equalisation rather than equality, with both friends giving the other what they 'deserve'. As we will see, this has important political implications in terms of the relations between citizens under the various types of constitutions that Aristotle outlines in the *Politics*. Finally, it is in the *Nicomachean Ethics* that Aristotle most explicitly discusses the idea of 'political friendship' (*philia politike*). It is this notion which is not only suggestive to contemporary thinkers, but which Aristotle also explicitly connects to the idea that there is a kind of friendship between citizens. This is intriguing as it places friendship at the heart of political relations. Moreover, taken as a whole, it is this idea of political friendship and the primacy of friendship for any community (including the political community) that helps to link the observations and purposes of the *Nicomachean Ethics* to those of the *Politics*. It is the

---

[110] AWH Adkins, 'The Connection between Aristotle's *Ethics* and *Politics*', *Political Theory* 12(1), 1984. It should be noted that the *Nichomachean Ethics* is not the only place where Aristotle discusses friendship. A *similar* discussion can be found in his *Eudemian Ethics*. The topic is also discussed (programmatically) in the *Rhetoric*.
[111] Aristotle, *Nicomachean Ethics*, 1155a20-25.

connection between friendship, justice, and equality that helps to inform the theoretical and practical discussions of not only the correct and deviant constitutions of the later treatise, but also the purpose and potential of the polis as a community directed towards the good life itself.

Friendship: The origin of the species

In approaching Aristotle's account of friendship in the *Nicomachean Ethics* it is important not to lose sight of how his treatment of this particular theme fits within his thought as a whole. First, the *Nicomachean Ethics* and the *Politics* are concerned to identify and discuss the hierarchy of goods and ends of human beings. In particular, they are concerned with the highest end that is the focus of 'political science' which (by virtue of its focus on the highest end and its control of the other sciences) is therefore the 'ruling science'.[112] The approach is at once both theoretical and practical. Second, Aristotle's usual method is to understand a phenomenon in relation to its ultimate aim or purpose. In the realm of human affairs this is always some (apparent) good. The aim or ends of human activity are found to be both natural and normative. It is in this way that Aristotle takes an interest in the 'deviant' or 'incomplete' things which, although not perfect, may have some value nonetheless. This is all played out in Aristotle's account of the polis. The polis is the over-arching community that contains all the partial communities which it encompasses.[113] However, it is much more than the sum of its parts. Given that the true aim of man is to live beyond necessity and the realise his ethical potential, the polis is the community that all other communities ultimately aim towards and (in some sense) their existence is justified by the life of the polis.[114] It is only within the polis that a full opportunity for virtue is offered. What we see here is not simply the advancement of an ideal and the denigration of all that falls short of this, but an ethical assessment of the gamut of political arrangements and the offering of practical advice as to how the best may be made of them.

Aristotle's account of friendship in the *Nicomachean Ethics* fits into and follows the contours of this overall scheme. For Aristotle, friendship is a way of understanding the partial communities which fit into this overarching community and their aims and purposes. Moreover, for Aristotle the polis is understood to be characterised as a

---

[112] Aristotle, *Nicomachean Ethics*, 1094a25ff. Cf. Adkins, 'The Connection between Aristotle's *Ethics* and *Politics*'.

[113] Aristotle, *Nicomachean Ethics*, 1160a10-30. Aristotle, *The Politics*, 1252a1-6.

[114] For a discussion of this idea of priority see Kraut, *Aristotle: Political Philosophy*, pp. 253-273.

form of friendship (and, as we shall see, this is reflected most clearly in his discussion of the various constitutions). In the *Nicomachean Ethics* Aristotle famously advances three 'causes' of friendship: utility, pleasure, and virtue. These three causes result in three different (and basic) species of friendship (although later this will be brought into question). Of these, only the friendship of good men is described as being complete. Whilst they aim at some good, the good of the other two species of friendship is said to be limited and relative. In light of this it is important to note that Aristotle is not, in the first instance, claiming that the incomplete friendships are incomplete *because* they are not virtuous.[115] In fact, in the opening of his discussion Aristotle is comparing all these species of friendship to a generic template. It is this template which is definitive; but it is also a template which is drawn from the common features of the things that Aristotle's contemporaries commonly called friendship. The three species of friendship map on to this generic account as possible instances of specific things which are lovable. For, whilst it is true that Aristotle holds virtue friendship in particular regard as most fully realising the generic account, and although virtue friendship is sometimes treated as virtually synonymous with the generic account, the two should not be confused.[116] To do so would be to misunderstand the value that Aristotle finds in the other two species of friendship. It would also be to misunderstand the role that these friendships can play in the life of the communities that form the polis.

In the generic account Aristotle argues that the object (or aim) of friendship is what is loveable, and that each person loves what *appears* good for him.[117] Thus, there is a possible disjuncture between relative and absolute good, but the possibility is also left open that different things could be good for different people.[118] As we will see, this has important implications for what Aristotle will go on to say about justice and equality within friendship. It is this claim concerning the apparent good being the aim of friendship which leads Aristotle to the identification of the three causes of love. The three causes are instances of this open-ended definition. However, this is not the only condition

---

[115] WW Fortenbaugh, 'Aristotle's Analysis of Friendship: Function and Analogy, Resemblance, and Focal Meaning', *Phronesis* 20(1), 1975, p. 58.

[116] Fortenbaugh, 'Aristotle's Analysis of Friendship: Function and Analogy, Resemblance, and Focal Meaning'. This insightful article has been crucial for the thinking developed here. See also John M Cooper, 'Aristotle on the Forms of Friendship', *Review of Metaphysics* 30(4), 1977a, p. 629.

[117] Aristotle, *Nicomachean Ethics*, 1155b15-25. On Aristotle's consistency on this point see Cooper, 'Aristotle on the Forms of Friendship', p. 626.

[118] John M Cooper, 'Friendship and the Good in Aristotle', *The Philosophical Review* 86(3), 1977b, p. 290.

for friendship. Between 1155b25 and 1156a5 Aristotle further specifies what is meant by friendship culminating in the claim that to be friends people 'must have goodwill to each other, wish goods and be aware of it, from one of the causes mentioned above [i.e. utility, pleasure, virtue]'. In other words, friendship is the mutual awareness of reciprocated goodwill (which is more than mere well-wishing).[119] This reciprocated goodwill is based on the love of utility, pleasure, or virtue. Thus, Aristotle is not (in the first instance) taking 'virtue' friendship as the ultimate end of all friendship, by which the other two forms of friendship can be judged to be inferior. Under this scheme there are three distinct species of friendship, and each conforms to the contours of the generic model. It is true that later Aristotle will offer considerable praise for virtue friendship and even recognise it as the most complete of the forms of friendship. However, to confuse this development with the idea that virtue friendship is the one true form of the friendship is to misapprehend Aristotle's typology, and leads to misunderstanding of the relative worth of the three species of friendship.

We can see from the start that Aristotle's objective in the *Nicomachean Ethics* is not simply to recommend one 'perfect' account of friendship, but to identify the generic features of all forms of friendship and to investigate the specific manifestations in their own terms. In this respect Aristotle's account of friendship (*philia*) is far more inclusive than the contemporary English term 'friendship' might allow. This is especially so when Aristotle applies this term to relations between what in English we would consider the diverse groupings of business associates, citizens, and the family. This observation might give us pause for thought. Although in contemporary English the term 'friendship' tends to be reserved for close, intimate, and acquired relationships based on reciprocated affection, it is nonetheless possible to describe the relations between business associates, citizens, and family members as being 'friendly'. Indeed, to refuse to do so would be somewhat perverse. Aristotle's inclusiveness reflects the intention to associate and theorise a group of phenomena which are concerned with the attractions and connections between persons. Aristotle's understanding of friendship can be considered to be the answer to the question of what binds communities together. What is important about this investigation is that its answer indicates that whilst all such relations are motivated by the aim to achieve some good, there is

---

[119] Cf. Cooper, 'Aristotle on the Forms of Friendship', pp. 633-636. See too SJ Theodore Tracy, 'Perfect Friendship in Aristotle's *Nicomachean Ethics*', *Illinois Classical Studies* 4(1979), p. 66.

significant variation in the goods aimed at. As a result there is also variation in the purposes and kinds of friendship.[120]

Aristotle's typology therefore maps on to the complex structure of the relations that form the polis and the intricate overlapping of the communities within it. Although there are three basic species of friendship this is by no means the end of division. In identifying both business associates and family members as sharing in friendship Aristotle recognises that friendship can have both an acquired and structural basis. Friendship can also be subdivided by the relative equality of the friends and what they bring to the friendship. Some friendships are based on the equality of persons (the friendship between virtuous people, for example) whilst others are based on inequality (such as the superiority of a father over his son).[121] Furthermore, because the goods of friendship are relative to the persons involved, various mixed forms of friendship are possible (utility might be matched with pleasure, for example). It is the combination of these features which not only governs the appropriate forms of behaviour within the friendships, but also determines whether they are formed between similar or dissimilar persons, their relative stability and instability, and the numerical limits of their extension.

Equality and Justice

So far we have noted that for Aristotle the defining feature of all friendship is the acknowledgement and reciprocation of goodwill motivated by something that appears good to the friends. This results in three basic species of friendship aiming at utility, pleasure, and virtue. Although virtue-friendship provides an exemplary case as it is both the most desirable and most complete form of friendship, it should not be confused with friendship *per se*. Despite this, the friendship of good men does highlight a feature of friendship that we might suppose to be intrinsic to the relationship itself: equality.[122]

The issue of equality in friendship is vexed and it is prone to lead thought to travel in at least two directions. One approach sees this

---

[120] Fortenbaugh, 'Aristotle's Analysis of Friendship: Function and Analogy, Resemblance, and Focal Meaning', p. 52. It should be noted that these goods are both necessary and choice-worthy cf. Theodore Tracy, 'Perfect Friendship in Aristotle's *Nicomachean Ethics*', p. 66; Ferdinand Schoeman, 'Aristotle on the Good of Friendship', *Australasian Journal of Philosophy* 63(3), 1985, p. 269.

[121] For a general discussion of these points see Lorraine Smith Pangle, *Aristotle and the Philosophy of Friendship* (Cambridge: Cambridge University Press, 2003).

[122] Aristotle, *Nicomachean Ethics*, 1157b35. Cooper makes the point that virtue friendship should not be considered the preserve of moral heroes. Although it can be perfected decent citizen can still partake of it. Cooper, 'Aristotle on the Forms of Friendship', p. 643.

cashed out in terms of the relative *worth* of the friends. Clearly this is what Aristotle has in mind when he mentions some of the difficulties an excellent person would face in forming and maintaining a friendship with a morally inferior man who held political power.[123] Here the idea seems to be that friends will be similar in some way. In this sense we would expect good men to form friendships with other good men. In fact two themes are merged here. The first is the idea that the friends have some *equivalence* in moral status. This sees the friends *share characteristics*. This all echoes the puzzles that Socrates is seen to struggle with concerning the possibility and source of the friendship between good men, and the question of whether like really does attract to like (a question central to *Lysis*). It will be remembered that whilst the former is an ethical question the latter need not be, and this is true for the two themes as woven together in this approach to the Aristotelian case. However, to the modern mind comparing the 'worth' of human beings inevitably leads to objections: it militates against the basic equality of all people that forms the bedrock of most moral and political assumptions. If this is what Aristotle is saying then (presumably) it is not an outlook that modern minds are in a position to either entertain or endorse. If it is to have currency then it must be converted into its non-moral denomination. Here it might be argued that different people seek and make different contributions on friendship. However, there is still a sense in which some people are 'better' friends than others. The idea here is that they are better at fulfilling the requirements of a friend. This does not mean that they are morally superior people in the sense of worth, but they are certainly better (or more 'successful') friends.

The second approach might consider equality in terms of the *balance* of reciprocated goodwill and beneficent acts that the friends perform for each other. Again, Aristotle points to the importance of this issue when he discusses disputes in friendships for utility.[124] The contemporary perspective would readily admit that there must be some kind of balance of beneficence within a friendship. We grow suspicious of relationships claiming the title friendship where one party aids the other but receives nothing in return. However, the temptation might be to think that whilst there should be some kind of balance within a friendship that this is a delicate and elusive thing. Against the view that the focus of equality in friendship should be worked out as a balance of benefits, it might be assumed that any equation of favour for favour is not calculable as such. Indeed, it might

---

[123] Aristotle, *Nicomachean Ethics*, 1158a25-35 and 1159a30-35.
[124] Aristotle, *Nicomachean Ethics*, 1163b35-1164b20.

be though that such concerns only come into consideration in failing friendships. The calculation of the return of favours becomes important in such cases not because it is an intrinsic feature of friendship, but because it reflects the failure of one of the parties to understand what friendship means. We do not simply accuse our friends of failing to return a favour, but failing to be our friends in the right kind of way. The external manifestation of reciprocation is assumed to reflect a mental or emotional attitude towards the other. Calculation is not necessary, indeed it might even be thought to be pernicious. Sometimes, acknowledging the effort of the other is enough.

Given these two directions, the modern mind might tend to favour a modified version of the former rather than the latter. The problem with the latter position is that it seems to make friendship too calculating and dependent on reciprocation and exchange. As has been suggested, friendship is about an appropriate response and disposition towards the other, not the calculation of benefit and loss. A reinterpretation of the former position would see the 'worth' of a person modified by the language of the appropriateness of their moral and emotional attitudes towards us and the friendship. Of course, when others do us good we should respond in kind when asked, but this kind of exchange should not be the basis of the friendship. Thus, we can simultaneously recognise the basic moral equality of all persons, whilst also recognising that our dispositions and actions towards each other should be met with particular (and appropriate) responses and consequences. We simply owe more to those who have done us good. Appropriate though this response is (when and however we are able), it should not be considered a condition of the good deed itself. Friendships are held together because we are attracted to the other *person*, not because of what they can do for us. We might even be tempted to assume that Aristotle had something like this in mind (given that possessing the virtues reflects having the right motives and capacities). However, this temptation reflects more about our sharing in the emphasis of the contemporary view that genuine friendship should be based on a form of moral altruism rather than an appreciation of Aristotle's position. For, as we shall see, Aristotle's view is much closer to the second of these alternatives, a view which ties any talk of equality in friendship to a kind of equality of return and an instance of reciprocation.[125]

To see why this is the case it is important to note the context and manner in which equality first enters into Aristotle's discussion of

---

[125] Smith Pangle, *Aristotle and the Philosophy of Friendship*, p. 103.

friendship. 'Equality' first appears in the discussion at 1157b35 where Aristotle tells us that in the friendship of good men:

> Each of them loves what is good for himself, and repays in equal measure the wish and pleasantness of his friend; for friendship is said to be equality. And this is true above all in the friendship of good people.

There are three things to be said about this. First, this comment is at best semi-detached from the opening generic account of friendship that Aristotle offers between 1155b15-1156a10. In this generic account friendship exists between people who 'have goodwill to each other, wish goods and [are] aware of it, from one of the causes mentioned above [i.e. utility, pleasure, and virtue]'.[126] There is no mention of equality here. Indeed, Aristotle manages to discuss the contrasts and similarities between the three species of friendship (including their relative completeness) before making this comment. Second, the subject of the comment itself (the supposed connection between friendship and equality) is not taken-up directly at this point. Indeed, there seems to be some hesitation on Aristotle's part to give his unconditional endorsement to this popular assumption. Aristotle merely notes that friendship *is said* to be equality. He seems to endorse this insofar as it applies to the case of the friendship of good men. It might also be noted that it is not clear what 'repayment' might mean here, either. Nor is it clear in what sense this leads to equality. Third, after this comment, Aristotle briefly continues his comparison between the three species of friendship before taking up the issue of equality more directly at 1158b7. Here Aristotle considers friendships where one party is in some way superior to the other (his examples include a father towards his son, and a ruler towards those he rules). However, whilst this implies that Aristotle has been treating the three species of friendship that have formed the focus of his discussion so far as having (some kind of) equality, it does not mean that we should conclude that equality is intrinsic to friendship (or how else could Aristotle now claim to be talking about the friendships of father and son, ruler and ruled?), nor should we assume anything about how Aristotle might happen to find equality in these previously discussed relationships. In itself, this shift of focus does not resolve our previous question about the *kind* of equality present in friendship (i.e. between equality of quality [worth], and equality of quantity [reciprocation]).

The key for understanding Aristotle's views on the relationships between friendship and equality is to be found in his comments that contrast friendship and equality with justice and equality. Previous to

---

[126] Aristotle, *Nicomachean Ethics*, 1156a5.

his discussion of friendship, Aristotle has explored the notion of justice in Book V of the *Nicomachean Ethics*. Pointing-out that 'justice' is a homonym, Aristotle then goes on to outline two categories: one general and one particular (or 'special').[127] The general type is found to pertain to the laws of a political community. It represents not only what is contained in the general laws, but also the customs and mores of the community. Here the basic idea is that in a well-ordered political community the laws will promote the virtues. The particular form of justice is connected much more closely to the idea of 'fairness'. Here Aristotle is concerned primarily with what might be described as the mechanisms of distribution, rectification, and exchange. In other words, whereas general justice is concerned with the value-system and pattern of social intercourse, special justice is concerned with the application of the rules concerning the effects of specific actions and claims. Moreover, whereas failings in the first form of justice are the result of a more general failure to display the virtues, failures in the particular form of justice seem to be motivated by the specific characteristic of *pleonexia* (greed). In particular justice we haven't just failed, we are motivated by the desire to take more than our fair share and to deprive others of theirs.[128]

Particular justice is further subdivided in the three ways already indicated: distribution, rectification, and exchange (although it is not entirely clear as to whether Aristotle intends exchange to be a separate category, or a subset of rectification). In any event, it is in justice as distribution and rectification that equality plays a central role. However, there is a differentiation as to what counts as being the relevant concern of equality in both. In justice as distribution those who are equal in *worth* are to receive equal shares.[129] Aristotle leaves open the question as to what is a relevant qualification for worth, noting that this is often disputed (although this is what is established by general justice). This thought connects directly to what Aristotle has to say about equality in the *Politics*. In the later work, when discussing the specific issue of the basis of the constitutional arrangements for the distribution of power, Aristotle claims that:

---

[127] Aristotle, *Nicomachean Ethics*, 1129a25-30. See also Kraut, *Aristotle: Political Philosophy*, pp. 102-4. It might also be that we have made a mistake about justice. This more charitable assessment of the failure to understand justice is made in *The Politics*. However, it should also be noted that 'economic interest' also plays a significant role here.

[128] For a more detailed discussion of this point see Kraut, *Aristotle: Political Philosophy*, pp. 136-141.

[129] Aristotle, *Nicomachean Ethics*, 1131a20-25.

> ...it is thought that justice is equality; and so it is, but not for all persons, only for those that are equal. Inequality also is thought to be just; and so it is, but not for all, only the unequal. We make bad mistakes if we neglect this 'for whom' when we are deciding what is just.[130]

In other words, in distribution the key is in assigning the appropriate goods to the people with the appropriate qualities. The qualities of different people lead to them having different shares of different things (albeit that those with the same qualities should have an equal share of the same things). The important point is that Aristotle does not argue that the 'starting point' for justice in distribution is to assume that all people receive an equal share in the sense of 'the same' and that their qualities should be ignored. Aristotle contrasts this notion with his claims about rectification. Here the concern is not the initial distribution (or more properly, the basis of the initial distribution), but only with the more limited concern of rectifying imbalances caused by the actions of individuals. Thus, Aristotle claims that in these cases:

> ...it does not matter if a decent person has taken from a base person, or a base person from a decent person, or if a decent or base person has committed adultery. Rather, the law looks only at differences in the harm [inflicted], and treats the people involved as equals...[131]

The thought here is that it is the role of rectificatory justice to *restore* a balance. It makes no comment on the criteria for the initial assignment of goods (as in the case of distributive justice). In this sense justice as rectification is obviously dependent on justice as distribution. It is for this reason that we can consider justice in distribution to take 'priority' as an account of justice over that of rectification (with a consideration of exchange as a special case of rectification).

The relevance of these observations can be seen when we consider what Aristotle has to say on his discussion of friendship at 1158b30. Here it is Aristotle's claim that whilst it is the case that proportional loving leads to a kind of equality, this is to be *contrasted* with the equality found in justice. We can suppose that Aristotle must have particular rather than general justice in mind as equality is the defining feature of the former rather than the latter. Aristotle writes that:

---

[130] Aristotle, *The Politics*, 1280a7.
[131] Aristotle, *Nicomachean Ethics*, 1132a1-5.

> Equality, however, does not appear to be the same in friendship as in justice. For in justice equality is equality primarily in worth and secondarily in quantity; but in friendship it is equality primarily in quantity and secondarily in worth.

What is the significance of this contrast? Here Aristotle relates but differentiates the forms of equality found in friendship and justice. As we will see, there is a relationship between the three ideas as Aristotle will not only claim that equality is a feature of both friendship and justice (albeit equality in different primary senses), but he will also claim that friendship and justice exist together (indeed, the implication is that the latter is dependent to some degree on the former, and that in this sense they are coextensive). However, whilst there is a contrast between the form of equality found in friendship and justice, Aristotle is not claiming that in justice equality is only to be understood as equality of worth, and that in friendship equality is only to be understood as equality of quantity. Instead, there is a two-tier understanding of equality in each with a primary and secondary sense. As we have seen, in the case of justice this two-tier process involves a narrowing of the focus and scope of justice. General justice is focused on virtuous acts as a whole and concerns treating others in an appropriate way. Here 'appropriate' is determined by the differing worth of self and others. The good man has distinct ways of behaving towards his fellow citizens, his wife, children, and slaves. From an Aristotelian standpoint we would not expect a good man to treat them all the same as if there were no difference in worth between them. He stands in a different relation to each. Behaving appropriately to these different people also means attributing different goods to each (such as honour, power, and wealth). It is only when equality of quality is settled (through justice taken in the widest sense to include the mores, customs, and beliefs of the community) that the secondary and more particular form of justice plays a role. In the particular form of justice the concern is not with quality as such but with ensuring that individuals receive and retain their 'fair share'. Thus, having decided what constitutes a 'just distribution' and what counts as a 'like case', particular justice is concerned with the more prescribed tasks of distribution in the sense of assigning like goods to like persons; rectification in the sense of rebalancing imbalances that appear through human actions; and exchange (which is really a subset of rectification). Thus, justice can be said to be primarily concerned with equality as quality, and only secondarily as equality as quantity.

Friendship reverses this priority. To see how and why this is the case we need to remember that for Aristotle an account of friendship must cover both the paradigm and non-paradigm cases. The non-paradigm cases are still friendships even if they are not complete or ideal friendships. As such, the claims about the equality of friendship being primarily equality of quantity must apply not only to the three cases that Aristotle sets out at the start of his discussion (virtue, pleasure, and utility), but it must also apply to both the non-structural and structural cases, and the cases where there is clear equality of worth in the friendship as well as cases where there is inequality of worth. For Aristotle, the prime example of a structural friendship where there is inequality of worth is that of the relations between parents and children. From this perspective it is interesting to note where Aristotle's claim about the equality in friendship being primarily concerned with quantity appears in his discussion. For the bulk of the discussion prior to making this claim Aristotle's focus had been on the three *causes* of friendship. However, the lines before Aristotle makes his claim have significantly refocused the discussion. For now Aristotle takes up 'a different *species* of friendship ... the one that corresponds to superiority'.[132]

Given this change of focus, we might be forgiven for assuming that the discussion until this point has supposed that the friendships in question are between equals in worth. Why else introduce the idea of friendships where persons are of unequal worth? This conclusion is initially plausible, but does not seem to be borne out by attention to Aristotle's argument itself. The first thing to note is that Aristotle has not, in the most generic case, specified 'equality' as being a feature of friendship. Indeed, it is only being brought in at this later stage, and here it is clearly focused on equality of quantity rather than equality of quality (albeit this being only a primary focus). Clearly Aristotle is *inclined* to recognise that equality is a feature of friendships (and thus, presumably, a feature of the most generic type).[133] More significantly, Aristotle's introduction of this claim now, and specifically in relation to unequal friendships, might make us reconsider what—exactly—is being claimed about the previous three species of friendship. In particular, it might make us draw away from confusing the features of the paradigm case with the features of the generic case (and thus supposing what happens to be true about the paradigm case is also true of the non-paradigm cases). For whilst it might be assumed that virtue-friends are similar in virtue and thus equal in the sense of quality, there is nothing to lead us to assume that this is also true of the non-

---

[132] Aristotle, *Nicomachean Ethics*, 1158b10 (*emphasis* added).
[133] This relates back to the ambivalence that Aristotle seems to display over the notion of equality in friendship when it was first raised at 1157b35.

paradigm cases. In fact, it is reasonable to assume that in many cases this would not be so: good men can have friendships based around pleasure with significantly less good men, and the same is obviously true for utility.

Seen from this perspective, we might assume that most friendships are not friendships based on the similar worth of the friends: indeed, bad and good men can be friends if their friendship is based around the attainment of pleasure or utility, although we might agree that we would not expect this to endure. What is common to each of these relationships is not equality of worth, but equality of quantity. That is to say, the friendships for pleasure endure insofar as pleasure is exchanged and reciprocated, and the friendships for utility endure insofar as the friends receive equal benefits from each other.[134] This also opens the way to the mixed cases of friendship (for example, where one friend seeks pleasure and the other profit). What all this points to is that whilst it can be concluded that in the case of virtue friends there is a similarity of worth, this is not at all the case for the other forms of friendship. We must conclude that the paradigm case is a happy coincidence of both equality of worth and equality of quantity, and perhaps what makes it paradigmatic is that it combines equality in both the primary and secondary senses. Primarily it is an equality of the reciprocation of virtuous activity. It just so happens that in this case equality of worth (virtue) makes this possible. In other words, what ties the friends together in *all* the forms of friendship is their shared (and reciprocated) pursuit of benefits: virtue, pleasure, and utility. Thus, the equality is an equality of quantity not quality for if the reciprocation is uneven then the friendship will dissolve.

This, then, covers the vast array of both common friendships and the paradigm case. However, this does not completely deal with the observation that led to this line of thought: Aristotle's shift in focus from the three cases based around virtue, pleasure, and utility to an explicit consideration of friendships where 'superiority' exists. This shift is somewhat puzzling because here Aristotle not only seems to introduce equality as a feature of friendship, he also seems to introduce a fourth 'species' of friendship (and possibly another cause).[135] For in describing the friendships based around superiority (which also tend to be structural friendships) Aristotle says that they have 'different causes of love'.[136] It is not clear whether this means that the relationships have a variety of causes of love (i.e. virtue, pleasure, utility), or—perhaps

---

[134] Cooper, 'Aristotle on the Forms of Friendship', p. 633.
[135] Schoeman, 'Aristotle on the Good of Friendship', p. 276.
[136] Aristotle, *Nicomachean Ethics*, 1158b15-20.

more plausibly — some new (but unnamed) cause of love. In any case, here we have instances where equality of quality is clearly not achieved (as might have initially been assumed about the cases of virtue, pleasure, and utility). What can Aristotle therefore mean by equality of quantity in these instances? Are these structural friendships (e.g. that of the family) to be considered less complete than the incomplete friendships of pleasure and utility? Our modern inclination would be to say that they are somehow more loosely related to what we would term friendship — but can this be the case for Aristotle? After all, these friendships do display the characteristics of the most general type, and the relationship between father and son would seem to have much more in common with the friendship for virtue than those of utility and pleasure (and even the modern prejudice would have to concede this — and perhaps even hope it). So, given that the primary focus of equality in these friendships is obviously not equality of worth (and thus cannot be virtue friendship — at least not at first), and given that it is difficult (and unattractive) to think of them as being primarily about the exchange of pleasure and utility, in what sense can these friendships be considered to display equality through the primary sense of quantity?

Aristotle's answer can be found in the following claim: '[in] friendships corresponding to superiority, the loving must also be proportional, e.g. the better person, and the more beneficial… must be loved more than he loves'.[137] In these relationships there is, then, a form of equalisation in exchange, but it is not an exchange of the same things (and nor is it a form of reciprocation based on one of the goods outlined in Aristotle's three species of friendship). It might well be that fathers draw pleasure from the existence of their children, and that children gain benefits from their fathers, but the primary form that equality takes in these forms of friendship is the return of honour to a benefactor. In this respect Aristotle is keen to remind us that in the case of fathers and their children, the father must be viewed as the ultimate benefactor because whilst he may draw pleasure and even some utility from his virtuous activity of creation, it is the child who is the ultimate beneficiary dependent on the father for their very being (which is to be considered the highest good).[138] Thus, this relationship seems to exist on the outer limits of the forms of structural friendship (and perhaps offers a parallel paradigm to the case of virtue friendship in the non-structural forms). For Aristotle is clear that the superiority of the gods makes friendship impossible with them (and seemingly unlimited

---

[137] Aristotle, *Nicomachean Ethics*, 1158b25.
[138] Aristotle, *Nicomachean Ethics*, 1158b20.

reverence is due),[139] and the same must surely be thought of for those who are significantly below the standards of human worthiness (such as slaves and animals). Thus, even in the structurally unequal forms of friendship the focus can be seen to be on equality of quantity. If insufficient honour is paid to parents, or benefactors of whatever variety, then the friendship is liable to dissolve in the same way as in the other species of friendship where the reciprocation of benefits breaks down.

Friendship in the polis

In the account developed so far it has been seen that for Aristotle friendship and justice are co-extensive.[140] Furthermore, Aristotle has claimed that both features define the extent of community, and that in different sorts of community friendship and justice take different forms and have different demands. It has also been noted that for Aristotle it is the friendship of the virtuous that forms the paradigm case. It is this form of friendship that displays the fullest range of features of friendship and thus is its most complete realisation. However, it remains to be seen how this general account of friendship can contribute to an understanding of the form of community and ends realised by the polis. Indeed, although the general connection to the political has been partially drawn out, this needs to be sharpened. In addition, we also need to attend to the specific ways in which friendship is connected to the forms of politics found in the polis. In what remains this issue will be taken up. We shall see that although Aristotle makes use of the phrase 'political friendship' (*politike philia*) this cannot be considered to indicate a single and specialised form of friendship in the polis. Instead, the phrase denotes a more general idea that friendships in the realm of politics are especially characterised by concord (*homonia*) and have a particular relationship to the forms of community and justice promoted by a constitution. In this way, it is the relationship between fellow citizens which can best be said to characterise the political friendship found in the polis. Thus Aristotle's account shows political friendship to have both general and specific aspects. Friendship provides the basis for the bonds between the various subgroups (such as the family) that form the framework of the polis as an institution; but more specifically, a certain form of

---

[139] Aristotle, *Nicomachean Ethics*, 1159a5. For a discussion of this intriguing point see Jens Timmermann, 'Why We Cannot Want Our Friends to Be Gods. Some Notes on "NE" 1159a5-12', *Phronesis* 40(2), 1995.

[140] Aristotle, *Nicomachean Ethics*, 1159b25 and 1161a10. See also Lorraine Smith Pangle, *Aristotle and the Philosophy of Friendship* (Cambridge: Cambridge University Press, 2003), p. 81.

friendship can be said to be the characteristic of the uniquely political relationship of citizenship.

Before these issues can be explored in more depth something needs to be said about Aristotle's use of 'political friendship'. Our expectations about what this term might indicate are perhaps most obviously informed by Aristotle's more strident claims about the polis in the *Politics*. Even the most casual perusal of this tract leaves the reader in no doubt of one central point: the polis is something more than a mere association—it is the fulfilment of what it means to be a human being capable of moral action. In the *Politics* Aristotle makes the quasi-historical claim that the polis is formed from smaller (and less complete) associations of the household and the village. They are 'less complete' because whilst they obviously can survive on their own, they do not (and cannot) successfully realise man's true potential. The state appears when several villages come together. Aristotle portrays this as a natural development of the process of mutual need and exchange that brought the household and then the village together. However, Aristotle stresses that 'while the state came about as a means of securing life itself, it continues in being to secure the *good* life'.[141] As a result of this the state has an eye on what is both necessary and fine, and it forms the end of the earlier associations which remain subordinate (although re-infused given their foundational role in providing the necessities for the state).[142] Moreover, it is the claim of the *Nicomachean Ethics* that the virtuous person's concern with 'political science' furthers not only his own ends, but his ends as a member of a polis. As Aristotle boldly claims 'while it is satisfactory to acquire and preserve the good even for an individual, it is finer and more divine to acquire and preserve it for a people and for cities'.[143]

Given his claims about the place of the polis as the moral pinnacle of human endeavour, and given the importance Aristotle has placed on the connections between community, justice, and friendship, we would be forgiven for now expecting Aristotle to make a direct (and clear) connection between the virtuous aspects of friendship and the most virtuous aspirations and achievements of the community of the polis. We might anticipate either drawing a direct line from virtue-friendship

---

[141] Aristotle, *The Politics*, 1252b27 (*emphasis* added). See also 1280b29 where 'The state is an association intended to enable it members, in their households and the kinships [*gene*], to live *well*; its purpose is a perfect and self-sufficient life.' See also Bernard Yack, 'Community and Conflict in Aristotle's Political Philosophy', *The Review of Politics* 47(1), 1985, p. 97.

[142] Aristotle, *The Politics*, 1252a27, 1253a18. Cf. Aristotle, *Nicomachean Ethics*, 1160a10-25. See also Terence Irwin, 'The Good of Political Activity', in Günther Patzig (ed.), *Aristoteles' Politik*, p. 74.

[143] Aristotle, *Nicomachean Ethics*, 1094b10.

to virtuous political activity, or developing a specifically political form of friendship aimed at virtue. Our interest might be further piqued by Aristotle's introduction of the phrase 'political friendship'. However, tempting though it is to be inspired by this line of thought and to focus labour on this phrase, our approach must remain somewhat deflationary. Significant restraint is called for as whilst Aristotle does use the phrase in both the *Nicomachean Ethics* and in the *Eudemian Ethics* it is used sparingly, and it is clearly absent as a significant ordering term in the place where we might expect it to be expanded in full: the *Politics*.[144] Furthermore, where Aristotle does have cause to comment on 'political friendship' he is unequivocal in declaring it is a friendship for advantage.[145] Set against expectations formed in the light of Aristotle's high praise of virtue friendship and the moral nature of the polis this is all somewhat disappointing. From this perspective we might have hoped that not only would Aristotle have been a little more forthcoming on the issue of 'political friendship', but that he would also somehow incorporate it into an account of the highest ends and activities of the best men in the most flourishing polis.[146]

The problem here is not as it seems: the problem is not with the scant attention paid to the phrase 'political friendship' in Aristotle's works, but in our assumptions that this is the only indicator of Aristotle's engagement with the connection between friendship and politics. A wider perspective (the perspective already pursued throughout this discussion of Aristotle and this enquiry as a whole) has already shown that Aristotle connects friendship to the political. We should not lose sight of Aristotle's indication that friendship is co-extensive with justice, is found in all communities, and is a necessary feature of the best and self-sufficient life. Moreover, friendship is inherently political in Aristotle's thought as it provides the central

---

[144] Suzanne Stern-Gillet, *Aristotle's Philosophy of Friendship* (New York: State University of New York Press, 1995), p. 149. See too Richard Mulgan, 'The Role of Friendship in Aristotle's Political Theory', *Critical Review of International Social and Political Philosophy* 2(4), 1999, p. 16.

[145] Aristotle, *Nicomachean Ethics*, 1167b. and *Eudemian Ethics*, 1242b22-23.

[146] For some of the attempts to identify what Aristotle means by 'political friendship' see Yack, 'Community and Conflict in Aristotle's Political Philosophy'; Bernard Yack, 'Political Friendship and the Second Self in Aristotle's *Nicomachean Ethics*', *Innovations: A Journal of Politics* 5(2004-2005; Irwin, 'The Good of Political Activity', and John M Cooper, 'Political Animals and Civic Friendship', in Günther Patzig (ed.), *Aristoteles' "Politik"*; Susan Bickford, 'Beyond Friendship: Aristotle on Conflict, Deliberation, and Attention', *The Journal of Politics* 58(2), 1996; Mulgan, 'The Role of Friendship'; Smith Pangle, *Aristotle and the Philosophy of Friendship*; Stern-Gillet, *Aristotle's Philosophy of Friendship*; Francis Vander Valk, 'Political Friendship and the Second Self in Aristotle's *Nicomachean Ethics*', *Innovations: A Journal of Politics* 5(2004-2005).

category for the theorisation of the bonds between person and person. It is the causes and dynamics of these bonds which generate the claims to justice, and which enable men to be something more than 'just' social animals. It is in these bonds that we find the fabric necessary for the political.

To understand the connection between friendship and the political, then, it is neither desirable nor necessary to focus all our attention on just one phrase (much less to hope to develop a political theory around it). Instead we must keep the connections between friendship, equality, and justice in sight, along with the claim that friendship takes different forms in different communities. It is this perspective which will best enable us to make sense of the role of friendship in politics in both the *Nicomachean Ethics* and the *Politics*. As we shall see, it is also this perspective which will best give us an insight into citizenship as an especially political form of friendship concerned with equality, justice and concord (*homonia*).

Citizenship as friendship: Concord and the constitutions

Citizenship can be understood to be both a status and a term that indicates the bonds between people in an explicitly political capacity. As a status it is a title or role which is conferred upon individuals. As a bond it indicates a discrete set of activities and dispositions that characterise the political community. As will be shown, citizenship can be considered to be a form of friendship (indeed, Aristotle uses it as an example in precisely this way). Moreover, it should be considered to be the paradigm form of political friendship (i.e. the form of friendship which is most completely both friendship and political). Contrary to his usual practice, when discussing citizenship it is clear that this is one occasion where Aristotle does not attempt to simply reconcile and develop the common accounts. Indeed, as the *Politics* makes clear, for Aristotle 'citizenship' is to be defined in a formal rather than a pragmatic way. Aristotle writes that:

> What effectively distinguishes the citizen proper from all others is his participation in giving judgement and holding office.[147]

And that:

---

[147] Aristotle, *The Politics*, 1275a22.

... as soon as a man becomes entitled to participate in office, deliberative or judicial, we deem him to be a citizen of that state; and a number of such persons large enough to secure a self-sufficient life we may, by and large, call a state.[148]

This somewhat uncompromising statement is not intended to completely capture the extent of common usage of the term 'citizen' but to provide a logical basis for the idea.[149] In fact, Aristotle is quick to point out that this very formal definition of citizenship immediately points to a much deeper and more interesting set of questions. First, reminding his audience of the three correct and three deviant constitutions, Aristotle notes that 'A citizen, therefore, will vary according to the constitution in each case'.[150] This prepares the ground for the central problem of citizenship (and one of the central themes of the *Politics* itself). As Aristotle has it: 'The question here is not "Are these persons citizens?", but whether they are citizens justly or unjustly'.[151] The formalism of Aristotle's initial definition is used as a device to generate a concern with the merits of the distribution of political power and (more importantly from our current perspective) the binding principles of the various constitutions which structure communities.

Citizenship, then, is a special set of relationships within a community ordered by a constitution. A constitution is not simply a written document, it is any general agreement on customs, laws, and procedures that frame the life of a community.[152] Importantly it is agreement on the just claims to power. Thus the constitution answers the question of 'Who should rule and why?'. The extent of this agreement about justice is also the extent of the friendship within the political community. The answer is not expected to be univocal, and in different kinds of political community this question will be answered in different ways.[153] Thus, the realisation of citizenship under the various constitutions (both correct and deviant) manifests in different groups of men being admitted into citizenship for different reasons. For example, this can be seen in the famous distinction between the deviant constitutions of oligarchy and democracy where 'oligarchy occurs

---

[148] Aristotle, *The Politics*, 1275b13.
[149] Irwin, 'The Good of Political Activity', p. 82.
[150] Aristotle, *The Politics*, 1275a34.
[151] Aristotle, *The Politics*, 1275b34.
[152] Cf. Stern-Gillet, *Aristotle's Philosophy of Friendship*, p. 154; Yack, 'Community and Conflict in Aristotle's Political Philosophy', p. 98.
[153] Aristotle, *The Politics*, 1241b10. See also Stern-Gillet, *Aristotle's Philosophy of Friendship*, p. 160; Yack, 'Community and Conflict in Aristotle's Political Philosophy', p. 99.

when the sovereign power of the constitution is in the hands of those with possessions, democracy when it is in the hands of those who have no stock of possessions and are without means'.[154] However, although the different constitutions use different criteria for the identification of who should share in power, all the forms nevertheless recognise some form of equality as the basis for the application of their respective criteria. In other words, if wealth is taken as the mark of citizenship (i.e. the relevant quality that entitles a person to share in power) then all those with this mark are to be admitted as citizens. Equality thus plays a dual role in citizenship: it acts as a principle for inclusion and exclusion, and it characterises the relationship between all those who are included.[155]

In this sense we can see two forms of political friendship operating in the polis. The first kind is based around differentiation and is characterised as a variety of the unequal friendships that Aristotle outlines in the *Nicomachean Ethics*. Those who are citizens stand in vertical relation to those who are excluded. The citizens represent the active, deliberative, and rational part of the state which exercises power and control over the other elements. Nevertheless, whilst citizens may well rule in their own interests, this should not (necessarily) be thought of as being somehow antithetical to the interests of non-citizens or as being merely exploitative. Just as Aristotle has already argued that this is not the case in the pairings which form the household, nor should it be assumed in the polis. The real distinction concerning rulership in the household and the polis falls along two axes. First, is the rule over free and equal persons or 'inferiors'? Second, is the rule the result of rationality and aimed at the common good, or does it result from desire or ignorance and focus on sectional interest? All of this is traceable to the *Nicomachean Ethics* where Aristotle identifies the resemblances between the correct constitutions and the relations within the household.[156] In the correct constitutions the citizens should take an interest in the common good of the entire polis. The wider relations of the polis are the necessary foundation and well from which the resources are drawn to make political activity possible. Thus the relationships must be characterised by utility, but clearly utility (in the best constitutions) is not mere 'use of others' let alone exploitation; it is to be understood as *mutual* advantage.

---

[154] Aristotle, *The Politics*, 1279b16.
[155] It might be objected that monarchy (the rule of one) does not admit to this principle. In fact, the claim of the monarch (be he king or tyrant) is precisely that he has no relevant equal (and therefore should not be treated like other men).
[156] Aristotle, *Nicomachean Ethics*, 1161a10 ff. Aristotle repeats this observation in *The Eudemian Ethics*, 1241b25-35.

In contrast, the relations between citizens (*qua* citizens) can be thought of as being strictly horizontal. Of course, this does not mean that citizens are equal in all respects as men, but they are to be considered and treated as equal in respect to rulership. Whatever happens to differentiate them as men, as citizens they all possess the relevant quality in respect to the criteria for sharing power. It is in this sense that they are considered equal. This is important because, as we have seen, in this respect the friendship between citizens can be said to *resemble* the paradigm case of friendship in important ways. However, in drawing these resemblances it is important not to confuse the features of friendship in citizenship with the primary case.

So far we have seen that citizenship shares in one of the features of the paradigm case of friendship: equality. This has been played-out in terms of citizenship being a relationship between those sharing power. It has been further noted that this form of friendship adds additional structure to the more generalised and asymmetric friendships that form the wider polis. The exact form that citizenship takes (and the tenor of the friendships as a whole) is conditioned by the particular form of the constitution. These observations can help us to understand two further points about citizenship as a form of friendship that (at first) might appear to be at odds with one another. The first concerns Aristotle's central claim about citizenship: that it is an exemplary case of *concord*.[157] It should be carefully noted that it is *not* Aristotle's claim that concord is *only* found in political friendship. Indeed, attention reveals that concord is a feature of all friendship, including the most complete type. However, it remains the case that the concord found in citizenship is of a particularly noteworthy variety: it is agreement about the most general things which affect the life of a community. In other words, it is found to be agreement about the constitution, the nature of justice, and the procedures for political action. The second point to be examined concerns Aristotle's repeated claim that political friendship (and thus citizenship) are friendships for advantage. Whereas the first claim would seem to draw citizenship towards the paradigm case, the second claim seems to push it away. It is this second claim that seems to sit somewhat uncomfortably with the view that the polis is aimed not merely at a secure and pleasant life, but at a life infused with virtue.

Concord is a form of agreement but it is not merely this. It is agreement where deliberation is required. Thus two people are not in concord if they merely happen to share a belief. At a minimum they must be mutually aware that they share the same belief. Furthermore, concord does not relate to matters where mere procedure or

---

[157] Aristotle, *Nicomachean Ethics*, 1167b.

demonstration can settle the dispute. Concord concerns precisely those matters where the answer is uncertain, but action is demanded.[158] In this way Aristotle's account of concord can be seen to repeat the steps he took to establish goodwill as a feature of friendship. As with goodwill, concord requires mutual awareness and reciprocated action. In concord it would seem that this awareness is created by individuals deliberating, choosing, and acting in concert.

It is easy to see how Aristotle moves from this account of concord to the close link that he makes between this form of agreement and political friendship. It is in citizenship that we can most readily envisage individuals coming together to deliberate and act together over the matters that concern them as a community. Even in contemporary mass democracies there is a clear sense in which citizens choose together and are considered a part of the same deliberative processes even if their direct interactions with others are relatively localised. However, whilst the concord of citizens might be a necessary component for the realisation of the virtuous aims of the polis, its *direct* cause should not be conflated with this. Concord between citizens rests not on their focus on virtue, but on attention and agreement to practical matters of mutual advantage. In the *Nicomachean Ethics* Aristotle informs us that:

> ...a city is said to be in concord when [its citizens] agree about what is advantageous, make the same decision, and act on their common resolution.

And that:

> Concord, then, is apparently political friendship, as indeed it is said to be; for it is concerned with advantage and with what affects life [as a whole].[159]

Thus, in general the concord of citizens plays only a supporting role in the cultivation of good men. Whilst it is a desirable foundation for the exercise of this virtue it is not directly concerned with virtue itself. This follows not only from the explicit focus of the form of concord that Aristotle ascribes to citizenship (agreement about the constitution), it also follows from Aristotle's claims that what it means to be a citizen (and the standards of justice within the six constitutions) is variable from case to case. Neither citizenship *per se*, nor the feature of concord, can be taken to indicate a *direct* concern with virtue. Each of the six

---

[158] Aristotle, *Nicomachean Ethics*, 1167a25. On this topic see Bickford, 'Beyond Friendship: Aristotle on Conflict, Deliberation, and Attention', pp. 400-402; Kraut, *Aristotle: Political Philosophy*, pp. 467-470.

[159] Aristotle, *Nicomachean Ethics*, 1167a25 and 1167b.

types of regime require different 'virtues' of their citizens.[160] It is the cultivation of these particular and relative virtues of citizenship that Aristotle believes is so important in education.[161] Without the relative virtues of citizenship the regimes would not be stable. Instability arises not through disagreement about virtue in general, or through a lack of fully virtuous men. Instability arises when citizens fail to agree on practical matters. Without agreement about the constitution and justice there will be a constant struggle for power. This is why Aristotle claims that stability can be achieved even in the deviant constitutions of democracy and oligarchy if there is sufficient concord or support for the constitution. If Aristotle held the position that concord in politics aimed at virtue, or is dependent on virtuous people then he would not be able to hold out any hope of achieving stability in these deviant regimes.

Seen in this way it is precisely the prospect of achieving stability through the agreement about the constitution of ordinary but decent people that makes 'polity' such a pragmatic option for Aristotle. Here the regime of polity utilises the like-mindedness and equality of its numerous middle class, but does not assume that these men are better than they are. It is in polity that 'men whose virtue does not rise above that of ordinary people' share in a constitution which 'alone is free from factions'.[162] Only in the regimes of aristocracy and kingship may we hope that citizenship and complete virtue can coincide. In such regimes we would expect citizens to be able to extend their collective concerns beyond expediency; but such regimes are rare. Thus, whilst aristocracy might be the best regime that it is reasonable to hope for, polity is all that can be reasonably expected. With the descent from the correct constitutions to their deviant alter-egos we also see a parting of the possibilities of a connection between virtue taken in its unqualified sense and citizenship. Only in the best regimes could we expect such a connection. In the regimes which seem most common and achievable (polity, democracy, and oligarchy) the virtue of the citizens is qualified. It is curtailed by the conceptions of justice which are pursued by these constitutions. Therefore, what can be said of all the forms of citizenship—which must include the deviant as well as the correct forms—is that what is aimed for is not virtue in an unqualified sense, but the virtues that are appropriate to the constitutions in question.[163]

---

[160] Aristotle, *The Politics*, 1309a33. This also explains Aristotle's motivation for his discussion of how far the good man should be distinguished from the good citizen in *The Politics*.
[161] Aristotle, *The Politics*, 1310a12.
[162] Aristotle, *The Politics*, 1295a25, and 1296a7 respectively.
[163] Aristotle, *The Politics*, 1276b20.

Insofar as citizens are able to see advantage in this and to coalesce around a constitution there is concord and stability.

The final aspect of citizenship as a form of friendship has been anticipated by the discussion of the practical aspects of concord: citizenship is a friendship for utility or advantage. Indeed, in the *Eudemian Ethics* Aristotle is quick to point out that quarrels (and by implication political instability) arise when individuals give their political friendships greater pretensions.[164] In thinking about citizenship in this way we must be mindful of avoiding two related mistakes. First we should not conclude that political friendship is unworthy of the name 'friendship' because it is not based upon or aimed at virtue. Second, we should not think of friendships for advantage as being inherently exploitative or undesirable. In respect to the first point, it is true that friendships for utility fall short when compared to the paradigm case of virtue friendship. However, to focus on this fallaciously reifies the paradigm case. Virtue friendship is an especially complete example of friendship, but it is only one instance of a wider phenomenon. Its completeness makes it the best example, but an example none the less. Indeed, it should not be forgotten that the completeness of virtue friendship means that its virtue is accompanied by pleasure and utility. That utility is a feature of virtue friendship indicates that finding others useful, or seeking our advantage, cannot be objectionable *per se*. Thus (in respect to the second point) we can distinguish between relationships which are exploitative (which are not really deserving of the name 'friendship') and those relationships where there is mutual, recognised, and reciprocated goodwill that results in an equal exchange. Utility friendships cease to be if the friends do not take care to maintain their justice and equality.

By recognising that utility friendship is to be contrasted to mere exploitation we can also appreciate that utility friendship is more nuanced than mere exchange. Indeed, we should think of simple exchange as being a kind of lower limit for this kind of friendship. Reflection on experience will show that the vast majority of these friendships are more sophisticated. In the majority of these kinds of friendships exchange is supported by elements of well-wishing, justice, and trust (for our own sake and that of our friend).[165] At its fullest, friendship for utility is a sustained relationship with another which is focused not merely on coordinated activity, but cooperation and shared benefits. Utility friendship can thus be thought not merely to be about exchange, but the advantage that can be gained from working with

---

[164] Aristotle, *The Eudemian Ethics*, 1242b35-1243a5.
[165] Cooper, 'Aristotle on the Forms of Friendship'.

others. As such friends are not merely (and narrowly) concerned about what accrues to them individually, they are also concerned about the health and stability of their overall enterprise. Such a concern leads them to consider the well-being of their friend, to aid them, and to ensure that justice is done.

Seen from this perspective the advantage pursued by citizens can be said to have either a narrow or a wide focus. This links back to what we have already noted about one of the cardinal differences between the coalescence of citizens around the correct and deviant constitutions. In the deviant constitutions citizens fail to understand justice as a whole (or justice in the unqualified sense). Although they have a conception of justice it is partial. As a result the claims that they make to their right to share in power are actually the claims of sectional interest. They mistake an aspect for the whole.[166] Of course it is true that the citizens of deviant constitutions hold interests in common and even have a form of common interest. This common interest is, however, the interests of their faction. As Aristotle makes all too clear, this interest is more often than not advanced to the detriment of the claims and interests of other groups. Much of books four, five, and six of the *Politics* are concerned with not only making this point but warning against it. Thus, in these deviant constitutions the friendship of citizens aims at advantage in a narrow sense. In such constitutions citizens come in mobs and their rule is that of the cartel.

The correct constitutions offer a contrast to this picture. Whilst still a friendship for utility, in the correct constitutions citizens have a more developed sense of their relationship and their understanding of justice. They pursue their advantage in the widest sense and this means looking not simply to the interests of their faction, but to the common life of the polis. The common interest is not simply understood as the immediate interest of the group to which the citizens happen to belong, but the long-term health of the community as a whole. Although there are differences between the three correct regimes (and especially that of kingship), ultimately what benefits those who rule cannot be gained at the expense of others. What benefits those who rule is what benefits all: the stability and friendship generated and preserved by the balance of claims, an agreed sense of justice which is seen to be fair to all, and the rule of law. In aristocracy and polity this means that power must be shared amongst equals, and used not only for their own advantage but also for the benefit of those who do not have access to such power. Thus, rather than using politics to gain common advantages at the expense of others (a practice that ultimately leads to discord even

---

[166] Aristotle, *The Politics*, 1280a7.

within the ruling faction), citizens in the correct constitutions use politics to pursue mutual and shared advantages. Insofar as they aim for this and it is achieved the degree of their sharing is both deeper and more extended than that which is common to the citizens in the deviant constitutions. As such it is a more complete form of friendship.

Aristotle: Friendship in principle and practice

Of all the Ancient accounts of friendship, Aristotle's is perhaps the best known and the one that many have found most attractive. There is much to recommend it. As we have seen, Aristotle is both a great systematiser and what might be described as a pragmatist (in the sense that he has a concern with practicalities). As systematiser, Aristotle's account of friendship brings together both a comprehensive taxonomy and a focus on the features of their underlying order. Various *species* of friendship are thus identified, and what is essential to the class is separated from what is accidental. Aristotle repeats this when identifying the *causes* of friendship. Insofar as Aristotle attempts to reconcile our own search for what is good for us with a concern for the good of another, he seems to put his finger on something that friendship is especially well placed to address. In doing so he also places his finger on a chief concern for those trying to theorise friendship in contemporary times.

To recognise Aristotle as a kind of pragmatist is not to say that he lacks principles. Aristotle has his own normative commitments. However, he is also keen to see what can be made of the material and situations into which we are thrown. Aristotle's taxonomy of the species and causes of friendship shows itself to be comprehensive and encompassing. This is not simply an account of the best form of friendship, but an account of friendship in all its variety. This gives Aristotle's theory a practical edge that sometimes seems to be lacking in other theories. As a result, the more limited forms of friendship also receive attention and discussion. Mirroring his discussion of the 'deviant' constitutions in the *Politics*, Aristotle seems keen to explain both how actual friendships work and what is likely to prolong them and maximise their benefits. Even incomplete friendship is better than no friendship at all. In taking this approach Aristotle not only tends to reconcile his theory to ordinary opinion, he also highlights the connective bonds between person and person which form the fabric of all communities.

Attractive as it may be, Aristotle's account is not without potential hazard to the contemporary theorist. Once read, Aristotle's account is not easily forgotten. Once read, it is hard to think *outside* of Aristotle's taxonomy. Thus the default quickly slides into converting theory back into Aristotle's terms, and to trying to match contemporary thinking to his structure. This enticement must be resisted. For whilst Aristotle's account can illuminate much for us, it is a mistake to think that this illumination either shows us all that there is to see, or to ignore the assumptions in Aristotle's framework which make the illumination possible. The fact that Aristotle is endorsing the structure of a hierarchical society which rests on the exclusion of women from politics and the institution of slavery is obvious. Repellent though this is to the contemporary mind, it is not the only difficulty here. It might be thought that Aristotle's account can be removed from this particular context and transplanted into our own thus leaving these hierarchical assumptions in the past, and replacing them with our own assumptions about equality, liberty, and the like. It is not clear that this kind of move is entirely possible. What would be left of Aristotle's virtue friendships without a fixed and hierarchical ethical standard? Moreover, even if it were possible to transpose Aristotle's theory, it is not clear that we thus escape other difficulties and limitations of the account.

The first question that arises in Aristotle's account concerns how the other person is actually theorised. In a sense, Aristotle's account faces similar difficulties to that of Plato in this regard. Aristotle has the friends recognise and return goodwill to each other. He also identifies friendship as wishing goods to the other for the sake of the other. However, for Aristotle friendship is primarily an activity. It is true that he describes it as both a state and an activity in the *Nicomachean Ethics*, but he goes on to note that *if* the friendship lays dormant for too long then it will dissolve. Moreover, Aristotle's stress throughout the *Nicomachean Ethics* is on what the friends do together. Chief amongst these for the most complete forms of friendship is living together (which obviously involves regular and sustained interaction). This sense of activity is also reflected in the friendship derived from the three main causes of friendship. In friendships of utility the friends provide services for each other. In friendship of pleasure the friends must act in ways that produce pleasure and which are pleasing. Even in virtue friendship (where we might think that the state of character would have the largest role to play) Aristotle stresses that the friends must display virtue. Here being virtuous is not simply a state of character, but an activity between the friends and the world.

Aristotle's stress on activity is not especially objectionable in itself, but it does tend to have a distorting effect on his view of relationships. In terms of his view of friendship, Aristotle concludes that it is loving (rather than being loved) which is the true virtue of friends. This conclusion raises questions concerning the potential for emotional openness and connectivity in friendship. One of the features of friendship that we might think is especially valuable is the ability of the friends to share their thoughts and emotions with each other. Of course, this isn't a feature of *all* forms of friendship, but in many friendships the feeling that the friends are 'in it together' is significant. In part this feeling marks the friends as being friends—they are not simply aware of the emotional states of others, but share these states in some deeper sense. What affects one tends to affect the other, and something might be thought amiss if this were not to be the case. Aristotle's focus on loving as an activity seems to undermine the potential for this to occur. For in order for one person to be active in loving, another has to be the recipient of that love. Yet, Aristotle sees the recipient of love as playing second fiddle to the person actively loving. Here the friend is active insofar as they are giving to the other. The value of simply sharing emotions and a connection is thus obscured. To the contemporary mind it might be thought that it is the emotional openness of the friend which helps to sustain the relationship. Moreover, the ability of the friends to experience each other's emotional state is thought to be important in being able to claim that the friends understand one another. On this view, then, friendship is not simply a way of *acting towards* others (as stressed by Aristotle), it is a way of *being with* them.

It is significant that Aristotle does not focus on this sharing of an emotional life. His most complete friendship appears to be the sharing of intellectual activity and noble deeds. It is true that he does not rule out the life of the emotions, but he clearly views it as a danger to friendship. For example, he advises us not to share sorrow as seeing our friends in grief adds to our own. Nor do we find the sharing of emotions (or the emotions in general) to be included amongst the *causes* of friendship. The one place where this might be said to occur is in family life. As we have seen, Aristotle is somewhat ambivalent about this (the love found in families might be a cause of friendship, but it is not named). If this is the case then the emotions (like the family itself) are sidelined and confined to the household. Thus, we are brought back to the same kinds of concerns that were raised about Plato's account: in what sense are the friends concerned with each other as particular selves? By ignoring or downplaying the emotional side of friendship Aristotle appears to be downplaying the particularity of the friends. Moreover, he also appears to be missing out on something which we might think is important in at least some kinds of friendship.

These concerns about the particularity of the friends and what is shared also have a limiting effect on Aristotle's ability to generate a distinctively political friendship. As we have seen, Aristotle's account here is rather thin. In addition to being a friendship for advantage, the focus of the friendship is concord. In making this move Aristotle is producing a theory which is consistent with some of what he will go on to say in the *Politics*. Any thicker view of political friendship would mean that it could not be adapted to the constitutions that Aristotle identifies in that later text. The focus of this political friendship is agreement about large constitutional issues: it is therefore an agreement about political justice. Setting political friendship up in this way has two consequences. The first is that such political friendship points away from pluralism. Aristotle's view of political friendship connects it with the subscription to a standard of justice which all the citizens share. In a sense we would expect this. However, it should also be remembered that this is set against a normative view of justice in general, and a view about the unity of the virtues. Although less rigid than Plato's view it simply is not the case that a polis bound by the kind of political friendship that Aristotle envisages would be especially plural. There would be no real discussion of who gets what and why. Indeed, Aristotle sees such discussions as potentially leading to factions in the polis. Furthermore, it is hard to see how such a state of affairs would promote alternative ways of life. In short, it seems somewhat inadequate to deal with the complex political arrangements of mass societies characterised as they are by multi-culture and overlapping political, social, and religious loyalties.

Second, Aristotle's focus on political friendship as being a kind of friendship for advantage limits its ability to realise virtue within the polis. In effect, although Aristotle recognises that the purpose of the polis is to give men a chance at living a virtuous life, politics itself seems to be stripped of the tools needed to fully realise this. Indeed, it might be asked whether the kind of political friendship that Aristotle does identify is strong enough to command loyalty to a constitution given that the motivation for this form of friendship is advantage. This does not seem to sit very happily with Aristotle's stronger claims about the priority of the polis to its parts. Here a more sympathetic view concerning the openness and connectivity in friendship might be of help. Whilst citizens can be said to agree about large scale issues (such as the constitutions) it could be suggested that this agreement is underpinned by some emotional attachments to these issues, and between the citizens themselves. It is important that citizens do not simply 'subscribe' to the traditions and principles of their state. Something deeper is often needed to motivate citizens to act for the state and for each other. Even in the mass societies of the contemporary era citizens often *feel* something in relation to the state, rather than simply endorsing it in an intellectual fashion. It is *their* state, not just *the* state. It is this feeling a part of something, and the feelings that citizens have for each other, which is an important part of the explicitly political bonds between citizens. Such a deeper commitment also opens the door to the possibilities of pluralism. Although citizens might have disagreements about justice itself, they are nonetheless committed and connected to each other.

Aristotle's account of friendship repays close study. In it we see a whole range of friendships (and their causes), and Aristotle's contribution is to show not only this variety, but also how different kinds of friendships make differing contributions to our lives. However, we should not become too ready to simply accept Aristotle's account. Whilst it is undoubtedly a great example, it also sets limitations and makes assumptions that we would do well to avoid and overcome. Aristotle's failure to fully appreciate the emotional aspects of friendship—and especially the importance of what might be termed understanding and belonging—set him at odds with a feature of friendship that we might think important in the contemporary setting. It is clear that there is now considerable doubt as to the purpose of politics. That the purpose of politics is to set of the stage for the attainment of virtue (or a particular set of virtues) is doubted by both the theorists and citizens alike. If Aristotle is now to be of use to us then we must find a way of moving beyond his 'most complete' form of friendship, and focus instead on what he elides and obscures. Such a task need not focus politics on the irrational or purely emotional, but it will need to address and understand the fact of pluralism. The task of the contemporary theorist is to understand how person can be bonded to person in a world characterised by such pluralism.

Part II

Three Modern Transformations

Chapter Four
Kierkegaard

SØREN KIERKEGAARD was born and died in Copenhagen. To attempt to move beyond this most meagre of statements is to step on to a web of intrigue. For in approaching Søren Kierkegaard very little is as it seems. Even the simplest things turn out to be intricately and sometimes surprisingly connected to others. The task is to try to escape, to try to see the true structure spun by the Danish Arachne. The more we follow these threads the more we find we are struggling; and the more we struggle the more we become ensnared. In his native Copenhagen Kierkegaard was both respected and a figure of fun. He subscribed to none of the leading philosophical, cultural, and political movements of his day, and rejected 'Christendom'. Yet it was his thought that has come to have such a lasting influence on some of the movements of the following century and beyond, not least in our understanding of Christianity. Even his personal affairs and friendships (which we might take to have been entirely private) take the air of public performance. His life is subject to interpretation and reinterpretation as much at his own hands as those of others. His books themselves offer no real respite. Indeed, they intensify and provoke the difficulties. Kierkegaard's copious writings—for other thinkers a final testament of thought offered to posterity—oscillate between the profound and the playful to the point of perversion. Pseudonym is edited by pseudonym, and one flatly rebukes and contradicts the other. Kierkegaard admits the paternity of them all only to disown them. In those books, and in his life, we can discern concerns that not only consumed him and his pseudonyms as thinkers, but trouble us too. The problems of understanding and achieving authentic selfhood, of relating in a meaningful and ethical way to others, and of a political context where levelling, envy, empty reflection, and chatter are the defining features, are all problems which have prescience for us as well as for Kierkegaard and his contemporaries. Who could have predicted that

Kierkegaard's 'Danish backwater' flowed into the deepest currents of modernity itself?

The problem of escaping Kierkegaard's web is real; but a strategy is needed to avoid further entanglement. What is needed is a way to negotiate the pseudonyms and the ruses without creating more confusion and intrigue. One way to move beyond this is to take Kierkegaard's Christianity seriously.[167] We can 'spring out' of Kierkegaard's web if we use the image of the man in prayer as our means of momentum. This is an image of a man who is quiet and still. It is also an image of the utmost seriousness and communication. For the man in prayer is not simply reciting an empty and formulaic liturgy. The man in prayer is attempting to reach out to God; the man in prayer is attempting to communicate with God. This is no easy task. For in order to reach out we must know who we are and what we wish to say; but the man in prayer is praying precisely because he is not transparent to himself. As he searches for himself he appears to himself in many forms. He is both guide and deceiver. Despite this *self-deception* God is not deceived. God sees the man for what and who he is. In order to become transparent to himself the man must see himself as God sees him. In order to do this he must relate himself not to himself, but to God. As Kierkegaard writes himself concerning prayer 'the prayer does not change God, but it changes the one who prays'.[168]

It is this need to relate oneself to God which supports the web that Kierkegaard and his pseudonyms weave. It is the possibility of this relationship which makes the web taut so as an escape is not effected by hopeless struggle but a springing propulsion from the web itself. A person's relationship with God forms the central dynamic of their life — or should do. Indeed, such a relationship opens them to the very possibility of constituting the self. However, this relationship with God is neither solipsistic nor cause for quietism.[169] On the contrary, this central relationship demands a radical response to others. It is this

---

[167] Bruce H Kirmmse, '"But I am Almost Never Understood..." Or, Who Killed Søren Kierkegaard?' in George Pattison and Steven Shakespeare (eds.), *Kierkegaard: The Self in Society*, pp. 189-90. The political significance of this is clearly recognised by Marcuse who writes that 'Kierkegaard's work is the last great attempt to restore religion as the ultimate organon for liberating humanity from the destructive impact of an oppressive social order' later adding 'He thus restores Christianity to its combative and revolutionary force', Herbert Marcuse, *Reason and Revolution* (London: Routledge and Kegan Paul, 1941), pp. 264, 265 (respectively).

[168] Søren Kierkegaard, *Upbuilding Discourses in Various Spirits*, Howard V Hong and Edna H Hong trans. (Princeton, New Jersey: Princeton University Press, 1993 [1847]), p. 22.

[169] See Harvie Ferguson, *Melancholy and the Critique of Modernity* (London and New York: Routledge, 1995), p. 57; Anthony Rudd, *Kierkegaard and the Limits of the Ethical* (Oxford: Clarendon Press, 1993), p. 24.

central relationship which underwrites the frailties of other human bonds, and guarantees that they do not become deviant. In this way, Kierkegaard's thought is immediately and inescapably concerned with friendship understood as the bonds between person and person, and the foundations for any such sociality. Furthermore, for Kierkegaard the personal and the political are conjoined.[170] Without attention to a correctly related self, all forms of human association (from the family, to friendship, to political community) are doomed to failure. What is more, they are all instances of despair.[171] Thus, Kierkegaard offers us a penetrating analysis of the possibilities of friendship. He takes the forms of friendship so highly prized and celebrated by the Ancients — and transformed into key elements of civil and ethical society in his own time — and shows them to be deeply lacking. Both romantic love and philosophical friendship are found to be based on the instability of the passions, preference, and a reciprocity which is really the love of the self. In contrast, Kierkegaard promotes a form of human bonding based on the command of God. This radical response to others, which views them as spiritual equals to whom we have infinite obligations, Kierkegaard calls the relation of 'the neighbour'.[172] Kierkegaard's express concern is to contrast friendship and the neighbour as purely human and spiritual respectively. Nonetheless the neighbour is presented as a form of human binding, and is thus considered here as a form of friendship. Indeed, in some ways the neighbour can be seen as a specifically *spiritualised friendship* whereby true equality is practised and the friends love each other in the right way. Without this spiritual transformation, people relate only in their purely human capacities. Thus, these relations are fractured and prone to the human qualities of selfishness, envy, and limitation.

However, before we can address the issues of friendship and the neighbour two small detours are required. The first is to say something about Kierkegaard's authorship as a whole. As the next section will argue, Kierkegaard's authorship must be understood as having a *Christian* purpose. Ultimately Kierkegaard wishes to confront his reader with the importance of transcending the merely aesthetic and ethical and making a commitment to faith and a Christian existence.

---

[170] Cf. John W Elrod, *Kierkegaard and Christendom* (New Jersey: Princeton University Press, 1981), pp. 93-4, 116-7; Robert L Perkins, 'Climacan Politics: Polis and Person in Kierkegaard's *Postscript*', in George Pattison and Steven Shakespeare (eds.), *Kierkegaard: The Self in Society*, p. 44.

[171] For a further discussion of the link between despair and the political see Graham M Smith, 'Kierkegaard From the Point of View of the Political', *History of European Ideas* 31(1), 2005.

[172] Elrod, *Kierkegaard and Christendom*, pp. 123-4.

The second detour continues this theme by looking at the issue of despair. Despair is a mis-relation of the self. This is important as unless the self is correctly constituted in relation to God, human relationships are doomed to failure. It is on the first of these detours which we now embark.

Kierkegaard and his doubles

Who was Søren Kierkegaard and why did he write in the way that he did? Moreover, what is the relationship between Kierkegaard's pseudonymous writings and those to which he appended his own name? These questions are of perennial concern to Kierkegaardian scholarship, and their answer takes us to the heart of what Kierkegaard's thought is about.[173] In particular, they raise the issue of the possibility of a central message in Kierkegaard's writings, a message that shows his output not only to have an overall coherence, but also an overall strategy. To make such as claim is not to deny that Kierkegaard was opposed to systematisation.[174] What Kierkegaard was opposed to were moves to enclose all existence within a system which was understandable by human reason alone. Nevertheless, Kierkegaard's writings show a sustained concern with the coherence of human life. Central to this coherence is the recognition that human experience shows that something extends beyond human reason. It is the relationship with the divine that becomes the central theme of Kierkegaard's output (both that of the pseudonyms and his own signed authorship). It is also this relationship that not only gives coherence to the authorship as a whole, but also to Kierkegaard's concern with correctly grounding our bonds with others both in our personal and political lives.

There is a strong temptation with Kierkegaard to attempt to understand his authorship through his biography. Unless we subscribe to the notion that all thought is somehow reducible to context, caution should be employed. Despite this—and possibly with the sole exception of the 'psychotic' Nietzsche—perhaps no other modern

---

[173] For a survey of the discussions surrounding Kierkegaard's authorship (and especially the relationship between Kierkegaard and his pseudonyms) please consult Stephen D Crites, 'The Author and the Authorship: Recent Kierkegaardian Literature', *Journal of the American Academy of Religion* 38(1), 1970; Seung-Goo Lee, *Kierkegaard on Becoming and Being a Christian* (Meinema: Uitgeverij Meinema-Zoetermeer, 2006); Poul Lübcke, 'Kierkegaard and Indirect Communication', *History of European Ideas* 12(1), 1990; George Pattison, *Kierkegaard: The Aesthetic and the Religious* (London: Macmillan, 1992); Rudd, *Kierkegaard and the Limits of the Ethical*; Mark C Taylor, *Kierkegaard's Pseudonymous Authorship* (Princeton, New Jersey: Princeton University Press, 1975).

[174] Alastair Hannay, *Kierkegaard* (London and New York: Routledge, 1982), pp. 144-7.

thinker has been subjected to so many attempts to show that his thought is principally guided by his personal experiences and especially psychological landmarks. For a thinker who almost never strayed from Copenhagen Kierkegaard's biography still seems to provide rich pickings for the psycho-analyst. There is the melancholy 'inherited' from the father and the brooding secret disclosed to Søren that he carried to his grave; the broken engagement 'we are all sick of hearing about'; the 'provoked... feud with a satirical weekly called Corsair' and the death-bed refusal of his brother, and of the Eucharist from all but a 'hard to arrange' layman 'Then I die without it'.[175] However this temptation is compounded by Kierkegaard's own attempts to obscure and distance himself from what he (or his pseudonyms) wrote. This is implicit in Kierkegaard's very use of pseudonyms, and evident in his flagging of his technique and interests in his dissertation on 'irony'. It is also made explicit both at the end of the *Concluding Unscientific Postscript* and again in the *Point of View*. Such prohibitions virtually invite trespass, and certainly raise the lure of temptation by a greater power.

It is perhaps fair to say that if Kierkegaard had not written in this way then comment upon the relationship between life-author-work would be less complex, and less tempting. However, in a way Kierkegaard's biography does give us a clue to understanding some of the motivations to his thought. Its relationship however must be considered in the light of the reverse of what we would otherwise suppose. For rather than considering the events in Kierkegaard's life as being the chief influencing factors of his thought, why not start by considering his thought (and the focus of this thought) to have been the influencing factors on how he lived? The truth is suspected to be found somewhere between these positions. The suggestion is useful as it provides a corrective that allows us to focus on Kierkegaard's thought as an independent and guiding principle, albeit one that is subject to development and change. Significantly Kierkegaard was concerned with two questions that he viewed as being inter-related: what it means to be a person, and what it means to be a Christian. These twin questions run through Kierkegaard's life and thought, and both his life and thought can be seen as attempts to grapple with and resolve them.

Most thinkers attempt to say what they mean. However illusionary the dream of the transmission of thought, their aim is to convey a

---

[175] See (respectively): Walter Lowrie, *A Short Life of Kierkegaard* (New Jersey: Princeton University Press, 1970), p. 25; Crites, 'The Author and the Authorship: Recent Kierkegaardian Literature', p. 38; Hannay, *Kierkegaard*, p. 6; Kirmmse, '"But I am Almost Never Understood..." Or, Who Killed Søren Kierkegaard?', p. 173.

message to their readers. To be sure, this does not mean that what writers commit to paper is always clear and unambiguous. Nor does it mean that thinkers never change their mind or are immune to contradiction; but the former is usually openly acknowledged and the latter a source of embarrassment. Kierkegaard is not of this kind. It is not possible to read Kierkegaard's books as a simple direct transmission of what he thought.[176] Indeed, commenting on the difficulties of reading and explaining Kierkegaard's texts, Roger Poole argues that the efforts of a 'blank reader' are doomed to failure.[177] Kierkegaard's style is one of 'indirect communication' and he plays on irony, the comic and the aesthetic. By using forms of indirect communication (such as pseudonyms) Kierkegaard is able to address his reader as a 'single individual' where the reader already stands. Kierkegaard's aim, then, is not to state his position in opposition to the views of his readers. His aim is to make his readers think through their positions for themselves.[178] In this way the reader is encouraged to know themselves in a thorough, committed and authentic way. Kierkegaard's writings are to be considered *existential*: his reader has to think and experience reality for themselves and first hand. Kierkegaard's message cannot be transmitted through text alone, but only through a process of engagement.[179]

It is this method of indirect communication and the need to address the reader from where they stand and to encourage them to articulate and engage with their own position that helps to explain Kierkegaard's method of using both pseudonymous and signed works. Kierkegaard's authorship can be (roughly) divided into two parallel series.[180] The first

---

[176] Bernard Zelechow, 'Fear and Trembling and Joyful Wisdom — The Same Book; A Look at Metaphoric Communication', *History of European Ideas* 12(1), 1990, p. 94; Ferguson, *Melancholy and the Critique of Modernity*, p. 37 but also p. 84.

[177] Roger Poole, 'The Unknown Kierkegaard: Twentieth-Century Receptions', in Alastair Hannay and Gordon D Marino (eds.), *The Cambridge Companion to Kierkegaard*, pp. 58-62.

[178] Søren Kierkegaard, *The Point of View*, Howard V Hong and Edna H Hong trans. (New Jersey: Princeton University Press, 1998), pp. 45-47. See also Jim Perkinson, 'A 'Socio-reading' of the Kierkegaardian Self: Or, the Space of Lowliness in the Time of the Disciple', in George Pattison and Steven Shakespeare (eds.), *Kierkegaard: The Self in Society*, p. 161.

[179] Lübcke, 'Kierkegaard and Indirect Communication', p. 33.

[180] The pseudonyms form the basis of a vertical split in Kierkegaard's authorship — or at least would appear to. This is the line that is pursued (although with some caveats) by Mark C Taylor in Taylor, *Kierkegaard's Pseudonymous Authorship*. Thus, as Taylor suggests we might trace the pseudonyms up until (and including) *The Concluding Unscientific Postscript*. However, this does not provide an entirely satisfactory foundation for answering the 'question' of the pseudonyms. Two further points must be taken into consideration. First, the pseudonyms do not end after this book: Anti-Climacus is a case in point. Second,

contains those books written under the names of pseudonyms. The second contains those produced under his own name. However Kierkegaard's authorship is more complex than a simple contrasting between the pseudonyms and the signed works. Whereas the signed works are discourses and deliberations, the pseudonymous works are generally 'aesthetic' in approach.[181] The aesthetic works explore a number of issues confronting the individual and bearing on the problem of friendship, especially the problems of choice, freedom, authority and selfhood. The pseudonymous works explore these issues within the sphere of the aesthetic and the ethical.[182] Ultimately Kierkegaard is to reject this aesthetic sphere as a mode of existence, showing its bankruptcy both in its own terms and when contrasted to and understood from the sphere of the religious (and ultimately *truly* Christian). However, it is important to note that it is not Kierkegaard but the pseudonyms who explore these issues. The works are written and presented from *their* point of view.[183] Indeed, Kierkegaard claims that it would be 'ludicrously confusing' to attribute the works of the pseudonyms to him.[184]

Nowhere is this separation of Kierkegaard from the views of his pseudonyms demonstrated more clearly than in what is possibly Kierkegaard's most famous work *Either/Or*. Here we have a whole variety of pseudonyms in play. Actually written by Kierkegaard it is edited by Victor Eremita, and presents the papers and letters of the young aesthete 'A' and his older friend Judge William. We are even confronted with 'The Seducer's Diary' amongst the papers of A, which forms a book within a book (and even within that we are presented with Cordelia's letters). There are multiple layers of complexity and personality here which remove and distance Kierkegaard himself from the claims, statements, positions and presentations within the book. Kierkegaard is also concerned that the aesthetic nature of the early pseudonymous works do not result in all that he has written being 'dragged down into the aesthetic'.[185] It is this observation that also enables Kierkegaard to defend his authorship against the view that he

---

this move also overlooks the fact that even whilst producing works under/by pseudonyms, Kierkegaard also produced a corresponding series under his own name. Kierkegaard himself points this out. See Kierkegaard, *Point of View*, pp. 7-8.

[181] Cf. Pattison, *Kierkegaard: The Aesthetic and the Religious*.

[182] George Pattison and Steven Shakespeare (eds)., *Kierkegaard: The Self in Society* (Great Britain: Macmillan, 1998), p. 76ff.

[183] Gene Outka, 'Equality and Individuality: Thoughts on Two Themes in Kierkegaard', *The Journal of Religious Ethics* 10(2), 1982, p. 173.

[184] Kierkegaard, *Point of View*, p. 288.

[185] *Journals and Papers* 6: 6361).

started as an aesthetic author, and only later become a religious author. As Kierkegaard writes:

> [the authorship] began maieutically with aesthetic production, and all the pseudonymous writings are maieutic in nature. Therefore this writing was also pseudonymous, whereas the directly religious — which from the beginning was present in the gleam of an indication — carried my name. The directly religious was present from the beginning; *Two Upbuilding Discourses* (1843) is in fact concurrent with *Either/Or*.[186]

So, whilst the pseudonymous authorship might appear to have aesthetic elements, it has non-aesthetic purpose. The aesthetic works are a means to an end, and according to Kierkegaard are intended from the outset to serve that end. This end is neither aesthetic, nor ethical, but religious in nature (indeed, it is *Christian*). In this way the terms 'aesthetic' and 'religious' have particular meanings when used by Kierkegaard and applied to his authorship. The 'aesthetic' works are aesthetic not in the sense that they are written for pleasure as such, but that they explore world-views from a non-religious point of view. They are aesthetic in the sense that they present complete characters and their world-views. The best example of this is clearly the two correspondents in *Either/Or* where the first 'A' represents a person who lives his life through the pursuit of pleasure, and the second is Judge William who lives his life through a kind of civil ethic. What the aesthetic literature attempts to achieve is an exploration and demonstration of the possibilities of a life lived without genuine commitment to Christianity; forms of existence which Kierkegaard believes are ultimately bankrupt. As we will see, the 'religious' writing is explicitly Christian, and often takes the forms of sermons or discourses on biblical themes. It presupposes Christianity as its worldview, and is therefore not an exploration of non-Christian possibilities of personhood, but is strictly for Christian edification.

It is the religious writings that form the second series of Kierkegaard's authorship, a series which he authors under his own name. They start from the position that the reader has decided to *become a Christian*. This phrase is loaded with meaning. First the reader has to have made a decision or a choice. For Kierkegaard one is not a Christian by tradition, habit, or accident of birth. One certainly was not a Christian because one belonged to a Christian state. Second, the reader is to *become* a Christian. Christianity is not simply an achieved status or subscription to a prescribed set of teachings: it requires strenuous effort on the part of the individual, commitment, and

---

[186] Kierkegaard, *Point of View*, pp. 7-8 cf. also pp. 6, 47-50.

constant renewal. Third, the term Christian itself raises the question as to what a Christian is. More correctly, it raises the question as to what the Christian life entails. Being a Christian does not simply entail a faith in Christ and God, but the accomplishment of a way of life. That way of life involves a three-fold relation with God, self, and others. Kierkegaard's claim is that in the present age being a Christian has become separated from its distinctive way of life and a distinctive way of being with others. Christianity has become a reflection game, rather than a lived and passionate experience. The decision to become a Christian also requires that the reader move beyond the purely aesthetic and even the ethical. The writings of the second series are therefore self-confessedly Christian, and serve the purpose of exploring with the reader what Christianity means, or more correctly, what it means to become Christian. However, this does not mean that the aesthetic works are in no way related to the Christian. On the contrary, the purpose of the first series is to bring the reader to the Christian point of view not through proselytising or imparting religious truths and teachings, but by showing the bankruptcy of non-Christian and pseudo-Christian (or bourgeois Christian) points of view through an exploration and demonstration of them in the thoughts and 'persons' of the pseudonyms. Moreover, it is to make a sharp contrast between the Christian and non-Christian world-views, and to bring the reader to a point of decision.[187]

This reinforces what we have already said about the use of the pseudonyms as a whole. Kierkegaard's use of the pseudonyms links to his purpose with the authorship as a whole, and are his starting point towards that purpose. The purpose of the authorship as a whole is to choose to set out on the road to becoming a Christian. For Kierkegaard this is the religious-ethical task of selfhood. The starting-point for

---

[187] A slight complication to this picture is added by what we may consider a third series. This series would consist of Kierkegaard's many and varied Journal entries and unpublished notes. We might consider these writings a 'shadow' series. Of course, these would appear under Kierkegaard's own name, but there are two distinct features of the Journal entries that separate them from the other signed works. First, the Journals are not published works. This separates them from the polished published works under Kierkegaard's own name (and indeed the names of pseudonyms). The second feature is that it is not clear to see exactly how we are to relate the Journal entries to the other two categories of writing. They add an increasingly personal tone to what Kierkegaard claims in other places. However, perhaps we should not automatically take this personal tone as being the real Kierkegaard: we must bear in mind that the pseudonyms are written by 'personalities' and that the 'signed' works are personal in the sense of being 'authorised'. The Journal entries may simply be experimental rather than especially illuminating or definitive. Indeed, maybe they were only ever intended for Søren Kierkegaard himself.

Kierkegaard's authorship is the individual where he stands. Kierkegaard assumes that communication of any point rests not just with the one who is attempting to express their point of view, but also upon the one who is to receive, or being communicated with.[188] In this way it is wrong-headed to begin by asserting the truth or correctness of one's own position. In order to convince and transform we must start by 'taking the other's delusion at face value'.[189] In this way the receiver of the communication is taken through a birthing process where they explore and expose the contradictions and bankruptcy of their own position for themselves. For Kierkegaard this has a dual purpose. Not only is it the most effective and realistic ground for the reader's search for selfhood, it is also the only grounds for a successful exploration and development of the self. It is not possible to tell another how to form a self, or the details of the self that is to be developed. In Kierkegaardian terms, if selfhood is to be achieved then the individuals must first choose to become a Christian, and develop their own self existentially. This is how we are to understand Kierkegaard's 'maieutic' method. The works help the reader to realise what they already know, rather than 'impart' or teach knowledge.

Therefore, in the use of the pseudonyms we do not see Kierkegaard simply masking his own views. Nor do we see a move from the aesthetic to the religious. The purpose of the pseudonymous authorship is to allow the reader to explore the position that they are in. In fact, the pseudonymous authorship employs the reader's prejudices against the reader themselves. The pseudonyms present stages in self-understanding which are both detailed and complete like characters in novels. In this way Kierkegaard's purpose is to bring those who live in the aesthetic and ethical spheres to the point of deciding to become a Christian: that is, deciding to become a self. However, the pseudonyms offer little relief for those who consider themselves to be Christians within Christendom. The pseudonyms encourage such Christians to challenge their own assumptions and practices, and to ask whether they are really Christians at all, or whether they simply accept Christianity in a mere aesthetic or ethical manner. As Kierkegaard notes:

---

[188] Kierkegaard, *Point of View*, p. 54.
[189] Kierkegaard, *Point of View*, p. 54.

The situation (becoming a Christian in Christendom, where consequently one is a Christian)—the situation, which, as every dialectician sees, casts everything into reflection, also makes an indirect method necessary, because the task here must be to take measures against the illusion: calling oneself a Christian, perhaps deluding oneself into thinking one is without being that.[190]

Despair and double-mindedness

So far it has been argued that the task of choosing to become a Christian is central to Kierkegaard's enterprise. This task is also central to his account and critique of purely human forms of friendship. It is also clear that for Kierkegaard many who already consider themselves Christians are not. Indeed, in some respects those who consider themselves *to be* Christians are further from the task of becoming a Christian than those without faith. Whilst the former languish in complacency, the latter are at least in a position to make a conscious choice. However, more needs to be said to fill-out the notion of choosing to become a Christian. In order to understand what this means, we need to explore another Kierkegaardian notion: despair. As we shall see, despair is a kind of mis-relation of the self. Furthermore, despair is important to fully appreciating Kierkegaard's understanding of the failings of earthly friendship, and the normativity of his alternative of neighbourliness.

What, specifically, does Kierkegaard have in mind when he announces becoming a Christian as a task? This task centres around the question of achieving selfhood. Put simply, for Kierkegaard human beings are a synthesis of opposites. They are both finite and infinite, subject to both freedom and necessity, composed of mind, body *and* spirit. In Kierkegaard's account they are potential selves which are ordered (or actualised) by the way that they choose to relate to their condition. A human being can choose (or will) to relate to any number of schemes, projects, and worldviews. In the words of Julia Watkin's concise summary 'The self develops through the process of its relationship to the core ideal(s) chosen by the individual who strives to implement them'.[191] Thus the self is never settled or achieved, but is in

---

[190] Kierkegaard, *Point of View*, p. 8 footnote 2. Cf. also Elrod who writes that 'Kierkegaard viewed his task as the Socratic one awaking his reader from three illusions: his ignorance about himself as a being who egotistically loves himself and desires to achieve a publicly recognisable and valued identity; his self-deception that he is a Christian; and his belief that Denmark is a Christian state.' Elrod, *Kierkegaard and Christendom*, p. xviii.

[191] Julia Watkin, *Historical Dictionary of Kierkegaard's Philosophy* (Maryland, Toronto, and Oxford: The Scarecrow Press, Inc., 2001), p. 231. Cf. also Rudd, *Kierkegaard and the Limits of the Ethical*, p. 75.

a constant state of becoming. It is both dynamic and relational. Dynamic because it is subject to and capable of transformation (and this process is set in the context of freedom); relational because the self achieves realisation through awareness of possibility, difference, and choice (and the process of internalising and externalising this). However, Kierkegaard's point is that to be fully (and correctly) constituted as a self then we must realise the *true* potential of spiritual freedom. Although this freedom can be directed (or *mis*directed) at any number of projects and worldviews, human beings only truly start on the road to selfhood when their freedom is recognised to be *spiritual* and directed towards that one, unchanging (and therefore unfailing) end. In other words, we must choose to form a relationship with God.[192] Thus, by choosing to become a Christian an individual is choosing to attempt to centre their life around their relationship with God. In so doing they are placing their life on the only sound footing that is possible: the eternal. The success of this relationship is both normative and rare.

What we find in Kierkegaard's authorship is not so much one account of selfhood, but a whole taxonomy of examples of how individuals can fall short of achieving spiritual selfhood. In short, all of these individuals achieve something, but their achievements are unfulfilling and precarious from the only unchanging and meaningful point of view. The discussion of the vast majority of cases of selfhood forms a significant strand of Kierkegaard's authorship. Indeed, many of the positions of the pseudonyms represent just such failed attempts. Despite this negative focus Kierkegaard's account of the failure to develop a self is still instructive of the normative case, and this is *especially* true when the cases under scrutiny are found to be ostensibly Christian. For Kierkegaard, all of these failed attempts at selfhood are manifestations of 'despair' and 'double-mindedness'. These conditions are not necessarily experienced subjectively as melancholy and confusion, but are an *objective* condition that individuals can be said to be in if they fail in the ultimate task of selfhood: to choose to become a Christian.

Kierkegaard makes the connection between 'despair' and 'double-mindedness' in his signed work of 1847 *Upbuilding Discourses in Various Spirits* (and specifically in the first section often referred to a *The Purity*

---

[192] MG Piety, 'The Place of the World in Kierkegaard's Ethics', in George Pattison and Steven Shakespeare (eds.), *Kierkegaard: The Self in Society*, pp. 27-28; Perkinson, 'A 'Socio-reading' of the Kierkegaardian Self: Or, the Space of Lowliness in the Time of the Disciple', p. 159; Rudd, *Kierkegaard and the Limits of the Ethical*, p. 24.

of Heart is to Will One Thing).¹⁹³ Although he treats the notions somewhat differently there is a synonymity between them. This can be seen when we compare the account of double-mindedness offered in *Purity of Heart* to that of the account of despair later offered by the pseudonym Anti-Climacus in *The Sickness Unto Death*.¹⁹⁴ A comparison of these books reveals close parallels in the structure of treatment and function of the concepts, although the overall focus differs. In *Purity of Heart* Kierkegaard's concern is explicitly with the focus of the will. This is not explicitly played out in terms of selfhood. Instead it is framed in terms of bringing the reader to a better understanding of what it means to will to focus on the truth and to underpin their life with the foundation of the eternal.¹⁹⁵ In *Sickness* Anti-Climacus starts with an account of the (relational) self. However, his main purpose is to show that despair is precisely the failure to relate to the eternal in the correct way. In other words, individuals are inherently spiritual beings (whether they recognise this or not) and despair is a choosing not to live in accordance with this and its demands.¹⁹⁶ In both despair and double-mindedness the individual misplaces their true spiritual relation. Instead of focusing in the right way on the eternal, they substitute this with all manner of temporal relations.¹⁹⁷

In *Sickness* Anti-Climacus identifies three basic forms of despair. In despair as ignorance the individual fails to even recognise the possibility that they are a spiritual being. Such an individual is therefore conditioned by the world around them, their circumstances, and their relations with others.¹⁹⁸ Second there is despair in weakness. The individual realises that they have the potential to recognise and actualise their spiritual self, but they abandon that task. The individual wishes to take on the form of a self which they would consider acceptable, but realise that they are very far from this achievement. Thus, they reject the self that they are. Finally, there is despair as defiance. Here the individual recognises themselves as a spiritual self,

---

[193] Kierkegaard, *Upbuilding Discourses in Various Spirits*, pp. 30-31.
[194] For a much fuller account of 'despair' as explored in *Sickness* see Hannay, *Kierkegaard*, p. 157ff.
[195] Cf. Rudd, *Kierkegaard and the Limits of the Ethical*, p. 137.
[196] James Collins, *The Mind of Kierkegaard* (Chicago: Henry Regenry Company, 1953), p. 81.
[197] Søren Kierkegaard, *The Sickness Unto Death*, Howard V Hong and Edna H Hong trans. (New Jersey: Princeton University Press, 1980 [1849]), p. 33; Ibid., *Two Ages*, Howard V Hong and Edna H Hong trans. (Princeton: Princeton University Press, 1978 [1846]), p. 62.
[198] Kierkegaard, *Sickness*, pp. 42-47; Søren Kierkegaard, *Søren Kierkegaard's Journals and Papers*, Howard V Hong and Edna H Hong trans., vol. 3 (Bloomington and London: Indiana University Press, 1975), § 2999.

but they wish to separate this self from the power which constituted it: God. In other words, such an individual realises what is required of them, but openly and actively opposes these requirements. Thus, with the exception of despair as ignorance (which, in a sense is not really despair at all insofar as it is not qualified by consciousness) despair can be seen to be a misrelation of the self which is based on the choice of the individual. It is in this sense that we can see Kierkegaard's meaning in *Purity of Heart* that all despair is double-mindedness. For double-mindedness is precisely the misrelation which is brought about by the individual choosing something other than the correct spiritual relation with the eternal. Thus, the kinds of double-mindedness in *Purity of Heart* mirror the main positions outlined in *Sickness*.

In *Purity of Heart* Kierkegaard focuses on those forms of despair where consciousness goes astray. He focuses on the forms of double-mindedness where an individual seeks to will one thing, but where that individual is either confused about the true object of willing one thing;[199] where the individual seeks to temper this demanding task with willing something else simultaneously (and in a fashion that they deceive themselves into thinking is harmonious with willing one thing); or where the individual wills one thing not for its own sake but for the sake of something else (such as the avoidance of punishment, the attainment of reward, or their own victory).[200] Thus, double-mindedness and despair prove to be alternative presentations of the same basic misrelation that Kierkegaard identifies at the heart of the human condition. His ambition is to show how this sickness infects the individual both *singly and in relation*, and in their understanding of their role in affairs both sacred and profane.[201]

Friendship in the *Works of Love*

'Sociality' is the key concern of Kierkegaard's publication of 1847 *Works of Love*.[202] Kierkegaard explores this concern through the notion of love. In so doing he focuses directly on the concerns of friendship; what Kierkegaard is attempting to find in *Works* is the ultimate foundation of all human bonds. However, Kierkegaard's book is also a Christian deliberation. Thus, his concern is not simply with what *happens* to bind

---

[199] Cf. Kierkegaard, *Upbuilding Discourses in Various Spirits*, p. 26.
[200] Cf. Kierkegaard, *Upbuilding Discourses in Various Spirits*, pp. 37, 44, 60.
[201] Hannay, *Kierkegaard*, p. 169.
[202] For two fuller and exemplary treatments of this book please consult: M Jamie Ferreira, *Love's Grateful Striving* (Oxford: Oxford University Press, 2001); Paul Müller, *Kierkegaard's 'Works of Love' Christian Ethics and the Maieutic Ideal*, C Stephen Evans and Jan Evans trans. (Denmark: CA Reitzel, 1993). Both of these commentaries have been influential on the account given here.

person to person (and the various manifestations of this). Kierkegaard's ultimate concern is the true and normative foundation of human sociality. Such a sociality creates normative conditions for the bonds between person and person. For Kierkegaard this sociality is found not in ourselves or in others (*qua* humans), but is generated as a consequence of our attempts to become selves before God. It is our relationship with God that dictates the contours of our bonds with others, and these bonds are understood as placing on us demands to love all others as spiritual equals. For Kierkegaard, this is the meaning of being a *neighbour*. For Kierkegaard all other forms of sociality are not only opposed to this, but are also doomed to limitation, self-contradiction, and failure.

It is in the account of the neighbour that we find Kierkegaard's theorisation of the bonds between person and person taken normatively. Laying at the root of this relationship is the human need for love. However, this need 'originates darkly in the deep spring' of God's love.[203] Thus, whilst becoming a neighbour to others is what all should aim for, it is sadly far from usual. The need for love can manifest and develop in a whole variety of ways. Here the bonds that Kierkegaard promotes under 'the neighbour' are contrasted to others. This contrast becomes one of the primary ways in which Kierkegaard stages his discourse. For early in *Works* Kierkegaard solemnly warns his reader that 'To defraud oneself of love is the most terrible, is an eternal loss, for which there is no compensation either in time or in eternity'.[204] It is precisely the ways in which people do deceive themselves out of love and the correct form of bonds with others that is the central concern of the opening chapters of *Works*. Here Kierkegaard examines the meaning of the commandment 'You shall love the neighbour' and in doing so shows how this spiritual understanding of human bonds is superior to that of a human friendship. We now turn to the features of friendship that Kierkegaard identifies (preference, passion, and reciprocation) which lead him to conclude that a purely human friendship is ultimately a selfish relationship mired in despair.

Preference, particularity, and partiality

For Kierkegaard all friendship is a form of preference. Indeed, this is one of its central and defining features.[205] In friendship the friends are thought to be tied together in a closer way than in their relations with

---

[203] Søren Kierkegaard, *Works of Love: Some Christian Deliberations in the Form of Discourses*, Howard V Hong and Edna H Hong trans. (Princeton: Princeton University Press, 1995 [1847]), pp. 9-10.
[204] Kierkegaard, *Works*, pp. 5-6.
[205] Kierkegaard, *Works*, pp. 19, 44-46, 52-69.

those outside of the friendship. It is this closeness that generates some of the appeal of friendship and even underpins the ethical obligations friends are thought to have to each other.[206] In making this observation Kierkegaard is also drawing from the tradition that associates and even merges our ethical and emotional duties. As we have seen, this tradition finds expression in the theorisation of friendship offered through the concerns of *eros* and *philia* articulated by Plato and Aristotle. Under Kierkegaard's pen the preferential aspects of friendship tie into these variations, and also to what modernity would term 'erotic' (that is romantic) love. In making this connection Kierkegaard writes that:

> The same holds true of friendship as erotic love, inasmuch as this, too, is based on preference: to love this one person above all others, to love him in contrast to all others. Therefore the object of both erotic love and friendship has preference's name, 'the beloved,' 'the friend,' who is loved in contrast to the whole world.[207]

Kierkegaard's characterisation of erotic love and friendship is one that also associates the relationships with a kind of closed, encircling exclusivity and intimacy. This is easily recognised in the case of erotic love. Here the romantic image is one of two people deeply and passionately committed to each other. In the most dramatic depictions of this kind of relationship the lovers are cautious of others encroaching on their intimacy. Indeed, it is clear that others cannot share in the bond of the lovers, and this bond can drive the lovers to sacrifice themselves for each other. The lovers not only contrast themselves to the world, in a sense they also forsake it for each other. In the case of friendship this sense of 'contrast to the whole world' is somewhat harder to see. Kierkegaard's point can be discerned when we take his connection between friendship and love seriously. Whilst we are not accustomed to viewing the relationship of friendship as one that is based on the same levels of intensity and exclusivity that characterises a love affair, nevertheless it follows the same basic contours. It is this logical relation (which also slips over into an experiential relation) that Kierkegaard is keen to expose. This can be seen when we think about friendship circles. Such circles cannot be extended *ad infinitum*. There is

---

[206] In raising the issue of partiality Kierkegaard highlights a feature of friendship that has also found some attention in contemporary philosophical debate. In particular, there has been some discussion within the analytic tradition as to whether friends are justified in displaying partiality from an ethical point of view. See, for example, Bernard Williams, *Moral Luck* (Cambridge: Cambridge University Press, 1981); Lawrence Blum, *Friendship, Altruism and Morality* (London and New York: Routledge, 1980).

[207] Kierkegaard, *Works*, p. 19.

a very real sense in which an individual can only have a friendship with a very small number of people: personal friendship places emotional and ethical obligations on individuals which simply cannot be generalised and retain their intensity and value. In part the intensity and value of friendship comes from the very fact that the friends do not seek to generalise it. Thus, in the 'ideal' friendship—that is to say, the idealised friendship as imagined by poets and authors—the friends are bound to each other much in the same way as the lovers are bound together. In friendship, as in romance, preference and fidelity are linked; a preference and fidelity that makes both sacrifice and betrayal real possibilities.

Seen in this way Kierkegaard's focus on the preferential aspects of friendship is not especially controversial. Indeed, even his connection of friendship to erotic love does not appear peculiar when we consider the longer tradition that tends to blur these distinctions, and the logical similarity that is exposed when we consider their dynamics. However, the particular direction in which Kierkegaard develops his account of this feature is less than uncontroversial. As we have seen, Kierkegaard associates friendship with erotic love on account of the preference that both display. It is this preference that makes both relationships the subject of the poet's admiration.[208] It is the *partiality* of friendship (that the poets celebrate) that becomes the focus of Kierkegaard's attack. Kierkegaard has two strands to this attack. The first is to claim that the 'preference' of friendship develops to the *exclusion* of others, and is actually a preference for the human aspects of the friend.[209] The friend is the object of admiration, but Kierkegaard suggests that it is a specific set of characteristics that are admired (or the possibility of the relationship itself). It is not the other person as a total self that is admired, but a particular set of features of that self. Friends do not simply show preference, but the notion of preference is determined by the possibility of differentiation. What differentiates person from person are the particular characteristics, traits, dispositions, qualities, actions and achievements that they display. Thus, for Kierkegaard, friendship is not just *partial* but *particular*. It would seem that this would have to be conceded by any account of friendship (understood as a personal relation). In addition, the friend does not simply admire the other's self as such (or aspects of that self) but they are concerned that their friend will admire and relate to them. In short, the preference

---

[208] Kierkegaard, *Works*, pp. 19, 46.
[209] Kierkegaard, *Works*, pp. 52, 56-57.

of friendship must be reciprocal.[210] Without reciprocity the friendship will perish.

This focus on partiality and particularity is problematic for Kierkegaard not only because it is exclusionary, but also because it is subject to change. Kierkegaard points out that the poet seeks to 'join' the friends in their relationship, and that friendship is praised precisely because the friends promise to remain true to each other in eternity.[211] This adds a new dimension to Kierkegaard's earlier observation that the friends prefer each other in contrast to the whole world. From Kierkegaard's point of view the focus of the friend's relationship is doomed as the friends cannot secure themselves against change, and so the ideal of remaining *true* to the friend cannot be achieved. The friends cannot secure themselves against change not only because they are a part of the temporal sphere where change is inevitable, but because what they really admire about each other is not the other person as such, but some specific and particular human features of the other person. From the start the bond is doomed to failure as it is dependent not only upon arbitrary particularities, but also factors outside the friends' control. What is more, the pursuit of particularity and partiality can only lead to a deviant formation of the self. As we have seen, for Kierkegaard selfhood is relational, but true selfhood can only be achieved and maintained when focused on its correct object: God.

The focus on the specificity of the other person opens space for Kierkegaard's second line of attack. Here Kierkegaard argues that the preference shown in friendship is essentially *selfish*. As we shall see, Kierkegaard attaches various degrees of depth to this claim, and ultimately it is this claim that distinguishes Christian neighbourliness from all other forms of sociality (including friendship of both a romantic and philosophical kind). In anticipation of what is to come, we can say that for Kierkegaard the preference in reflecting love of some feature of the other ultimately leads back to the love of the human self. Friends relate only to the other as *specific human* selves. They do so by making the friendship the highest good: but can do so only at the expense of a correct formulation of their own self. That the friends do this is brought to our attention by Kierkegaard's reminder that philosophers call the friend the 'other self' or 'other I'.[212] However, this focus on the human self is really a variety of despair. That is to say it is a mis-relation of the self. Despair threatens all forms of purely human

---

[210] Kierkegaard, *Works*, pp. 34, 54-55. This feature will be discussed in more depth shortly.
[211] Kierkegaard, *Works*, pp. 30-31, 168-70.
[212] Kierkegaard, *Works*, p. 53.

sociality. Before we can move to discuss the relation between selfishness, despair and partiality, we need to spend some time outlining and clarifying Kierkegaard's second claim concerning friendship: that it is based on the emotional life of individuals.

The passions of the self

We have seen that for Kierkegaard 'preference' — understood as a focus on specificity — is ultimately loving one in contrast to the whole world. Thus, the poetic celebration of love and friendship is revealed not to be simple romanticisation. Idealistic as it is, the poets' view of love and friendship is an accurate portrayal of the logical structure of its subject. What remains to be explained is how this 'preference' is to come about. In other words, why is it that the friends are drawn to each other (in particular) and not to others? It will be recalled that this question traces its origin at least as far back as the concerns of Socrates in *Lysis*. Indeed, the question is fundamental in demarcating one of the dimensions of the field of concern that friendship theorises.

In order to explain the phenomenon of preference in friendship and love Kierkegaard turns his attention to the inner life of the individual. In so doing he has no compunction in confronting directly the passion that characterises the underlying emotional life of the self and which shapes our friendships.[213] However, whilst the passions that lead to preference might be a necessary part of the human self, their particular expression is always contingent and accidental. Much depends on where we find ourselves and who we happen to meet. Much also depends on forces beyond our (direct) control. Thus, whilst friendship is the result of a deeply human passion, it is not the result of choice. As such it can never be truly reflective (it cannot be chosen) nor secure (it cannot be guaranteed). Friendship might well be praised by the poet, but such a poet praises a relation which is deeply and necessarily insecure, uncertain, and flawed. Thus, friendship can be praised by the poet (*qua* poet) but it cannot be praised by the Christian (*qua* Christian).[214] As we shall see, in Kierkegaard's final analysis friendship and erotic love are not simply 'inferior' to the Christian relation of loving the neighbour, they are diametrically and decisively opposed.[215]

Kierkegaard's account of friendship and love places passion and emotion at their foundation. Friends join with each other because of

---

[213] Kierkegaard, *Works*, pp. 44-45, 49, 52.
[214] Kierkegaard, *Works*, pp. 45-46.
[215] Amy Laura Hall, *Kierkegaard and the Treachery of Love* (Cambridge: Cambridge University Press, 2002), p. 14; Müller, *Kierkegaard's "Works of Love"*, p. ix; Peter George, 'Something Anti-Social About *Works of Love*', in George Pattison and Steven Shakespeare (eds.), *Kierkegaard: The Self in Society*, p. 71.

feelings that they experience. Of course, these feelings can develop over time. Indeed, it is in some ways crucial to Kierkegaard's account that this is possible as it is this passion that partly leads to the exclusion of others.[216] The enclosure of the passion of friends can become intoxicating (and in its highest and most celebrated forms is praised as such). It is also passion which helps to explain the mutual identification of the friends as 'other selves'.[217] We will see in the next section that this notion (common to all the main accounts of friendship) has significant implications for Kierkegaard (not least in establishing friendship as being selfish). For now, however, it is sufficient to note that in friendship the passion of the friend is said to focus on the self of the other. It is that particular self who is shown preference and to whom the emotions of the friend attach. As Montaigne has it in describing his friendship with La Boétie: 'If you press me to tell why I loved him, I feel that this cannot be expressed, except by answering: Because it was he, because it was I'.[218]

For Kierkegaard whilst these poetical celebrations of passion are commonplace both in terms of poetry itself and in the relations and aspirations of individuals, they are also deeply and hopelessly flawed. Such celebrations are possible precisely because such deep and lasting friendships are both rare and subject to the threat of instability. In the first instance friendship is subject to instability as a result of preference. As we have seen, the relationship cannot tolerate the introduction of 'a third' into its dynamic. However, there is a deeper way in which friendship is subject to instability. For, whilst the emotional foundations of friendship are uniquely human they are not within human control. Fidelity may be demanded by passion, but passion itself is a fickle master. It transforms and departs as quickly as it flares up. Kierkegaard presents a picture that is easily recognised in both erotic-love and friendship when he writes that:

> Spontaneous love can be changed within itself; it can be changed into its opposite, into *hate*. Hate is a love that has become its opposite, a love that has perished.[219]

And a few paragraphs later Kierkegaard observes that:

---

[216] Kierkegaard, *Works*, p. 52. The expression 'other selves' is perhaps most closely associated with the thought of Aristotle (see *Nichomachean Ethics* 1170b5). However, what Kierkegaard stresses, and what seems absent from Aristotle's account, is precisely the element of emotion.

[217] Kierkegaard, *Works*, p. 56.

[218] Pakaluk (ed.), *Other Selves*, p. 192. Indeed, Montaigne's essay, although short, is an excellent example of many of the common assumptions about friendship as the idea enters modernity.

[219] Kierkegaard, *Works*, p. 34.

> Spontaneously love can be changed *from itself*, it can be changed over the years, and is frequently enough seen. The love loses its ardour, its joy, its originality, its freshness.[220]

The force of what Kierkegaard is claiming here should not be mistaken. It would be easy (perhaps even poetical) to accept this observation as a mere danger that friendship faces. This would allow the poet to 'ascend' into an idealised form of friendship which is to be aimed at even if it is ultimately unattainable. Thus, whilst many (possibly *all*) existing friendships meet the fate of failure, the ideal of friendship is saved by an act of wishful reification. For Kierkegaard this response would be deeply mistaken. The problem is not that actual friendships fail, but the friendship itself is a failed ideal. Kierkegaard's point here is that as friendship is generated by drives and inclinations, it is *inherently* unstable both in its realised and potential form. This instability occurs in two ways. In the first it might simply be that the passion or emotion that forms the basis of the friendship wanes. Of course, the friends might attempt any manner of rouses to prevent this. Such rouses are ultimately futile; they can no more prevent passion from waning than they can engender its appearance. In the second, the very attempt to secure the friendship leads to an intensification of its instability. Both friends fear change and seek assurances of the fidelity of their friend.[221] In effect, the assurance is a promise against change. However, this is neither in the gift of the friends, nor can they produce the 'proof' that the friendship requires. For the friendship can only be 'proven' in eternity. If the friendship is truly secured against change then this can only be known retrospectively. Friendship, on the other hand, is a dynamic relation which—whilst the contemplation of past events may contribute to its dynamic—is a present relationship which is future orientated. It is this future orientation which is a source of uncertainty for the friends. Their endeavour is brought into peril by the possibility of infidelity and the transformation of feeling. This creates a logical contradiction for the friends. For the test against the future is eternity, and it is this test that the friends seek to apply, but can never wish to apply. As Kierkegaard argues, the test of friendship betrays the fact that the friends are uncertain in their relationship.[222] Indeed, seeking to test the friendship is either a sign that the friendship does not yet exist (if it did then its security would be self evident and it would not need to be tested), or it is a sign of distrust in an existing friendship and so a betrayal of the fidelity that is supposed to bind the

---

[220] Kierkegaard, *Works*, p. 36.
[221] Kierkegaard, *Works*, p. 31.
[222] Kierkegaard, *Works*, p. 33.

friends in the first place. Yet, without such a test the friends cannot be secure.

The persistence of friendship as ethics: Ancient and Modern

As we have seen, if we accept Kierkegaard's claim that friendship is rooted in emotion then difficulties arise for the prospects of maintaining the bond. The emotional foundation of friendship cannot be secured by mere human effort; it is not a case of will or choice. In the best case the friends might act *as if* they liked or even loved one another, but they cannot force the emotion, nor wish it into existence. This raises the question as to whether such relationships are friendships at all. Of course, individuals in such a relationship might behave in a friendly manner, but without emotional underpinnings it is difficult to claim that they either share in a friendship or are fully each a friend to the other. The lack of emotional attachment on the part of one (or both) of the friends might even occasion accusation. The relationship is maintained as a formalism, courtesy, or from social expectation. Friends, it would seem, do not simply act in a friendly manner, but do so because they are correctly motivated. Such motivation finds its source in the heart not simply in the head. Thus, for friendship to be 'complete' it is usually assumed that the special consideration that is shown within friendship is ultimately a result of inclination rather than obligation or prudence.

These kinds of considerations lead Kierkegaard to make the claim that friendship contains no 'moral task'.[223] This is important as it might be thought that friendship was a primary site for ethical behaviour. In contrast to this view Kierkegaard maintains that we cannot be obligated to seek friendship (or a friend), nor is friendship the expression of ethical behaviour. To those who would consider friendship to be the demonstration of selfless if not altruistic behaviour Kierkegaard has an uncompromising response: friendship is ultimately selfish. This second claim, which is central to Kierkegaard's criticisms of 'friendship' will be taken up shortly. First a word or two needs to be said about the notion that friendship cannot be a moral task as it is this claim that also sees Kierkegaard militate against the accounts of the Ancients, and especially those of Plato and Aristotle. An examination of this skirmish not only shows what is distinctive to each account, but it also helps us to understand Kierkegaard's more damning conclusion that friendship is selfish.

In Ancient thought friendship constitutes something amounting to a 'moral task', and Kierkegaard's thought draws from this idea. We have

---

[223] Kierkegaard, *Works*, p. 51.

already had occasion to explore this in the thought of Plato and Aristotle, but it is a common theme in many of the classical writers. For example, in his *De Amicitia* Cicero has Laelius claim that friendship results not from any 'inadequacy' found in the individual, but from a love of virtue.[224] The view expressed here is that far from being a sign that the individual is incomplete, friendship is a demonstration of a person attempting to extend their virtue and to foster it in others. Cicero's text observes that the extension of friendship rests on virtue, and that it is necessary for the maintenance of the social order.[225] For his part Seneca clearly sees a connection between friendship and the extension of ethical activity. For him, friendship must be sought and cultivated so as our 'noble qualities may not lie dormant'.[226] Presumably the idea here is not only that friendship allows us to act in a virtuous way, but that it is a forum which encourages us to do so. As a further instance, Plutarch's view is not wildly dissimilar. He views friendship as an important corrective to the unworthy side of the person. The irrational side is both inclined to falsehood and emotion. In contrast the rational side is governed by honour and reason. Friends act as 'advocates' and 'physicians' playing an important role in fostering the rational, honourable, and reasonable.[227] Insofar as friendship fosters the desire for and understanding of honour it promotes a socio-political virtue. In these accounts the theme of friendship is being considered not only as a personal relation, but a relation with social and political consequences. Friendship, then, is not merely to be cultivated by accident and for personal satisfaction, it is a task that all truly good, noble, and virtuous men should endeavour to achieve.

These later developments of the ethical task of friendship are prefigured in the accounts of Plato and Aristotle. As we have seen, in Plato's account friendship is intimately connected to both the philosophical pursuit of the truth and the good, and the establishment of the good political community. Friendship (as epitomised in dialogues such as the *Symposium*) is presented as a form of bonding which is capable of developing an appreciation of truth and virtue in its participants. In this account physical and emotional attraction must be transformed from the particular to the general, and then on to the

---

[224] Pakaluk (ed.), *Other Selves*, p. 90.
[225] Pakaluk (ed.), *Other Selves*, p. 88. Here Cicero notes that 'if the mutual love of friends were to be removed from the world, there is no single house, no single state that would go on existing; even agriculture would cease to be'.
[226] Seneca, *Ad Lucilium Epiestulae Morals*, Richard M Gummere trans., vol. 1 (Nassachusetss: Harvard University Press, 1917), p. 120.
[227] Plutarch 'Moralia' in Philip Blosser and Marshell Carl Bradley (eds.), *Friendship: Philosophic Reflections on a Perennial Concern* (Lantham, New York, and Oxford: University Press of America, 1997), p. 111.

abstract. It is turned outwards from the immediate cause of desire (the lover and his beloved) to the beauty to be found in all people, and finally to the beauty of truth and goodness itself. Although there are clearly lower and higher forms of this relationship, all friendship between lover and beloved aims (in some way) at the apprehension of the good. Moreover, in the highest forms not only is the good apprehended, but it is cultivated and fostered not only in the friendship itself, but in wider social and political life. In the *Republic* Plato is seen to make friendship the complement of justice. It is an important force for binding the citizens together, and is also important in motivating the Guardians not only to seek the truth and goodness, but to take on the task of governing others and fostering these ideals within the earthly city. Thus, for Plato not only is friendship a forum for ethical activity, but ethics is not possible without the foundation provided by friendship.

In like manner Aristotle also develops the close association between friendship, ethics, and politics. It will be recalled that in contrast to Plato, Aristotle's account is somewhat more attuned to the variation of the forms of friendship and attempts to reconcile theory with everyday practice. In this vein, whereas Plato develops one true account of friendship to mirror his one true account of the good, Aristotle identifies a most complete form of friendship based around 'virtue' but is less inclined to see other forms of friendship as *merely* defective. Indeed, Aristotle recognises that whilst all friendship aims at 'some good' different friendships aim at different goods (virtue, pleasure, and utility). What is significant about the case of virtue-friendship is that in contrast to Kierkegaard's own focus on emotion, this form of friendship is presented as being somewhat sober.

In this respect we can see how Kierkegaard's view in *Works* stands in contrast to that of one of his earlier pseudonyms (Judge William) who explicitly draws on Aristotle's view of friendship to develop his own.[228] In *Either/Or* the judge seeks to correct his young correspondent (the aesthete A) whose views reflect his own inability (or unwillingness) to live beyond the aesthetic sphere where the only structure to life is the self-imposed challenge to accumulate new experiences. A's view of friendship is conditioned by this over-arching aestheticism. According to Judge William, A considers the relationship to be 'an enigma; a fog'[229] its sole attraction being the possibility that it might temporarily relieve boredom. Such a position is expounded in

---

[228] Søren Kierkegaard, *Either/Or*, Howard V Hong and Edna H Hong trans., 2 vols., vol. II (Princeton: Princeton University Press, 1987 [1843]), p. 322.

[229] Kierkegaard, *Either/Or II*, p. 319.

'The Rotation of the Crops' although the dangers of an unchanging friend are also stressed there:

> ...one quite consistently hopes to meet one's old friends and acquaintances in a better world but does not share the crowd's fear that they may have changed so much that one could not recognise them again. One fears, instead, that they may be altogether unchanged.[230]

In contrast to the view expounded by his young correspondent, the judge connects friendship to the ethical life. He praises it alongside marriage as being one of the highpoints of a life lived according to ethical lights. Such a friendship can only be cultivated by an individual who has not confused it with an inferior version of erotic love, or has not experienced erotic love too early and abandoned it for friendship.[231] According to Judge William, what is needed for friendship is 'unity in a life-view'.[232] Such a life-view gives direction and meaning to relationships and action. It is edifying for both of the friends in much the same way as Aristotle conceives of the friendship of the virtuous. Thus, Judge William can claim that:

> Unity in a life-view is the constituting element in friendship. If this is present, the friendship lasts even if the friend dies, inasmuch as the transfigured friend lives on in the other; if this ceases, the friendship is over even if the friend goes on living.[233]

What the judge is pointing to here is that true friendship is a real possibility, but it is only a possibility for those who seek friendship as a result of first obtaining a positive life-view. This echoes the views of Aristotle who says that the virtuous seek the friendship of the virtuous, which indicates that these men are already virtuous. Virtue-friendship confirms, sustains, and enhances their understanding and common life of virtue. Similarly for Judge William the life-view both sustains and is sustained by friendship; it is what the friendship is based on and around and what the friends share. As a common project that has both personal, interpersonal, and social consequences it not only forms the common material of their relationship but also contributes to the fabric of society itself. Friendship not only connects person to person (and makes public life possible), it also points to something beyond itself: the ethical. Thus, for Judge William such a view is only achievable if an individual bases their life on ethical foundations. If it is based on such foundations, friendship is not caught in the fleeting whims of pleasure

---

[230] Kierkegaard, *Either/Or I*, p. 296.
[231] Kierkegaard, *Either/Or II*, pp. 317-318.
[232] Kierkegaard, *Either/Or II*, p. 319.
[233] Kierkegaard, *Either/Or II*, pp. 321-322.

and utility, but secured by rational appreciation of universal ethical considerations and duties. Without such a foundation friendship is doomed to perish as it is not rooted in permanence but subject to human inclination (and here the judge's view accords with that of Kierkegaard himself). Furthermore, such aesthetic friendships can provide no lasting satisfaction as rather than contribute to a fully ethical life they are merely a distraction from it. Judge William concludes that:

> The person who views friendship ethically sees it, then, as a duty. Therefore, I could say that it is every person's duty to have a friend.[234]

The judge's view is a clear echo of the views of the Ancient writers. For the judge the duty to have a friend is a part of the duties of an ethical individual as a social self. In the judge's account friendship is a personal relationship, which is a component of and bolsters ethical life in the wider community. Thus, it is edifying not only in setting the friends on a mutually supportive appreciation of their ethical status and duties, it also leads the friends to play their roles in society more generally.[235]

Kierkegaard *contra* Aristotle and Judge William

Despite the pedigree of the view that connects friendship and the idea of a moral task, Kierkegaard's position in *Works* is a clear rejection of this line of association. How then does Kierkegaard respond to this model which stands in contrast to his own (be it presented by Aristotle or Judge William)? Any such response must do more than simply address the claim that there is an ethical dimension to friendship; it must also tackle the shift in the foundation of friendship from 'emotion' to 'rationality'. So far Kierkegaard's account is often directed at 'poetic love' which (as we have seen) is both preferential and passionate. The relationship of friendship as Aristotle describes it does not appear to fall under this rubric. Indeed, for Aristotle virtue-friendship is based around contemplation and not passion, and the same seems largely true for the account offered by Judge William. In effect, the foundation of friendship is moved from the particularity (and contingency) of emotion to the abstract and general that can be apprehended by reason.

To anticipate what is to come in response to these questions it can be noted that ultimately there are two major differences between the

---

[234] Kierkegaard, *Either/Or II*, p. 322. However, it should be noted that the judge uses this conclusion as a platform to enthuse about the importance of the duty to 'become open'.

[235] Which reflects Judge William's quasi-Hegelian outlook more generally. See, for example, his views on the institution of marriage.

structure of the accounts of friendship offered by Kierkegaard and Aristotle. These differences relate to the source of bonding in the wider structure of their thought. However, the differences not only provide points of contrast between their accounts, they also render their accounts irreconcilable. These differences are also mirrored in the differences between Kierkegaard's views and those of Judge William despite the latter's profession of Christianity. Thus, by implication, the account of friendship that Kierkegaard offers in *Works* is also irreconcilable with the promotion of the relationship by Judge William. In respect to Aristotle, the first difference relates to the role and connection of *telos* and *eudemonia*. The second (which we will discuss in full under the third feature of Kierkegaard's account of friendship) is the notion of the self and selfhood itself. In respect to Judge William the difference is somewhat harder to discern as Judge William considers himself a Christian. However, the difference becomes apparent when we consider the explicitly Christian understanding of selfhood and our duty in *Works* (which can be considered a truly religious—that is to say truly *Christian* understanding) and contrast it to the *ethical* understanding that Judge William offers in *Either/Or*.[236] In other words, whilst Judge William clothes his ethics in religious garb, their foundation remains rooted in human reason. For Kierkegaard, this fails to appreciate the rupturing presence of the divine.

First, let us take up the issue of *telos* in Aristotle's thought (and *human telos* in particular). Although this is a complex and nuanced concept the general idea is that for human beings there is a final end to which their actions are aimed, and the attempt to achieve this end can be understood to be the cause of their actions. We have already seen that for Aristotle human beings desire some good (i.e. that they desire what is good for them). However, here 'desire' should not merely be thought of as an emotion or longing. It is perhaps better described as an interest (be that immediate or long-term). For Aristotle ultimately only *eudemonia* is a complete end, and other things considered goods are said to be good insofar as they contribute to this final end.[237] What it is also important to note about these notions of *telos* and *eudemonia* is that in Aristotle's scheme they are apprehended and realised through human intelligence and decision. Fundamentally, human beings are able to use their reason to discern knowledge not only of the physical world but also of the ethical. The criteria of such ethical knowledge (and the principles for action which follow from it) is what will lead to the fullest achievement of *eudemonia*.

---

[236] Lee, *Kierkegaard on Becoming and Being a Christian*, p. 48.
[237] Aristotle, *Nicomachean Ethics*, 1094a1-20.

Given this account of Aristotle's overall scheme it is not difficult to see how friendship finds its place. If we take the three basic causes of friendship mapped by Aristotle in the *Nicomachean Ethics* (i.e. virtue, pleasure, and utility) we can see that they all aim at some good, and that those goods are components that help to contribute towards the most complete life (i.e. the life where *eudemonia* is most fully achieved). The goods that each friendship aim for are goods that rational people would choose. Clearly whilst both utility and pleasure are a necessary component of the fullest life, they are not sufficient in themselves. Indeed, Aristotle is clear in his *Nicomachean Ethics* as to the limitations of mere pleasure which can lead to a slavish existence.[238] So, although for Aristotle there might well be an emotional side to friendship, it is not its primary basis. Indeed, this might be why he appears somewhat equivocal about the relations within the family which appear to have a more immediate and apparent emotional basis, but a basis that (presumably) must be chosen nonetheless. Be this as it may, it would seem that for Aristotle emotional attachment in friendship is not its primary motivation or the basis for the relationship. Emotions that do exist in friendships must be endorsed by choice. Seen from this perspective when Aristotle observes that friendship underpins the socio-political order he is not merely making a 'sociological' claim. His claim is both sociological and ethical, for not only can friendship *be seen* to underpin the social order, but this underpinning can also be chosen by rational decision. It is not merely how human beings happen to live, it is how they should live. Primarily, this choice has little (if anything) to do with how individuals might feel about each other: it has everything to do with their rational choice in relation to each other.

Kierkegaard's account of friendship in *Works* can be shown to be not only critical of such a scheme but can be viewed as being diametrically opposed to it. Whilst an account such as Aristotle's shifts the focus for the foundation of friendship it fails to fully resolve its problems. By constructing friendship around the rational appreciation of particular goods Aristotle's account downplays its relationship to emotion. This is not to say that emotion plays no role at all, but the feelings that the friends happen to have for each other must be brought under rational control. Presumably (although it is never entertained by Aristotle) the flip-side of such an account of the emotions in friendship would also entail fostering the correct emotions towards those worthy of friendship. This economy of the emotions seems somewhat difficult to achieve — but perhaps this is why the fullest friendship is reserved for those of superior virtue who may be able to better respond to this

---

[238] Aristotle, *Nicomachean Ethics*, 1095b5-20.

challenge. In any event, bringing the emotions under rational control would avoid the pitfalls of the contingency of emotion, but only at a cost. The cost would be that as the relationship is now dependent on rational judgement and not only is it something likely to be rare (as noted, few can be said to be able to truly order their emotions), but it also does virtually nothing to overcome the charges of 'preference', 'particularity' and 'partiality'. Indeed, in some ways Aristotle's account only serves to increase the force of these complaints. Now it seems that friends choose each other not because of natural inclination or a passion for each other, but because of particular choice-worthy actions, dispositions, and qualities. In the case of friendship for utility and pleasure this has an even narrower range than in virtue friendship. Moreover, Aristotle is clear that friendship generates its own justice and whilst friends should not act in unjust ways to others, they are not only justified but actually obliged to show preference and to have a special concern for their friends. The displacement of emotion does not seem to lead to a corresponding displacement of Kierkegaard's main criticisms (i.e. those relating to preference, partiality, and particularity) because now friendship is not possible unless others display particular qualities.

However, even if this were not the case Aristotle's account of friendship remains rooted in the realm of ethics. This is a realm which is limited and incomplete for Kierkegaard unless it is transfused by an apprehension of the religious. In short, ethics *qua* ethics is based on human reason. As such it mistakes a limited part of what it means to be a person for the whole. Indeed, for Kierkegaard different ethical considerations and systems must be considered equally valid (from an ethical point of view) as there is no external purpose or direction with which they can orientate themselves. The only way such ethical systems can differentiate themselves is if they have a transcendent element. Therefore, we see that Aristotle's and Kierkegaard's accounts of friendship are diametrically opposed. Aristotle's account of friendship sees the friends aim at diverse goods. Nevertheless there is a sense in which we are concerned for the friend 'for his own sake'. This is because friends wish to see their friends receive what they deserve. From Kierkegaard's perspective this fails to recognise the true aim of human association: God. Without a self constituted in relation to God no other associations are possible. Friendship becomes, then, a kind of mis-relation. This is made all the worse by the supposed ethical character of friendship. Far from advancing the individual towards their true *telos* Kierkegaard sees it as diverting our course. It is clear then that these two accounts do not, and cannot, speak to each other as they fail to recognise the starting-points of the other's account as being legitimate.

The second feature that separates the accounts of Aristotle and Kierkegaard is their respective notions of what selfhood entails. Kierkegaard cannot accept Aristotle's ethical notion and understanding of the self. As Kierkegaard writes in a journal entry:

> Aristotle has not understood the self deeply enough, for only in the aesthetic sense does contemplative thought have an entelechy, and the felicity of the gods does not reside in contemplation but in eternal communication. — Aristotle has not perceived the specification of spirit.[239]

It is this distinction between contemplating the self as merely a temporal being, and that of a self as a spiritual being, that leads us to our third, and as we shall see for Kierkegaard decisive, feature of friendship: friendship's distinctive conception of the relationship of selves, which Kierkegaard comes to characterise as being selfish and despairing.

Reciprocity and selfishness: A return to despair

Thus far we have explored Kierkegaard's claims that friendship is both 'partial' and based upon 'drives and inclinations'. However, to fully appreciate Kierkegaard's criticisms of friendship it is important to understand how it is possible for Kierkegaard to claim that friendship is selfish. This claim is central as it connects friendship to despair. As we have seen, despair is a misrelation of the self. Specifically, those in despair fail to recognise or relate to the eternal that is a part of their self to God. However, despite his criticisms of friendship, Kierkegaard does not reject friendship completely. He merely rejects it as a despairing existence if it is not underpinned by living in recognition to spiritual selfhood. It can form a component of a Christian existence *if* the individual underpins and transforms the relationship by recognising and obeying the command to 'love the neighbour'.

Unlike Kierkegaard's previous claims concerning the features of friendship, to claim that friendship is selfish appears to militate against our intuitions. It would not be at all controversial to claim that our common understanding of friendship conjures up an image of a relationship characterised by mutual concern for others. Indeed, in friendship it could be supposed that the focus was on the *other* person rather than a focus on the self. Yet this view must be somewhat modified for if the relationship is to be characterised as friendship we

---

[239] Kierkegaard, *Works*, p. 397.

would be inclined to add that this concern for the other is displayed by both of the friends. In this sense, friendship is not a one-way street. Friendship can be said to be at least mutually other-orientated. Given this picture (at once both descriptive and normative), it is perhaps surprising to us when we read that this is *also* a picture of friendship that Kierkegaard recognises. How, then, does Kierkegaard maintain that the relationship is selfish and ultimately despairing?

In claiming that friendship is selfish Kierkegaard challenges our assumptions concerning friendship in three ways. He does so by taking the idea of friendship as being a relationship between selves seriously. The first challenge is to claim that the preferential and emotional aspects of friendship reveal the relationship to be 'selfish' insofar as the focus is ostensibly on the 'self' of the other person.[240] Such a move might appear to be simply highlighting a semantic fact, but it is actually pivotal for what is to come. As we shall see, this semantic 'clarification' has more to it than meets the eye. Having pointed out the focus of friendship, Kierkegaard's second move is to argue that the concentration on the self is coupled with the importance that the friends place on *reciprocation*. The aspect of reciprocation begins to expose the true focus of friendship which is not the self of the other, but the self of the 'I'. Reciprocation (especially the reciprocation of fidelity and love) is to pose the question not of *do I love the other?*, but instead to replace this question with the question of *does the other really love me?* Finally, the third and most significant claim of Kierkegaard's in relation to the selfish nature of friendship is that the friendship focuses on the human aspects of self. For Kierkegaard the spiritual is neglected. In this sense Kierkegaard's and Aristotle's estimations of friendship are not only opposed, but they actually start with mutually exclusive assumptions. This brings us back to despair. Taken either aesthetically or ethically friendship is actually a mis-relation as the individual fails to relate primarily to God. For Kierkegaard this means that it fails to provide the grounds for genuine selfhood. As a relationship of despair, friendship is doomed to failure. Here there is a triple mis-relation: to God, to ourselves, and to the other. The focus on the self is thus far from trivial. It is undermining of some of the ethical attractiveness of friendship. Kierkegaard's reader now faces a choice: to turn away from basing their relationships with others on selfishness and to look for a new foundation, or to continue to relate to others in this way knowing that it is ultimately possible only by deceiving both self and other. To return to friendship after understanding Kierkegaard's account is to live in a category of conscious despair. The only possible return to

---

[240] Kierkegaard, *Works*, pp. 53-60, 266-7.

friendship is to see the relationship as being underpinned and therefore transformed by first becoming a neighbour.

We have seen that a central strand of Kierkegaard's criticisms of friendship is that rather than loving the other person *per se*, in fact friends love a particular aspect of the friend, or a particular collection of aspects. Of course, it should be noted that these aspects may, or may not, be present: the friend loves a particular image of the other. However, the true force of this claim is only realised when Kierkegaard turns his attention to reciprocity.[241] It is the reciprocal aspect of friendship that reveals the true misguided nature of the love involved in friendship, its connection to selfishness, and the associated despairing experience of self. It is perhaps worth considering how Kierkegaard describes the relation in *Works*. Here Kierkegaard claims that:

> To admire another person is certainly not self-love, but to be the one and only friend of this one and only admired person—would not this relation turn back in an alarming way into the I from which we proceeded?[242]

Kierkegaard's claim is that it is perfectly possible to admire the qualities of another person, but that in friendship there is a degree of exclusivity and intensity that takes the friends beyond simple admiration and into the desire to claim or possess the other. The fidelity of the friendship, which is manifested in a partial love and admiration, must be reciprocated if the friendship is to survive. Indeed, the very notion of friendship entails a reciprocal relationship: friends always come in pairs.

Here Kierkegaard is able to link the preferential and emotional elements of friendship to the most thoroughgoing notion of selfishness. It is perhaps surprising that what appears to be friendship's attempt to be other-orientated proves to be so telling of its failure. Kierkegaard concludes that the partiality and passion of friendship lead to both exclusivity and the jealousy which he claims is 'always fundamentally present in erotic love and friendship'.[243] The friends themselves seek validation of their own self in the response of the other. They turn away from the world. Others are a threat to their union. As Kierkegaard claims: 'The more securely one I and another I join to become one I, the more this united I selfishly cuts itself off from everyone else'.[244] This

---

[241] Kierkegaard, *Works*, pp. 18-19, 54-55, 236-38, 267, 349-51.
[242] Kierkegaard, *Works*, pp. 54-55.
[243] Kierkegaard, *Works*, pp. 52, 54, 55.
[244] Kierkegaard, *Works*, p. 56.

union is not complete. Indeed, although it is enclosing the friends remain apart. Under the illusion that they share a self, the friends actually focus on their own self.[245] Far from encouraging or laying the foundations for a wider sociality, the reciprocity in friendship actually prevents a selfless or other-orientated approach. Within the relationship itself reciprocity see friendship become a secret calculation and exchange of benefits or an exchange of assurances and admiration.[246] If reciprocity is removed, so is the admiration for the other. All friends hope and expect their affection and respect to be returned to them.[247] This last claim of Kierkegaard's is extremely hard to avoid, as it is difficult to see how reciprocity could not be a feature of friendship. This is betrayed in both ordinary and philosophical talk of friendship, where we speak of the friends supporting and caring for each other, and even the friends' choosing of each other. It is easily recognised that friendship cannot be a one-way-street. The reciprocal feature of friendship is also essential if we are to distinguish it from other relationships and attitudes such as mere civility, goodwill or well-wishing — a point of which Aristotle is also keen to make us aware.

Having focused our attention on the reciprocal dimension of friendship, it is now possible to see how Kierkegaard's account of friendship extends beyond what at first appear to be the fairly narrow confines of an especially intimate and intense relationship. It is true that Kierkegaard's main focus is on what we might term the 'highest' form of friendship, but it is important that Kierkegaard can discount this form of friendship as it is the most promising of alternative social relationships. Whilst other social relationships have merits, it is only in friendship that they combine to create the potential for a fulfilling and ethical human sociality. What Kierkegaard achieves through his examination of the reciprocal dimension of friendship is the exposure that even this most ideal of relationships is laced with selfishness, exclusivity and jealousy (and if this is the case for the 'ideal', how much more so for those relationships which aspire towards this apex?). Moreover, Kierkegaard has attempted to show that not only is this often the case, or even potentially the case, but that this is necessarily so because of the nature of the relationship itself. Reciprocity is one of friendship's defining features and one of its most celebrated merits: Kierkegaard's analysis attempts to expose it as also being one of friendship's deepest flaws.

---

[245] Kierkegaard, *Works*, pp. 266-69.
[246] Kierkegaard, *Works*, pp. 155-56, 237, 267.
[247] Kierkegaard, *Works*, p. 351.

It is now possible to see how we can link Kierkegaard's analysis of friendship back to his wider notion and experience of despair. It can be said that friendship is a despairing relationship in three main senses. First, friendship in both its philosophical and poetic forms fails to recognise the centrality of spirit in the formation of self. It is true that friendship can recognise the spiritual aspects of persons, but it fails to build upon the full implications of this. In Kierkegaard's account friendship ignores or displaces the God-relationship and focuses on the purely human aspects of self, or transforms spirit into a human category. Second, this misconception concerning spirit not only fails to place God at the centre of the relationality, but deifies the human. The loyalty, fidelity and love shown towards the friend is not only a secret reflection of selfishness, but is also an impossible foundation for human sociality. As Kierkegaard has claimed, friendship is made into the highest good, or finds its place in a plurality of equal goods. This results in either the worldly ethical being placed as the highest good, or the human self becoming deified. From Kierkegaard's point of view this is a manifestation of despair. Moreover, to love in this way is to have a duplicity at the core of existence and cannot be Christian, which is simply to have the purity of heart to 'will one thing'. It is in this way that Judge William's Christianity represents a bourgeois-ethical approach to life, rather than a truly Christian existence. The judge justifies friendship through a largely ethical understanding (and practice) of Christianity. Here Christianity is largely taken to be a system of ethics understood by human reason. This helps to frame the context for the judge's practice of Christianity which appears somewhat legalistic, formulaic, 'civil', and thus distanced from Christianity's radical and even socially disruptive life-force. Third, Kierkegaard's view and account of the features of friendship, and especially the insecurities created by its reciprocal and selfish aspects and its misplacement of spirit, makes the relationship doomed to failure. Those who cling to friendship can only do so despairingly. Friendship can exist purely in the realms of the aesthetic and the ethical. As such it fails unless it is also underscored by the religious.

Neighbourliness: Every tree is known by its fruit

We have now seen in detail as to why Kierkegaard rejects friendship as a foundation for a lasting and fulfilling sociality. According to Kierkegaard's account we must conclude that friendship (even on its strongest account) falls victim to despair.[248] However, Kierkegaard

---

[248] Linell E Cady, 'Alternative Interpretations of Love in Kierkegaard and Royce', *The Journal of Religious Ethics* 10(2), 1982, pp. 238-263.

does not completely abandon friendship (or, indeed, erotic love). These relationships can be fulfilling if they are underpinned by the primary and normative relationship of neighbourliness.[249] Even so, it is important to note that for Kierkegaard Christianity does not praise erotic love and friendship as *Christian* relations.[250] Whilst Kierkegaard indicates that non-Christian relations are unavoidable and may even help the person's development they are not sufficient in themselves.[251] For Kierkegaard neighbourliness should and must be the *primary* human relation and is the key to his views on society, the ills of the age, and the development of selfhood. It should be stressed that Kierkegaard uses the neighbour in direct and explicit contrast to the conception of both romantic love and friendship that he has explored. Nevertheless, from our current perspective which views friendship as a more general field of concern focusing on the bonds between person and person, Kierkegaard's account of 'neighbourliness' may be identified as a form of friendship. For what Kierkegaard is exploring is not simply a philosophical or even theological category, but the very conditions which bring person in relation to person and the bonds — both ontological and normative — which connect person to person. Indeed, it is valuable to us insofar as it theorises the bonds between person and person on two levels which are transposed. The first is what might be termed a spiritual friendship. Here we see the true and normative connections between person and person (understood as spiritual selves before God) which Kierkegaard explores under the banner of 'the neighbour'. The second layer is built up and shaped by the first layer. The bonds between person and person which exist in our everyday relations and political relations are a direct result of our success to apprehend and act upon the potential of our primary bonds as neighbours.

In what follows three aspects of neighbourliness will be discussed. First we will concern ourselves with the notion and implications that we are *commanded* to love the neighbour as ourselves. Here the

---

[249] Kierkegaard, *Works*, pp. 61-62, 141-43, 147.
[250] Kierkegaard, *Works*, p. 45; LC Keeley, 'Subjectivity and World in *Works of Love*', in George B Connell and C Stephen Evans (eds.), *Foundations of Kierkegaard's Vision of Community: Religion, Ethics and Politics in Kierkegaard*, p. 100; Bruce H Kirmmse, 'Call Me Ishmael — Call Everybody Ishmael: Kierkegaard on the Coming-of-Age Crisis of Modern Times', in George B Connell and C Stephen Evans (eds.), *Foundations of Kierkegaard's Vision of Community: Religion, Ethics and Politics in Kierkegaard*, p. 177; M Andic, 'Is Love of Neighbour Love of and Individual?' in George Pattison and Steven Shakespeare (eds.), *Kierkegaard: The Self in Society*, p. 117; Müller, *Kierkegaard's 'Works of Love'*, pp. x, 11; M Holmes Hartshorne, *Kierkegaard Godly Deceiver* (New York: Columbia University Press, 1990), pp. 53-4.
[251] Kierkegaard, *Works*, pp. 52-3; Ibid., *Upbuilding Discourses in Various Spirits*, p. 35.

significance of the act of commanding love will be outlined as it is not immediately apparent that love can be commanded. We will also draw out the implications of the wording of the command: specifically, that it is both possible to love others and ourselves. The second aspect is Kierkegaard's use of the notion of the neighbour. Here we will see that Kierkegaard's identification of the neighbour is achieved not through meditation on who the neighbour might be, or on our emotional attachments to others, but through our actions and attitude in responding to others. Furthermore, the neighbour is based on commanded love. As such God forms the middle term of the relationship and *all* individuals must be recognised *equally* as neighbours. For Kierkegaard the neighbour is a recognition that we are all spiritually equal before God. Finally, we will conclude our sketch by focusing on aspects of neighbourliness in a central passage in *Works*: 'The Work of Love in Recollecting One Who is Dead'.[252] This passage is important as it is here that Kierkegaard appears to hold up love for the dead as a test and a model for neighbour love. For some this has caused concern, and potentially undermines notions of sociality in *Works*.[253] However, this model actually highlights some of the strongest features of Kierkegaard's account of neighbour-love in that it is non-partial, changeless, other-orientated, and 'upbuilding'. Moreover, the model of loving the dead reinforces the notion that we are beings who can and should both love and be loved.

The commandment: 'You shall love your neighbour as yourself'

For Kierkegaard acting as a neighbour requires nothing more (and nothing less) than obedience to the command of God. No understanding of a complex theology or jurisprudence is required to identify the neighbour or to understand what they are: the neighbour is quite simply every other human being. The commandment therefore exposes a relation between self and other, a relation which places a clear but infinite demand on the self. Such a relation is also a spiritual imperative. It is to be pursued by all people. To become a neighbour we must seek to recognise and treat all others as neighbours. Human (or temporal) friendship, based on the contingencies of inclination and

---

[252] This passage has been identified as being of importance by several commentators including: George, 'Kierkegaard: The Self in Society', HS Pyper, 'Cities of the Dead: The Relation of Person and Polis in Kierkegaard's *Works of Love*', in George Pattison and Steven Shakespeare (eds.), *Kierkegaard: The Self in Society*; Keeley, 'Foundations of Kierkegaard's Vision of Community', Ferreira, *Love's Grateful Striving*.

[253] George, 'Kierkegaard: The Self in Society'.

preference, and its need for reciprocation could not achieve this. Kierkegaard's central claim in relation to our ability to fulfil this task is that human love finds is source in God's love.[254] By paying close attention to the commandment to 'love the neighbour as yourself' Kierkegaard also counters two of the main lines of criticism of the notion of Christian neighbourliness. These criticisms point in opposite directions. The first argues that people are primarily concerned with self-love and so are either reluctant to love others, or (in the worse case) cannot truly love others. In contrast, the second line of criticism argues that the truly religious person would love others *more* than they love themselves (that they would be totally self-sacrificing). Before we turn to the implications for grounding the command to love in God's love (which will lead to our discussion of the question of identifying the neighbour), let us first turn to the two criticisms of the command, focusing first on the concerns about the 'limiting' factors of self-love.

'Self-love' is a somewhat peculiar term, but the notion (in one form of another) is not alien to ethical and political philosophy. It is often assumed that whatever people are capable of they have (or develop at a primary stage) some form of self-regard or self-respect that serves to motivate their preservation or way in life. This is an especially common theme in modernity. Whilst some would find it hard to support the idea that humans are sympathetic or even geared towards loving others, even the most ardent and inventive critics of the potential for humans to be sociable and to co-exist in a civil society generally concede that people are characterised by self-love. Indeed, for some it is the notion of self-love itself, manifested as the need for survival (or to protect the integrity and self-sufficiency of the individual), which is actually the very impediment to sociability and the common good (for example Hobbes' position in *Leviathan*). In others, self-love leads to social goods either directly (Rousseau, Hume) or indirectly (Adam Smith). Kierkegaard would not find particular quarrel with these accounts of self-love. However, he would point out that from the spiritual point of view they are irredeemably 'worldly'. That is to say, they are accounts of self-love which remain attached to the 'bourgeois individualism' they serve.[255] What Kierkegaard aims for in neighbourliness is a notion of self-love that (if rightly understood and performed) can be the basis of a higher and complete sociality. Kierkegaard claims that the command to love the neighbour both

---

[254] Kierkegaard, *Works*, pp. 154, 160-1; Ibid., *Upbuilding Discourses in Various Spirits*, p. 276; Müller, *Kierkegaard's "Works of Love"*, p. 14.

[255] M Nicoletti, 'Politics and Religion in Kierkegaard's Thought: Secularisation and the Martyr', in George B Connell and C Stephen Evans (eds.), *Foundations of Kierkegaard's Vision of Community: Religion, Ethics, Politics*.

transforms and redirects self-love.[256] In doing so it transforms both the love *and* the person. This is achieved through a recognition and transformation of the object of love. The person changes the way they love themselves and others through recognising and treating the neighbour *as* the neighbour.[257] As we shall see, Kierkegaard generates an up-building spiral: in recognising the neighbour we recognise them as spiritual beings, equal to ourselves before God. In recognising ourselves as spiritual beings before God, we *must* simultaneously recognise all others in this way. We are the neighbour of everyone, and everyone is our neighbour.

Thus, Kierkegaard's starting point is an acknowledgement of the fact of love. However, as indicated there are many forms of love and Kierkegaard is keen to contrast the Christian form of neighbour-love with the 'worldly', 'poetic' and 'philosophical' forms. The defining difference between neighbour-love and *all* other forms of love is that neighbour-love is commanded by God.[258] As such any account of love must recognise the human capacity and need to both love themselves and others, and to be loved.[259] For Kierkegaard the fact of love is not in contention, although it should be stressed that it is an act of faith to believe in and *act* upon this love.[260] This powerful emotion is therefore quite literally a God-given aspect of the human being. It is the spiritual task of the human to take the reality of love and actualise it through the transformation wrought of obeying the neighbour-command. In other words, the individual begins to actualise their potential through neighbour-love. The need to love and to be loved cannot be removed or eradicated and so always seeks its fulfilment.[261] If untransformed the givenness of this drive might lead to expressions that are far from desirable or (in Kierkegaard's terms) 'upbuilding'.[262] Love might remain hidden, or we might seek to deceive ourselves about love.[263]

It is the thwarted and deviant manifestation of love that we can readily see in Kierkegaard's concern with the individual flourishing into a social being. For in the present age, love might manifest in a limited way expressed only through the almost animalistic need for 'companions'.[264] Whilst the fulfilment of the need for companionship is

---

[256] Kierkegaard, *Works*, p. 12.
[257] Andic, 'Is Love of Neighbour Love of and Individual?' in, p. 115.
[258] Kierkegaard, *Works*, p. 24.
[259] Kierkegaard, *Works*, p. 67.
[260] Kierkegaard, *Works*, pp. 5, 16.
[261] Kierkegaard, *Works*, p. 219; Müller, *Kierkegaard's 'Works of Love'*, pp. 13-14.
[262] Kierkegaard, *Works*, pp. 5-6, 118-19, 120-21, 127-29.
[263] Kierkegaard, *Works*, pp. 5-6.
[264] Kierkegaard, *Works*, p. 154ff.

desirable and permissible for the person, the association must develop beyond this and must be founded upon something deeper than this. In addition, companionship and association should not become a detour away from the task of selfhood and its recognition of *individual responsibility*. Left unguided self-love is prone to producing a society of egotistical, self-serving and envious people.[265] Under these circumstances it is not really possible to speak of either community, or perhaps even society. Crucially, if self-love is not transformed by the commandment of neighbourliness then it is also prone to lead the individual to a conceited self-deification, either of themselves or of others.[266] Thus, the social bond (as with temporal friendship and romantic love) is shown to be one based on reciprocation, selfishness, and despair. They are expressions of love, but a love whose potential is misunderstood and misapplied.[267]

In Kierkegaard's view what all of these manifestations of love have in common is not only a failure to recognise and obey the command to love the neighbour, but that the primary failure of the individual is to recognise and acknowledge God as the source of love and of their being. In this way Kierkegaard believes that neighbourliness can solve the problems of love and enable it to achieve actuality. Unlike temporal friendship, neighbourliness is under no illusions as to what it means to be a human being: a physical-psychical-spiritual being the self of which is relational.[268] Such a being's freedom and love are grounded in the power which created it: God. To fail to recognise this is to be in despair or sin.[269] The commandment of neighbourliness does not falter here as it 'contains what is presupposed, that every person loves himself'.[270] Here Kierkegaard uses the command to play self-love off against itself. Every person loves himself (as a matter of worldly fact), and every person *can and should* love himself *in the correct way*.[271]

We can now anticipate how Kierkegaard deals with the second line of criticism of neighbour-love, that we should not simply love the neighbour as ourselves, but should love the neighbour *more* than ourselves. Of course, in one way Kierkegaard could simply reply that this is not what God has commanded. However, his emphasis is not

---

[265] Kierkegaard, *Works*, pp. 59-60, 121-2; Ibid., *Two Ages*, pp. 81-4.
[266] Kierkegaard, *Works*, pp. 19-20; Hartshorne, *Kierkegaard Godly Deceiver*, p. 47.
[267] Cf. Cady, 'Alternative Interpretations of Love in Kierkegaard and Royce', p. 244. Müller, *Kierkegaard's 'Works of Love'*, p. 10.
[268] Kierkegaard, *Works*, pp. 56-7. This is also an account which is developed in *The Sickness Unto Death*.
[269] Kierkegaard, *Upbuilding Discourses in Various Spirits*, pp. 101, 269.
[270] Kierkegaard, *Works*, p. 17.
[271] Kierkegaard, *Works*, pp. 18, 22-3.

simply on obeying a command that could be doomed to failure, but to actually showing that the command of love is not only spiritually edifying, but also achievable. In this case Kierkegaard's focus is on the impossibility of achieving the command if it is extended beyond the basis of self-love, and even the contradiction that would lay at the core of extending this command. The command cannot be extended as self-love cannot simply be extended in this way. If this were the case then we would hardly even need a command to love the neighbour at all. Moreover, to attempt to love another *more* than ourselves is to fail to love ourselves in the correct way. It is both unnatural and unnecessary.

For Kierkegaard, then, the true source and object of our love is God.[272] But God directs our love that we rightly owe to Him to others. It should not be at all difficult to love others as ourselves as they are our spiritual equals. The command is in some ways a reminder of this, but also a recognition that, because we are immersed in the world of despairing relationships, we need motivation or prompting to love. It is not that we cannot achieve this, it is simply that (left to our preferences) without the imperative of a command, we would be inclined to be neglectful of what we owe to others. In this way, we do not posses our own love, nor do we (necessarily) affect a change in our neighbour. The object of love truly remains God, and the love that we owe to Him is reflected back, and activated by, the neighbour (and ourselves) as a spiritual being.

The neighbour: 'Unconditionally every human being'

Who, then, is the neighbour? Although Kierkegaard claims that idle speculation and the evasion of duty can be ended by simply recognising that the neighbour is 'all people' and that by 'acknowledging your duty you easily discover who your neighbour is' he perhaps ushers us forward a little too hastily.[273] Of course, in one way it *is* perfectly simple to claim that the neighbour is everyone we meet, excluding none. However, what we are looking for (and what Kierkegaard provides, perhaps even despite himself) is a theoretical underpinning for this radical and inclusive equality. Kierkegaard does not *simply* mean by 'neighbour' everyone that we meet or encounter (although he clearly does mean to include this in his definition). Kierkegaard also means to use 'neighbour' as a spiritual term that refers not just to others as individuals in temporality, but also to indicate that all are spiritually equal before God. Indeed, one of the major observations (and criticisms) that Kierkegaard makes of non-

---

[272] Kierkegaard, *Works*, p. 107.
[273] Kierkegaard, *Works*, pp. 21-22.

Christian forms of relationality is that they cannot understand or recognise the neighbour precisely because they cannot understand what it means to be a spiritual self before God.[274]

Despite these observations it is clear that Kierkegaard's direction is not one of mere speculation but an exhortation to practice.[275] Just as Kierkegaard's stress when dealing with love was not to show the complexity of Christian love but rather to focus on its compelling yet transforming simplicity and depth in performance, so too Kierkegaard places the stress of neighbourliness on *being* a good neighbour. The focus of what Kierkegaard says is not so much on knowing about or understanding the other as such, but on our response and attitude towards that other. Citing the parable of the good Samaritan, Kierkegaard observes that 'Christ does not speak about *knowing* the neighbour but about *becoming* a neighbour oneself'.[276] As with the notion of 'loving oneself' there is a double movement here. In recognising the other as neighbour and acting accordingly we ourselves become the neighbour: in acting as a neighbour to others, in knowing that we are the neighbour, others become neighbours to us. The neighbour is located neither in ourselves nor in the other but in our mutual relation. To say that the relation is mutual is not to claim that it is *necessarily* reciprocated, or that it is dependent upon reciprocation. Nor is it to say that there must be a simultaneous recognition by individuals of each other as 'neighbours'. The relation is mutual as we are mutually related as spiritual equals before God, and have a mutual obligation to love each other that takes the form of a mutual debt (whether we realise this and act on it, or not).[277]

This view of bonding is a major step away from the models of temporal friendship outlined earlier. Whilst these models involved reciprocity, neighbourliness is a relation that is determined not by the other, but solely by our relation to them. There can be no concern in neighbourliness about the fidelity of the neighbour. The neighbour is the neighbour not because of their relation to us as such, but because of our mutual relation with them to God. It is this relation that defines the relation of the neighbour to us. In friendship there is no such 'middle term' or 'point of reference' and the friends only have each other and the friendship to cling to. *Qua* human beings the friends cannot use themselves as a point of reference because they are subject to change.

---

[274] Kierkegaard, *Works*, p. 44.
[275] Kierkegaard, *Works*, p. 46.
[276] Kierkegaard, *Works*, p. 22 (italics added).
[277] Cf. Cady, 'Alternative Interpretations of Love in Kierkegaard and Royce', p. 243; Müller, *Kierkegaard's "Works of Love"*, p. 25; Hartshorne, *Kierkegaard Godly Deceiver*, p. 51; Andic, 'Is Love of Neighbour Love of and Individual?', p. 115.

As such instability and doubt is a factor in the relationship, and one that threatens to undermine its continuance. The relationship is not secured by the changelessness of God, and depends as much on the other person as on ourselves.

Loving those that we see

As we have already seen, Kierkegaard is not against the correct form of self-love. Indeed, the correct form can lead to the recognition of, and response to, the neighbour. However, we must also bear in mind that the self is relational. It is in a continual process of becoming. As such, whilst in a state of despair we have reality as human beings, but lack actuality. That is to say, Kierkegaard does not question the existence of the physical-psychical aspects of the individual. However, he comments further that whilst in despair the individual has not yet apprehended and accepted their spiritual freedom, its source (God), and the obligations that this entails. To do so would be to overcome despair and to achieve actuality: it would be to become what we are (even though there is still the possibility that we will fall back into despair). As expressed by MG Piety 'a person's actuality is equivalent to an agreement of his concrete existence with God's idea of how we ought to exist'.[278] When we act and recognise others as neighbours, we act in accordance with our actuality. The neighbour is how we both can and ought to be. As neighbours we have a spiritual relationship with, and an obligation to, the *reality* of other people. Ultimately the reality of others rests on their potential for actuality, but we are not obligated to this possible or future person. We are obligated to the immediate 'flesh-and-blood' human being who we encounter in temporality.[279]

In *Works of Love* Kierkegaard expresses this obligation to the reality of others in a variety of ways, but of special interest is what he has to say in the section 'Our Duty To Love the People We See'. Here Kierkegaard refocuses the notion of neighbourliness by taking an apparent detour from it. In this section Kierkegaard points out that we must start loving from where we stand. This is the world of preferential and partial relationships, characterised as they are by passions and uncertainties. The task becomes not to find the loveable object, but to find those who we already love loveable, and to secure this love against change.[280] In this way Kierkegaard accepts that it is natural for us to have preferential relationships. What he is concerned with here is to

---

[278] Piety, 'The Place of the World in Kierkegaard's Ethics', p. 27.
[279] Hartshorne, *Kierkegaard Godly Deceiver*, p. 51; Keeley, 'Foundations of Kierkegaard's Vision of Community', p. 96.
[280] Kierkegaard, *Works*, pp. 159-60.

ground these relationships in something other than despair, and to prevent people from avoiding their temporal duties and obligations to each other in the name of Christianity.[281] We must love the people we see as there is a danger that we will end-up loving no one if we merely seek to love what is not seen.[282] This involves loving the person as they are, and not an image of that person. It is important to avoid focusing solely on their excellences, or on the hope of some future person that they might become.[283] We must not fall into the trap of loving others simply because they can change. As we shall see, Kierkegaard holds the 'unchanging dead' up as a curious model for Christian love. What Kierkegaard is aiming for is a form of Christian love that recognises difference without loving difference or partiality as such, and that can accommodate but not engender temporal change. The person that we see can indeed change, but somehow our love must remain constant because the person is always there.[284]

What this amounts to is a recognition of the other's claim to be a person (which is simultaneously a recognition of our own claim to be a person).[285] As human beings we have no real problem in loving ourselves despite our own changing personhood: so we can and must love the other's too. In effect, it is an acknowledgement of the humanity of the other even as a spiritual being. As Hartshorne explains:

> It is a recognition of his or her claim to be recognised as a person... It teaches us to accept any and all persons *as persons*, regardless of inclination of interest.[286]

The recognition of others as persons not only activates our recognition of our equality with them as spiritual beings, and their claim to our love, but also makes communication possible. Communication becomes possible as in treating others as neighbours we recognise and act upon our responsibilities to them. Ultimately Kierkegaard sees this in terms of helping them to become a self through Christianity. However, what neighbourliness creates (in Kierkegaardian terms) is a self-aware individual who is unified in thought, passion and action. This manifests in the individual's relationship with God, their own self, and others as the neighbour. The

---

[281] Müller, *Kierkegaard's "Works of Love"*, p. 27.
[282] Kierkegaard, *Works*, p. 161.
[283] Kierkegaard, *Works*, pp. 164, 173; Andic, 'Is Love of Neighbour Love of and Individual?', p. 118.
[284] Kierkegaard, *Works*, pp. 167, 172.
[285] Hartshorne, *Kierkegaard Godly Deceiver*, p. 49.
[286] Hartshorne, *Kierkegaard Godly Deceiver*, pp. 50-1. See also Piety, 'The Place of the World in Kierkegaard's Ethics', p. 35.

relationship of the neighbour is to include all people, in both their spiritual and worldly aspects. This involves us recognising both ourselves and them as neighbours; but crucially it is not dependent upon a recognition of us as a neighbour by them. Whilst this recognition can be hoped for, it cannot become a condition for us treating them as a neighbour. It is in this way that we can see how we are to 'love' our enemies. The person does not remain unchanged, but that change is effected inwardly: it is a change in their relation to God and therefore to others.

Loving the dead

One of the most intriguing and revealing passages in *Works* is Kierkegaard's chapter on 'The Work of Love in Recollecting One Who Is Dead'. This chapter is pivotal for Kierkegaard's account of Christian love as in it Kierkegaard exposes the true focus, depth and nature of neighbour-love. Early in the chapter Kierkegaard claims that 'death is the best summary of life'.[287] The statement is shown to have a double-meaning. First, Kierkegaard means that death is the summary of life insofar as a person's life can only be understood as a whole when death has completed that life. However, Kierkegaard also means that death can show what is *best* in life. Indeed, Kierkegaard's central point is that in loving the dead we show '*the most unselfish love*'.[288] Kierkegaard holds-up the work of love in recollecting one who is dead as being the highest exemplification of Christian love, and a model for the love that we must show to those who we see (i.e. the living).

For Kierkegaard the unselfishness of loving the dead is a logical necessity, and a necessity which also follows from his critique of temporal friendship. We have already commented that Kierkegaard argues that friendship is ultimately a selfish form of love. By this Kierkegaard meant that it both focuses on the love of the self, but that it also demands a form of reciprocation. However, this chapter would appear to develop this theme, and *imply* that there are degrees of selfishness. Selfishness is seen to have two dimensions. The first is that *either* the love is focused on the self, *or* that it is not focused on the self. The second dimension is a matter of degree: if the love is focused on the self, how deep does that love extend? In this way Kierkegaard appears to concede (at least in part) that although neighbour love is the ideal that we should strive for, we are also benighted by difficulties when trying to overcome our selfishness.

---

[287] Kierkegaard, *Works*, p. 345.
[288] Kierkegaard, *Works*, p. 349 (emphasis in the original).

What Kierkegaard attempts in this chapter is to make our love for the dead the *measure* of our love for the living. In examining our love for the dead, Kierkegaard also allows us to recognise our duty to love and to measure the completeness of our response to it. It is here the unselfishness of loving the dead comes to the fore. On one level it would appear absurd to suggest that a person selfishly performed their duty, as a duty necessarily implies an obligation to others. However, the relationship between the living and the dead is a one-way-street. This is crucial for Kierkegaard as in this relationship it is not the dead who are exposed, but the living person's own expression and form of love as 'one who is dead is no actual object', and 'is only the occasion that... discloses what resides in the one living who relates himself to him'.[289] The dead are the absolutely unchanging and absolutely unresponsive recipients of our love. It is here that we can see how our previous two features of neighbour love are best highlighted by Kierkegaard's account of loving the dead: loving the dead exemplifies a love which is not based on the wrong variety of self-love, and which represents an absolute equality. In addition, loving the dead is both stable and enduring as it is a duty. Loving the dead, then, is held as the supreme example of such a Christian form of love. It is the highest example as it tests only the person who performs the work of love. The subject of the love (like the neighbour) can play no part in the love itself. They can neither change, nor respond, nor show signs that the love will be repaid in any way. Nor, it can be stressed, can the dead demand our love. Thus, love given in this way 'is the most unselfish, the freest, the most faithful love'.[290]

It will be remembered that in his account of neighbour-love Kierkegaard sought to stress the elements of that love which make it both stable and enduring. In order to achieve such a relation the love is based not upon our drives and inclinations (as in temporal friendship and erotic love) but in our duty towards God, and our innate need to love and be loved. Spiritual equality bases love not on particularities, or similar views, but on the personhood (or potential personhood) of the other.[291] We have already seen that Kierkegaard objects to non-Christian forms of love precisely because they are based on the particularity of the other person, and as such the object of the love is not the other person as a spiritual being, but some accidental quality about them, or the contingent passions of the lover. Ultimately Kierkegaard fears the dangers of reciprocity and selfishness.

---

[289] Kierkegaard, *Works*, p. 347.
[290] Kierkegaard, *Works*, p. 358.
[291] Kierkegaard, *Works*, p. 346.

Clearly this cannot be the case in loving the dead. The dead can neither return our love, or change in any way. In this way loving the dead is freer than loving the living as there is no prospect of repayment at all.[292] Kierkegaard implies that the closest that we can come to this in loving the living is the love of a parent for their child, although he argues that here there is at least the 'prospect' of some form of repayment—presumably through a return of the love.[293] Indeed, unlike the living, the dead are easy to 'be rid of' as they do not cast recriminations at the break of faith.[294] This makes loving the dead even freer than loving the living as there is 'something compelling, daily sight and habit if nothing else' that binds us to loving the living.[295] Indeed, sometimes the 'alliance' itself is what holds the living together in their love.[296] None of this is possible with the dead. In this way Kierkegaard sees this as the most unselfish and freest form of love as not only does it not return the love, there is no compulsion to love, and no possibility of a return. The love that we show to the dead is then an ideal form of love; but it is also an ideal by which we measure the love that we show towards those that we see.

Kierkegaard: *Either* friendship *or* the neighbour?

Kierkegaard's account of purely human friendship starts from common and easily accepted romantic and philosophical assumptions. It ends-up by employing these against the relationship, turning the assumptions about what they entail, and how they might be valuable, on their heads. Kierkegaard's account of the neighbour (as a form of spiritual friendship) promises to reconcile the purely human with the spiritual aspects of a person. Such a reconciliation promises that persons will relate to each other as spiritual equals mediated through God. Here we see a continuation of the pattern of relations started by Socrates-Plato and developed afresh in the later Christian tradition. This pattern sees individuals drawn together by what is truly valuable. Whereas in the Ancient tradition this was the Good, in the Christian tradition it becomes God. In so doing the relationship is transformed as God need not be remote and cold, but can be thought of as a living and animating presence in the relationship between two individuals. Indeed, it could be thought that God can transform the individuals making them truly open to Him and each other. The stress here is on

---

[292] Kierkegaard, *Works*, p. 351.
[293] Kierkegaard, *Works*, p. 350.
[294] Kierkegaard, *Works*, p. 352.
[295] Kierkegaard, *Works*, p. 354.
[296] Kierkegaard, *Works*, p. 355.

responding to the people that we see. This kind of bonding is thus focused not on what others could become, but on what they are. In Kierkegaard's thought this form of bonding is attractive insofar as it identifies aspects of the person which are both inalienable and possess eternal value. Unlike the earlier Ancient tradition these aspects are *uniquely* situated in each *person*. It is harder to think of them as being connected to some larger generic (and undifferentiated) whole or ideal. Thus, in Kierkegaard's thought there is a stronger focus on the person of the other. This understanding of the self as spiritual also enables Kierkegaard to show how the correct form of self-love need not be objectionable. It is right to love what is eternal in ourselves, and it is also right to extend that recognition and love to others.

Insofar as he follows the Platonic pattern Kierkegaard's thought on human sociality echoes a pre-modern paradigm. Indeed, his adherence to a personalised view of Christianity as a dynamic and lived experience might make him seem at odds with modernity itself. However, it would be a mistake to think that Kierkegaard simply wishes to turn return to another age. Although his thought draws on a pre-modern tradition, Kierkegaard is acutely aware of the changes that modernity has wrought around him. Indeed, his thought can be considered to be a modern transformation of the older tradition; a transformation that not only accepts but actually radicalises some of the traits of modernity. For in Kierkegaard's thought of friendship and the neighbour we see examples of the modern anxiety about particularity and the passions. We also see reflected a concern with the individual. Kierkegaard recognises that both friendship and neighbourliness are relationships between individuals. A part of his focus is to consider how to extend these relationships without the individuals becoming lost in a crowd. Although clearly not devoid of an engagement with the social, Kierkegaard's thought is centred about the experience and development of the individual. Kierkegaard's thought also sees friendship and the neighbour played out in terms of both the universal and the abstract. The features of the friend and the neighbour are found in individuals but evaluated against a concern for their ability to be both generic and generalised. Individuals are unique, but the relationship of the neighbour is achievable by all.

However, in another way Kierkegaard's thinking shows signs of the pre-modern. It posits an absolute value and eschews pluralism. For Kierkegaard there are normatively correct ways to live our lives with others, and our relations with others can be measured against standards. Furthermore, it warns against a sociality that is purely grounded in reason, the economy, or the emotions. Kierkegaard's sociality is not ethical, but religious. Ethics cannot be the resting place for sociality unless it is transformed. In thinking in this way Kierkegaard sees human beings in a renewed light. He sees for them a normative selfhood which involves connections to others, and it is this that he places back at the heart of the political. It is paradoxical that in Kierkegaard's thought normative human bonding is the product of an intensified focus on the individual. However, insofar as he addresses these forms of bonding and tries to find a lasting foundation for them in a normative selfhood Kierkegaard provides a kind of corrective to the view of the political which cannot move beyond individual self-interest and where there is no greater aspiration than prudence. Human beings are something more than calculating machines. True sociality can only be achieved by a turn to the self, which is simultaneously a turn to both a higher power and a recognition of our equality with others. Kierkegaard's thought, then, places a limit on the political by stressing that the primary value of society comes from recognising our own value and the value of others.

Laudable though some of Kierkegaard's aspirations are, his account of the bonds between person and person are not a total success. Kierkegaard's account never quite seems to meet its promise to resolve the tensions between the human and the divine—or at least to find a way to transform the former though an engagement with the latter. What Kierkegaard leaves us with is stark contrast. On the one hand there are the forms of non-Christian love, and specifically friendship, which he rejects as primary bases for human bonding. He does so because he views these forms of approaching the other to be based on preference, emotions, and reciprocity. Kierkegaard undermines the possibility of friendship containing a moral task. Ultimately he sees it as both unstable and selfish. In doing so Kierkegaard turns his back on the vast majority of human relationships. Yet we cannot help but wonder whether Kierkegaard casts them aside not because they contain no good, but simply because they fail to meet his exacting standards. This is especially true of the motivation to seek friendship with another. Friendship falls victim to Kierkegaard's exhortation that purity of heart is to will one thing. It is not clear how this demand could be met. Nor is it clear that in the realm of human bonding it is necessary to do so. Must reciprocation be considered such a bad thing? Reciprocation is a form of recognition of the other and a response to them. Moreover, before reciprocation can occur one of the parties must make an initial gesture. Reciprocation grows out of an openness to the other. It builds trust and concern between individuals. It can be a part of a supportive relationship between self and other in which the needs, wishes, and hopes of both are recognised and attended to. In any event, even by Kierkegaard's own lights we might be considered to be failing to love ourselves in the proper way if we didn't seek recognition from others — after all, that is what we expect to offer them.

On the other hand, Kierkegaard promotes his ideal of a Christian neighbourliness. Here we love the other as a duty, a duty which is directed by constituting our self through God. However, whilst Kierkegaard's criticisms of friendship are far reaching and forceful, especially when he examines the idea in its own (secular) terms, his notion of neighbourliness is not entirely satisfactory. Although Kierkegaard's notion of neighbourliness does overcome some of the problems associated with friendship, it is far from clear as to whether this relationship pays enough attention to the human sides of our self. Of course, the other is approached as a spiritual equal before God, and Kierkegaard overcomes the dangers of a selfish reciprocation by making our duty dependent on the other's spiritual status. Kierkegaard's account of neighbourliness thus shows some ways in which the difficulties of temporal friendship might be overcome or avoided, but places a heavy burden on those who would seek to practise it. It is a truly radical response to otherness, and its ultimate value appears to be not that it is always achieved, but that the Christian should strive to achieve it, and in doing so realise their own weaknesses and limitations as a human being before an eternal and life-giving God to whom their debt is infinite. However, Kierkegaard's focus on this God makes the corresponding spiritual aspect of neighbour-love somewhat remote. Indeed, it strikes the reader as both demanding and austere. Although Kierkegaard's stress is on the *works* of love, there appears to be little regard for the feelings and emotions of either the receiver of these works, or the performer. The danger here is that Kierkegaard's construction of neighbourliness will avoid reciprocation only to also eliminate any possibility of true communication or communion. This impression is certainly not helped by the ideal of neighbour love being that of loving the dead. Nor is it softened by Kierkegaard's more general stress on the single individual. Could anyone really love another in the way that Kierkegaard demands?

Although Kierkegaard holds it up as a spiritual norm, neighbourliness seems to be somewhat devoid of the basic human joys that sociality and caring about another can bring. Kierkegaard indicates that like so much else in the realm of ethics, friendship can continue if it is underpinned by neighbourliness. However, this is an unconvincing sleight-of-hand. Mundane friendship underpinned by a spiritual relation ceases to be *purely* mundane. Things simply cannot carry on as normal if we recognise ourselves as spiritual beings. Furthermore, by placing neighbourliness and friendship in this order (and not rescinding any of his criticisms of mundane friendship) Kierkegaard has demonstrated where his sympathies and priorities lie. In the final analysis Kierkegaard leaves us with one of the choices that is synonymous with his name. *Either* friendship *or* the neighbour. For Kierkegaard, a choice must be made, and a priority must be established. Either we continue to live in the limited and finite world of human friendships, with all their complexity, instability, and change; or we accept ourselves as spiritual beings and strive to become a neighbour. Either we accept partiality and preference, or we ignore difference and temporal inequality to view all as spiritual equals. Either we limit our bonds or we extend them indefinitely. Either we accept the limitations of the temporal, or embrace the infinity offered by the divine. Either God or the human. Given that this logic underpins Kierkegaard's account of friendship and the neighbour it is not clear how we should choose—or if there could be any reason for doing so. Both might be thought to be equally as demanding and equally in need of our attention. For Kierkegaard there could be no *reasons* for such a choice—we might question whether this has to be a choice at all.

Chapter Five
Nietzsche

FRIEDRICH NIETZSCHE has sometimes been portrayed as an uncompromising iconoclast. Bombastic and prescient, Nietzsche said of himself that he wasn't a man but dynamite.[297] Posthumously Nietzsche has been taken-up into that pantheon inhabited by the images of those who have shaped our social and political milieu such as Marx and Freud. Nietzsche both anticipated and dreaded such an afterlife.[298] Nietzsche also shares the fate of those thus elevated; his last word has sometimes been taken as a summary of the whole. Most scholars of Nietzsche are now careful to avoid this assumption. Indeed, in recent decades a body of scholarship has developed which traces the development of Nietzsche's thought showing that it is not monolithic.[299] If we are attentive to this idea then we can see that Nietzsche's thought displays variety and difference. It is in this context that we locate our concern with friendship. For whilst it is true that enmity and solitude become more dominant themes in the later period (especially from *Beyond Good and Evil* onwards), these themes cannot be fully appreciated without us also taking cognisance of their relationship to Nietzsche's previous views on friendship. Indeed, it could be said that it is Nietzsche's initial entertainment of friendship and his eventual disillusionment with it that leaves the hostile landscape of solitude and enmity. Whilst in the later period we hear talk of philosophers who are both hard and solitary, in the writings from *Human, All Too Human* leading up to *Thus Spoke Zarathustra* we catch glimpses of philosophers who are not only 'free spirits' but also

---

[297] Nietzsche, *Ecce Homo*, 'Why I am Destiny', §1.
[298] Nietzsche, *Ecce Homo*, 'Why I am Destiny', §1.
[299] For a sample of such accounts see: Ruth Abbey, *Nietzsche's Middle Period* (Oxford: Oxford University Press, 2000); Rüdiger Safranski, *Nietzsche: A Philosophical Biography*, Shelly Frisch trans. (London: Granta Books, 2003); Bernd Magnus and Kathleen M Higgins, 'Nietzsche's Works and Their Themes', in Bernd Magnus and Kathleen M Higgins (eds.), *The Cambridge Companion to Nietzsche*.

form a community of future friends. Thus, Nietzsche connects *genuine* friendship to a kind of philosophical-cum-spiritual elite. This elite not only points to the possibilities of a kind of worthwhile and desirable human bonding, it also provides the zenith of human bonding itself.

In this chapter the development of Nietzsche's thinking on friendship will be set in the context of the overall development of his thought. In terms of this development, *Thus Spoke Zarathustra* can be considered the pivotal text. In the writings preceding *Zarathustra* there is a strong indication that individuals realise themselves through better self-understanding (the implication being that there is something waiting to be discovered). By way of contrast, in *Zarathustra* and the writings which follow it, the emphasis tends towards the identification of more general drives and self-realisation comes though sculpting, fashioning, and forging the self. The fate of friendship in Nietzsche's thought is tied to these wider transformations. Before it is eclipsed Nietzsche sees an important role for friendship. Friendship acts as a mechanism for the central philosophical task of self-discovery. Friendship is portrayed as simultaneously analytic, therapeutic, and agonistic. In the later work this supportive form of bonding is increasingly seen as inadequate and perhaps even dangerous to the philosopher. *Zarathustra* thus becomes pivotal as friendship is linked with the ideas of enmity and the Übermensch. Ultimately both displace friendship, intensifying its agonism into antagonism, and leading the individual into a sovereign solitude. Friends now overcome themselves and each other to live at an icy remoteness. Although Nietzsche seems to have turned back from complete isolation in his later works, he never really returns to the questions of positive and productive human bonding based on the possibility of intimacy and sharing with others. In Nietzsche's later thought friendship is attached to the ideas of aristocracy and nobility that he seeks to promote — but his active focus is elsewhere.

Friendships found and lost

The trail of friendship in Nietzsche's thought must be picked-out from his aphorisms over numerous books.[300] As Ruth Abbey has argued, this trail starts in Nietzsche's 'middle period'.[301] Nietzsche's middle period has been an identified 'stage' in his authorship for as least as long as serious scholarship of his work has existed. Consisting of the works

---

[300] John E Smith, 'Two Perspectives on Friendship: Aristotle and Nitezsche', in Leroy S Rouner (ed.), *The Changing Face of Friendship*, p. 59.
[301] Ruth Abbey, 'Circles, Ladders and Stars: Nietzsche on Friendship', *Critical Review of International Social and Political Philosophy* 2(4), 1999, pp. 50-51.

from 1878 to 1882 these texts can be considered to be some of Nietzsche's most adept and insightful, and yet attention to this period has only really become serious in recent decades.[302] One of the most notable features of Nietzsche's entry into his middle period is not only his intellectual concern with friendship, but how this concern comes to structure his view of relationships in his own life. In Nietzsche's case there is no easy way to separate thinker and thought, and this period is characterised by the ebb and flow of friendships both found and lost. Nietzsche's letters during this period record an intensity of feeling and hope, but also a deep concern about his own 'incommunicability of the heart' and the 'strangeness of his mind'.[303] Entering into this period are the older figures of Malwida von Meysenbug and Jacob Burckhardt; but also Carl von Gersdorff, Peter Gast, Franz Overbeck, and Erwin Rohde.[304] They would all reach out to Nietzsche in various ways, be pushed and pulled by his personality and phases, until his final years of 1888 and beyond. It should also be noted that during this period Nietzsche continued to hold fast to his desire to found a kind of philosophical-cultural fraternity.[305] This community of friends echoes Nietzsche's early identification with the circle portrayed in Plato's *Symposium*.[306] Importantly, this is also the period when Nietzsche becomes entangled in the now notorious trio which would see him photographed with his friend Paul Rée and the 'free spirit' Lou

---

[302] Of these accounts Ruth Abbey's work has found a place as the seminal account. Abbey is also especially attentive to the notion of friendship in Nietzsche's thought during this period. See Abbey, *Nietzsche's Middle Period*; Ibid., 'Circles, Ladders and Stars'.

[303] Christopher Middleton, ed., *Selected Letters of Friedrich Nietzsche* (Indianapolis: Hackett Publishing Company, Inc., 1969), p. xi.

[304] Accounts of these relations can be found in the following: Karl Jaspers, *Nietzsche: An Introduction to the Understanding of His Philosophical Activity*, Charles F Walldaff and Frederick J Schmitz trans. (Baltimore, Maryland: The Johns Hopkins University Press, 1997 [1936]); Joachim Köhler, *Zarathustra's Secret: The Interior Life of Friedrich Nietzsche*, Ronald Taylor trans. (New Haven and London: Yale University Press, 2002); Safranski, *Nietzsche*.

[305] Joachim Köhler, *Nietzsche and Wagner: A Lesson in Subjugation*, Ronald Taylor trans. (New Haven and London: Yale University Press, 1998), p. 116. Christopher Middleton notes that this continues even as late as 1884. Middleton writes that 'Until about 1876, when he was thirty-two, Nietzsche's letters do contain protestations of friendship: with Gersdorff, with Rohde, with the motherly Malwida von Meysenbug. It was to be a system of friends, with a spiritual centre in Bayreuth, that should regenerate and transform German society, in the names of Schopenhauer and Wagner. As late as 1884, he is dreaming of a 'Brotherhood of the *Gaya Scienza*' to be assembled in Nice.' Middleton (ed.), *Selected Letters*, p. xi.

[306] Walter Kaufmann, *Nietzsche: Philosopher, Psychologist, Antichrist*, Fourth ed. (Princeton: Princeton University Press, 1974), p. 23.

Salomé.[307] In this friendship the pursuit of knowledge, philosophy, and unrequited love were mixed in a heady cocktail. Unlike his erstwhile adversary Socrates, Nietzsche was unable to swallow the draught of *eros* without consequence. The hangover was severe, but it resulted in *Zarathustra*.[308] Some of these friendships have a double significance: they are the occasion for Nietzsche's thought but they also tend to act as prototypes of the kinds philosophical-cultural friendships that he wished to develop.[309] These friendships are not merely for personal satisfaction, comfort, and pleasure, but are part and parcel of Nietzsche's task as a philosopher. That task concerns not just the enquiry into and debunking of all that is mistaken, but the rejuvenation of European civilization.

Despite this concern to develop friendships it cannot be overlooked that the first book of this period (*Human, All Too Human*) also coincides with the dissolution and breaking of a pivotal 'friendship': that between Nietzsche and Wagner. There has been much analysis of this relationship, a trend which was started by Nietzsche himself. What type of a person was Wagner? Why were so many attracted to him, and what did his hold over others represent? Contemporary commentators have tended to call the equality and reciprocity of this relationship into question.[310] There is little doubt that the relationship revolved around a power dynamic which saw the younger Nietzsche treated badly (if not openly exploited and then humiliated) by Wagner.[311] What is crucial is that Nietzsche had pinned his hopes of a kind of artistic and cultural revival on Wagner and his music. He had hoped that Wagner's music would provide a focus for a kind of Germanic cultural community, and what he saw in Wagner was the personification of creativity and genius. Thus, from an early stage Nietzsche was drawn towards Wagner. However, whereas Nietzsche saw the relationship as one of a joint cultural and intellectual endeavour (albeit with the majestic Wagner as the grander and senior partner), it is far from certain that Wagner was ever quite so genuine. What Wagner saw in Nietzsche

---

[307] For a discussion of the mutual influence of Nietzsche and Rée see Brendan Donnellan, 'Friedrich Nietzsche and Paul Rée: Cooperation and Conflict', *Journal of the History of Ideas* 43(4), 1982.
[308] For an account of this period see Safranski, *Nietzsche*, pp. 248-257.
[309] See Jaspers, *Nietzsche*, pp. 76-87.
[310] See Köhler, *Nietzsche and Wagner*, p. 99.
[311] Daniel Halévy, *The Life of Friedrich Nietzsche*, JM Hone trans. (London: Unwin, 1917), p. chapters II and IV; RJ Hollingdale, *Nietzsche: The Man and his Philosophy* (London: Routledge and Kegan Paul, 1965), Part II; Ibid., *Nietzsche* (London and Boston: Routledge and Kegan Paul, 1973); Kaufmann, *Nietzsche: Philosopher, Psychologist, Antichrist*, pp. 30-41; R Hayman, *Nietzsche: A Critical Life* (London: Weidenfeld and Nicolson, 1980), Chapters V and VI.

(beyond a source of gratification) was the chance to bolster his own notoriety. Ultimately Wagner was to outgrow the benefit that he could draw from association with Nietzsche, and Nietzsche found himself (like others before him) cast down from Wagner's magic circle.[312]

It became clear to Nietzsche from his experience of Bayreuth that his hopes were ill-founded. For in Bayreuth Wagner's German nationalism, anti-Semitism, and eventually fawning Christianity were all to come to the fore. This was all laced with his personal traits of spite and arrogance. Nietzsche may well have been able to overlook Wagner's views in private. Perhaps there was even an element of denial. Nietzsche would have been aware that his friendship with Wagner had deep implications for his other friendships, not least with the Jew Paul Rée.[313] For the sake of the friendship it may well have been possible to initially ignore Wagner's growing anti-Semitism, German nationalism, and his attraction to the Reich, but their increasingly becoming the focus of public celebration at Bayreuth could not be denied or tolerated.[314] What is significant about Nietzsche's relationship with Wagner is the fact that in the *persona* of Wagner the young Nietzsche encountered creativity and greatness at close hand.[315] In this relationship Nietzsche saw both greatness and pettiness, both liberating ideals and a tawdry politics. Much later, in a letter to Georg Brandes (dated 10th April 1888) Nietzsche recalls his intimacy with Wagner writing that 'for several years we shared all our great and small experiences— there was limitless confidence between us'.[316] Yet, despite this retrospective confession, by the summer of 1882 this confidence was presumably in ruins. Nietzsche refuses an invitation to Bayreuth from his sister lamenting:

---

[312] Köhler, *Nietzsche and Wagner*, p. 139ff. esp. p. 143, where Nietzsche is rumoured to engage in 'unnatural proclivities'. On the question of the significance of the conjecture of Nietzsche's homosexuality see Safranski, *Nietzsche*, pp. 245-248.
[313] Köhler, *Nietzsche and Wagner*, p. 142. See also Schacht 'Introduction' in Friedrich Nietzsche, *Human, All Too Human: A Book for Free Spirits*, p. xiv.
[314] Kaufmann, *Nietzsche: Philosopher, Psychologist, Antichrist*, p. 38; Keith Ansell-Pearson, *An Introduction to Nietzsche as Political Thinker* (Cambridge: Cambridge University Press, 1994), pp. 26-27; Smith, 'Two Perspectives on Friendship', p. 70.
[315] Jaspers, *Nietzsche*, pp. 65-69.
[316] Middleton (ed.), *Selected Letters*, letter 168.

I had sought for so long a man who was superior to me and who actually looked beyond me. I thought I had found such a man in Wagner, I was wrong. [...] My Wagner mania certainly cost me dear. Has not his nerve-shattering music ruined my health? And the disillusionment and leaving Wagner—was not that putting my very life in danger? Have I not needed almost six years to recover from that pain?[317]

In issuing *Human* Nietzsche must have known that it would court the ire of Wagner.[318] Retrospectively Nietzsche clearly acknowledges as much in *Ecce Homo* when he discusses his estrangement from the Bayreuth festival.[319] Indeed, here Nietzsche goes on to describe the crossing of his own book with a copy of *Parsifal* sent to him by Wagner as the crossing of swords.[320] It is also a period that Nietzsche describes as a return to himself. For what this period marks is the final break with any idealism and a focusing on the dimensions of the human condition which were revealed through empiricism. Such a refocusing eschews dogmatism, metaphysics, and sentimentality. Such a view would see Nietzsche lose and gain friendships. It would also give him cause to consider the role of friendship in philosophy and culture itself.

Ventilating friendship: Greek origins

An illuminating starting-point for appreciating Nietzsche's view of friendship and its role in this period is to pick it up as an aspect of his continuing dialogue with Greek culture. Nietzsche's hopes were not simply based around an idealistic and naively impossible *re*-creation of the Greek achievement. Instead, they were focused on the reinvestigation of the questions and problems that Greek culture raised as tasks as both an example and a resource to address contemporary problems. It is in this spirit that Nietzsche raises again the *question* of friendship. In *Human* Nietzsche observes that:

> The Greeks, who knew so well what a friend is—of all peoples they alone often and repeatedly ventilated the subject of friendship, so that they were the first, and so far the last, to whom the friend has appeared a problem worth solving...[321]

And later in *Daybreak*:

---

[317] Middleton (ed.), *Selected Letters*, letter 180.
[318] Cf. Richard Schacht in his 'Introduction' to *Human, All Too Human*, p. ix.
[319] Nietzsche, *Ecce Homo*, 'Human, All Too Human', §2.
[320] Nietzsche, *Ecce Homo*, 'Human, All Too Human', §5.
[321] Nietzsche, *Human*, §354.

Antiquity lived and reflected on friendship to the limit, and almost buried friendship in its own grave.[322]

Nietzsche clearly knew the Greek case. It is also more than reasonable to suppose that the connection made by Socrates, Plato, and Aristotle between the notion and practice of friendship and the endeavour of philosophy was not lost on him. However, Nietzsche does not simply transpose or reproduce the Greek view of friendship. On the contrary, whilst the theme of friendship as a problem in need of ventilation has Greek roots (and Greek exemplars), the notion must be rethought and reinvented for contemporary conditions. Thus, in this period Nietzsche opens again what are discovered to be two interrelated questions. The first concerns the *function* or *purpose* of friendship. The second asks what *kinds of people* can be friends. On these two questions there is evident variation in the Greek position. Nevertheless the terrain covered is comparable in both the cases of Socrates-Plato (on the one hand) and Aristotle (on the other). All these thinkers have a basic conception of the 'best' kind of friendship playing a role in the philosophical life. Such a life is focused around knowledge of the true and good. Knowledge is pursued through friendship acting as a forum for both its apprehension and its application. In the 'best' friendship men seek the good in and for others as they seek it in and for themselves. Self, others and knowledge are tied together and reach for the truth as good.

Although he was to follow the Greeks in raising the question of friendship, and even though he was to follow a path concerned with knowledge, self-knowledge, and the development of character, ultimately Nietzsche's development of friendship is wholly un-Greek (or un-Socratic, at least). Socrates and his heirs had all adhered to variations on one central set of tenets: that there was such a thing as truth, that this truth was unitary, and that it was valuable to apprehend it. These tenets shaped the Socratic (and post-Socratic) understanding of friendship. Nietzsche was unable to embrace this position. Indeed, Nietzsche now began to develop a method and outlook which would have made a return to the Socratic view of friendship impossible even if he had wished it: *perspectivism*.

Perspectivism, knowledge, and the divided self

Human and the works leading up to *Zarathustra* see the correlation of Nietzsche's concern with friendship and the development his

---

[322] Friedrich Nietzsche, *Daybreak*, §503. See also Friedrich Nietzsche, *The Gay Science*, §61.

perspectivism.³²³ As we shall see, this correlation is not simply coincidence but a correspondence. Understood as an *approach* to truth and knowledge, Nietzsche's perspectivism can be seen to actively encourage and endorse the kinds of dynamics and discoveries that friendship yields. Nietzsche's perspectivism was to reach its fullest (and most self-conscious) expression in his post-*Zarathustra* writings.³²⁴ However, the very style and presentation of the works from *Human* to the pre-*Zarathustra* books of *The Gay Science* are a demonstration of perspectivism in practice. Put concisely, Nietzsche held that what philosophers have taken to be timeless and eternal truths impervious to change, are exposable as either empty (and unjustified) abstraction, or demonstrated to be the 'products' of long historical, social, psychical and physiological processes.³²⁵ Thus, Nietzsche did not simply deny the possibility of truth and knowledge outright. Nor was he concerned to 'prove' or 'disprove' in an absolute way the tenets or premises of any given position.³²⁶ Instead he was concerned with a conception and practice of philosophy which did not start from the *pre*-conception (or blind assumption) that truth and knowledge are eternal, unchanging, and accessible only in limited ways. Nietzsche's perspectivism was an attempt to approach truth and knowledge from a variety of angles thus increasing understanding by multiplying and juxtaposing numerous perspectives.³²⁷ Such a juxtaposing saw knowledge and the subject of knowledge not as fixed but as changing.³²⁸

As such, Nietzsche's perspectivism is a technique rather than a position. That is to say, although it is sometimes portrayed as a contribution to what might be traditionally considered debates in epistemology and ontology, Nietzsche's perspectivism is perhaps better appreciated as an approach to the apprehension of knowledge and

---

[323] Schacht in Nietzsche, *Human*, p. xvi.
[324] There are various reconstructions and commentaries on Nietzsche's account of perspectivism. Many of these are recreated through a focus on his post-*Zarathustra* writings. As examples of these see Arthur C Danto, *Nietzsche as Philosopher* (New York: Columbia University Press, 1980); Alexander Nehamas, *Nietzsche: Life as Literature* (Cambridge, Massachusetts: Harvard University Press, 1985); Richard Schacht, 'Nietzsche's Kind of Philosophy', in Bernd Magnus and Kathleen M Higgins (eds.), *The Cambridge Companion to Nietzsche*.
[325] Nietzsche, *Human*, §15.
[326] See Danto, *Nietzsche as Philosopher*, p. 70. Richard Schacht argues Nietzsche is not so much *offering arguments*, but *making cases*. See Schacht, 'Nietzsche's Kind of Philosophy', pp. 156-159.
[327] Richard Schacht, *The Arguments of the Philosophers: Nietzsche* (London: Routledge and Kegan Paul, 1983), pp. 116-117; Sheridan Hough, *Nietzsche's Noontide Friend: The Self as Metaphoric Double* (Pennsylvania: The Pennsylvania State University Press, 1997), p. 75.
[328] Cf. Nietzsche, *Human*, §§9, 20. See also Danto, *Nietzsche as Philosopher*, p. 77.

truth.[329] It is an approach which (in *Human* and the books leading-up to *Zarathustra*) Nietzsche could view as taking the Enlightenment to a more radical and more rigorous stage. The method sought to foster as wide and as comprehensive view of a topic as possible.[330] Such a task involved both multiple perspectives and experimentation rather than the doctrinal pursuit of a single perspective. Thus, whilst Nietzsche's perspectivism recognises that knowledge and truth are human aspirations motivated by human hopes, desires, and drives, it is not the case that his perspectivism collapses into mere relativism or subjectivism.[331] On the contrary, perspectives do not 'invalidate' what is seen, and those views which combine the greatest variety of perspectives are to be considered more comprehensive and ultimately to be favoured. Perspectivism suggests an approach to knowledge but does not presuppose the unity and permanence of that knowledge. However, perspectivism is an understanding and approach not only to knowledge, but also an approach to the self as a condition of knowledge.[332]

That perspectivism has an internal as well as an external dimension both underlines that the knowledge is a human production, and raises questions about the nature of the self. Nietzsche was sufficiently Socratic to pursue philosophy through the Delphic injunction to 'know thyself' (albeit an injunction that he viewed as 'almost malicious').[333] The kind of self that Nietzsche came to know was radically different from that which had hitherto held a central place in both the Judeao-Christian inheritance and the dominant assumptions of Western philosophy. For the self is not immune to the perspectivism that Nietzsche advocates as an attitude towards knowledge in general and the positions that entails. The view that Nietzsche is rejecting holds that whilst there may be component parts to the person, there is also a rightful order and a sovereign part. This sovereign part of the individual was identified with the true person and often played-out in both abstract and eternal terms: the soul, the ego, the self, the consciousness. This abstracted part of the person is said to stand *behind* thoughts, experiences, attributes, and actions. This real and enduring individual was the true concern of philosophy and religion.

---

[329] On the issue of Nietzsche's 'pragmatism' see Danto, *Nietzsche as Philosopher*, pp. 76-81; Nehamas, *Nietzsche*, pp. 52-57; Hough, *Nietzsche's Noontide Friend*, p. 63.
[330] Nietzsche would come to view this striving for the truth as one need amongst many, but 'dominant' due to its cultivation by Socrates then Christianity. Cf. Nietzsche, *The Gay Science*, §110.
[331] Nehamas, *Nietzsche*, pp. 72-73. See also Hough, *Nietzsche's Noontide Friend*, p. 63.
[332] Cf. Hough, *Nietzsche's Noontide Friend*, p. 64.
[333] Nietzsche, *The Gay Science*, §335.

From an early stage Nietzsche seeks to challenge this view.[334] In its place he devises a picture of the self as a multiplicity of drives and passions with no central core. This view of the self dispenses with the metaphysical reference to an unchanging ego, self, or soul standing behind the thoughts, passions, experiences, and actions of the individual. This view of the self as both divided and without an essential core was clearly a key insight for Nietzsche.[335] Whilst it was in keeping with his claims about perspectivism and his scepticism about the 'thing-in-itself' it was also to greatly complicate the task of acquiring both knowledge and developing the self. For now not only are there a variety of vantage-points which could be adopted to look 'outwards', so too are there multiple vantage-points for looking 'inwards'. Furthermore, just as the world displays multiplicity, variety and change, looking inwards also reveals a self in flux and subject to continuous (re)formation.

Friendship and the discovery of the self

Given these observations it is possible to anticipate the role that friendship could play in such a scheme. The friend takes the role of another observer who can offer a fresh perspective. Such a perspective might complement or challenge that of the original observer, and in so doing both contribute to the growth of their knowledge and aid their ability to make evaluations. Yet, although such a conclusion about the role of friendship heads in the right direction, it does not fully anticipate the terrain that it is to encounter. This terrain is complex because Nietzsche does not maintain the internal-external distinction in his thinking about knowledge and perspectivism. On the contrary, his divided view of the self undermines this distinction. As we have noted, the observer is a changing and transforming complex that does not offer a point of stability. Thus, if knowledge of the so-called external world is difficult, knowledge of the internal world is positively treacherous. Indeed, given his account of how the individual is not only

---

[334] Hillis J Miller, 'The Disarticulation of the Self in Nietzsche', *The Monist* 69(2), 1981, p. 248.

[335] For a fuller discussion of Nietzsche's view of the self the following will be useful: David Booth, 'Nietzsche on "The Subject as Multiplicity"', *Man and World* 18(2), 1985; Leslie Paul Thiele, *Friedrich Nietzsche and the Politics of the Soul: A Study in Heroic Individualism* (Princeton: Princeton University Press, 1990), pp. 51-65; William McNeill, 'The Poverty of the Regent: Nietzsche's Critique of the "Subject"', *Epoché* 8(2), 2004; Schacht, *Nietzsche*, pp. 130-140, 268-279; Miller, 'The Disarticulation of the Self in Nietzsche'; Walter A Brogan, 'The Decentred Self: Nietzsche's Transgression of Metaphysical Subjectivity', *The Southern Journal of Philosophy* 29(4), 1991; Michael Lackey, 'Killing God, Liberating the "Subject": Nietzsche and Post-God Freedom', *The Journal of the History of Ideas* 60(4), 1999.

ignorant of the forces and drives of which they are composed, but that active self-deception is also at work, we might conclude that for Nietzsche self-knowledge is the greatest and hardest task of all.

It is perhaps fair to say that whilst he recognised the difficulties with the attainment of self-knowledge as a central problem of human existence Nietzsche never really offers an entirely satisfactory solution as to how this is to be overcome. Indeed, it might be that no solution is possible. What Nietzsche does offer are some techniques and strategies for mitigating this problem, and thus a strategy to make human existence liveable and the task of knowledge bearable. Here friendship is one such strategy.[336] In order to see how this is the case consider what Nietzsche has to say in §491 of *Human*:

> *Self-observation.* Man is very well defended against himself, against being reconnoitred and besieged by himself, he is usually able to perceive of himself only his outer walls. The actual fortress is inaccessible, even invisible to him, unless his friends and enemies play the traitor and conduct him in by a secret path.[337]

In this aphorism the problem of man's inaccessibility to himself is made evident. The role of the friend is to provide a path to access the self. However, it is important to note Nietzsche's metaphor here. The person is seen to be in conflict with their own self. The self is not (as some philosophers have argued) either unified or transparent. Indeed, self-knowledge is a struggle. Furthermore, the idea of the friend is linked to that of the enemy. Although there is the possibility of the friend offering a way into the self, it is an act of *treachery* to lead an individual into the fortress of their self. This might run counter to what we might initially expect. If self-knowledge is so important to Nietzsche, then why is the friend considered a traitor in aiding the individual's assault on their own self?

Part of the answer to this is suggested by §489 (obviously positioned closely to §491). In this aphorism Nietzsche writes:

---

[336] Cf. Fredrick Appel, *Nietzsche Contra Democracy* (Ithica and London: Cornell University Press, 1999), p. 87.

[337] The difficulty highlighted in this passage echoes a problem that Nietzsche had previously grappled with in the unpublished essay of 1873 'On Truth and Lying in a Non-Moral Sense'. In this essay Nietzsche writes: 'What do human beings really know about themselves? Are they even capable of perceiving themselves in their entirety just once, stretched out as in an illuminated glass case?' Friedrich Nietzsche, *The Birth of Tragedy and Other Writings*, Ronald Spiers trans. (Cambridge: Cambridge University Press, 1999), p. 142. It is also restated in *Gay Science* §335 where Nietzsche writes: 'How many people know how to observe something? Of the few who do, how many observe themselves? "Everybody is farthest away — from himself"…'.

Not too deep. People who comprehend a thing to its very depths rarely stay faithful to it forever. For they have brought its depths into the light of day: and in the depths there is always much that is unpleasant to see.

Clearly there is a danger in knowing the truth about something that it hidden: the danger of unfaithfulness. Nietzsche will later make much of the murky depths and base origins of human affairs and especially morality in his account of the development of the concepts of good and evil (with the story told in *Genealogy* being the prime example). In the case of friendship and knowledge of the self the danger is clear enough. By bringing-up the depths of another, the friend is in danger of finding something tawdry or repulsive. By exposing themselves to this knowledge the friend is likely to become disillusioned with the other. By exposing this knowledge to the other the friend is likely to cause them occasion for disillusionment over their self, or disillusionment with the friend who has been so 'treacherous' as to expose these depths. In either scenario, a dissolution or rupture in the friendship is in the making.[338]

So friendship presents a kind of irresistible and necessary danger. This danger is inherent to the relationship and linked to the degree that the friends can truly pursue their friendship (insofar as it is connected to disclosure). It seems that Nietzsche recognises that there are contradictory forces at play in friendship: the desire for disclosure and the need for masks and deceit.[339] On the one hand friends offer an alternative perspective on the self and so an opportunity for greater self-knowledge. The best friend would therefore be someone who knows us intimately (perhaps even knowing us better than we know ourselves). In this sense, intimacy is to be welcomed. On the other hand, such a friendship also threatens the self. To extend Nietzsche's metaphor, the knowledge brought by the treachery of friendship might see the citadel fall and the occupants fall into confusion and disarray. Even the besieger will consider such a victory pyrrhic. Whilst an individual might seek self-knowledge Nietzsche is also aware of the need to prevent the anarchy of the senses and the need to marshal the drives and forces of the person into a 'unity'.[340]

This tension is heightened by the nature of the self. As we have seen, for Nietzsche the self is a fluid complex. Nevertheless, in order to

---

[338] Compare what Nietzsche has to say on 'judging falsely', Nietzsche, *Human*, §352.
[339] On this topic see the interesting discussion in van Tongeren's article: Paul J M van Tongeren, 'Politics, Friendship and Solitude in Nietzsche (Confronting Derrida's Reading of Nietzsche in 'Politics of Friendship')', *South African Journal of Philosophy* 19(3), 2000, pp. 216-218.
[340] Thiele, *Friedrich Nietzsche and the Politics of the Soul*, p. 63.

survive some integration and order is required, and to some extent Nietzsche judges individuals according to their success in balancing such an achievement in their honesty about their inner being. In terms of friendship a peculiar danger now emerges. Whilst Nietzsche recognises that friendship and sharing might be both necessary and desirable, he cannot bring himself to countenance the possibility (or perhaps desirability) of a *shared* selfhood. Here friendship offers a danger as the intimacy of friendship could conceivably lead to the blurring of the friends. Such a shared self would threaten the cause of individuality and its contribution to culture—at least as far as Nietzsche is concerned. In the later works all of this is cashed-out coldly in terms of domination and power.

Friendship, then, is to be an important aid in the attainment of knowledge and the development of character. However, Nietzsche is acutely aware that not all that counts as intimacy and especially 'commonality' also counts as friendship. True friendship is rare. Although Nietzsche's perspectivism divested him of the classical apparatus with which to evaluate friendship, he does have a measure for the kinds of friendship that he thinks that a philosopher (or free spirit) should seek and cultivate. In a sense these friendships are not so much focused on the persons of the friends but in their shared endeavour. This shared endeavour focuses around the attainment of knowledge and the understanding and development of character. This is not without risk. Friendship is a kind of perilous game whereby the benefit that can be offered to the other and drawn from their friendship must be balanced against the inherent destructiveness that friendship poses for the formation of a coherent and individuated self. Even though it is an act of friendship to offer it, the knowledge that friendship exposes is not always welcomed by the friend. Sometimes the true friend is one who has the courage to allow the dissolution of the friendship and to go their own way.

Friendship as *gift*: The thing given

We have seen then that Nietzsche's account of both perspectivism and the self have implications for his view of friendship. Not least, the friends are engaged in an attempt to obtain a perspective on, and knowledge of, their own self. Given that this 'self' is revealed to be a changing multiplicity this task is potentially a somewhat destabilising one. However, there are other ways in which Nietzsche plays out his thought on friendship. One important metaphor that Nietzsche employs when discussing friendship is the idea that friendship is a gift. This metaphor is brought out in what can be considered a key passage on friendship found at *Human* §368 where he identifies two types with such a gift 'the ladder' and 'the circle'. There are two main ideas at play here. First, that friendship is a gift or talent in the sense that it is a skill or ability. Given what has already been said about the perils of friendship and its peculiar task, it is reasonable to suppose that a sense of what this entails has already been offered: the skill of friendship is found in attracting suitable friends and navigating the dangers of friendship. The complexities of this will be drawn out in the next section. Before that, the metaphor of friendship as a gift will be explored in its sense of 'the thing given'.

In characterising friendship as a gift Nietzsche is invoking a powerful metaphor. For far from being a simple and uncomplicated act, Nietzsche shows that giving to others is a sophisticated movement in the economy of power. For gifts, like other aspects of human relations, are an attempt to exert control and influence over another and to have them recognise our own power. In the case of the gift it can be noted that there is no automatic reciprocation or exchange. Nor are gifts granted by the demands of right or justice. It would seem that the gift is given *and* received freely, and without prior terms or conditions. Yet, there is more here than meets the eye. It is Nietzsche's view that gifts are not merely the tokens of power, but acts of power. In Nietzsche's scheme the benefactor has exercised power in relation to the recipient. The response of the recipient is also understood in terms of power for Nietzsche. Our initial intuitions might be that the recipient has received some aid from the benefactor then the appropriate response should be gratitude. In effect, gratitude is a recognition of the gift. It might be thought that it is a symbolic display that the benefactor has sacrificed something in favour of the beneficiary, and that the beneficiary has gained by this. This is not Nietzsche's view. Whilst he identifies gratitude as a kind of recognition for something given, he is more cynical about the meaning of gratitude. For Nietzsche what is, in fact, being 'recognised' in gratitude is an act of power. Far from being welcomed, these acts might be resented. Thus, in *Human* §323, Nietzsche counsels that:

> *Ingratitude to be expected.* He who bestows something great receives no gratitude; for the recipient is already overburdened by the act of taking.

In Nietzsche's account the difficulty in gift-giving does not always lie with the ability of an individual to give a gift, but with the ability of another to receive it. Gratitude should not always be expected as the gift can be a kind of burden. Indeed, Nietzsche considers the gift to be a kind of disruption of the self. This difficulty can be measured along lines of proportionality relating to both the size of the gift in relation to the resources of both the giver and the receiver, and the ratio of the relative degrees of power between the giver and receiver. Where the ratios are greatest Nietzsche's tendency is to characterise gratitude as a form of revenge.[341] Gratitude is a means by which men return the intrusion on their own power by their benefactors. However, not all 'revenge' need be violent and basely motivated. Nietzsche tells us that a powerful community 'place[s] gratitude among its first duties'.[342] Acts of beneficence and gratitude (and thus friendship as an economy of gift giving) are possible between men of power who share a kind of equality *on that account*.[343] In such an environment a 'noble soul' will neither avoid occasions when they might be obligated to show gratitude, nor show their gratitude in an uncontrolled and damaging way.[344] They can accept gifts and return appropriate gratitude (i.e. acknowledge acts of power and rebalance the relationship) as the power of others is not seen as a menace to their own. Gift-giving and gratitude form a kind of exchange, an exchange that binds the parties together. It is in recognition of the possibility of an equality of character and power.

In contrast, those whom Nietzsche terms 'baser souls' find acts of beneficence either demeaning to receive or 'miraculous'.[345] In both cases the consciousness of the power of another in relation to their own lack of power is the source of the response. Therefore, whilst some seek to avoid all occasions when they might be required to show gratitude, others exaggerate their display of gratitude. As has been noted, such gratitude is a form of revenge and here the revenge is predicated on the feeling of powerlessness. The greater the gratitude the greater the consciousness of (and distress caused by) the disproportion of power; and the greater the desire for the compensation of revenge. In the case of those who are prone to affectation in gratitude the response is as harmful for them as it is to their intended target. Nietzsche notes that in such cases baser souls 'choke themselves with the cord of gratitude'.[346] As with Nietzsche's later theme of *resentiment*, the baser soul can never fully discharge the need for revenge or overcome the slight which has been demonstrated to them. Thus, the baser kind might be judged by Nietzsche as unsuitable for friendship as they cannot accommodate the demands of power as beneficence and gratitude.

---

[341] Nietzsche, *Daybreak*, §138. For a fuller account of Nietzsche's view of revenge see Friedrich Nietzsche, *Human, All Too Human: The Wanderer and His Shadow*, §33.
[342] Nietzsche, *Human*, §44.
[343] Nietzsche, *Human*, §92.
[344] Nietzsche, *Human*, §366.
[345] Nietzsche, *Human*, §366.
[346] Nietzsche, *Human*, §550.

Given these considerations, this view of friendship as a gift seriously limits those capable of such a relationship; and as a result the possibility of genuine friendship itself. What is perhaps novel in Nietzsche's thought is his connection of the ideas of friendship and power, and his refusal to abandon the relationship (and its endeavour) on account of this. For others, the transposition of these concepts would be utterly objectionable. This connection between beneficence and power is maintained throughout the books of this period and into Nietzsche's other works. The key appears to be the ability of the participants to recognise and assimilate this aspect of their relations. In §13 of *Gay Science* we see a typical instance of this. Here Nietzsche notes that 'benefiting and hurting others are ways of exercising one's power upon others'.[347] Nevertheless, Nietzsche stresses that 'proud natures' are 'doubly obliging toward their *peers* whom it would be honourable to fight if the occasion should ever arise' (again, echoing the thoughts of *Human* §44). What Nietzsche is pointing to in this passage is that power need not be a simple force that manifests in a zero-sum-game of domination or repulsion. This might well be the experience of baser souls, but it is not the experience of all. Under the right circumstances the power that is expressed in acts of beneficence and gratitude can be considered to be beneficial to men of a rough equality and a source of bonding.[348] It is this kind of attention to social obligation between differentiated equals—who are none the less aware of their own power and the power of their peers—which Nietzsche has in mind when he speaks of aristocracy. Indeed, Nietzsche repeatedly characterises aristocracy as being an hierarchical organism of differentiated parts. Such an understanding of aristocracy allows Nietzsche to apply it to the whole gamut of human associations and relations from political community, to relations between individuals, to relations 'within' individuals themselves.[349]

Nietzsche's thought leaves open a space for the kinds of differentiated relationships bound through gift and gratitude. In

---

[347] Cf. also Nietzsche, *Human*, §§337, 348; Ibid., *Daybreak*, §112; Ibid., *Wanderer*, §256.

[348] Cf. the account of 'justice' as a form of exchange between men of equal power (and the connection to Nietzsche makes between this and gratitude) in Nietzsche, *Human*, §92. On the shift on justice and power from the middle to the late period see Lester H Hunt, *Nietzsche and the Origin of Virtue* (London and New York: Routledge, 1991), pp. 100-104. Ruth Abbey discusses Nietzsche's account of the role of 'benevolence' as a form of social bond as a kind of controlled egoism which 'can give without counting the cost', Abbey, *Nietzsche's Middle Period*, pp. 65-66.

[349] Thiele, *Friedrich Nietzsche and the Politics of the Soul*, pp. 66-67, but cf. p. 4. For a more general account see Ansell-Pearson, *An Introduction to Nietzsche as Political Thinker*, pp. 39-44. On aristocracy in the middle period see Abbey, *Nietzsche's Middle Period*, pp. 93-98.

characterising friendship as a gift Nietzsche brings the relationship into this sphere of power. Nevertheless, Nietzsche does not find this destructive to the possibilities of genuine friendship. Indeed, friendship as a gift shares some intriguing possibilities of a community of peers. Despite this it should also be noted that in *Gay Science* Nietzsche's more accommodating view is beginning to wane. Although it is by no means solidified, an increasingly uncompromising view of power comes to dominate and close-down the subtleties that his thought would otherwise afford. This view understands power not only as a function of egoism, but of a more robust individualism. One example of this can be seen in how Nietzsche now tends to see human relations in terms of the desire to master through possession. Although this tendency is already indicated in *Human* (for example, where Nietzsche refers to a woman's attitude towards 'a man of consequence'),[350] in *Gay Science* §14 this is repeated and generalised. Nietzsche asserts that 'our pleasure in ourselves tries to maintain itself by again and again changing something new *into ourselves*; that is what possession means'.[351] Love is here identified as a form of egoism. Later in this same passage Nietzsche writes:

> Here and there on earth we may encounter a kind of continuation of love in which this possessive craving of two people for each other gives way to a new desire and lust for possession — a *shared* higher thirst for an ideal above them. But who knows such love? Who has experienced it? Its right name is *friendship*.

There are, of course, echoes of the Socratic-Platonic ideal here as announced in the *Symposium* (and, indeed, Nietzsche has just been discussing Sophocles and Eros). What this shared higher ideal is Nietzsche does not make clear (if, indeed, it is any one thing). Perhaps friendship itself is the ideal. If so, then this would make friendship a kind of shared striving for friendship. Perhaps it is the shared desire to remain bound to another despite the danger it poses to the self. For some, the danger motivates this desire. This notion of an ideal which is set above the friends is a theme that Nietzsche uses to characterise friendship both within this period and beyond.[352] However, if §14 of *Gay Science* is anything to go by, the basis of friendship is power understood as possession, and to fully move beyond this is either something immensely rare or even impossible. Significantly Nietzsche

---

[350] Nietzsche, *Human*, §401.
[351] Cf. Nietzsche, *The Gay Science*, §334.
[352] In *Zarathustra* the friends share the goal of the Übermensch; and in *Beyond Good and Evil* the friends share the goal of preparing the way for the philosophers of the future and their own independence.

is not disturbed by the role of power within friendship (or other human relationships), and it is not entirely clear that *he* needs to be so. We might not find the two so comfortably reconciled.

Friendship as *gift*: The ability or disposition

The second way in which Nietzsche uses the idea of friendship as a gift is in the sense of a skill or disposition. Nietzsche is trading on the various overlapping meanings of the idea of a gift in this passage. It has already been suggested that the talent required in friendship is connected to some form of skill or ability to respond in an appropriate way to the danger presented by knowledge within friendship. The preceding discussion of the notion of gratitude has shown one particular aspect of this. However, Nietzsche's identification of friendship as an ability or disposition develops this. In particular, Nietzsche shows that whilst the talent for friendship is desirable it is also restricted. Furthermore, in the two types that Nietzsche identifies as having a particular talent for friendship (the ladder and the circle), the friendships are played-out or conducted in contrasting ways. Thus, it would seem that the talent for friendship is not likely to be acquired by those who do not already posses it, and those who do possess it will display it in diverse manners which are unique to their particular situation.

As a starting-point to thinking about friendship as a talent it is worth making a few brief comments on the common associations with the notion of talent. The first, and perhaps most obvious point, is that talent is usually highly-prized. The talent is something which is valuable to both its possessor and others. Indeed, in some cases others value the talent more highly than its possessor. Second, and related to the value of talents, we often think that talents can be put to proper and improper use. The talent itself is often thought of as being a kind of generic disposition or ability (which can be used in a variety of ways), or as a specific skill relating to a specific task or activity. Third, there is some debate as to whether such talents and dispositions are natural (that is to say innate) or have to be acquired and developed. Usually there is a sense in which specific skills develop over time, but that they are based upon innate qualities of the individual (and if not innate, certainly dispositions acquired at an early age). Finally, and not without relevance, there is a general inclination to forgive the talented for other shortcomings that they might have, and even 'character defects'. No one expects another to have the full range of skills and abilities. Furthermore, should someone be especially talented, it is sometimes the case that this either eclipses negative features of their character, or are even thought to be somehow connected to it (we might think here of the image conjured of the 'brilliant yet troubled' artist).

These common associations with the idea of talent are at play in Nietzsche's own account of friendship as a talent. Indeed, in *Human* §263 and §264 he discusses these very issues. In the first aphorism Nietzsche tells us that everyone has access to many talents and possesses 'inborn talent'. Here Nietzsche's thought seems to be that there are two sources of talents: internal disposition and external range. He goes on to note that not everyone has either the internal disposition or 'acquired toughness' to actually 'become a talent'. Thus, Nietzsche leaves it open as to whether talents are truly inborn or acquired, but indicates that there are dispositions and situations which are necessary for the development of talent. However, Nietzsche also makes it clear that talents are not simply dispositions but are displayed in action. Nietzsche writes that not everyone has the ability 'to *become* what he *is*: which means to discharge it [talent] in works and actions'. Thus, in this passage talent (and in particular *being* a talent) is not simply an appendage to the person, but is the person themselves. The self is expressed not merely through the talent of works and actions, but is in some sense constituted by these. In the second aphorism (§264) Nietzsche discusses how different kinds of talented or gifted people over-value or under-value each other. The main contrast here is between non-scientific people (such as artists) and scientific people. The former seek anyone who will 'inflame' them and 'spur them on' (irrespective of whether they are on the 'right track or not'). The latter seek pleasure in 'the real, valid, genuine' which might not appear exciting at all. As we shall see, these different ways of being gifted are played out in Nietzsche's wider thinking on friendship, and in particular his two types, the ladder and the circle.

The ladder: Friendship as agonism[353]

As indicated, in *Human* §368 Nietzsche writes that amongst those who possess the talent for friendship two types predominate: the ladder and the circle. The ladder seeks a friend for each step of his development, whereas the circle attracts a variety of personalities who cluster around him. The ladder appears to be in a state of ascent, and his friends form a series. Nietzsche notes that such a series will often be characterised by discord. In contrast, the circle appears to hold differences together and rupture is not a feature of this form of friendship. Thus, the aphorism is

---

[353] On the connection between this and the Greek view of friendship made by Burkhardt see Smith, 'Two Perspectives on Friendship', p. 67. For a more general discussion see Appel, *Nietzsche Contra Democracy*, p. 89ff.

significant as in it Nietzsche recognises and presents two forms of human bonding: one based on agonism and one on harmony. In what follows the ideas of this aphorism will be opened-up and explored. Specifically they will be connected with Nietzsche's treatment of friendship, and placed within the context of his overall themes and motifs.

One way to approach the type of the ladder is to consider it as a possible generalisation of Nietzsche's own friendship with Wagner.[354] In particular, this relationship illustrates two key points. The first is that the pattern of the ladder is connected to the role of friendship in the attainment of knowledge about the self and especially self-development. The second is that the relationship and subsequent split in both Nietzsche's friendship with Wagner, and the pattern of the ladder in general, connect to considerations of the wider dynamics within friendship itself. It also suggests how former friends should view their friendship and each other—at least if they wish to develop as individuals and possess nobility of character.

We have already seen that a part of Nietzsche's attraction to Wagner was motivated by the fact that Nietzsche 'sought for so long a man who was superior [to him] and actually looked beyond [him]'.[355] This echoes Nietzsche's thinking on the ladder, but also his later rather cryptic comment that friends desire 'a *shared* higher thirst for an ideal above them' offered in *Gay Science* §14. In the early stages of his own ladder-friendship with Wagner Nietzsche is clearly not only drawn to the personality of Wagner, but also towards what the composer is trying to achieve and what he represents. In this sense Wagner was an 'appropriate' friend for Nietzsche's stage of development. However, during and after the break with Wagner Nietzsche is more prone to see Wagner's shortcomings. Moreover, Nietzsche tends to see his own development as an overcoming of Wagner or an emergence from a

---

[354] Wagner is the most obvious example of Nietzsche 'overcoming' one of his friends, and thus illustrating the idea of the ladder. It is not suggested here that Nietzsche had Wagner in mind when he wrote this aphorism. As a generalisation of a particular type of friendship others might also fall into this category, not least Rée and Salomé. The question of Nietzsche's relationship with Schopenhauer is also suggestive of this (albeit a relationship which is carried on through Nietzsche's engagement with Schopenhauer's thought in text). This thought might not be as strange as it first appears. For Nietzsche addresses his own (unknown) readers as friends, and even has a sense of his friendship with future readers. Moreover, as Nietzsche makes clear in his writings, it is perfectly possible to have a relationship with an author through their writing—in this sense books represent not just thoughts but also personality. How far this can be taken is, of course, a moot point—but perhaps it should not simply be rejected out-of-hand.

[355] Middleton (ed.), *Selected Letters*, letter 93.

sickness. This break was clearly over-determined, but one of the key reasons from Nietzsche's point of view seems to be Wagner's failure to change and develop (at least, to change and develop with Nietzsche). An example of this can be found in a letter from Nietzsche to Peter Gast dated 31st May 1878 after the publication of *Human*:

> In Beyreuth the book [*Human*] has been placed under a sort of ban, and it seems that excommunication has been decreed for its author at the same time... Wagner has missed a golden opportunity to show greatness of character. I must not let this distort my opinion of him, or myself.[356]

Here the type of the ladder is illustrated in Nietzsche's attitude towards Wagner. It is important to note that Nietzsche is trying to maintain a balance between admitting the failures of his friend (and perhaps his own, insofar as he courted Wagner as a friend), and acknowledging and even endorsing what was valuable in that friendship and each other. For although both men were far from perfect, the key to Nietzsche's view about the break-up is suggested in a letter to Reinhard von Seydlitz dated 11th June 1878:

> [Wagner's] aspirations and mine keep drawing apart. This pains me considerably. But in the service of truth one must be prepared for any sacrifice.[357]

It is this higher goal — the search for truth, knowledge, and honesty of character — that brings the friends together. They recognise each other as being on the same but separate quests. There is clearly a sense in which intimacy, affection, and even a form of love are not contrary to Nietzsche's understanding of friendship here.[358] Indeed, in his letters

---

[356] Peter Fuss and Henry Shapiro (eds.), *Nietzsche: A Self-Portrait from His Letters* (Cambridge, Massachusetts: Harvard University Press, 1971), letter 49. The problem of the split with Wagner affecting Nietzsche's judgement is reflected in *Assorted Opinions and Maxims* §229 where Nietzsche claims that our climbing higher than those we have admired makes them appear 'to have sunk and fallen lower'.

[357] Fuss and Shapiro (eds.), *Nietzsche*, p. letter 50. This view is repeated two years later to Malwida von Meysbug in a letter dated 14th January 1880. Here Nietzsche writes: 'I knew long ago that Wagner, as soon as he realised that our aims had diverged, would do just that [abandon Nietzsche]... I am still grateful to him for having inspired me to strive passionately for independence of spirit.' Ibid. letter 59.

[358] Again this observation is borne out most obviously in how he addresses his own friends — and talks about friendship — in his letters. For one example of this, see the letters to Peter Gast in Fuss and Shapiro, eds., *Nietzsche*, letter 62. Here 'one stops loving oneself properly when one stops loving others. Which is why the latter is a very bad idea. (I speak from experience.)'. As Fuss and Shapiro usefully note, this idea is expressed in aphoristic form in *Daybreak* §401.

friendship is often connected to these notions, and it is something that Nietzsche complains of losing after the split with Wagner.[359] However, the true focus of the relationship is to be found in the notions of self-discovery and the shared ideal that stands above the friendship.[360]

The talent of the ladder is thus revealed not only in their ability to find an appropriate friend, but also in overcoming that friend. Thus, Nietzsche tells us that a sign of humanity in respect to 'closer association with others' is to follow the spirit of the expression that 'If you are going towards the morning I shall draw towards the evening'.[361] Moreover, the real talent is perhaps shown in being able to remain focused and to pursue the ultimate goal of the friendship. This is reflected in being capable of not only breaking the friendship, but also in being able to continue to appreciate the friend (and the contribution of the friendship to the individual's development) after the break. As Nietzsche makes clear in *Gay Science* §99, one remains faithful to what is 'true and authentic' in another. Wagner may well have had his 'intellectual tempers and cramps' and have even been 'so often in the wrong'. However, the encounter with Wagner enabled Nietzsche (and perhaps others) to 'grow and blossom out of ourselves'.

The ladder, then, is as much about breaks as it is about attraction. There is room in this model for a mutual affection and perhaps even genuine concern for another. However, although the task that stands above the friends may well bring them together, ultimately it is a task that they both pursue for themselves and as individuals. Thus, the dominant image of the ladder is overcoming and ascent. It is within this context of the growth and transformation wrought by friendship that Nietzsche has occasion to consider the meeting of old and former friends. Somewhat roguishly we might term this the 'afterlife' of friendship as these encounters hover between friendship and non-friendship, neither truly one thing nor the other. This also reflects the very language that Nietzsche uses in two of the aphorisms in *Maxims* (§242 and §259) where he discusses the question of how former friends should acknowledge and respond to each other; passages which also bring the idea of the balance between development and residual affection and acknowledgement to the fore. In the two passages the theme is that of the 'ghost'. In the first of these aphorisms Nietzsche suggests that 'If we greatly transform ourselves, those friends of ours who have not been transformed become ghosts of our past'.[362] Here the

---

[359] Fuss and Shapiro (eds.), *Nietzsche*, letter 63.
[360] For an example of how this focus can affect the end of a friendship see Nietzsche, *Daybreak*, §287.
[361] Friedrich Nietzsche, *Human, All Too Human: Assorted Opinions and Maxims*, §231.
[362] Nietzsche, *Maxims*, §242.

implication is that the individual who has transformed is somehow more substantial and more complete than the shadowy friend. Moreover, the image of the ghost invokes ideas of haunting. The friend is now an unsettling presence which is out of time in the present. A presence which the transformed individual should now lay to rest or avoid. The image of the friend as ghost is also used to describe the relation between two friends who have changed. Conversations with such former friends, where interest is 'feigned', are 'like those in the realm of the dead'.[363] Here the image is one of a meeting where the life and vitality has been drained from the encounter. The friendship has stopped being a dynamic and living relationship, and further development of the person through the friendship is no longer possible. Indeed, Nietzsche indicates that in such an encounter we might be afraid of finding out what the other has now become. Again, the former friend becomes a spectral presence. The vitality suggested by the ladder has now gone.

The final place where Nietzsche discusses the relationship between former friends is in the much admired passage in *Gay Science* entitled 'Star friendship'.[364] In this passage Nietzsche describes the friends as ships who have travelled together but have now parted. However, the parting (or estrangement) should not be a source of shame. In this passage Nietzsche gives a real sense of the tragic necessity of parting (and thus the passage links back to the metaphor of the ladder). For although the ships may have *appeared* to have the same goal their goals were, in fact, separate. The fate of the ships is not to rest together. On the contrary, Nietzsche writes that:

> the almighty force of our tasks drove us apart again into different seas... our exposure to different seas and suns has changed us. That we have to become estranged is the law *above* us; by the same token we should also become more venerable for each other—and the memory of our former friendship more sacred.

Here Nietzsche identifies the 'tasks' of the friends as being the cause of their separation. However, it is not entirely clear as to what 'the law above' the friends might be. At first it is tempting to think of the law being the product of a deity, or perhaps 'fate', or some form of teleology. Of course, Nietzsche cannot have recourse to any of these. Could it be that the 'law above us' is connected to the tasks of the friends? It would seem that here Nietzsche adds weight to the

---

[363] Nietzsche, *Maxims*, §259.
[364] Nietzsche, *The Gay Science*, §279. See also Abbey, 'Circles, Ladders and Stars'; Robin Small, *Nietzsche and Rée: A Star Friendship* (Oxford: Clarendon Press, 2005). Both of these commentators also discuss and are impressed by this passage.

suggestion that the tasks of the friends (self-knowledge and self-development) are what both draw them together, but ultimately cast them apart. Without such a break the friends would cease to develop (and remain moored on a calm and sunny sea). Thus, the separation is not to be regretted. Nor is the former friend to be thought of badly. The fact that the friends have both met and separated is something which is to be held as 'sacred' (i.e. an extraordinary and valuable event), and something that both of the friends should continue to 'believe' in despite its sublime aspects.

The circle: Friendship as harmony

In the pattern of friendship suggested by the circle the friend is represented as a centre-point of a constellation of differing characters. In words which echo his own assessment of his 'solar system of loving friendship'[365] during his Wagner years, Nietzsche tells us that the friends are bound together by the centre-point and that 'in him this solidarity between such different natures and dispositions must in some way be prefigured'.[366] Here the emphasis is very much on the possibilities of friendships holding differing (perhaps even juxtaposing) elements *together*. In this sense the friendship of the circle stands in contrast to that of the ladder; although it is not clear whether the models are assumed to be exclusive or complementary. Thus, if we summarise the model of friendship illustrated by the ladder as being 'agonistic', then that of the circle is 'harmonic'.

In many ways this harmonic view of friendship might be thought to be attractive. It certainly lacks some of the more turbulent elements of the agonistic relationship suggested by the ladder. It would also seem to steer clear of the fateful conclusion that those relationships seem to imply, especially the possibility of mutual recrimination to the detriment of both parties. Clearly the talent of the circle is to draw friends who reflect and embody aspects of the circle's own personality and character. The circle of friends can be considered to be an external representation of the internal composition of the circle himself. Two further conclusions can be developed from this view. The first is that in this externalisation the circle brings together not only aspects of their own personality but also (presumably) new aspects belonging to the characters of the friends that are drawn into the circle. The character of the circle is a complex whole. The collection of friends reflect this complex whole and are prefigured in the complexity inherent in the character of the circle himself. In addition, each member of the

---

[365] Middleton (ed.), *Selected Letters*, letter 48.
[366] Nietzsche, *Human*, §368.

friendship circle also has their own complex character. Some of these aspects of character they share with the centre of the circle, but some they do not. Therefore, the circle not only brings together and combines different aspects of their own character in their choice of friends, they are also introduced to new aspects brought by their friends which are not prefigured within them. It can also be assumed that the friends of the circle have the potential to come into contact with each other. In this way, the friends of the circle bring new aspects to not only the circle himself, but to his other friends. The *talent* of the circle is in not only holding the differing aspects of themselves into a coherent whole, but also in holding the different aspects of their friends together in the circle.

This leads naturally to the second conclusion which connects the ideas implied in the image of the circle back with the themes of perspectivism and self-discovery. It has already been suggested that the friends of the circle are an external embodiment of internal characteristics (at least in part). Such an embodiment allows that circle to both appreciate and even interact with different aspects of their own character. In a sense, the friends of the circle form a mirror around the circle in which the circle's own composition is reflected back in a more fragmented but more analysable way. However, the friends of the circle do not *simply* act as mirrors. As we have noted, they bring with them not only aspects of the circle, but also aspects of their own characters, dispositions, and biographies. Thus, the mirroring is one which allows the circle not only to develop a self-perspective, but also to enhance that view with the additional qualities brought by those acting as the mirrors. Here, then, something new is brought to the circle, and this might be thought to aid not only self-knowledge but also development.

Overcoming friends for friendship

Both the type of the ladder and the type of the circle answer some of the questions that are raised by the possibilities of human bonding, but they also raise fresh questions of their own. These questions revolve around the themes of independence and instability. Some of the answers are unsettling to Nietzsche's wider views. In the case of the circle, in particular, there is a danger of a merging of the selves as so much is prefigured and shared. Ultimately it might be thought that the answers and challenges to these questions draw Nietzsche away from his central commitments, and it is perhaps for these reasons that Nietzsche's later views reflect the agonistic images suggested by the ladder. The type of the ladder suggests that the friends come together to either complement each other (which would seem to suggest lack), or because they are at parallel stages of development (which would seem to suggest similarity). However, the emphasis of the friendship of the ladder is as much on separation and independence as it is on attraction. In an inversion of the Ancient ideal, the best friendship is inherently unstable. Indeed, ladder-friendship seems to seek instability. This sense of independence is less clear in the case of the circle. In contrast to the instability connected to development exhibited by the ladder, for the circle there seems to be an economy of difference which may have its own internal circulation (and thus not remain entirely static), but which also suggests that the introduction of new traits or development beyond its bounds is unlikely and perhaps even impossible. In the friendship of the circle there is a reordering of the same.

This emphasis on 'prefiguring' and 'solidarity' in the case of the circle also raises the question of the true independence of the friends in a way that the ladder avoids. This concern comes back to the central issue of the Nietzschean view of the self. We have already seen that Nietzsche's view of the self is one which eschews some core or essence for an account which sees the self as being composed of various (and even competing) drives and emotions. This is not to say that some drive does not seek to bring some kind of order to this maelstrom. As we have seen friendship can be an aid to such a task. Nietzsche notes that the ability to abide with ourselves—despite our complexity and contradictions—is the very model for our ability to abide with our friends. Thus, as in the case of the circle, unity does not mean the eradication of difference. In §376 of *Human* Nietzsche comments on the accidental nature of friendship. Ultimately, it rests on the friends being attracted to each other in a state of 'error and deception' about each other's true nature. Nietzsche goes on to write that:

> Are there not people who would be mortally wounded if they discovered what their dearest friends actually know about them?— Through knowing ourselves, and regarding our own nature as a moveable sphere of moods and opinions, and thus learning to despise ourselves a little, we restore our proper equilibrium with others. It is true that we have good reason to think little of each of our acquaintances, even the greatest of them; but equally good reason to direct this feeling back onto ourself.—And so, since we can endure ourself, let us also endure other people...

This passage brings together a number of themes. The first is the idea that friends might (initially) be attracted to each other as a result of erroneous judgements about each other. Nietzsche then reverses this as the erroneous image that the friend has of the other is then replaced by some insight. It is this fresh perspective that makes friendship a potentially useful tool in self-knowledge. However, Nietzsche *also* stresses that this knowledge might result in the friend being 'mortally wounded' should it be revealed or reflected back to them. Here Nietzsche's thinking links-up with what he will go on to write about 'self-observation' in *Human* §491. Self-knowledge is potentially dangerous both to ourselves and to our friendships.

The second thing which is striking about this passage is that here Nietzsche indicates that although friendship is based on misunderstanding, and although this might be replaced by disagreeable truths about ourselves and others, there is a possibility for it to endure. We can live with the faults of our friends insofar as we are able to live with our own shortcomings.[367] This connects back to the idea of the circle who externalises aspects of their own character in the friendships that they form with others. As in the passage which introduces the type of the circle, in this passage there is a sense of reconciliation rather than overcoming. Whilst this might appear attractive, from Nietzsche's perspective it represents a creeping danger. The harmony of the circle is certainly an achievement. Such a form of harmony might even include some tensions if they are incorporated into a greater whole. However, it also appears that the dynamism and introduction of new elements which are needed for self-discovery and self-development are lacking in the case of the circle (and especially when compared to the type of the ladder). It seems that the circle might get us so far, but then things are prone to stagnate.

The more serious fear which is raised by the possibilities of friendship, and suggested most strongly in the case of the circle, is the possibility of merging. This possibility is exacerbated by Nietzsche's account of the self. The tension is brought out as whilst Nietzsche wishes to see the self as a cluster of drives without a permanent core or essence, he also wishes to understand and advocate the notion of individuality. The question now arises as to where one person ends and another begins, and the notions of sharing and especially affection for the other in friendship aggravate this.[368] Whilst in the case of the ladder this problem is ultimately side-stepped by the emphasis on attraction *and* separation, it is not so clear that those concerns are avoided in the case of the circle. In the case of the circle the sharing (and thus the possible risk of blurring) is much more pronounced. Nietzsche himself is obviously well-aware of this tension. In *Maxims* §241 he defines a good friendship by the maintenance of careful

---

[367] Cf. van Tongeren, 'Politics, Friendship and Solitude in Nietzsche', p. 217.
[368] We might think here of Nietzsche's own experience of his struggle to separate his thought from that of Paul Rée; see Small, *Nietzsche and Rée*.

distances, and especially avoiding 'the confounding of I and Thou'. It is difference that marks the friends, and although they share something this does not mean that they must share everything or become each other. Indeed, one of the marks of friendship is precisely that the true friend does not wish others to share all of their judgements and experiences.

Nietzsche's view of friendship in the works leading-up to *Zarathustra* is thus mixed. However, what is important is that there is a role for friendship. Friendship is to be a mechanism of self-discovery. It is also a way for those engaged on the endeavour of philosophy to form a mutual bond and to aid each other. This is not to say that the relationship isn't without its tensions. Indeed, it is the agonistic view of friendship practised by the type of the ladder which seems to be the favoured model. Intimacy, trust, and a kind of concern for the other can be generated by this kind of friendship—but ultimately the friend is something to be overcome. This is the view that is taken up by *Zarathustra*—and intensified.

Zarathustra: From star to disaster friendship[369]

It is sometimes said that *Zarathustra* is a kind of creative eruption of intellectual and emotional forces that Nietzsche struggled with during the beginning of the 1880s.[370] This is undoubtedly true, and Nietzsche's own letters reflect this struggle.[371] If *Zarathustra* is to be considered an eruption, then it is an eruption that also changes the landscape in which it is situated. For after the instability of *Zarathustra* Nietzsche's thinking solidifies into a new terrain. It is in this struggle, both personal and philosophical, we also see played-out what was to be Nietzsche's final resolution of the tension between his thinking and practice of friendship and solitude. As we have seen, from an early stage Nietzsche sought companions who could understand his work as a philosopher. Such philosophical companions must appreciate that Nietzsche's philosophy was not simply doctrine but an approach to life itself. It was intellectual *and* experiential. As a result Nietzsche sought not devotees or disciples, but true companions who would travel with him in the heights and depths of philosophy understood as a *spiritual*

---

[369] For accounts of the role that the metaphor of 'stars' play in Nietzsche' thoughts on friendship see Small, *Nietzsche and Rée*; Abbey, 'Circles, Ladders and Stars'.

[370] Hollingdale in Friedrich Nietzsche, *Thus Spoke Zarathustra: A Book for Everyone and No One*, p. 11.

[371] See, for example, Nietzsche's comments to Overbeck in December 1882, 'Unless I discover the alchemical trick of turning this – muck into gold, I am lost.' in Middleton (ed.), *Selected Letters*, letter 109.

endeavour.[372] Perhaps it was the case that he would find no one equal to the task that he had taken on for himself.[373] Perhaps it was the case that no one could be his equal. Most troubling of all was the thought that philosophy might necessitate solitude, but that ultimately it revealed isolation. That these thoughts trouble Nietzsche's mind and finally prevail can be seen in both his correspondence leading up to *Zarathustra* and beyond the book itself. By the mid to late 1880s this is complete and overt. For example, in a letter to Rhode dated 23rd February 1886 Nietzsche confesses that his hopes of companionship have evaporated:

> ... life has proposed my duty to me with the terrible condition that I should fulfil that duty in *solitude*. It is difficult for people to follow my feelings; I almost assume now, even among acquaintances, that I shall be crassly misunderstood...[374]

This painful desperation is repeated again to Malwida von Meysenbug in 1887 where Nietzsche claims that Meysenbug is 'the only person who could make me have this wish [for company]; for the rest, I feel *condemned* to my solitude and fortress'.[375] The next year Nietzsche writes to Meysenbug again lamenting that: 'There is indeed a great *emptiness* around me. Literally, there is no one who could understand my situation'.[376] In the same year he tells Reinhart von Seydlitz that 'A friendly voice seldom reaches me nowadays. I am alone now, absurdly alone'.[377] Over the course of the 1880s something clearly changes for Nietzsche. Increasingly he focuses on the difficulties of intimacy and communicating his thoughts and feelings. As such, there is a growing distance between Nietzsche and his friends, and his tendency is to cast himself in the role of an outsider or hermit.

Perhaps the clearest illustration of the tensions that lead Nietzsche along this trajectory are illustrated by the now notorious intrigue with Rée and Salomé.[378] Regardless of the exact nature of any romantic hopes that Nietzsche placed in Salomé, the relationship between the three held out the possibility of philosophical companionship.[379] We

---

[372] Cf. Hollingdale in Nietzsche, *Zarathustra*, pp. 11-12.
[373] Safranski, *Nietzsche*, p. 270.
[374] Middleton (ed.), *Selected Letters*, letter 141.
[375] This thought links to what Nietzsche will later say about 'indolent' friends in *Beyond* §27.
[376] Middleton, ed., *Selected Letters*, letter 173.
[377] Middleton, ed., *Selected Letters*, letter 163.
[378] For a fuller treatment of this episode see Safranski, *Nietzsche*; Small, *Nietzsche and Rée*.
[379] Safranski, *Nietzsche*, pp. 254-257. Cf. also Fuss and Shapiro (eds.), *Nietzsche*, letters 73, 74, and 80.

have already noted that this feature of the relationship sets it with the other attempts at philosophical companionship during Nietzsche's life. What sets this particular constellation apart is that it becomes disastrously misaligned. This misalignment casts the thought, emotions, and affairs of Nietzsche into disarray. In the confusion, Nietzsche was simultaneously drawn towards reconciliation and what he might have thought of as being the shrewder policy of maintaining a studied distance. Clearly Nietzsche's conflicted thoughts and emotions over the lost intimacy and hope of companionship, and whether this failure is his own or his friends, advocates caution. In a letter to Rée in mid-December 1882 Nietzsche talks of the need for forgiveness from Lou in order that he can forgive her. He then comments that 'It is harder to forgive one's friends than one's enemies'.[380] This is near to the time of the end of any contact that Nietzsche would have with Rée and Salomé, with Nietzsche realising that they were much closer to each other than they would ever be to him.

What this relationship must have reinforced for Nietzsche is the very danger of intimacy, and especially being mistaken in intimacy. It also reinforces for him the difficulties that one individual has in truly expressing themselves to another. Indeed, it began to suggest the sheer impossibility of this. By February 1883 Nietzsche has the following regret to relate to Overbeck 'I mean to find my health by the same means as before, in complete seclusion. My mistake last year was to give up solitude'.[381] Nietzsche presents solitude as a choice, but there is also a sense in which it is necessitated. If Nietzsche could not find the philosophical companions who were to be worthy of him and his task would he rather live and work alone? Could he take any solace in the half-measures of those who were bound to see him 'crassly misunderstood'? Indeed, was any form of solace a mistake and a symptom of his own failure? As the later period draws to its collapsing close Nietzsche becomes increasingly aware of his isolated fate.

This all stands in stark contrast to the hopes of a circle of *gaya scienza* that Nietzsche entertained in his earlier years, and his obvious deep affinity with both Wagner and even Rée and Salomé. Whatever the cause of the decline in their relations, Nietzsche's loneliness in his later period is simultaneously both a product of this decline, and a perpetuation of it. Previously in May 1884 Nietzsche confesses to Elisabeth that 'Almost all my human relationships have resulted from

---

[380] Middleton (ed.), *Selected Letters*, letter 108. See too Middleton (ed.), *Selected Letters*, letter 109.
[381] Middleton (ed.), *Selected Letters*, letter 112.

attacks of a feeling of isolation'.[382] Nietzsche's complaint here is that his relationships have not been the product of something worthwhile in themselves, but as a result of a need within him when he has felt isolated. Nietzsche retreats. He cannot (or cannot let himself) fully share in rewarding human relationships. He has had to 'playact somewhat instead of refreshing [himself] in people'.[383] Again, the problem here seems not to be that this kind of communication is impossible, or undesirable in itself, but that it is almost impossible to find the person with whom Nietzsche can communicate. In June 1884 he writes to Malwida von Meysenbug that he has experienced his solitude 'ever since my earliest childhood! This secretiveness, even in the most intimate relationships!' and that 'I have never found anyone to whom I could talk as I talk to myself'.[384] Friendship it seems is internalised — even amongst friends. This tension between the need for companions to share and develop Nietzsche's task, and the need for solitude, are played out in the drama of *Zarathustra*. So, too, are the increasingly troubling themes of struggle and war.

Zarathustra's Quest

Zarathustra was the book for which Nietzsche had the greatest pride.[385] Despite its fame, the book can be said to be the least representative of Nietzsche's publications. There are two reasons for such a judgement. First, unlike Nietzsche's other books, this piece is written as a narrative. Thus, stylistically, it is unlike anything that Nietzsche wrote previously or would write afterwards. Second, even though the book heralds some of Nietzsche's most notorious ideas such as the Übermensch (Superman) and Eternal Recurrence these ideas are never really expanded or developed in his later thought — at least not as much as one might expect.[386] Thus, it is not unfair to say that the book has had a disproportionate role in our understanding of Nietzsche's thought.

---

[382] Middleton (ed.), *Selected Letters*, letter 134.
[383] Middleton (ed.), *Selected Letters*, letter 134.
[384] Middleton (ed.), *Selected Letters*, note to letter 125.
[385] See, for example, what Nietzsche has to say about the book and himself in *Ecce Homo* where one day 'perhaps even chairs for the interpretation of Zarathustra will be established' and where Nietzsche goes on to berate his critics (no modesty spared one might think!), Nietzsche, *Ecce Homo*, 'Why I Write Such Excellent Books', §1.
[386] It is a matter of debate as to what can and should be made of the idea of the Übermensch (and, indeed, the Eternal Recurrence). Much depends on whether scholars accept the authority of Nietzsche's unpublished notes. The case for the relevance of the unpublished notes (and the implications for the wider significance of the Übermensch), is made in a judicious article by Bernd Magnus, 'Nietzsche's Philosophy in 1888: *The Will to Power* and the *Übermensch*', *Journal of the History of Philosophy* 24(1), 1986. Here (on p. 93) Magnus argues that 'the

The book itself presents the reader with significant questions concerning how it is to be understood.[387] These are legion and notorious. The first, thing which is noticed about *Zarathustra* is that it is a narrative with drama and characters. Ostensibly it is the story of Zarathustra's quest to find an audience for his teachings. This quest takes him from his cave and solitude to the town of Motley Cow, to teaching his disciples, to another period of wandering, and finally with assembling the Higher Men. The drama relates Zarathustra's various encounters and his inner life, but most of the book is made up of what can be described as his 'sermons' or 'teachings'. The manner and themes of these sermons allude to both Biblical and Socratic teachings (as does the style of the book as a whole).[388]

All of this raises two questions which need to be addressed in some fashion for a fuller appreciation of the book. The first concerns the sense in which the story of the book can be considered the story of a success. Whilst the figure of Zarathustra is clearly central to the message of the book, it is far from evident that he fulfils his mission.[389] Indeed, not only does he seem to be unable to locate the right ears for his gospel, at times he also seems unable to live-up to its demands

---

notion of an Übermensch virtually disappears from Nietzsche's published *and unpublished* writings after *Zarathustra'*. This is not to say, however, that the notion isn't central to *Zarathustra* itself. Nevertheless, the significance of the notion for Nietzsche's wider thought has continued to draw considerable attention. For two representative accounts (linking the notion of the Übermensch to that of the Eternal Recurrence) see Kaufmann, *Nietzsche: Philosopher, Psychologist, Antichrist*, pp. 307-333; Danto, *Nietzsche as Philosopher*, pp. 195-213.

[387] As Keith Ansell-Pearson has observed 'Despite some major studies by philosophers of the work in recent years, there still exists no consensus as to the meaning and significance of the principal teachings of the book'. Ansell-Pearson, *An Introduction to Nietzsche as Political Thinker*, p. 101.

[388] Kathleen M Higgins, 'Reading Zarathustra', in Robert C Solomon and Kathleen M Higgins (eds.), Reading Nietzsche, pp. 135-136.

[389] For examples of these 'failures' see the following: Robert John Ackermann, *Nietzsche: A Frenzied Look* (Amherst: The University of Massachusetts Press, 1990), p. 45. where Zarathustra 'is a signpost on a tragic route of thought'; Peter Berkowitz, *Nietzsche: The Ethics of an Immoralist* (Cambridge, Massachusetts: Harvard University Press, 1995), pp. 128-130, 211-213, where we see Zarathustra's shortcomings and errors, and where Part IV is considered a 'descent into farce ... in part a consequence of [Zarathustra's] failing to fulfil, or live in accordance with, the superhuman requirements imposed by his new ethics'; Ansell-Pearson, *An Introduction to Nietzsche as Political Thinker*, p. 120, where what Zarathustra learns is the nature of 'his own sickness and morbid, dissatisfied condition'; Higgins, 'Reading *Zarathustra*', p. 138, who concludes that 'at the end of the book Zarathustra fails to communicate even with the few disciples in whom he still had confidence.'; and David Owen, *Nietzsche, Politics and Modernity: A Critique of Liberal Reason* (London: Sage Publications, 1995), pp. 129-130.

himself.[390] His actions seem to square somewhat uneasily with his exhortations to remain true to the earth and not to seek otherworldly solutions to the challenges of this world. The end of the book might lead us to seriously doubt whether Zarathustra himself is truly capable of living in this world *as it is* given his rejection of the Higher Men and his enthusiasm for the somewhat redemptive figure of the Übermensch. Thus it is possible to wonder whether Zarathustra succeeds, and whether if he doesn't this can be attributed to his own weaknesses, contradictions in his message, or the contrivance of Nietzsche as author. This leads to the second question: how far can we identify Zarathustra's views with those of Nietzsche? There is a strong temptation to view Zarathustra as the mouthpiece of Nietzsche, and it is certainly true that Nietzsche explicitly identifies with the book as a whole. However, the question remains as to why Nietzsche chose this particular medium for his message; and whether Nietzsche's later writings are truly elaborations on the central themes of *Zarathustra* or departures from it.[391]

Having said all of this, the book is still important and it is significant to understanding Nietzsche's view of friendship. The text is pivotal in the exploration of the theme of friendship in two ways. First, *Zarathustra* itself is the result of a particular crisis in Nietzsche's own life. This crisis is both biographical and intellectual. Nietzsche is concerned about his own relationships, prompted by the fateful breakdown of relations with Rée and Salomé. Nietzsche comes to worry about his own ability to form intimate relationships which true expression and communication might take place and confirms the role and importance of solitude. Intellectually, Nietzsche's series of aphoristic writings from *Human* to *Gay Science* had pushed his philosophy to its very limits. These books had explored the roots of European civilisation and values showing that far from exalted origins pointing to higher truths, much in fact results from the limitations of the human being ruled by hidden and drives which were animalistic, irrational, and often destructive. The project had been one of following a path of deconstruction—albeit one that Nietzsche hoped would be liberating and produce a kind of cheerfulness free from illusion and

---

[390] For example, despite his teachings Zarathustra still has compassion for the priests, see Stanley Rosen, *The Mask of Enlightenment: Nietzsche's Zarathustra* (New Haven and London: Yale University Press, 2004), p. 147. It has also been observed that whilst Zarathustra claims that he has rejected the multitude and others to do so too, he still seeks their attention, see Berkowitz, *Nietzsche*, p. 140. Others have suspected Zarathustra of lapsing into idealism, see Daniel W Conway, *Nietzsche and the Political* (London and New York: Routledge, 1997), p. 21.

[391] See Berkowitz, *Nietzsche*, p. 227; Ackermann, *Nietzsche: A Frenzied Look*, p. 48; Conway, *Nietzsche and the Political*, p. 21.

fear. However, something more was now needed. Could something more positive be built on the space that had been cleared and using the tools that Nietzsche had fashioned? *Zarathustra* and the works which follow it are Nietzsche's attempt to answer in the affirmative.

The second way in which *Zarathustra* is a pivotal in understanding Nietzsche's view of friendship is that it develops a new attitude towards the idea. However, the ambivalence of the works leading up to *Zarathustra* persists. On the one hand friendship is now seen as a possible means for the realisation of the Übermensch. As such, it becomes connected to the task of creation, and a means for the individual to shore-up against the entropy of the age. In this sense friendship is a thing to be celebrated. On the other hand, both solitude and enmity come to play a much more prominent role in what is written in *Zarathustra*, and these themes are connected in a much clearer way both to friendship and its possible work. In the end, it seems that the need for independence comes to eclipse friendship, and the only friendship which is possible is with the men of the future. Zarathustra is thus presented as a teacher of friendship; but the friendship he has to teach is an intensified version of the ladder friendship sketched in *Human*. Now friendship is creative only in agonism, caring only insofar as the friends are unyielding, and ultimately a relationship to be overcome. The Übermensch becomes symbolic of the possibilities of this kind of friendship: hard, unyielding, and connected to others through struggle.

Seeking friendship: The narrative of *Zarathustra*

One of the central themes of *Zarathustra* is the concern with Zarathustra's search for suitable companions.[392] It is this search, as much as anything else, which drives the narrative of the book. It is also this search which helps us to better appreciate the themes of Zarathustra's speeches and to make connections between them. These speeches represent a developing whole. Thus, the most overt treatment of friendship in *Zarathustra* (the section in Part I entitled 'Of the Friend') cannot be treated in isolation. It must be seen in the context of Zarathustra's other pronouncements on the related themes of self-overcoming and creation, neighbourliness, enmity and solitude, and

---

[392] For comment on the centrality of Zarathustra's search for companions see Rosen, *The Mask of Enlightenment*, p. 66; Laurence Lampert, *Nietzsche's Teaching: An Interpretation of Thus Spoke Zarathustra* (New Haven and London: Yale University Press, 1986), p. 13; Higgins, 'Reading *Zarathustra*', p. 138; Richard Avramenko, 'Zarathustra and His Asinine Friends: Nietzsche and Taste as the Groundless Ground of Friendship', in Richard Avramenko and John von Heyking (eds.), *Friendship and Politics: Essays in Political Thought*, pp. 304-306.

the Übermensch. It must also be seen as an aspect of Zarathustra's wider struggle for companionship and his retreats back into solitude. In order to better understand the significance of Zarathustra's search for companions and what this tells us about friendship it is worth highlighting some of the forms of fellowship that Zarathustra pursues in the book. This is necessarily both selective and somewhat impressionistic.[393] Here three will be highlighted: Zarathustra's friendship with his animals; Zarathustra's attempts to communicate with the people of Motley Cow and the tight-rope walker; and Zarathustra's 'disciples'.[394]

Although we usually think of friendship as existing between human beings, Zarathustra's first form of companionship sets up a relationship between a human being and beings from the realm of nature: the eagle and the snake. Whilst the eagle and the snake represent aspects of both Zarathustra's personality and his task (connecting the sky to the earth, and nobility and pride to cunning and even evil), they remain unsatisfactory as companions.[395] Of course, Zarathustra's message is intended for human beings as they must be the ones to act upon it, but the eagle and the snake drawn attention to this insofar as they have 'fixed' forms. Whereas human beings are capable of change and have the possibility to become something new, animals do not.[396] This gives us an important insight into the kinds of companions for whom Zarathustra is searching, and the reason for seeking them. Zarathustra is seeking those who are capable of change. Whilst there might be something to be admired in both the eagle and the snake, and whilst their natures might be instructive, they are not the ultimate recipients for Zarathustra's wisdom.[397]

It is this notion of the malleability of the human being, and especially the potential for man to forge himself in a direction of his

---

[393] For a fuller account of these see Lampert, *Nietzsche's Teaching*; Rosen, *The Mask of Enlightenment*.

[394] We could add others to this list, notably the 'Higher Men' of Part IV. These men are significant as both they and Zarathustra clearly attempt some form of companionship. It is not at all clear that this is a success for either the Higher Men or Zarathustra. The Higher Men seem to misunderstand Zarathsutra, and Zarathustra seems unable to reconcile himself to the fact that these men are the 'best' the earth has produced. Interested readers might consult Weaver Santaniello, *Zarathsutra's Last Supper: Nietzsche's Higher Men in Thus Spoke Zarathustra* (Aldershot: Ashgate, 2005); Kathleen M Higgins, *Nietzsche's Zarathustra* (New York: Lexington Books, 2010); Francesca Cauchi, *Zarathustra Contra Zarathustra* (Aldershot: Ashgate, 1998).

[395] See Avramenko, 'Zarathustra and His Asinine Friends', pp. 306-307.

[396] Rosen, *The Mask of Enlightenment*, p. 26.

[397] Indeed it has been noted that the animals are an expression of Zarathustra's loneliness, see Rosen, *The Mask of Enlightenment*, p. 26.

own choosing, that informs Zarathustra's attempts to find ears in the town of Motley Cow and leads to the fatal accident of the tight-rope walker. Although the addresses in this episode are most often discussed in terms of the contrast between the hopes for the Übermensch and Zarathustra's admonishment of the Last Man, there is also a sense in which *if* Zarathustra found those both capable and willing to understand his message then this would form the basis of a new political community based around the realisation of the Übermensch. The self-overcoming and affirmation of life promised by the Übermensch is either ignored or misunderstood, and—all too predictably—the townsfolk identify with the Last Man instead. Rather than the adventure and daring suggested by the Übermensch, the townsfolk choose the fearful huddling and nihilistic merging of safety and the avoidance of suffering. Such a choice demonstrates to Zarathustra that not only are such men unworthy of his message, but that they are incapable of true companionship.

Without doubt the fall and death of the tight-rope walker is one of the major dramatic moments of the Prologue and Part I more generally. Much has been made of this, and it has rightly been taken to be a highly significant episode rich in symbolic meaning. Here just two comments are made about this incident and its aftermath. The first concerns Zarathustra's affinity with the tight-rope walker. The meeting of Zarathustra and the tight-rope walker is purely coincidental, yet the connection between the two men which is a feature of the confusion of the townsfolk is both mistaken but strangely appropriate. For the endeavour and fate of the tight-rope walker illustrates the contents of Zarathustra's speeches. Indeed, Zarathsutra describes man as a 'rope, fastened between animal and Superman' and the sense of a precarious going-across between two banks over an abyss is a recurrent theme.[398] In addition, the fall and subsequent death of the tight-rope walker draw Zarathustra and the artiste together as companions in choosing danger. In Zarathustra's assessment, although the tight-rope walker's life has ended in misfortune, his life has not been worthless or a failure. Indeed, in choosing danger the tight-rope walker has affirmed the value of life. Zarathustra tells the dying artiste that: 'You have made danger your calling, there is nothing in that to despise. Now you perish through your calling: so I will bury you with my own hands'.[399] What attracts Zarathustra to the tight-rope walker is that the performer embraces risk and danger. Although it is not mentioned, we might also think of the discipline (both physical and psychical) that is required for

---

[398] Nietzsche, *Zarathustra*, Prologue §4.
[399] Nietzsche, *Zarathustra*, Prologue §6.

such a feat. The tight-rope walker overcomes fear. Thus, insofar as the tight-rope walker chooses danger he exhibits one of the qualities that are to characterise both the Übermensch and what Zarathustra is to seek in his friends. Zarathustra's friends are to be contrasted entirely with the picture of the Last Man so readily embraced by the townsfolk of Motley Cow. Instead they are to be seekers of challenge and danger, and to seek this in others too. Zarathustra's message is right for such men because it is not one of consolation and comfort, but a chaotic mix of revaluation, liberation, and foreboding.

The second comment is related closely to the first. In acknowledging his affinity with the fallen tight-rope walker Zarathustra also has cause to reflect upon his efforts to reach an audience in Motley Cow. It is his affinity with the tight-rope walker that brings Zarathustra to the realisation that if he is to find those capable of understanding and acting on his teaching then he needs to refocus his search. After 'burying' the tight-rope walker in a hollowed-out tree, Zarathustra speaks to his own heart admitting that 'A light has dawned for me: Zarathustra shall not speak to people but to companions! Zarathustra shall not be herdsman and of the herd! To lure many away from the herd—that is why I have come.'[400] Importantly, the tight-rope walker can be considered to be someone who embodies this message in his art and performance. For Zarathustra his message is not one that can simply be 'understood'. On the contrary, it is not so much a set of teachings in the doctrinal sense (Zarathustra does not wish for 'dead companions and corpses'), but a teaching that is more akin to an ethos, attitude, or approach to life, self, and others.[401] Not everyone is capable of adopting such a stance. Zarathustra's companions will be destroyers of tables of values, fellow creators, and will follow Zarathustra because they follow themselves. It is from this perspective that Zarathustra names the fallen tight-rope walker as his *first* companion.

This turn from the crowd to solitary individuals is an important shift as it also refocuses Zarathustra's conception of community. Now companionship will be restricted amongst the few, and it will be this smaller group whose efforts will result in the higher cultural production. However, who are these few? And how do they relate to Zarathustra? We are given little indication of who these people are in *Zarathustra*, although by the midsection of Part I they are described as Zarathustra's disciples. This term should not mislead. For Zarathustra makes it clear that his expectations of discipleship are contrasted to religious and especially Biblical accounts. Whereas in the New

---

[400] Nietzsche, *Zarathustra*, §9.
[401] Cf. Magnus and Higgins, 'Nietzsche's Works and Their Themes', p. 40.

Testament the primary aspect of discipleship of Jesus Christ was to have faith in the truth of Jesus, Zarathustra inverts this. Zarathustra stresses that his followers must both 'lose me and find yourselves; and only when you have all denied me will I return to you' (Of the Bestowing Virtue). Only in this way will Zarathustra's 'believers' become his 'friends'.

It is also against this backdrop that we can assess Zarathustra's warning at the end of Part I that he may have 'deceived' his disciples. On the face of it this is a rather peculiar thing for a teacher to suggest especially one who claims to teach 'the friend'. However, this is entirely in keeping with the kinds of companions that Zarathustra hopes to attract and journey with. Zarathustra does not wish to cultivate followers, but companions who will embrace his teaching as an example of how one can reinvigorate life. Such followers embrace life in its totality. That Zarathustra might deceive his followers is direct encouragement for them to challenge and test what he has taught, and in so doing either find the wisdom of his teachings to be true, or forge a wisdom for themselves. However, Zarathustra's challenge is also to turn what is seemingly closest to his followers into what is furthest. In other words, Zarathustra's challenge places him in role of deceiver rather than truth-teller, and thus potential harmer and enemy rather than friend. In this speech (as elsewhere) Zarathustra seeks to blur the distinctions between the friend and enemy, making the source of creativity, growth, and 'aid' ambiguous. This can be seen not only in Zarathustra's instructions to his followers to 'lose me and find yourselves' but also in his mischievous amendment to *Matthew* 5:43-44 'The man of knowledge must be able not only to love his enemies but also to hate his friends'.[402] Provocative though this is, it is not simply devilry. Seen in the context of the wider project of both seeking worthy companions, and creating ambiguity for the friend-enemy distinction, it is an attempt by Zarathustra to redefine the meaning of friendship in relationship to its higher task. In the first instance Zarathustra is asserting that we have something to learn even from our enemies, indeed, that the harm that our enemies might seek to do us might in some way aid our development. Moreover, Zarathustra is asserting that the kind of friendship that he has in mind is far from the world of mutual comfort. It is a creative and assertive friendship which is based around the provocation of the other. As such, it could easily be replaced by the experience of enmity — albeit of a decent rather than a poisonous variety.

---

[402] Nietzsche, *Zarathustra*, 'Of the Bestowing Virtue' §3.

Teaching friendship: The discourses of *Zarathustra*

The three forms of companionship that have been sketched here illustrate some of the main features of Zarathustra's quest for friendship. This quest is revealed to be one of finding individuals who are capable of understanding his message. It is also a quest for individuals who are going to embrace the ethos of that message in their own lives and to travel with Zarathustra in its development. Crucially, these companions of Zarathustra can remain his friends even if their development of this new ethos takes them in directions which are not only new but different and even opposed to Zarathustra's own. As we have seen, this dramatic context provides the complement to what is said about friendship. Indeed, in exploring the dramatic context some connection with Zarathustra's teaching has already been made. Seen in this way the idea of companionship has an important place in *Zarathustra* as a whole, and friendship forms a particular connective thread (especially in Part I). This connective thread will now be traced showing both how it develops a distinctively Zarathustrian account of friendship, and how that account is related to other Zarathustrian themes.

One of the central themes of the discourses of Part I is the identification of the kind of relationships that Zarathustra seeks to establish. The discourses address both what is desirable and to be promoted in human fellowship, and what is to be considered degenerate and to be avoided or rejected. In the first of these categories are the ideas of enmity and friendship as extolled in 'Of War and Warriors' and 'Of the Friend'. Although these ideas might seem antithetical, Zarathustra relates them closely. As we will see, there is considerable overlap in the ways in which friendship and enmity function in Zarathustra's thought. Zarathustra also connects these qualities of the kinds of disciples who are capable of both understanding and developing his message. It should be noted that for Zarathustra both friendship and enmity are not merely structural relations, but are acquired through (and characterised by) striving. This process is dynamic and fraught with the difficulties of creation and self-overcoming. Ultimately it involves both confrontation and danger.

By way of contrast to these standards, Zarathustra also identifies the kinds of fellowship and community that he implores his disciples to reject. In a sense, the ability to recognise these forms of community as being unworthy and then to reject them and to move beyond them is one of the marks of both Zarathustra's disciples and the kind of person who is fit for friendship. In any event, several kinds of relationship are identified by Zarathustra for criticism. Typically these are the relationships of the 'many-too-many'. The most obviously political of these types are criticised in 'Of the New Idol'. This discourse sees Zarathustra denounce the 'superfluous' existence of the 'nimble apes' preserved under the modern state. Continuing this theme, 'Of the Flies in the Market Place' is concerned with the 'poisonous flies' of the liberal democratic polity being condemned as both 'cowardly' and being capable only of a stagnant 'prudence'. Zarathustra does not think that the 'many-too-many' are fit for discipleship, and his judgement on their political arrangements and the desires and values which motivate them borders on pure contempt.

Zarathustra also reserves some ire for relationships based on uncontrolled drives and the perverted channelling of *eros*.[403] This is one of the messages of both 'On Chastity' and 'Of Marriage and Children'. Partnership and reproduction should not simply be the result of 'the animal and necessity', the inability to endure 'isolation', or as a result of a 'disharmony' of the self. For Zarathustra marriage should aim at creating something higher, and this is also a judgement on the kinds of people capable of marriage. Again, such people are different to the 'many-too-many' who enter into marriage as a result of their own weaknesses and flaws. Taken as a whole the discourses of Part I build on Zarathustra's insights in the Prologue, and have a special focus on his identification and cultivation of his disciples in the wake of his realisation prompted by the fall of the tight-rope walker.[404] Having noted this context, in what now follows Zarathustra's view of friendship will be retrieved by focusing on three aspects: the production of the Übermensch and creativity; the connection between friendship and enmity; and the dangers of pity, merging, and solitude. In so doing, we shall also have occasion to further contrast this affirmative message with the relationships of modernity from which Zarathustra turns away.

The Übermensch and creativity

One of the central features of Zarathustra's conception of friendship is its role in the production of the Übermensch.[405] As has been noted, the Übermensch is one of the possibilities focused on in the speeches which form Zarathustra's Prologue, and it is a dominant theme of Part I as a whole. At times this is so dominant that Zarathustra might be mistaken for a kind of John the Baptist figure in relation to the somewhat messianic and possibly divine Übermensch. In fact, to think of the

---

[403] Lampert, *Nietzsche's Teaching*, p. 57.
[404] Lampert, *Nietzsche's Teaching*, p. 53.
[405] Smith, 'Two Perspectives on Friendship', p. 70.

Übermensch in this way is to misunderstand Zarathustra's message. The notion that the Übermensch is somehow going to be a saviour figure stands in direct contrast to Zarathustra's warnings about otherworldly hopes and his direct admonishment to his followers to 'be silent about all gods' and to 'remain true to the earth'.[406] Instead of otherworldly hopes (which represent the longing for external intervention or a super-human ideal) Zarathustra's message of the Übermensch focuses squarely on the potential of his contemporaries. The production of the Übermensch is the task and goal of *existing* human beings.[407] It is also the goal of Zarathustrian friendship. In Zarathustra's discourses friendship serves the goal of the production of the Übermensch in two main ways. First, that the friends are a foretaste of the Übermensch. Second (and ambiguously) the friends somehow realise the goal of the Übermensch in themselves and each other.

In what sense does Zarathustra consider friendship a foretaste of the Übermensch? One of the most direct statements of this teaching is found in 'Of Love of One's Neighbour'. In this discourse friendship is contrasted to those who love their neighbour. Of course, the commandment to love the neighbour is central to Christ's gospel, and so Zarathustra's message is easily recognised as a direct attack on a core Christian teaching and mode of relating self to other.[408] Zarathustra's attack claims to penetrate behind the mask of 'selflessness' of such a commandment and ethic. Zarathustra tells his disciples that far from being an act of genuine love for the other, love of the neighbour betrays 'bad love for yourselves'. For Zarathustra such a doctrine is not only dishonestly self-serving ('you want to mislead your neighbour into love and gild yourselves with his mistake'), it is also a sign of the disarray of a character unable to bear solitude and confrontation with their unworthy self. In this vein Zarathustra announces that:

> One man runs to his neighbour because he is looking for himself, and another because he wants to lose himself. Your bad love of yourselves makes solitude a prison to you.[409]

---

[406] Nietzsche, *Zarathustra*, 'On the Blissful Islands' and Prologue §3, respectively.
[407] See Rosen, *The Mask of Enlightenment*, pp. 15, 39; Ackermann, *Nietzsche: A Frenzied Look*, p. 44; Conway, *Nietzsche and the Political*, pp. 20-22.
[408] This teaching is central to Christ's doctrine as presented in the synoptic gospels: *Matthew* 19:19, *Mark* 12:31, and *Luke* 10:27. The theme is taken up by Paul in his letters (for example, *Romans* 13:9 and *Galations* 5:14). However, it should be observed that the injunction originates in the Old Testament, and that its use in the New Testament is often in direct reference to this heritage (see *Leviticus* 19:18).
[409] Nietzsche, *Zarathustra*, 'Of Love of One's Neighbour'.

In seeking the neighbour the individual is revealing their own emptiness. Furthermore, the neighbour is perhaps the worst possible remedy to this situation as they are just as devoid of character and strength as the person who seeks them. The neighbours are locked into a desperate embrace of mutual worthlessness and fear. As a result neighbourliness is not only damaging to those who practise it, but it is also damaging for the future hopes of others and especially the Übermensch. As Zarathustra makes all too clear: 'It is the distant man who pays for your love of the neighbour'.[410]

There seems to be no immediate remedy for this state of affairs. Indeed, it seems that many are doomed to this fate. Zarathustra indicates at the beginning of the discourse that this is ingrained as the result of a long historical process which has consecrated 'You' over the 'I'. However, for the few there is an alternative. Zarathustra's hopes rest on those choose to reject the crowd and who love the man of the future. Such individuals must turn their backs on neighbourliness and seek instead those willing to engage in the endeavour of friendship. Such individuals love themselves in the right way and thus can also love others. Far from the desperation *to be* loved exhibited in neighbourliness, this self-love consists in the affirmation of the self, its judgements, and experiences. In such friends 'the world stands complete' and the friend is 'a vessel of the good'.[411] Such friends are creative, making sense of their existence and that of others; their individual *and* joint goal being to cultivate the Übermensch. It is for these reasons that Zarathustra announces:

> I do not teach you the neighbour but the friend. May the friend be to you a festival of the earth and a foretaste of the Superman.[412]

In Zarathustra's view, friendship is motivated not by incompleteness or a lack but a kind of fullness and excess. The friend is said to be 'overflowing' and to have a 'complete world to bestow'. Of course, Zarathustra's view of friendship is cut-loose from the ethical framework of the Greeks. Thus, there is no *prima-facie* tension between individuals who are already complete seeking each other in a way that there is for the Socratic cases. In the Zarathustrian case, friendship is based around the ability to give and to receive.

Talk of giving and receiving might make us pause. This sounds very similar to some of Zarathustra's criticisms of neighbourliness. The comparison is, however, superficial. Whilst neighbours seek each other

---

[410] Nietzsche, *Zarathustra*, 'Of Love of One's Neighbour'.
[411] Nietzsche, *Zarathustra*, 'Of Love of One's Neighbour'.
[412] Nietzsche, *Zarathustra*, 'Of Love of One's Neighbour'.

because they are incomplete, friendship is based around fullness and confidence. Neighbours give in order that they might receive, their relationship is one of reciprocal equalisation. Zarathustrian friends give because it is in their character to do so, and their aim is to produce something beyond themselves (even if this leads to their destruction). In addition, Zarathustra's friends know how to receive from each other. Such receiving is not cause for secret resentment as is the case with neighbours. In this way friendship is a foretaste of the creativity, completeness, and self-confidence that Zarathustra associates with the Übermensch. The friends make the Übermensch their individual tasks and the task of their friendship, thus creating meaning for themselves and the world. In so doing the friends exhibit qualities that demonstrate both to their own self and to their friend that the Übermensch is possible.[413]

This presentation of friendship as a foretaste of the Übermensch, coupled with the idea that the shared goal of friendship is the cultivation of the Übermensch, leads to an intriguing suggestion: could friendship be a device to bring about such a realisation within the friends themselves? This suggestion is obviously speculative.[414] However, it is supported by the fact that many of the qualities that Zarathustra claims the friends must possess and develop in themselves and each other are also attributes of the Übermensch. Chief amongst these is the ability to overcome the self, discipline, creativity, confidence in action, and affirmation. The possibility is therefore held open that the difference between the friends and the Übermensch is one of scale rather than quality (albeit that the qualities of the Übermensch are amplified by scale). This suggestion draws further support from the ambiguity in Zarathustra's own pronouncements on the Übermensch. One way of understanding his reluctance to offer a detailed description of the Übermensch is that such a being represents a way of being rather than an end state. Such a way of being is effected by a transformation and development of the human being not into a new species, but into new forms of human life. The Übermensch represents the possibility realised when human beings marshal their potential (although this is clearly not open to all).[415] Such an understanding would echo what Zarathustra says in his Prologue (and repeats later) both that man is something to be overcome, and that man represents a rope tied

---

[413] Cf. Lampert, *Nietzsche's Teaching*, p. 58.
[414] Cf. Ackermann, *Nietzsche: A Frenzied Look*, pp. 51, 58. We should also note Lampert's observation that Zarathustra 'never once urges any of his hearers to aim at becoming the superman; rather he urges them to prepare the way for the superman', Lampert, *Nietzsche's Teaching*, p. 20.
[415] Rosen, *The Mask of Enlightenment*, p. 43.

between ape and Übermensch. Here what is great in a human being is that he is a going over: what is great in a human being is the ability to transform and to overcome limitations. If this understanding of the Übermensch is plausible, then credence is given to the additional understanding of the connection between friendship and the Übermensch as being one of the realisation of the Übermensch in the marshalling of the friends' capacity for self-overcoming, creativity, and affirmation. Such an understanding would see both friendship and the Übermensch as an immanent rather than future-orientated goal.

Friendship and enmity

The notions of friendship and enmity travel closely in Zarathustra's thought, a companionship already noted in the amendment to *Matthew* 5: 43-44. Although it might appear paradoxical, in *Zarathustra* not only are both friendship and enmity connected as desirable relationships for Zarathustra's followers to cultivate, they can also be understood to be two sides of the same coin. Friends must be capable of being enemies, and enemies are potential friends.[416] Indeed, it could be suggested that in *Zarathustra* the notions of friendship and enmity virtually collapse into one another. This conjunction of friendship and enmity can be said to have two aspects. The first is that the changeableness and even interchangeability of the term and role of friend and enemy is a reflection of the dynamism and malleability of human being itself. Human being is not fixed, and the relationships that it maintains are ultimately acquired. That friends can become enemies, and enemies friends, reflects this fluidity (and sometimes instability) in the human form. The second aspect is that it is possible to see in this formula echoes of an older tradition; that of the Greek dictum of 'helping friends and harming enemies'.[417] In Greek thought and practice this formula was both political and personal, and it helped to direct appropriate action to both friends and enemies. However, in Zarathustra's thought the closeness of the friend and enemy brings the simplicity of this dictum into question. For although it is clear how one should act towards friends and enemies, it is not necessarily clear who the friend and enemy are. Zarathustra's intertwining of the functions of friendship and enmity redirect the direction of this maxim. Now both the friend and the enemy can 'help' the individual insofar as they aid the individual (through complicity or opposition) in progressing towards

---

[416] Rosen, *The Mask of Enlightenment*, p. 122.
[417] See Mary Whitlock Blundell, *Helping Friends and Harming Enemies: A Study in Sophocles and Greek Ethics* (Cambridge: Cambridge University Press, 1989); Malcolm Schofield, *Saving the City: Philosopher-Kings and Other Classical Paradigms* (London: Routledge, 1999); Konstan, *Friendship in the Classical World*.

the goal of self-overcoming, creativity, and the Übermensch. Furthermore, both friends and enemies can be said to be 'harmful' to the individual insofar as they impede this goal in a way that debilitates and weakens the individual.

Set against these considerations it becomes clearer how and why Zarathustra connects enmity and friendship. The move is not as surprising as it might at first seem. For the link between friendship and enmity is explained by Zarathustra's overall task to find those who will understand and act on his message. Those who will do so will employ the necessary means to self-overcoming and creativity, and both the friend and the enemy are desirable for this process. Unlike the failed relationships that Zarathustra sets out in some of the discourses surrounding 'Of War and Warriors' and 'Of the Friend', friendship is by no means soft and yielding, a place of security, a refuge from the world and its challenges, or driven by the despair brought about by lack of self-discipline. On the contrary, the friend and the enemy are similar insofar as they encourage our development and creative overcoming not by indulging us or providing a place of permanent rest (and thus stagnation), but in challenging and opposing.[418] Later Nietzsche has Zarathustra describe the friend as a kind of 'camp-bed': a temporary and hard place of rest for the purposes of recommencing a journey.[419]

This 'harder' view of friendship is in keeping with the agonistic view of friendship developed by Nietzsche previously to *Zarathustra*, although the more explicit focus on the role of enmity is a new development.[420] The friend should not become too soft or yielding. Such a friendship not only threatens further development, but could even be destructive to the progress of the individual. The friend should be an inspiration and a spur upwards.[421] They should also prove a source of affirmation of life itself—in all its terrible aspects. It is this which also tells us something about Zarathustra's view of enmity, and its similarity to friendship. For Zarathustra is not promoting enmity *per se*, but the creative powers of the right kind of enmity. Such enemies are really opponents whose conflict leads not to the destruction and diminishing of the 'loser', but to mutual benefit and enhancement.[422]

---

[418] Rosen, *The Mask of Enlightenment*, p. 102.
[419] Nietzsche, *Zarathustra*, 'Of the Compassionate'. Cf. Smith, 'Two Perspectives on Friendship', p. 69.
[420] Abbey, *Nietzsche's Middle Period*, p. 86.
[421] Appel, *Nietzsche Contra Democracy*, pp. 90-92.
[422] Berkowitz, *Nietzsche*, p. 172. Indeed, Zarathustra claims to harm only out of an act of love, see Lampert, *Nietzsche's Teaching*, p. 51. We saw with the ladder that an appropriate friend must be found for each stage. Perhaps here an appropriate enemy is to be found too.

Enemies are thus considered to be a part of Zarathustra's happiness.[423] Seen from this perspective there is potentially little that separates the friend and the enemy in Zarathustra's thought.

What binds the friend-enemy nexus in Zarathustra's teaching, then, is not just that both friends and enemies can be helpful to the production of the Übermensch. It is also that the friends and enemies are not so dissimilar in terms of their character, and thus their evaluation of each other.[424] For just as Zarathustra does not want just *any* form of friendship, nor does he promote just *any* kind of enmity. The enemy, like the friend, must be respected and revered.[425] As Zarathustra says:

> You may have enemies whom you hate, but not enemies who you despise. You must be proud of your enemy: then the success of your enemy shall be your success too.[426]

The purpose of enmity is the same as that of friendship. It is to spur the individual to greater overcoming. Thus there is considerable overlap between the kinds of people who can be friends and enemies: indeed, they would appear to be within the same class. Just as the friend cannot be someone whom we despise or hold in contempt, nor can the true enemy. It is for this reason that Zarathustra does not declare war on the sick: they are not worthy enemies.[427] However, he is not afraid of provoking an enemy if he thinks that it will aid him, or the contest will aid his enemy.[428]

Pity, merging and solitude

In the preceding sections we have seen that Zarathustra's teaching of friendship is one that distances the relationship from notions of yielding and indulgence. This leads to a consideration of a final group of aspects relating to Zarathustrian friendship, here indicated by the terms pity, merging, and solitude. Zarathustra's struggle to find an

---

[423] Nietzsche, *Zarathustra*, 'The Child With the Mirror'.
[424] Lampert, *Nietzsche's Teaching*, p. 98; Rosen, *The Mask of Enlightenment*, pp. 103, 110.
[425] Nietzsche, *Zarathustra*, 'Of Old and New Law-Tablets'. See also Rosen, *The Mask of Enlightenment*, p. 106; Irving M Zeitlin, *Nietzsche: A Re-Examination* (Oxford: Polity Press, 1994), p. 32.
[426] Nietzsche, *Zarathustra*, 'Of War and Warriors'.
[427] See, for example, Nietzsche, *Zarathustra*, 'Of the Afterworldsmen'. Here Zarathustra claims that he 'is gentle with the sick. Truly, he is not angry at their manner of consolation and ingratitude. May they become convalescents and overcomers…'.
[428] Nietzsche, *Zarathustra*, 'Of the Tarantulas'. On this particular episode (and its wider meaning) see Lampert, *Nietzsche's Teaching*, pp. 52, 95; Rosen, *The Mask of Enlightenment*, pp. 150-152; Conway, *Nietzsche and the Political*, p. 57.

appropriate and sustainable response to suffering and failure is one of the central themes of *Zarathustra*. As one of the main drivers of the drama itself, it is seen repeated in numerous speeches and in Zarathustra's private thoughts.[429] When seen as an aspect of friendship the witness and sharing of suffering and failure presents a special danger. If pity and compassion are debilitating in general (especially when accompanied by the attendant notion of disgust), they are intensified and personalised in the case of friendship. This is the case as not only does Zarathustra place some of his highest hopes for the overcoming of these reactions in friendship, but he also builds into friendship some of his highest hopes for human existence itself. The friend is selected above all others as the channel of these hopes. The friends might expect failure and suffering to be unendurable by most, and the reactions of most to be petty and self-seeking. However, we might also think that the friend who is found wanting is a far greater calamity than even the mire pervading the relationships of the many-too-many. If, as Zarathustra teaches, friendship is a spur to the Übermensch and a festival of the earth, then the failure of the friends is also a failure of these greatest hopes. Zarathustra's own repeated disappointments point to this dynamic.

This is not the only danger. Pity and compassion in friendship also betray something about the characters of the friends themselves. In displaying compassion and pity the friends reveal that they are not treating each other as equals, that they are unworthy of each other, and perhaps even unworthy of friendship itself. Pity and compassion reduce both the person showing pity and the pitied. It is the relationship of unworthy equals. On the one hand the person showing pity reveals that they conceal a kind of superiority towards the other. Pity is reserved for those beneath the friend (who are fit to be its possible objects). Even so, Zarathustrian friends should be beyond pity even for their inferiors. As Zarathustra teaches (and shows in his own drama) it is a mistake to 'give in' to pity as suffering is a condition of existence. Failure to recognise this brings an individual into grave danger.[430] On the other hand, the friend who is being pitied is likely to resent being treated in this way. This resentment is born of their

---

[429] For examples see Nietzsche, *Zarathustra*, 'On the Blissful Islands', 'Of Passing By', and 'Of the Flies in the Market-Place', respectively. Cf. Rosen, *The Mask of Enlightenment*, p. 19. Berkowitz, *Nietzsche*, p. 140. Ansell-Pearson, *An Introduction to Nietzsche as Political Thinker*, p. 120.

[430] Nietzsche, *Zarathustra*, 'Of the Compassionate'. Here Zarathustra's help of a sufferer 'sorely injured his [the sufferer's] pride' and 'a small kindness is not forgotten it becomes a gnawing worm'. Much of what Zarathustra has to say about helping sufferers echoes what Nietzsche has already explored concerning gift-giving and gratitude as exercises of power in his middle period.

realisation that the other considers them inferior, and a fit subject for their own power.[431] Just as this poisons social life in general, so too it poisons the friends and their friendship.

It is for these reasons that Zarathustra counsels that the friends should 'fear nakedness' and that 'you cannot adorn yourself too well for your friend'.[432] The friends should hide both their pity (and reasons to be pitied) from each other. Failure to do so will upset the equilibrium of the friendship and it will also divert the friends from their goal of the Übermensch and self-overcoming. This is not, however, the full story. This advice is also given as a part of Zarathustra's observation that the friend is a mirror of the self. Whilst the face of the friend might well only be 'a rough and imperfect mirror' he is reflective nonetheless. What is reflected back in such a mirror is the face of the one who looks into it. From this it can be inferred that when Zarathustra asks whether one who has stared into the face of his friend is 'startled' at what he sees, Zarathustra is asking whether we are startled by our own self. Zarathustra seems to believe that we would have good cause to be so. We do not truly know ourselves, and we may not like what we see when we come face-to-face with ourselves. Such a reflection should provoke the gazer into self-overcoming. Thus, in adorning himself for his friend, the friend is also adorning himself for himself; and in eschewing pity for his friend, the friend is also eschewing pity for himself. However, whilst applying primarily to the observer, this dictum also has implications for the friendship itself. For in overcoming his own faults, limitations, and dependencies, the individual is also set to overcome the need and desire for friendship itself.

There is, then, a tension at the heart of Zarathustrian friendship. Whilst the friends are able to be brought together because of their similarities in terms of character and goal, ultimately friendship is cast as a resistance to the other with the supreme achievement of friendship being able to break free of the relationship. Whilst something higher might be the *common* goal of friendship, it is not clear from Zarathustra's account what is truly *shared*—or what could be. Indeed, Zarathustra stresses the need for the paths and persons of the friends to remain separate even as they travel and develop together. This distancing is made clear in the discourse 'Of the Friend'. Here Zarathustra proclaims that:

> You should honour even the enemy in your friend. Can you go near to your friend without going over to him?

---

[431] Nietzsche, *Zarathustra*, 'Of the Compassionate'. Cf. Zeitlin, *Nietzsche*, pp. 24-25.
[432] Nietzsche, *Zarathustra*, 'Of the Friend'.

In your friend you should possess your best enemy. Your heart should feel closest to him when you oppose him.

We have already seen that for Zarathustra the friend and enemy are linked.[433] This link is given renewed strength here as the qualities of opposition and otherness usually associated with enmity are stressed *within* friendship. Almost paradoxically, the friends are closest when they are opposed or in contest. The reason is made clear by the consideration as to whether a person can go near to their friend without going over to him. The danger here is that the association of the friends leaves them being too similar. The friend should not seek to create a replica of himself, or seek permanent intimacy, but a worthy opponent. Friends who are too similar lose their selves not because one comes to dominate the other but because they lose the spark and tension that drives each to self-overcoming and creativity. Initially the friends seek each other to prevent themselves from falling too deeply into the abyss that they find within their own selves.[434] However, for Zarathustra the person who has truly overcome himself is capable of solitude. That is to say, the friendship that Zarathustra teaches is how to be a friend to our own self. Such a friendship would enable us to truly be ourselves in the company of others, but it is also a friendship which undermines the need for us to be with others at all. This is reflected in the ambiguous story of Zarathustra's own search for friendship—it is also the foundation for Nietzsche's use of friendship in his later (post-*Zarathustra*) period.

'Every person is a prison': Friendship in the later work

After *Zarathustra* Nietzsche's intellectual terrain has been transformed. *Beyond Good and Evil* both demonstrates this and can be seen to be representative of what is to come. It might also be said that Nietzsche's focus is more panoramic, and his ambition greater. Now Nietzsche is clearly much more overtly concerned with the entire genesis and evolution of European civilization and how it can be further transformed. His ambitions now extend to what he will formulaically term 'a revaluation of all values'. Thus, creativity replaces discovery. With this transformation friendship is eclipsed as a focus, but perhaps can be said to remain as an *ethos*. *Zarathustra* prefigures some of the wider changes which make the terrain for developing friendship more inhospitable. One such change is the extension of the concern with self-

---

[433] Cf. Appel, *Nietzsche Contra Democracy*, p. 92.
[434] Nietzsche, *Zarathustra*, 'Of the Friend'. Here friends are seen as a 'cork' which prevents the self from sinking into an abyss.

discovery into *shaping* the self.[435] This turn displaces the role of friendship. Ultimately whilst friends might be useful in this process each is to develop independence.[436] What is now sought in the human being is not only self-knowledge, but also a kind of self-sufficiency. Only such a person can endure and understand the conditions of late modernity and transform them. In what now becomes a characteristically Nietzschean approach, this is also seen in terms of power.[437] The figure of the Übermensch is virtually abandoned in the later work, but the hopes that such a figure *represented* are now transferred to others. It is now 'aristocratic castes' and 'higher types' that populate Nietzsche's bestiary. Such aristocracies (whether spiritualised or not) are to raise themselves 'to [a] higher task and in general to a higher existence'.[438] Such higher states are seen as the justification of society and sacrifice. Nietzsche thus turns his attention and hopes to those whom Zarathustra seems to forsake. Nietzsche now also speaks to 'free spirits' urging them to prepare the way for the 'philosophers of the future'. Significantly, Nietzsche devotes an entire chapter of *Beyond* to address these experimenters and adventurers.[439] Such free sprits and philosophers of the future are characterised by their courage, independence, and freedom. Thus, the benefits and possibilities that friendship might suggest are sacrificed to a growing concern with individuality and self-sufficiency. Higher human bonding becomes precarious and perhaps even superfluous. The risk of friendship is potential weakness. Free spirits are liberated from the need for companionship and intimacy, although they might still use it in aid of their higher calling.

The tensions of *Zarathustra* — the need for friendship and the need to overcome the friend — are thus reflected in the opening of the Nietzsche's later period. Now the personal qualities of individuals clearly have much wider social and political consequences.[440] However, Nietzsche's views are now much more guarded and are set within his growing concern not only to transform the self but also society.

---

[435] See for example, Friedrich Nietzsche, *Beyond Good and Evil: Prelude to a Philosophy of the Future*, RJ Hollingdale trans. (London: Penguin, 1990 [1886]), §225, 260. As Abbey notes, this had always been a feature of Nietzsche's account of friendship and the self, Abbey, 'Circles, Ladders and Stars', p. 51. However, in *Zarathustra* and beyond it becomes more pronounced as a part of the wider recreation of values.
[436] Nietzsche, *Beyond*, §41, 42.
[437] Nietzsche, *Beyond*, §36, 259.
[438] Nietzsche, *Beyond*, §258.
[439] Nietzsche, *Beyond*, §42.
[440] Nietzsche, *Beyond*, §61, 203. Again, a view implicit in the previous works but brought to prominence in the 'Prologue' of *Zarathustra*.

Relations between members of 'the herd' remain mired in resentment, repressed self-loathing, and a debilitating fear of danger.[441] Nietzsche comes to warn his readers against being taken in by all that is 'common'. Commonality is desired in a 'people' (it binds and brings together), but it tends to make all things similar.[442] As such, for the higher types it destroys the conditions and possibilities of difference and independence.[443] As before, friendship—*true* friendship—remains the preserve of the few. Even so, these few must be judicious in seeking friendship. Do the higher types seek friendship for the right reasons? Moreover, are they motivated by the right kinds of impulses and traits? In answering these questions the higher types will come to evaluate the worth and function of their friendships correctly.

Within these friendships we see again a tension in Nietzsche's thought between our desire to know and our need to deceive. Not intimacy and truth, but distance and staging are the key. In the 'heads and hearts' of our friends we cannot roam exposed. Even here we are misunderstood and appear as masks.[444] Nietzsche also warns how free spirits can be led away from their task of independence and command. Independence must be continually tested. The free spirit must cling to nothing (including fatherland, pity, or virtue). Notably, first amongst Nietzsche's list is friendship itself. In this respect we are told that 'every person is a prison, also a nook and corner'.[445] Perhaps there is a double play of ideas here. Friends might become a prison for us either through our interest in them, or because they draw us away from ourselves. However, if we relate this idea to Nietzsche's concern about the (im)possibilities of genuine communication,[446] it might be that others are a prison insofar as they are locked within themselves and impenetrable to the outside world.

Most tellingly for Nietzsche's later view is that it seems that friendship can survive, but only if it is seen as a part of the economy of enmity and solitude. Nietzsche notes that enmity is needed to sustain friendship. Connecting both friendship and enmity to what is needed for a noble morality Nietzsche writes:

---

[441] Nietzsche, *Beyond*, §44, 201, 202.
[442] Nietzsche, *Beyond*, §268, 284.
[443] Nevertheless, independence is shown by being able to endure and learn from the crowd without succumbing to them. See Nietzsche, *Beyond*, §26.
[444] Nietzsche, *Beyond*, §40.
[445] Nietzsche, *Beyond*, §41.
[446] Friedrich Nietzsche, *Twilight of the Idols/ The Anti-Christ*, 'Expeditions of an Untimely Man', §26.

> The capacity for and the duty of protracted gratitude and protracted revenge—both only among one's equals—subtlety in requital, a refined conception of friendship, a certain need to have enemies (as conduit systems, as it were, for the emotions of envy, quarrelsomeness, arrogance—fundamentally so as to be able to be a good *friend*): all these are typical marks of noble morality...[447]

Such a morality can only exist amongst equals. It is not a morality that is to be extended to those who are inferior. It cannot be extended because what is needed is not equality in a formal sense, but an actual equality of common feelings, impulses, and valuations. This cannot be achieved by reason, it is a function of the kind of person an individual is.[448] One must experience as the other experiences. Nobility is rare, as is friendship. Central to this is the need to love oneself in the right way. We love ourselves in the right way when we do not need the approbation of others, and when we do not fear others and the harm that they might do to us. Such self-love speaks to independence and self-sufficiency. Thus the friends of the post-*Zarathustra* period come before each other in a much more completed state than those before *Zarathustra*. The purpose of their association also seems to have changed. Now their main role is to acknowledge each other rather than aid each other. This seems to be a role that friendship might have in common with enmity. In *Twilight of the Idols* Nietzsche will announce that it is an advantage to have and maintain enemies.[449] Increasingly Nietzsche sees enmity and opposition as the source of values and creativity. Values are created violently, forcefully through imposition.[450] Friendship, it seems, must submit to this too. In the later works friendship becomes something rare. It can be valuable when it is found, but it is not needed for the cataclysmic tasks that lie ahead.

Nietzsche: Overcoming friendship

Nietzsche draws our attention to friendship only to counsel that it is something that must be transcended. This paradoxical manoeuvre is instructive. Nietzsche's return to friendship plays a role in his attempt to think a way out of modernity. His return even suggests a route that would potentially lead him beyond some of modernity's most basic assumptions. Such a route would see a renewed account of friendship. However, Nietzsche fails to fully explore or develop the potential of

---

[447] Nietzsche, *Beyond*, §260.
[448] Cf. Nietzsche, *Beyond*, §43.
[449] Nietzsche, *Twilight*, 'Morality as Anti-Nature', §3.
[450] For examples of this see, *Beyond Good and Evil*, Parts V and IX, *Genealogy*, and *Twilight*, 'Foreword'.

friendship. Despite its promise, Nietzsche's thinking on friendship continues to be constrained by modernity. Yet Nietzsche's failure to overcome these constraints and to think through friendship indicates something wider about the fate of friendship in modernity. Here we witness a strange and surprising symmetry between Nietzsche's thought and modernity, a symmetry which is shaped by the limits of a self aiming at individuality, autonomy, and power.

How does Nietzsche's thought come to rest at this impasse? Given that friendship has not been a central theme of thought in modernity, Nietzsche might already be considered atypical in addressing it at all. Amongst those who have focused on friendship in modernity Nietzsche is atypical in another respect: drawing from the Greeks he views friendship as a *problem*. He also views it as being *dangerous*. Nietzsche's framing of the issue of friendship in this way indicates its significance for his endeavour. Nietzsche thought that friendship was something that was in need of resolution. It indicated a particularly powerful form of human bonding which could be both productive and destructive. As such, it was essential to analyse and understand friendship, to accommodate it and — if possible — put it to use. For one of Nietzsche's central concerns regarding friendship is to question whether this form of bonding can provide a basis for self-discovery and later a form of self-creation. Furthermore, Nietzsche realises that the products and effects of these features need not be limited to a *personal* relation. Nietzsche looks to the relationship to see whether it can provide a basis for a wider refashioning of values. Nietzsche's later view sees the higher types, aristocrats, free spirits, and the philosophers of the future brought into relation through their common task.

Friendship then, often considered one of the most personal and intimate of human connections, is entertained in Nietzsche's thought in terms of a wider and more encompassing task. Friends will use their abilities and persons to reshape self and others, and society itself is refashioned as a product of these bonds. Such a vision may well be elitist, but does hold out some possibility of a creative human bonding in which value can be enshrined. An elite might be preferable to nihilism. For Nietzsche it is the only way out. In this way Nietzsche takes the form of the philosophical circle of the Greeks with its aim of discovering the self, truth and the good and then extending these as widely as possible, and mixes it with his own concerns with self-creation and the revival of value, and entertains it as a nucleus for revitalising Europe as a whole.

In terms of the Greek heritage, Nietzsche sees friendship as a part of both the development of the self and as a good for the right sorts of people. He connects friendship to the Greek ideal of philosophy. As a philologist the connection between philosophy and friendship would have been obvious to Nietzsche both etymologically and conceptually. A truly philosophical life was a life spent with like-minded others. Such a life saw friendships which transcended the common motivations for bonding: utility, pleasure, sexual desire and kin. For Nietzsche it must also transcend fear and feebleness. The best friendships were both pure and rare. They were a mark of distinction. Nietzsche retains this view. However, in transferring friendship into the modern idiom Nietzsche restructures the framework that supported these conclusions. In Nietzsche's account friendship veers much more towards the *person* of the friends. This is a move which is pre-empted in the thought of Montaigne in the focus of his essay on friendship, but also in his stress on the uniqueness of his relationship with Boétie. Now friendship becomes connected not so much with standard characteristics of individuals who are capable of friendship (i.e. a character capable of displaying the virtues), but with what is unique and particular about the friends. In this idiom friendships are tailored to the individuals who form them and can take a variety of forms. Nietzsche must stress this uniqueness and particularity not only because he divests himself of the certainty of a moral framework, but also because he wishes friendship to be creative. In Nietzsche's view, friendship can only be creative if it is focused beyond what is common and merely formulaic.

Why, then, does Nietzsche go cold on friendship? Furthermore, what does this cooling indicate for us about not only Nietzsche's approach to friendship, but that of modernity more generally? The early promise of the middle period cannot withstand the strain placed on it in the more exacting and extreme structure of *Zarathsutra*. In the later works friendship is largely abandoned. It is replaced by the themes of solitude and struggle, and the attendant fear of isolation. This abandonment is partly forced by the development of Nietzsche's wider concerns. However, it would be a mistake to think these wider views are merely idiosyncratic to Nietzsche's thought. On the contrary, they are also indicative of some of the wider features of modernity which have closed down thinking on friendship. In this sense Nietzsche can be seen to both diagnose the dynamics of modernity and take them to their very limit. Friendship becomes victim to this drive. Although he is critical of the varieties of liberalism and the inheritance of Christianity, Nietzsche shares with liberalism and Christianity one important concern: a focus on individuality. In addition, in common with liberalism (and in a more subtle way with Christianity), Nietzsche also sees this played-out in terms of power. The individual seeks power over themselves and over others as a means to autonomy; at the very least, the individual seeks to preserve their autonomy by avoiding the threat of power from others. These concerns can be seen to be a part of the wider framework of modernity itself. Clearly Nietzsche is no liberal—not even an eccentric one. Diverse as its membership is, liberalism must mark Nietzsche out as *persona non grata*. His defence of inequality and suffering alone bar him from association. However, although Nietzsche rejects both the liberal and the Christian view of these themes, he develops radicalised variations of them in his own thinking. In particular he comes to place value in creative and autonomous individuals who have the power to organise and subdue both self and others. In so doing Nietzsche fails to think outside of modernity, albeit that he takes individuality and power to their very limits. Ultimately these themes prove obstacles for a more productive reworking of friendship in Nietzsche's thought, and a more productive reworking of friendship in modernity *per se*. They close down the possibilities for shared endeavours and ways of being with others which are not predicated on the detached, autonomous, and individual view of the self.

With respect to friendship and the self, Nietzsche's insight of the decentred self points to an unexplored avenue. Such a view of the self could have fashioned an extremely innovative view of friendship. Such a view would have the potential to be more novel than even the view that Nietzsche develops. As we have seen, the decentred self is the correlative of Nietzsche's perspectivism. The malleability of the self and its relations also does a good deal of work in Nietzsche's later thought when he turns his attention to the future of Europeans. Somewhat disappointingly, the possibilities of this view of the self suggested by the middle period and in *Zarathsutra* are closed down rather than explored and exploited. The decentred self that Nietzsche entertains suggests an alternative to the 'individuation' that is adopted in *Zarathsutra*, and the autonomous and self-sufficient individual of the later period. For rather than view the decentred self as being in need of individuation whereby that term is understood to denote a strict separation of self from other, it could be pursued in another direction. This direction would take Nietzsche's idea that there is no 'core' or 'stable' self more seriously. In so doing it might be thought that rather than a strict division between self and other, individuation points to not only what differentiates self from other, but also what selves share. Here something more is intended than simply pointing to features of selves which are the same, or paths on which they both happen to be developing. Sharing is intended to suggest that *if* a decentred view of the self is taken seriously then there are features suggested in friendship that cannot truly be said to belong to either of the friends, but exist to both only in relation.

This thought of shared selfhood and the intrinsic relationality of bonding is difficult as it is a challenge to the centred view of the self which predominates in both Ancient and Modern thought. Indeed, it is a view which is common to the Greeks, Christianity and liberalism. If this alternative view has merit, it would suggest that the bonds between person and person are established in a much more embedded way than is usually thought. Whilst individuation and even individuality might be promoted as an ideal, such an ideal can only be considered a partial abstraction from reality. Indeed, from the perspective offered by this view we might question whether 'individuality' as it is understood in modernity is either a realistic or desirable goal at all.

Nietzsche, of course, opens these possibilities in his account of friendship; but his focus and ambition is elsewhere. Intriguingly these possibilities are most clearly suggested by the figure of the circle where there is a good deal that is potentially shared. Nietzsche seems to abandon this metaphor in favour of the dynamics suggested by the ladder. Even here, there is a possibility of deeper sharing and even a shared self. In their *agon* the friends of the ladder-friendship help to shape each other. The friends are not their own creation—at least not entirely. Indeed, in the ladder-friendship development is predicated on the actions of another. If the friend cannot aid our development we are to find one who can. The selves of the friends in the ladder-friendship are dependent on others and perhaps not as distinct as Nietzsche would wish. Nietzsche obscures the implications of this. Perhaps he cannot move away from the prejudice that creativity and individuality are linked. Perhaps he cannot bring himself to distinguish between productive and debilitating forms of a shared identity. Nietzsche is surely missing something significant here, and ignoring too readily the creative possibilities of combination and sharing. Whatever his reasons, Nietzsche turns away from merging and sharing and comes to stress the need for 'hardness' in friendship.

In Nietzsche's later thought it is this sense of 'hardness' that comes to predominate. It shapes and restricts Nietzsche's search for a *use* for friendship. Here we see Nietzsche's ambivalence between valuing friendship in its own terms, and valuing friendship only insofar as it serves a particular function or purpose. Of course, Nietzsche is not the first thinker to view friendship as having a purpose—this is something already represented in views such as Francis Bacon's, and in some of the Graeco-Roman accounts. These views tend to stress that whilst friendship might bring some benefit to the participants, it is aimed at some other goal, be this a higher goal (as was Socrates' view) or a more practical and worldly goal (as was Bacon's view). As Nietzsche's thought develops we see friendship deployed to serve a variety of goals: self-discovering, self-shaping, a foretaste of the Übermensch, and preparation for the philosophers of the future. These shifts are similar insofar as they see a common task for friendship. It is easy enough to see how this could bring friends together. However, we might be tempted to note in the variations of the nature of the common tasks that Nietzsche sees for friendship that increasingly friendship becomes future orientated. Whereas self-discovery is connected to the idea of bringing something that is already present to light, the later views of friendship see a focus on realising something that is yet to be. Nietzsche's account of friendship sacrifices present benefits and sincerity for future hopes. There seems to be very little in the relationship which is worth preserving except that which enables the friends to move apart. This raises the question as to what really binds the friends in Nietzschean friendship—especially in its later incarnations. Increasingly Nietzsche pushes aside the possibility of a genuine and sustained intimacy. Having done so he is left with little to bind friendship. When this is coupled with his growing insistence on a strong sense of individuation and his focus on autonomy and power friendship is brought to a point of self-cancellation. Ultimately Nietzsche promotes the need to prove our independence by overcoming and moving beyond both the friend and friendship itself. Friends are bound together in acts of mutual resistance and repulsion.

In the final analysis, Nietzschean friends must overcome their friends, and the *purpose* of friendship is to transcend the *need* for friendship. Nietzsche infuses friendship with a sense of dynamism, discovery, and creativity. He fashions a view of friendship which stresses its uniqueness. It is a view of friendship which stresses the role of the *person*. It is perhaps regrettable that Nietzsche could not commit to a more positive view of friendship which broke away from the autonomous and individualised model of the self. That he could not tells us something not only about the obstacles that Nietzsche's thought faced in theorising friendship, but also something about the hazards thrown up by modernity itself.

Nietzsche, then, is an ambivalent friend of friendship. He touches again on friendship as a problem, and recognises that this form of bonding can have wider consequences. However, in remaining committed to some of the tenets of modernity he can only sustain his commitment to friendship if it is something which aims at the self-sufficiency of the individual. What is redeeming about Nietzsche's *ethos* is that he continues to dream of his friends—his later works can be seen as a calling out to them wherever they might be waiting. Moreover, Nietzsche continues to cherish the idea of friendship in his thoughts, letters and relationships with others. What is perhaps tragic about Nietzsche's thought is that his ideal of friendship is so demanding that it is unlikely that anyone could ever meet its challenge.

Chapter Six

Schmitt

CARL SCHMITT is one of the most trenchant and controversial thinkers of the Twentieth century. Diverse in scope—and with a tendency to mix theory with a critique of contemporary problems—Schmitt's thought has been variously cast in a number of political guises: authoritarian liberal, revolutionary conservative, advocate of *realpolitik*, supporter of differing shades of dictatorship, fascist, and apologist for Nazism.[451] In this respect, and especially given his association with

---

[451] For a general discussion of this reception (and attempts to 'define' Schmitt) see Renato Cristi, *Carl Schmitt and Authoritarian Liberalism: Strong State, Free Economy*, Political Philosophy Now (Cardiff: University of Wales Press, 1998), pp. 1-18. For views on Schmitt's location on the Right see Joseph W Bendersky, *Carl Schmitt: Theorist for the Reich* (Princeton, New Jersey: Princeton University Press, 1983), pp. 285-286. Bendersky argues that the 'crucial element' of Schmitt's thought is the state as 'Only the state can guarantee the basic human and societal requirements of order, peace, and stability'. Bendersky also notes that for Schmitt 'The state must also represent the interests of the nation as a whole and not merely sections of it'. Hirst takes a similar line, see Paul Hirst, 'Carl Schmitt's Decisionism', *Telos* 72(Summer), 1987, p. 22. Hirst views Schmitt as a supporter of 'commissarial dictatorship' which acts to restore stability. Both of these accounts seem to elide the issue of what—exactly—counted as the nation and stability for Schmitt. Others take a stronger line. Axtmann argues that 'Schmitt embraces the fascist *stato totalitario'*, see Roland Axtmann, 'Humanity or Enmity? Carl Schmitt on International Politics', *International Politics* 44(5), 2007, p. 531. Wolin argues that post-1927 Schmitt transforms 'his authoritarian political philosophy of the early 1920s into a protofascistic, conservative revolutionary partisanship for a totalitarian state', see Richard Wolin, 'Carl Schmitt: The Conservative Revolutionary Habitus and the Aesthetics of Horror', *Political Theory* 20(3), 1992, p. 440. Both Caldwell and Wiegandt link Schmitt's thought *directly* to that of the Nazi's, see Peter Caldwell, 'National Socialism and Constitutional Law: Carl Schmitt, Otto Koellreutter, and the Debate Over the Nature of the Nazi State, 1933-1937', *Cardozo Law Review* 16(December), 1994-1995; Manfred H Weigandt, 'The Alleged Unaccountability of the Academic: A Biographical Sketch of Carl Schmitt', *Cardozo Law Review* 16(5), 1994-1995. For Caldwell, 'Schmitt... fully accepted the two tenets of Nazi rule: the Fürher principle; and the principle of the essential unity of *Artgleichheit* (unity of species, type, or race) of the German Volk', p. 408. For Wiegandt 'there is a connection between the contents of Schmitt's work and his involvement in National Socialism', p, 1596. As will be seen, in this chapter the view is taken that

Nazism and his limbo of unrepentant disgrace following World War Two,[452] it is perhaps surprising that Schmitt's thought has come to influence not only the Right, but also the Left. Whereas the Right find in Schmitt's thought justification for 'exceptionalism' and the need for a strong state, the Left have been drawn to his critique of liberalism which they have attempted to reclaim for their own purposes. Thus, the positioning of Schmitt's thought, and the question as to whether it can ever be free from Nazi contamination, has been a site of intellectual warfare. Yet, in a sense, the importance of Schmitt's thought does not rest in the details of his exact position, or even in whether his thought can be rehabilitated and reclaimed.[453] For however it is framed, we simply cannot escape the conclusion that Schmitt is a thinker of the authoritarian Right. Nor can any amount of contextualisation conjure away the fact that Schmitt both applauded and supported the cause of fascism.[454]

Given his politics, Schmitt is not, therefore, a theorist whose views should be admired or emulated. However, it is hard to see how Schmitt's themes can be 'sanitised' by attempting to separate them from his politics. If separation is impossible then Schmitt is tainted and this threatens to contaminate others. If they can be separated then we are left with the question of why read Schmitt? What do we get from Schmitt that we cannot get from other sources (and without the complications)?[455] This is not the only problem. Schmitt's writings also have an almost inextricable tendency to draw the reader on to his terrain. This ground is already structured by assumptions about the nature and importance of entities such as the state and nation, and ideas such as homogeneity and sovereignty. Once we have ventured on to this terrain it is difficult to turn back. The consequences of this venturing are to begin to accept the possibilities and limitations created by the geography of Schmitt's authoritarian landscape, and to fall victim to his state-centric and nationalist logic. Given this, if any benefit

---

Schmitt's political thought is inescapably bound up with his normative promotion of a form of authoritarian *nation*-state. Thus his collaboration with the Nazis is *consistent* with his thought (although not a necessary conclusion). Schmitt's view of friendship is also conditioned by these normative commitments. It is therefore characterised by the themes of homogeneity, inequality, and violence.

[452] Weigandt, 'The Alleged Unaccountability of the Academic: A Biographical Sketch of Carl Schmitt', p. 1596.

[453] Cf. Benno Teschke, 'Decision and Indecisions', *New Left Review* 67(January-February), 2011, p. 79.

[454] See Richard Wolin, 'Carl Schmitt, Political Existentialism, and the Total State', *Theory and Society* 19(4), 1990.

[455] Andrew W Neal, *Exceptionalism and the Politics of Counter-Terrorism: Liberty, Security, and the War on Terror* (Abingdon: Routledge, 2010), p. 138.

is to be derived from reading Schmitt, it is to be drawn not so much from what he said, but from reflecting on *what* he thinks about, and *how* he thinks about it. Thus, Schmitt's value is not that he can offer us some especially novel political theory (by his own admission he often draws from, or works against, the insights of others), but that his thought can tell us something about a certain way of thinking. In particular, it is illuminating in what it has to show us about the assumptions that allow the neglect of friendship in modernity. This general approach thus concurs with the view of Andrew W. Neal, who has written that we need 'to be careful about reading Schmitt as a source of political wisdom rather than as a symptomatic figure who must be problematized'.[456]

It is against this backdrop — and its obvious dangers — that we locate our concern with friendship. Schmitt makes the link between the political and friendship most clearly (and polemically) in *The Concept of the Political*. It is here that it is claimed that 'The concept of the state presupposes the concept of the political' and that 'the specific distinction to which political actions and motives can be reduced is that between friend and enemy'.[457] Much has been said by commentators about what Schmitt means by 'the political'. However, whilst some attention has been given to 'the enemy', less has been said concerning what Schmitt might mean by 'the friend'.[458] We might be tempted to ask why this is the case. Such a question is important. As indicated, it has implications that span beyond an interest in Schmitt and connect to a trend in modernity itself. In order to address this question a little groundwork is needed. Here the approach to this question is configured along two main lines. First, Schmitt is recognised as a polemicist. This recognition is necessary if we are to understand how Schmitt intends his writings to operate, and how he approaches and frames problems. In this respect the aim of Schmitt's thought and writing is to politicise. That is to say, the purpose is not simply to make issues political, but to create opposing camps. As we shall see, there is thus a symmetry between Schmitt's use of politicisation and his view

---

[456] Neal, *Exceptionalism*. This chapter has benefited from the method that Neal uses to approach the issue of 'exceptionalism'.
[457] Carl Schmitt, *The Concept of the Political*, George Schwab trans. (Chicago and London: The University of Chicago Press, 1996 [1927, 1932]), pp. 19, 26.
[458] On 'the enemy' see especially Predrag Petrovic, 'Enemy as the Essence of the Political', *Western Balkans Security Observer* 13(April-June), 2009. On 'the friend' see Aryeh Botwinick, 'Same/Other verses Friend/Enemy: Levinas contra Schmitt', *Telos* 132(Fall), 2005; Gabriella Slomp, *Carl Schmitt and the Politics of Hostility, Violence and Terror* (Basingstoke, England: Palgrave Macmillan, 2009); Ibid., 'Carl Schmitt on Friendship: Polemics and Diagnostics', *Critical Review of International Social and Political Philosophy* 10(2), 2007.

and use of the friend-enemy distinction. Indeed, the friend-enemy distinction *itself* is a tool of polemicisation. Second, it is suggested that Schmitt's use of 'the friend' is best understood as a functional device which contributes towards his polemical objectives. As a result, Schmitt's interest in 'the friend' should not be taken at face-value. He says little of substance on the friend, but this 'empty' category is not simply to be considered a failure of definition. Instead it is a rhetorical trope which is employed to both help structure Schmitt's aim of asserting the normative importance of the nation-state, and to serve as a screen on to which the reader projects their own assumptions about friendship (assumptions which are conditioned by modernity and cultivated by Schmitt's prose). In this way Schmitt is able to channel our understanding of friendship and the political along his pre-determined lines and ultimately towards the conclusion that he wishes us to reach. Even if we do not accept his conclusions our thought is, nevertheless, held hostage on his territory.

Schmitt as polemicist

Under Schmitt's pen a link is forged between friendship and polemics, and Schmitt's use of 'the friend' is intimately connected to other aspects of his thought. In particular, the role that the friend plays is shaped by the very concrete and immediate problems and dilemmas that were often the stimuli for Schmitt's writing. In this light it is instructive to consider Schmitt's own claim about accounts of the political in *Concept*. Here Schmitt not only recognises the polemical nature of his *own* political thought; it is his claim that *all* political thought is polemical in nature. Schmitt writes that:

> ...all political concepts, images, and terms have a polemic meaning. They are focused on a specific conflict and bound to a concrete situation; the result (which manifests itself in war or revolution) is a friend-enemy grouping, and they turn into empty and ghostlike abstractions when this situation disappears.[459]

Schmitt's thought does not exist in a vacuum, nor is its primary approach an abstract investigation of the perennial questions and themes of political philosophy. Instead, Schmitt's thought is generated by the pressing questions and problems thrown-up by the concrete political situation in which he was situated. Thus his thought can be seen to be operating within a shifting context characterised by instability, and a crisis of authority and community before, during, and after the Second World War. In Schmitt's thought we see a response

---

[459] Schmitt, *Concept*, p. 30. See also Teschke, 'Decision and Indecisions', p. 90.

which is both tied to the importance of the state, but which recognises the shifting landscape in which the state is now adrift. The notion of the friend (and enemy) is crucial for Schmitt's re-conceptualisation of the political in this state of affairs, but it is also important in its role in reinforcing Schmitt's own view of the normative importance of the state. For the friend-enemy distinction is one which speaks both to polemics *and* to the logic of the nation-state. The friend-enemy distinction creates an inside and outside, and this maps on to both the nation-state and Schmitt's approach to identifying and 'resolving' political problems. For Schmitt, political problems are resolved by groups in conflict; and the identification and resolution of political problems is dependent on the friend-enemy distinction and the grouping that this entails.

Here, then, there is a symmetry between Schmitt's use of polemics and his invocation of the friend. In his hands both are devices which are intended to divide protagonists into groupings. Such a move is intended not only to bring a stark clarity to theoretical problems, but also to the dynamics and action required in concrete political situations.[460] Here, the friend is a way of analysing and responding to the very problems of political unity and political action that Schmitt diagnosed around him.[461] Thus, friendship is not merely polemical, but it is ultimately a tool of polemicisation. The polemical nature of Schmitt's work represents his own structuring of the political and his own decision about which side he was on regarding the concrete issues that challenged him and his milieu. As polemics, Schmitt's writings also challenge their reader. Can they resist coming on to Schmitt's territory and playing a game where Schmitt has set the rules?

Functional friendship

The second approach to understanding the role that friendship plays in Schmitt's thought is to consider it primarily in terms of *function*: what does the friend signify, and what are the consequences of Schmitt's construction of the friend for the coherence and attractiveness of his thought? This complements the view already suggested that the friend is a polemical device. If it is the case that the friend both divides

---

[460] Cf. Slomp's view of Schmitt's defence at Nurenberg. Slomp, 'Carl Schmitt on Friendship: Polemics and Diagnostics', p. 209.
[461] On this problem see the diagnosis of offered by Schmitt in *The Crisis of Parliamentary Democracy*. This book is especially clear on the *political* unity which is needed for democracy and how this conflicts with liberalism and parliamentarianism. See Carl Schmitt, *The Crisis of Parliamentary Democracy*, Ellen Kennedy trans. (Cambridge, Massachusetts, and London, England: The MIT Press, 1988 [1923, 1926]), pp. 22-32.

protagonists and makes issues political, then how is this achieved and what does it mean to talk of 'the friend'? In terms of filling out the notion of the friend, it has already been noted that contemporary commentators have tended to neglect this aspect of Schmitt's thought. However, in terms of a *definitional* enterprise they are not the only culprits—nor are they the first. For despite making the friend-enemy distinction crucial for an understanding of the political, Schmitt actually says surprisingly little about what the friend actually is. This observation should elicit a pause and raise a question: what is going on in Schmitt's writing that he leaves one of his central categories undefined? Moreover, what is Schmitt attempting to achieve by employing such an empty category?

It is virtually inconceivable that Schmitt's omission to produce a sustained and rounded definition of 'the friend' is an intellectual failing. Such a view is not only uncharitable, it also flies in the face of Schmitt's obvious intellectual capabilities. More importantly, it is also unnecessary to conclude this. Instead we should entertain the idea that Schmitt's contribution to our understanding of the friend is not all that it seems. As we shall see, Schmitt allows the category of the friend to be suggested but never truly demarcated or explored. It is a notion which stands empty. In using the friend in this way, Schmitt is able to deploy it as a structuring device for his argument as a whole. The reader is allowed to project their own assumptions into this space, and the temptation to challenge the construction that Schmitt provides is thereby evaded. Thus, the content of 'the friend' is inferred or assumed in two ways. First, it is inferred from what Schmitt says (more overtly and more fully) about 'the enemy'. As we shall see, 'the enemy' is framed as an 'existential threat' to the friend. Second, the meaning of friendship is implied to the reader from what Schmitt asserts about the supposed 'unity' required for (and imposed by) the state. In addition, where Schmitt does have something positive to say about friendship his view reflects and reinforces exclusionary, bellicose, and statist parameters and assumptions relying (as he does) on rather normatively dubious notions such as homogeneity, 'ways of life' and—much more disturbingly—ethnic identity. Schmitt's game is to leave his reader to fill in the blanks in a structure that he has already created. In so doing the reader is enticed into both completing and coalescing in the structure of Schmitt's thinking. In terms of the friend, the reader's complicity in filling in the blanks and accepting the basic premises of Schmitt's game leads to a position where it is strategically difficult to dismiss Schmitt's conclusions—however much the reader might wish to reject them in both theory and practice.

Challenging Schmitt on the friend

In what follows the role that friendship plays in Schmitt's thought will be investigated in terms of both its polemical and functional construction. Two texts will be of particular significance: *The Concept of the Political* and *Constitutional Theory*. By reading these two texts together, we can come to make Schmitt's polemical technique and his rhetorical use of an empty but functional friendship more apparent. We need to ask not only what Schmitt *means* by the friend, but also what *work* the friend does in legitimating Schmitt's normative assumptions about both the nation and the state. However, this investigation will also be framed by the view of friendship which underpins this enquiry as a whole: a concern with the bonds between person and person. Thus Schmitt's own polemics will be supplemented (and subverted) by highlighting what is obscured by his rhetoric in *Concept*. In contrast to Schmitt's own avoidance of providing a definition for the notion of the friend, a form of bonding can be discerned: the homogenous nation. It is this form of bonding which underpins both his account of the friend and his account of the state and the political more generally. Indeed, this form of bonding can be considered to be both an ontological and normative 'fact' of Schmitt's account of the political.

Thus, it is claimed that for Schmitt friendship is not *merely* the opposite of enmity (where enmity is conceived as an existential threat), although it is linked to it. On the contrary, Schmitt has in mind a grouping which is bound up with the foundations of the state: a people. A people is not any mere grouping, but an historical and homogenous bond typically based around a common way of life, land, and ethnicity. As a nation, it is an expression of unity, identity, and will. Schmitt's real legacy is to underwrite the notion of the friend with a normative view of this form of bonding, and to attach the notion of the friend to that of the state. Schmitt's presentation might well appear to be abstracted from these foundations, but they inform his enterprise nonetheless. For whereas in *Concept* Schmitt appears to leave the details of the friend open, he curtails the possibilities of friendship along contours established by his own (normative) preference for the nation-state. It is in *Constitutional* that we can see these contours more clearly, and it is here that Schmitt's commitment to 'peoples' understood a homogenous unity is made explicit. It is these groups which are capable of recognising themselves politically as nations, who bequeath themselves a constitution, and marshal the state. For Schmitt, they do so by recognising themselves as a friendship group (and thus having the possibility of identifying an enemy). They are the primary way in which Schmitt understands and theorises the bonds between person and person. Persons are only really of significance insofar as they contribute towards the life of the group.

Concept, then, should not be read alone, and should not be taken as Schmitt's final word on the notion of the friend. Indeed, as Gabriella Slomp has demonstrated, it is useful to supplement what Schmitt has to say in *Concept* with what he writes elsewhere.[462] In her illuminating study *Carl Schmitt and the Politics of Hostility* Slomp develops an account of friendship which maps on to Schmitt's development of the enemy concept in *The Theory of the Partisan* (1963).[463] Slomp uses Schmitt's typology of enmity to develop a typology of friendship. Here three forms of friendship are identified: (1) game-like friendship (the weakest form describing the connection between citizens in 'depoliticised' states); (2) existential or real friendship (which is much stronger and denotes the willingness to kill and be killed for others and is located in time and space); and finally (3) abstract friendship (which sees friends connected to unknown others through abstractions such as ideologies). The discussion here does not take issue with the categories in that account. As a way of approaching Schmitt on friendship in terms of a definitional endeavour they are useful. In this respect this discussion focuses almost exclusively on what Slomp would term 'existential or real friendship', the kind of friendship which is found *within* the state (although this has consequences for relations between states). This is the kind of friendship that Schmitt seems to have in mind in both *Constitutional* and *Concept*.

It is recognised that Slomp's work goes a long way in the direction of identifying and reconstructing a Schmittian account of friendship. However, the focus here is somewhat different to that of Slomp. The concern here is not so much with definition but with the *role* that friendship plays in the structure of Schmitt's thought. As a result three related moves are made. First, the endeavour is to undermine the logic of *Concept* which sets up the terms of the link between friendship and the political; second, to show how *Concept* allows Schmitt to deploy friendship to draw the reader into his own normative view of the state and the intractability of conflict; and finally to show how this view is expanded more openly in Schmitt's more general discussion of 'peoples' and 'nations' in *Constitutional*. It is here that Schmitt reveals that what he has in mind to fill the gap demarcated by friendship is not only a nation-state, but one which is homogenous and subordinates the individual—at least if it is to be 'successful' in its protection of ways of

---

[462] Slomp, 'Carl Schmitt on Friendship: Polemics and Diagnostics'; Ibid., *Carl Schmitt and the Politics of Hostility*.

[463] Slomp, *Carl Schmitt and the Politics of Hostility*, p.112ff. and esp.116-118.

life. It is this last observation which links Schmitt to the wider discourse of modernity: a discourse which also tends to view the bonds between person and person as being mediated via a sovereign nation-state.

Finding friendship: Schmitt's distillation of the political

The Concept of the Political is perhaps Schmitt's best-known book and the one that has particular fascination for those concerned with politics.[464] The ideas for the essay were beginning to be structured during Schmitt's seminar on 'Political Philosophy' at Bonn during 1925-1926.[465] The essay itself started life in 1927 and went through several revisions.[466] *Concept* presents its reader with two related theses. The first is that the defining criterion of the political is the friend-enemy distinction. It is this that sets the political apart from all other categories and considerations. The second is that human existence is grounded in the fact of conflict and the possibility of killing. For Schmitt violence cuts right-down and right-through human co-existence. The friend-enemy distinction is therefore presented by Schmitt as a decision by an entity about its self-preservation. However, it is a decision which crystallises the realisation of the most intense association and disassociation. In other words, Schmitt presents the decision as transforming the group—but presupposes that some group already exists to make the decision, or (more pertinently for Schmitt) to recognise and identify with the decision of another. In this way, Schmitt can present friendship as denoting the most irreducible homogeneity, and enmity heterogeneity (where the emphasis is on the Greek etymology of these terms). As such, friendship is irreducibly political and it subordinates all other concerns: first because it concerns matters of life and death; but second, because it suggests the basis of community and obligation to community. Ultimately friendship and enmity result in either killing or being killed by the enemy; and dying

---

[464] Thomas Moore, 'The Paradox of the Political: Carl Schmitt's Autonomous Account of Politics', *The European Legacy* 15(6), 2010, p. 721; Mark Lilla, *The Reckless Mind: Intellectuals in Politics* (New York: New York Review of Books, 2001), p. 56; Paul Gottfried, *Carl Schmitt: Politics and Theory* (London: Greenwood Press, 1990), p. 57.

[465] Bendersky, *Carl Schmitt*, p. 88. Bendersky also discusses the book's reception, pp. 85-103. For an examination of the book's relationship to Schmitt's wider reception (and especially the question of its connection to Nazism) see: Gottfried, *Carl Schmitt: Politics and Theory*, pp. 57-74.

[466] The history of these revisions can be found outlined and briefly discussed in the following: Cristi, *Carl Schmitt and Authoritarian Liberalism*, pp. 169-172. Cf. also Axtmann, 'Humanity or Enmity?' p. 535.

with or for friends.⁴⁶⁷ How, then, does Schmitt produce such a dangerous conclusion?

At the beginning of *Concept* Schmitt makes two related moves which attempt to draw the essence of the political out from domains and concepts with which it is otherwise confused. The first of these is the notion of the state. The second is concerned with what Schmitt identifies as realms of 'human endeavour' such as morality and economics. These moves are made by Schmitt not only to get to the essence of the political but also to claim that there is something *distinctive* and *autonomous* about it. As Schmitt writes, the political 'is independent of [the other endeavours] and as such can speak clearly for itself'.⁴⁶⁸ However, as we shall see, having identified the distinctiveness of the political (determined by the friend-enemy distinction), Schmitt then re-fuses this notion with the other elements to show the political in motion. Given Schmitt's initial insistance on the separation of the political from the state this move might seem to represent a slippage — perhaps even a mistake. In fact, what this reveals is Schmitt's assumptions about what the basic building blocks of the political really are: peoples. It is these that are bound together as basic friendship groups. Thus, what Schmitt is showing is not that the political *must* manifest in the state, but what a state which fully embraces the political would look like, and how it should behave. States which fail to recognise the truth about their political nature cede it to those who will. This, after all, was the very challenge that Schmitt thought was facing the Weimar Republic.⁴⁶⁹ It is also these assumptions which help to underpin the accounts of modern thinkers such as Hobbes, Locke, and Rousseau.

Let us turn first to Schmitt's move to attempt to separate the notion of the state from that of the political. Famously, Schmitt opens *Concept* with the claim that 'The concept of the state presupposes the concept of

---

⁴⁶⁷ Schmitt, *Concept*, pp. 27, 35, 37.
⁴⁶⁸ Schmitt, *Concept*, p. 26.
⁴⁶⁹ See Carl Schmitt, *State, Movement, People: The Triadic Structure of the Political Unity*, Simona Draghici trans. (Corvallis, Oragon: Plutarch Press, 2001 [1933]). In this essay (written after Hilter's seizure of power) Schmitt is unambiguous in his conclusion that the liberal-democratic Weimar Constitution was the author of its own demise. On p. 4 (and echoed on p. 34) Schmitt claims that it resulted in a 'suicidal neutrality, when there is no longer any equalisation or rather the absence of discrimination between the enemy of the State and the friend of the State, between the comrade of the people and the alien'. National-Socialism is presented as the solution to this suicidal inertia. Cf. Weigandt, 'The Alleged Unaccountability of the Academic: A Biographical Sketch of Carl Schmitt', pp. 1569-1571.

the political'.[470] Whereas the state is seen as merely a form or *instance* of politics, for Schmitt the political is a wider, more encompassing, and more fundamental notion.[471] On this reading the state and its concerns may well form a locus of politics, but it is more properly understood as one concrete manifestation of the political. What is also important about Schmitt's opening move here is what he goes on to say about the state itself. Schmitt claims that the state 'is the political status of an organised people in an enclosed territorial unit' and that 'in its historical appearance the state is a specific entity of a people'.[472] This indicates two things with the first being more apparent than the second. First, Schmitt is identifying the state as an historical entity. This is entirely consistent with his view of the state as being a derived manifestation of the political. The concept of the political has broad historical sweep (and can manifest in many ways) whereas the state is a particular manifestation of the political in modern times.[473] The second thing which is indicated here is more easily overlooked, and its meaning is less clear. Schmitt's opening to *Concept* links the idea of the state to the idea of 'a people'. Schmitt does not here elaborate what he has in mind by invoking this notion. Indeed, it is easy not to notice this as Schmitt's focus appears to be fixed on the task of isolating the state. However, this observation is noted here as the notion of a people is a central category for understanding both Schmitt's account of the state *and* the kind of bonding that 'the friend' indicates.

Regardless of the detail of what Schmitt might mean by invoking the idea of 'a people', linking it to the notion of 'the state' at this early stage raises two questions. These questions threaten to destabilise the

---

[470] Schmitt, *Concept*, p. 19. This is a claim that Schmitt repeats in Schmitt, *State, Movement, People*, p. 15.

[471] Nevertheless, it should also be noted that 'the state' is still a privileged term in Schmitt's thought (as we shall see, it is *normative*), and the problems of the political are worked-out through Schmitt's engagement with this historical entity. For discussions of this point see: Benjamin Arditi, 'On the Political: Schmitt contra Schmitt', *Telos* 142(Spring), 2008, pp. 7, 25; Axtmann, 'Humanity or Enmity?' pp. 540-541; Julien Freund, 'Schmitt's Political Thought', *Telos* 102(Winter), 1995, pp. 11-13; Moore, 'The Paradox of the Political', p. 721; William Rasch, 'Conflict as a Vocation: Carl Schmitt and the Possibility of Politics', *Theory, Culture and Society* 17(6), 2000, pp. 2-5; Gary Ulmen, 'Beyond Schmitt? Reply to Miglio', *Telos* 100(Summer), 1994, pp. 192-130.

[472] Schmitt, *Concept*, p. 19. Cf. Ellen Kennedy, '*Hostis* not *Inimicus*: Toward a Theory of the Public in the Work of Carl Schmitt', *Canadian Journal of Law and Jurisprudence* 10(1), 1997, p. 42; Ernst-Wolfgang Böckenförde, 'The Concept of the Political: A Key to Understanding Carl Schmitt's Constitutional Theory', *Canadian Journal of Law and Jurisprudence* 10(1), 1997, pp. 5-8; Freund, 'Schmitt's Political Thought', p. 15.

[473] See Arditi, 'On the Political', pp. 13-14, where 'we should not confuse the political with its historical modes of appearance'.

project of *Concept*. First, we are left wondering whether for Schmitt both the state *and* the people are to be considered historically contingent entities, or whether *only* the state is to be considered such. That is to say, although both states and peoples can have histories, is it the case that all history is necessarily about peoples, and only accidentally about states? This certainly seems to be the conclusion that Schmitt arrived at in *Constitutional*.[474] The second question takes the form of a deeper concern. Given that Schmitt has used 'a people' as one of the defining characteristics of 'the state', and given that it is far from clear as to what Schmitt intends by 'a people', do we really have justification to claim that we have understood the notion of 'the state' as deployed in *Concept*? This is not only problematic because it could lead to general analytical confusion. It is also problematic because it is Schmitt's mode of presentation to separate 'the political' from 'the state' as an *explicit means* of clarification. The consequences of the answer to this question are important for Schmitt's wider thought and for his notion of friendship.

These analytic questions are easily lost in the businesslike haste of the opening of *Concept*. What is perhaps also lost on the contemporary reader is the startling peculiarity of Schmitt's opening. For in asserting that the concept of the state *presupposes* the concept of the political Schmitt was actively reversing the priorities of the terms and direction of debate on this issue in Weimar — at least *explicitly*.[475] In making the state an instance of the political rather than the determinant of the political Schmitt is attempting two further moves. The first is connected to his critiques of liberal-parliamentarianism and pluralism. Schmitt was concerned that both the theory and practice of liberalism lead to a blurring of the boundaries between state and society. The state either becomes one equal and competing interest group amongst many; or the state had a tendency to extend ever deeper into the affairs of society subsuming all institutions, interests and concerns into its auspices.[476] To Schmitt's mind these tendencies and problems were all too evident in Weimar. What was needed was a clear understanding of what the political is. Such an understanding would act as a criterion for identifying genuine political activity and concerns from the non-political. This would rescue the state as in identifying its truly political

---

[474] Carl Schmitt, *Constitutional Theory*, Jeffrey Seitzer trans. (Durham and London: Duke University Press, 2008 [1928]), p. 102.
[475] Kennedy, '*Hostis* not *Inimicus*', p. 41.
[476] Schmitt, *Concept*, p. 22 ff.

role the state would be intensified but also limited.[477] Such a state would cease to be an 'impartial' arbiter of competing interests, or play the role of one equal interest group amongst many. In understanding itself as a manifestation of the political the state could assert itself as a carrier of the ultimate (and *decisive*) consideration. This consideration was not only to distinguish friend from enemy, but to protect the former and combat the latter.

Having shown that the notion of the state is derived from the notion of the political (at least to his own satisfaction), Schmitt moves to distinguish the political from what he calls 'the various relatively independent endeavours of human thought'.[478] Here Schmitt deploys the examples of morality, economics, and aesthetics. The purpose of this move is akin to that of the first: to try to identify what is distinctive about the political. For Schmitt, the political cannot simply be derived from these other spheres (or any combination of them) any more than it can simply be derived from the notion of the state.[479] We should bear in mind, however, that this separation is also important if Schmitt is to later maintain that his version of the political is superior to that of liberalism. The liberal view 'blurs' these boundaries. It is a project that claims both to limit conflict, and to offer the possibility of rational progress and justice in politics. For the liberal, the friend-enemy distinction can be transcended. The aim (at least in theory) is also to overcome the arbitrary separation of peoples and to achieve a rational, moral, and cosmopolitan world order. With this in mind, it is in this section of his argument that we see an instance of Schmitt's prejudice for dichotomy and mutual exclusion, both in his logic and in the ideas which underpin this. Schmitt claims that the other endeavours have their own special and exclusive concerns. They are characterised by a series of final distinctions (good and evil in morality; the profitable and unprofitable in economics; and beauty and ugliness in aesthetics). The conclusion drawn from this is that there must also be such a distinction that is unique to the political. Schmitt's next move is to use this pattern to assert that 'The specific political distinction to which political actions and motives can be reduced is that between friend and enemy'.[480]

Much is assumed in Schmitt's opening moves. Indeed, we might be inclined to think that a fair degree of question-begging is being ignored by Schmitt as he develops his argument. It is initially plausible that the

---

[477] On this question see Cristi, *Carl Schmitt and Authoritarian Liberalism*, pp. 179-199. See too Schmitt's address to the *Langnamverein* produced in Cristi's appendix 'Strong State and Sound Economy: An Address to Business Leaders' (1932).
[478] Schmitt, *Concept*, p. 25.
[479] Schmitt, *Concept*, pp. 26-27.
[480] Schmitt, *Concept*, p. 26.

'endeavours of human thought' are 'relatively independent' as Schmitt suggests—even though this can be seen to reflect his own prejudice for distinction and exclusivity. However, his own choices of morality, economics, and aesthetics do much to strengthen this sense of plausibility. We might ask whether we should accept this at face-value without further consideration. A question is suggested: is Schmitt's list of morality, economics, aesthetics (and then the political) supposed to be merely illustrative (and thus incomplete) or definitive (and thus exhaustive)? It seems somewhat unlikely that the list is to be considered definitive. First, Schmitt does not describe it as such. If he were to consider this list definitive why not add a sentence claiming that all other endeavours could be reduced to these three (exempting the political)? Second, *if* the list were to be considered exhaustive then much more would have to be done to establish this. It is reasonable to assume that Schmitt would have been aware of this. The conclusion seems to be that the list is *illustrative*, but it is allowed to trade on the status of a list which is more *definitive*.

The *illustrative* view is thus more accommodating, but the role that it plays in Schmitt's thought now raises questions of its own. The most obvious is to ask what could be included in such a list but is omitted by Schmitt. Indeed, later in *Concept* Schmitt appears to add 'the religious' to this list.[481] Along with Schmitt's addendum we might consider adding to this list any of the following: jurisprudence, history, psychology, or science. When this is considered the separation of the endeavours which Schmitt has attempted (each with their own antithesis) is brought into question. For although Schmitt has already qualified his claims (the endeavours are 'relatively' independent) it would now seem that they are much closer and a lot less discrete than Schmitt might have first implied. Indeed, in some cases not only is there significant overlapping (if not merging), but the idea of a central (and exclusive) antithesis is also brought into doubt.[482]

---

[481] Schmitt, *Concept*, p. 36.
[482] Interestingly Schmitt's own addition of 'the religious' is an especially disruptive case. What is the ultimate distinction or antithesis here? The religious clearly shares concerns with morality (the moral and the immoral). It could also be thought is as making a series of claims about reality (be they 'truth' claims or claims involving 'explanation'). If so, then how is 'the religious' separated from 'the scientific' or even 'the philosophical' (which might also be concerned with this distinction). Nor should we overlook the overlap between religion and jurisprudence (the just and unjust, the lawful and unlawful). Admittedly, these concerns need to be developed if they are to be substantiated. However, given that Schmitt does little to develop and support his own claims in this area, what is suggested here must be considered at least as *equally plausible* as Schmitt's account.

Regardless of whether Schmitt's examples are supposed to be exhaustive or merely illustrative, and regardless as to whether he is ultimately correct in claiming their relative independence, one further argumentative difficulty remains. In the examples that Schmitt uses he detects not only a concern specific to each (i.e each have their own criteria of distinction), he then seems to go on to *generalise* these observations.[483] This generalisation is what sets up his claims for the distinctive criteria of the political. Things are not, however, as straightforward as this. For although the thrust Schmitt's presentation might lead us to expect a strong connection between what he has outlined in the cases of morality, economics, and aesthetics with what he goes on to say about the political, in fact the connection is rather weak. Yet Schmitt presents these moves as if they were a part of a continuous argument. In other words, Schmitt seems to oscillate between presenting his account of the political as being somehow *derived* from his findings in the other endeavours (on the one hand), and simply following a weaker line of expectation based on an observable pattern (on the other). The reader is taken along partly because they are expecting to be following an argument. It is not clear that what Schmitt presents is an argument in this sense. If he does, it is not an especially strong one.

Unless we are careful to notice these features of Schmitt's argument, we are likely to be drawn into accepting his account of both the connection between friendship and the political, and the assumptions that he makes about the nature of this 'realm'. For without taking note of the moves that Schmitt makes in his argument we are prone to accept the friend-enemy distinction as a *solution* to a problem, rather than identifying it as a *problem* itself. Thus, in order to understand and to make clear what is going on here we must read Schmitt in another way—a way which disrupts his presentation. We need to look not so much at what Schmitt says, but to attempt to discern what Schmitt might be trying to achieve. Another way of approaching what Schmitt is trying to do is not to start from the position that he is abstracting from pre-established realms, but to start from the position that he is using abstract definitions to demarcate and establish these realms. Importantly, this view would consider Schmitt's account of the political to be the *primary* category, and that the other categories are introduced only to help elucidate and to contrast with this primary notion. This

---

[483] Schmitt's argument is both assertive and propositional. He makes his claims in such a way to suggest a continuous relation, but it is not entirely clear which of them he has *proved* by the end of the passage, and which of them *depend* on the others. To examine this short but pivotal passage in its entirely see Schmitt, *Concept*, pp. 25-27.

reading overcomes the obvious logical problems with his argument, and it makes some sense of Schmitt's otherwise puzzling opening moves (and doesn't just consider them to be a poor argument).[484]

This reversal of direction has significant consequences for Schmitt's project. Taken as an attempt to demarcate realms of endeavour Schmitt's assertion of the importance of a defining antithesis makes more sense. For in attempting to establish the categories (in contrast to merely describing and extrapolating what is already present) Schmitt is imposing a certain order on the world. Seen from this perspective the other spheres follow the model established by Schmitt's central category: that of the friend-enemy distinction. They are not pre-existent approaches to the world, but are generated by attempting to create order and distinctions. Once the friend-enemy category is established, the other spheres become what the friend-enemy distinction is not. Thus the force of the friend-enemy polemic is discerned. The friend-enemy distinction can now be recognised in its *role* as Schmitt's central category. It is this category which both demarcates and structures the others, and which politicises human existence by generating the imperative of hostile groupings. In addition, we come to see how this central category of the friend-enemy distinction (with its dynamics of division) is projected onto the other realms to give them the potential to *become* political. Schmitt weaves into the other realms the potential for conflict and division transferred from what is observed in the political with its friend-enemy distinction. This conflict and division cannot be resolved through rational means or appeals to higher norms. Seen from this perspective, far from being detached, the friend-enemy distinction is used to give the other realms the potential of politicisation; and once they are politicised they feed back into the central realm of the political itself. Thus, we must be attendant to what Schmitt 'smuggles' into his

---

[484] One way of thinking about the plausibility of this approach is to consider Schmitt's argument in a slightly different form. The argument could be reconstructed from the beginning of paragraph two where Schmitt asserts the friend-enemy distinction as being the 'specific political distinction'. It would be possible to take this as Schmitt's central thesis (which clearly it is) and then to read on. If we do this, then it becomes possible to see the importance (and even primacy) of the political. It is the claims about the independence of the political which are central to Schmitt's argument—not the claims about the other spheres. Indeed, taken in this light there could be considerable overlap between the other spheres without this compromising Schmitt's central claims concerning the political. However, such an attempt needs to be complemented with attendance to the polemical purpose of Schmitt's presentation. In other words, regardless of whether we can make Schmitt's argument work, we need to be aware of both what Schmitt is trying to do (to produce friend-enemy groupings and to politicise issues) and the normative assumptions that stand behind this endeavour (e.g the importance of the nation-state).

thought. In treating the friend-enemy distinction as a problem rather than the solution to a problem (i.e. an answer to the question what is the central distinction of the political), we can see that Schmitt's thought is characterised by a binary and exclusionary structure. It also builds conflict into that structure. This structure is never challenged by Schmitt, but it should (and must) be challenged by his readers. If this is not challenged we come to accept the assumptions that structure Schmitt's account of friendship and allow them to shape our own.

The *intensity* of friendship and enmity

As we have seen, Schmitt can be understood to be approaching the political from two directions. His opening moves take the appearance of abstracting the political *from* other realms. A series of endeavours with their own defining antithesis are set-up, and the political is derived from these by following their pattern. However, on inspection it would seem that these moves are more successfully understood as an attempt to define the political as being primary, and then to contrast the other realms to this. The other realms now appear as a kind of remainder to the political and subordinate to it.[485] Indeed, it has been suggested that their own distinctions are, in fact, shaped by the friend-enemy distinction that Schmitt claims for the political. The remainder of *Concept* is focused on demonstrating the unique ability of the political to determine action. As such, this antithesis is determined to be irreducible to the contents of the other realms. This method is one of contrast and analogy, where the realms are considered to be similar in *form*. Despite this there is an important way in which the notions of the friend and enemy differ from what is described in the other spheres. Whereas it might be said that the other spheres achieve their relative independence by applying their distinctive criteria to generate their subject matter, the same cannot be said for the political. In the other spheres the focus of the antithesis is definition and judgement. For example, although there might be disagreement about what counts as morality and immorality, this distinction points to a definitive sphere of human activity and enquiry. The criterion of the moral and immoral allows individuals to exclude certain concerns from that sphere and to make judgements about the status of actions and phenomena within it.

In contrast to the other realms, the political has no 'subject' of its own.[486] At first it appears that for Schmitt the sole consideration of the political is whether groups are prepared to fight and die in order to

---

[485] Cf. Moore, 'The Paradox of the Political', pp. 723, 730.
[486] Strauss, 'Notes on Carl Schmitt', in Schmitt, *Concept*, pp. 85-86. However, (as argued here), it does have a normative 'bearer' for Schmitt: a people.

maintain their existence. Thus, whereas the other realms suggest a definable subject matter and that something specific could be understood by the terms of their antithesis, this is not the case for the political. Friends and enemies are identified *existentially*.[487] Schmitt emphasises that the friend and the enemy do not conform to a pre-established pattern.[488] Instead the identification of the enemy (and thus the friend) 'can neither be decided by a previously determined general norm nor by the judgment of a disinterested and therefore neutral third party'.[489] The focus is on deciding who the friend and enemy is, and this decision can only be made by the parties involved.[490] As a result, the friend and enemy are generated not by conformity to theoretical definition and categorisation, but by the concrete decisions of existing entities.[491] This fluidity means that friends and enemies cannot be known in advance, and are subject to change over time.[492]

The focus on the mobility of the categories of the friend and enemy, and their links to the existential and concrete, separate the substance and characteristics of the political from that of the other realms. Here the crucial quality of both friendship and enmity is one of *intensity*.[493] For Schmitt 'The distinction of friend and enemy denotes the utmost degree of intensity of a union or separation, of an association or disassociation'.[494] This association is linked to the willingness to both kill and be killed.[495] Much turns on the question of killing, which is

---

[487] Schmitt, *Concept*, p. 27.
[488] Cf. Arditi, 'On the Political', p. 15. Here Arditi notes that 'the actual contours of the political are inevitably mobile as they follow the changing fortunes of the friend-enemy oppositions'. Furthermore, 'the political *does not refer to the constitution of a new autonomous domain but a type of relation* — the friend-enemy relation — that can arise anywhere' (emphasis added).
[489] Schmitt, *Concept*, p. 27. Cf. also *Concept*, p. 38 where the political 'does not describe its own substance'. See too Axtmann, 'Humanity or Enmity?' p. 535.
[490] Schmitt, *Concept*, p. 27.
[491] Schmitt, *Concept*, p. 28.
[492] Schmitt, *Concept*, pp. 34-35.
[493] Petrovic, 'Enemy as the Essence of the Political', p. 5; Kennedy, '*Hostis* not *Inimicus*', p. 43; Charles E Frye, 'Carl Schmitt's Concept of the Political', *The Journal of Politics* 28(4), 1966, p. 819.
[494] Schmitt, *Concept*, p. 26. This is a claim which is emphasised through repetition in *Concept*. See for example p. 29 where 'The political is the most intense and extreme antagonism', and then again at p. 38 where 'It [the political] does not describe its own substance, but only the intensity of an association or dissociation of human beings…'.
[495] Schmitt, *Concept*, pp. 27, 37, 45-46. See esp. p. 35 where the friend and enemy distinction is linked to the requirement to sacrifice life; and p. 47 where the power over life results in the political community transcending all others. On this issue (which is central to both enmity *and* friendship) see: Kennedy, '*Hostis* not *Inimicus*', p. 42; Moore, 'The Paradox of the Political', p. 733. Special attention should also be paid to Palaver who makes the connection between the killing of

central to this scheme. Indeed, it is perhaps the only constant and identifiable characteristic that Schmitt attaches to the friend and enemy in *Concept*. Stripped of the qualities of the other realms the friends stand naked before the reality of their willingness to fight and die for each other. The Ancient maxim of helping friends and harming enemies is thus taken to its limit and extreme. It is this particular intensity that characterises the union and disassociation of the friend and enemy, and sees them linked to homogeneity and heterogeneity, conformity and confrontation. It also helps to explain why the political must take priority over the other realms.[496] Until the question of who we are prepared to die for and who we are prepared to kill is answered, the antitheses of the other realms lack significance. This question also reveals our ultimate allegiance. In this sense it defines both our identity and that with which we are identified. In this way it can be said that the antithesis of the other realms are drawn within the limits of the political; but the political cannot be contained within their limits.

That the friend-enemy grouping is portrayed as being both irreducible to other realms and as taking a kind of sovereign priority over them is also consistent with Schmitt's rejection of a political normativism (albeit that his own normative view structures *Concept*). If it were the case that one of the other spheres held the key to determining the friend and enemy then the political would not be a matter of decision and judgement but of conforming to pre-established criteria. Furthermore, the sphere in question would take precedence over the other spheres. However, although the political emerges as sovereign over the other spheres due to its unique connection to the friend and the enemy and the issue of its hold over life, it is not completely divorced from them. Indeed, there is a sense in which Schmitt's emphasis on the intensity of the association of the friends and disassociation of the enemy (rather than on *defining* friendship and enmity) leaves the groupings peculiarly parasitic on the other realms.[497]

With this observation in mind, it could be asked whether Schmitt overplays the decisionism and vitalism that is found at the heart of his account of the friend and enemy.[498] It seems somewhat implausible (or even extreme) to suggest that the friend and enemy are identified on no

---

others and the sacrifice of self for friends. See Wolfgang Palaver, 'Schmitt's Critique of Liberalism', *Telos* 102(Winter), 1995.

[496] Schmitt, *Concept*, p. 47.
[497] For a full treatment of the various ways in which Schmitt asserts the 'autonomy' of the political see Moore, 'The Paradox of the Political'. Cf. also Arditi, 'On the Political', p. 20; Frye, 'Carl Schmitt's Concept of the Political', p. 821.
[498] On the role of vitalism in Schmitt's thought see: Wolin, 'Carl Schmitt', pp. 429-435.

other basis than the decision of a group; a decision which also has no basis in any other norm or ideal. If it is the case that the friend and enemy are connected to the real possibility of killing, what motivates the friends to both kill and be killed? Something more substantial seems to be required. As we have noted, although the friend and enemy must always exist, for Schmitt friends and enemies are presented as mobile configurations. As a result of this he cannot have recourse to the idea of *natural* friends and enemies.[499] It is possible to imagine that *individuals* might kill for a variety of reasons, and — *in the extreme case* — for no discernable reason at all. Individuals are prone to passion and are the prey of the irrational. However, it does not seem that this can be generalised to the level of the group. This is especially true of the large-scale groups of which Schmitt speaks. In order for these groups to select and kill an enemy something more is needed than passion or a moment of madness. For groups, killing must be sustained over time. Moreover, groups are expected to kill strangers.

Schmitt appears to be aware of these difficulties about motivation as his line is softened in two ways. This softening begins to reveal Schmitt's real assumptions about friendship groups. First, Schmitt's *primary* line is that the political remains both independent of, and ultimately undetermined by, the other realms. Nevertheless he concedes that there is a *de facto* relationship between them.[500] It is possible that antagonisms in these realms can intensify to such a scale as to *become* political. Schmitt writes that:

> ...religious, moral, and other antithesis can intensify to political ones and can bring about the decisive friend-or-enemy constellation. If, in fact, this occurs, then the relevant antithesis is no longer purely religious, moral, or economic, but political.[501]

This conclusion not only goes some of the way towards softening Schmitt's position, in doing so it helps its plausibility. We can now see how the friend and enemy grouping can be both mobile (i.e. have no specific descriptors of its own but merely be a reference to an intensity) and how this mobility connects to concrete situations and events. In a sense, when the antagonisms of the other spheres become sufficiently intense to spill-over into threatened and actual violence they cease to be

---

[499] Schmitt, *Concept*, pp. 34-35. The point being that if such natural enemies existed, then killing would be 'ontologically' motivated (as it were). The determination of friendship and enmity would be a 'brute fact' of the world — friends and enemies would be pitted against each other in the irresolvable antipathy of cats and dogs.

[500] Schmitt, *Concept*, p. 27. Cf. Wolin, 'Carl Schmitt, Political Existentialism, and the Total State', p. 407; Ibid., 'Carl Schmitt', p. 443.

[501] Schmitt, *Concept*, p. 36. Cf. *Concept*, p. 38.

characterised by their central antithesis (which is an organised remainder of the political) and can be seen to be linked to the formation of groups. Such groups are characterised by a special unity and intensity. The members are a band of friends opposed to and willing to fight their enemies. Such declarations are a *public* act.[502] That is to say, the friendship grouping is that of a political entity rather than that of a private association (such as a family).

It is worth pausing momentarily to note in more detail what Schmitt has in mind when he uses the term public. For in Schmitt's thought the idea of the public enemy is the correlate of his notion of the friend. Schmitt's ambition is to bring the notion of the friend and enemy back into political discourse not at the level of the individual but at the level of the group.[503] Whereas the relationship between friend and enemy is one of antagonism, within the friendship group the relationship is one of identification. Friendship denotes a loss of the individual to the group — a theme and position that Schmitt had pursued from an early stage of his thought.[504] Thus, whilst within the friendship grouping there might be discussion and even difference on lower order disputes (such as morality and economics) friendship becomes decisive at the moment of extreme identification. These lower-order disputes must be seen to lack the seriousness of the political. If individuals dispute this they thereby raise these other issues to the level of seriousness that is the political, and this then threatens the solidarity of the friendship group. Either this must be resolved or the polity will split. Civil war or revolution follows from such an eruption of intensity.[505] For Schmitt, such a situation is not merely regrettable but pathological. It is a sign

---

[502] Schmitt, *Concept*, pp. 28-29. See too, Kennedy, '*Hostis* not *Inimicus*'.

[503] Freund, 'Schmitt's Political Thought', p. 16; Alexandre Lefebvre, 'The Political Given: Decisionism in Schmitt's Concept of the Political', *Telos* 132(Fall), 2005, p. 89. Schmitt is at pains to point out that the considerations of morality apply only to individuals and not to groups. Focusing on the Christian commandment to 'love the enemy' Schmitt wriggles rather desperately to separate this command from the notion of a 'public enemy'. However, he might have done well not to draw attention to this issue. From one perspective this particular commandment might be considered the very negation of the friend-enemy distinction itself. Its radical implication could be (contrary to Schmitt's view) that the individual and their conduct are the central structuring force of human co-existence. Furthermore, in terms of loving the enemies of one's own people this — it seems — is precisely what Christ's command and ministry was about (consider the parable of the 'Good Samaritan'). Seen from this perspective, the message is one of a subversion of the kind of exclusionary and hostile identity politics that Schmitt promotes in the state system.

[504] See Palaver, 'Schmitt's Critique of Liberalism', p. 57; Weigandt, 'The Alleged Unaccountability of the Academic: A Biographical Sketch of Carl Schmitt', p. 1575; Wolin, 'Carl Schmitt, Political Existentialism, and the Total State', p. 403.

[505] Schmitt, *Concept*, p. 32.

that something has gone badly wrong for the state. As will become apparent in our discussion of *Constitutional* below, the problem here for Schmitt is not simply the fact of conflict, but that the normative structure of the state has broken down. Thus, in *Constitutional*, we see Schmitt invest states with the power to enforce the homogeneity of their people (a claim which is repeated as part of the basis for Schmitt's support of the Nazi take-over in *State, Movement, People*). Friendship, then, is not simply an indication of 'sameness' and those who we do not kill. In Schmitt's hands it is also a mechanism of homogenisation and hegemony.

When this is worked-up into concrete terms it provides a fuller basis for the motivation of friends to both kill and be killed. We have seen that the first way in which Schmitt softens his vitalism is to concede that the non-political antithesis can become political. Here Schmitt's second line is a development of his first which is taken to a thicker and more complex level. Here the attachment does not appear to be random but connected to concrete 'ways of life'.[506] Now it is not simply that a particular set of issues has reached the level of the political, but a whole system of values and relations have gained sufficient intensity to threaten violence. This seems much more plausible as a basis for motivation, especially when it is connected back to the state. Schmitt views the state as being connected to the notions of territory, ethnicity and culture,[507] and these would all seem to suggest a connection to a way of life. Furthermore, such thicker motivations also seem to provide a fuller and more realistic basis for friendship itself. Schmitt's vitalism is therefore not as thorough-going as it first appears.

This unravelling of Schmitt's position does not end here; a further thread also needs to be tugged. Although it is now convenient for Schmitt to have disputes in the other realms reach the intensity of the political (and thus motivate the friend-enemy grouping), it should not be forgotten that the divided nature of the other realms is something that Schmitt imports into them from the political itself. In other words, Schmitt has not *established* that these realms do, in fact, have antitheses. This is asserted — perhaps even plausibly — but not demonstrated or discussed. Moreover, although Schmitt links the friend-enemy distinction to the issue of killing, he does not demonstrate that this antithesis or conclusion is necessary. Schmitt trades on the idea that friends and enemies are opposites. However, what he builds into this is that any conflict between them is irresolvable via the means of reason,

---

[506] Lefebvre, 'The Political Given', p. 95; Ian Cook, 'Theorising Schmitt's Friend-Enemy Through Deleuzian Folding and First-Person Shooters', *Symploke* 17(1/2), 2010, p. 222.

[507] Schmitt, *Concept*, pp. 27, 49.

empathy, or appeals to higher authorities (either earthly or metaphysical). This leaves Schmitt with a free-hand to link the resolution of the conflict between friends and enemies to violence and killing. It is far from clear that he is justified in doing so. Furthermore, in linking the friend and enemy as an antithesis, Schmitt glosses over the complex relation between these terms. Schmitt simply cashes these out in terms of sameness and difference. There is no attention to the idea of differences which can exist between friends, or similarities which can exist between enemies (and thus provide a bridge to the resolution of conflict). Nor is the complex issue of those who fall between friends and enemies discussed: the stranger. As a result, Schmitt largely assumes what he is purporting to demonstrate.

Concept is thus acknowledged as Schmitt's most explicit treatment of friendship—but it must be approached with caution. A reading which accepts *Concept* at face-value is likely to draw the enquirer into Schmitt's terrain with no chance of back-tracking. Once in this terrain, the reader will find a view of friendship cast in terms of an especially intense association which pits the friends against others. It assumes that the friends share in something that their enemies do not, and that this difference leads to conflict. This view of friendship repeats the modern tropes of peace and war, inside and outside, and homogeneity and heterogeneity. Schmitt should not be followed on to this terrain. Instead, *Concept* should be approached from the point of view that it is a polemic. Its aim is to both crystallise and divide, and Schmitt's use of friendship repeats this technique. As has been suggested, Schmitt's conclusions can be avoided if we ask not what does friendship *mean* for Schmitt, but what *role* does it play. This question is to ask about function. This approach illuminates what Schmitt obscures: that friendship plays a part in his wider political aims to assert the normative priority of the sovereign nation-state. Such a state is homogenous, and hostile to heterogeneity. If this approach is taken then friendship is not a thing to be defined, or a solution to a problem, but is seen as a problem itself. Such a reading does not accept Schmitt's prejudice for binary oppositions and mutual exclusion, nor will it repeat Schmitt's statist and bellicose discourse. We are also in a position to identify and question what underlies and structures Schmitt's account of friendship. Whilst Schmitt's view of friendship is a tool of polemicisation, it succeeds only by assuming that the friends are an especially intense unity of equals. Such a group share an identity. In order for equality and unity to persist homogeneity must be recognised and cultivated. As such, the friendship group does not simply form out of nothing, but is established over time through the identification with others.[508] What this identification might amount to, and what the idea of the political unity of a people means, can be considered to have been worked out in *Constitutional Theory*.

Friendship and constituent power

As we have seen, in *Concept* Schmitt pairs friends and enemies as two poles in an antithesis: the ability of a group to self-identify in this way demarcates the political. This antithesis rests on the special intensity of the association or disassociation which sees the friends and enemies willing to undertake the extreme acts of both killing and being killed. The friendship grouping therefore takes precedence over all other groupings. In this respect it cannot be denied that the predominant language of *Concept* is bellicose. Despite his protestations to the contrary, it is hard to shake Schmitt's position free from the prospects of war which he does not attempt to avoid even if he is not intending to glorify it.[509] A world of mere economics and ethics — where differences can either be tolerated or reconciled — is clearly not enough for Schmitt.[510] After all, it is Schmitt himself who claims that the possibility of war gives life meaning.[511] Whichever way we look at it, the presentation of the antithesis of the friend-enemy in *Concept* appears to be inescapably tied to the idea of violence. This bellicosity surrounding the space of the friend makes it hard to think of friends in anything other than terms of armed comrades or a militaristic union. Underlying all of this is Schmitt's semi-veiled judgement that only the political collective carries significance and value, and his view that this is confirmed and realised through confrontation with others.

As we have seen, this framework is allowed both to stand unchallenged and to shape friendship precisely because Schmitt leaves

---

[508] Cf. Carl Schmitt, 'Ethic of State and Pluralistic State', in Chantal Mouffe (ed.), *The Challenge of Carl Schmitt*, p. 208. See too Böckenförde, 'The Concept of the Political: A Key to Understanding Carl Schmitt's Constitutional Theory', pp. 6, 8.

[509] Indeed, even Schmitt's attempts to show that war is an inescapable evil that can be curtailed by a recognition of the true nature of the political do not really persuade. For example, Schmitt informs us that the wars fought against enemies are not based on a moral judgement about such enemies (see *Concept*, p.48-49, 54-55, 66-68). Therefore (unlike wars in the name of humanity) the enemy does not need to be destroyed. This is unconvincing. First, if the enemy is *really* a threat to our way of life then this threat is unlikely to desist until the source of the threat is destroyed: the enemy. Second, in giving the enemy no moral status whatsoever Schmitt removes them and war entirely from a sphere which would place value on human life (and thus limit conflict). A war which sees the enemy as evil might be terribly misguided — but it can be called back to reason. A war which fails to see the enemy as even sharing a common moral plane might represent annihilation without end.

[510] Schmitt, *Concept*, p. 57.

[511] Schmitt, *Concept*, p. 35.

the category of 'the friend' largely devoid of content. The reader is left to infer that friendship is everything that enmity is not. Thus, a view of friendship emerges which relies on assumptions about homogeneity and unity, and this is encouraged by Schmitt's own comments about intensity. Moreover, his examples (which tend to focus on the state) reinforce this. All of this is *predicated* in *Concept*, but Schmitt's opening is constructed in such a way as to allow the reader to be drawn into thinking that the features of the friend, and the friend-enemy distinction itself, have somehow emerged from the observations that Schmitt makes in his opening pages. Here it has been suggested that Schmitt has not simply been drawing cards, but playing a hand. However, once we accept his schema — and fail to question it — then we have not only entered into the territory structured by Schmitt's binary and exclusive logic, but also his normative commitments (the state, the nation, and homogeneity). As a result, we also accept a view of friendship structured by these.

Yet a reading of *Concept* alone generates a somewhat incomplete picture of friendship. As we have already noted, a central idea in Schmitt's account of friendship in *Concept* is that of 'a people' and the connection between such a people and 'the state'. We have also noted that Schmitt doesn't simply leave his account of friendship to the mercy of an absolute decisionism. On the contrary, Schmitt concedes in *Concept* that those who identify themselves as friends tend to commit to and coalesce around some other position (in religion, or economics, for example). Schmitt also connects this grouping to the notions of homogeneity and a 'way of life'. It is here that we begin to see what Schmitt has in mind as the primary forms of bonding. In order to fill these notions out, attention can be drawn to Schmitt's seminal work of 1928 *Constitutional Theory*. In this book Schmitt elaborates on what is meant by the notion of a people. This grouping stands before politics and is considered the foundation of political unity. When understood as recognising themselves as a 'nation' Schmitt writes that the people are 'a unity capable of political action' (and thus rise above the status of simply belonging together on account of some common features).[512] Such a people acting politically as a nation are characterised by identity, equality, and homogeneity. As a nation they also have a will. It is the people who are endowed with the constituent decision making power. In *Constitutional* Schmitt focuses on the people as a seemingly irreducible and (when recognised as a nation) an especially intense unity or association. In this way, just as *Partisan* elaborates the meaning of the friend and enemy in the polarised world of the Cold War,

---

[512] Schmitt, *Constitutional*, p. 127.

Constitutional can be seen to fill in and complete the connection that Schmitt makes between friendship and the political during this earlier stage. Indeed, in some ways Schmitt's account of the state and people in *Constitution* might be considered a kind of groundwork for the discussion in *Concept*. As Ellen Kennedy has observed, the topic of *Constitutional* 'is the political association of friends that is possible in the modern world and within the legal structure of the modern state'.[513] Friendship, then, need not be tied to the somewhat reactive response to the presence of enemies. Whilst friendship groupings will generate the possibility of enemies, friendship can also be understood as a form of political unity based on mutual identification and a shared way of life. However, for Schmitt this boils down to not only life within a state, but a normative assumption about life inside an authoritarian nation-state.

The question of identity

In addressing the nature of friendship and the political as found in the state, *Constitutional* also takes up a theme which Schmitt had previously identified in *The Crisis of Parliamentary Democracy* in 1923. In *Crisis* Schmitt drew attention to the disjuncture between parliamentarianism (especially when allied to liberalism) and the idea of democracy. Whereas the former is based on the principle of procedure and discussion aimed at the establishment of rational laws, rights, and the resolution of conflicting interests,[514] the latter is focused on 'the assertion of an identity between law and the people's will'.[515] Thus, despite their historical coincidence, the principles of parliamentarianism and democracy are fundamentally opposed with each asserting priority over the other. Either political legitimacy is conferred as a result of rational discussion and appeal to higher norms (in which case the will of the people is irrelevant), or it is based on the decision of the people (in which case appeals to a higher authority and procedure are immaterial). Furthermore, the democratic principle need not be realised through elections and parliaments at all. In Schmitt's view democracy can be realised just as effectively in a dictatorship as it can as the product of a system of regular multi-party elections.[516]

What *Crisis* diagnoses, and what *Constitutional* develops, is a response to the foundations of the political that sees a central role for

---

[513] Ellen Kennedy, 'Foreword', in Schmitt, *Constitutional*, p. xv. See too Chantal Mouffe, 'Carl Schmitt and the Paradox of Liberal Democracy', in Chantal Mouffe (ed.), *The Challenge of Carl Schmitt*, p. 47.
[514] Schmitt, *Crisis*, pp. 42-44, 49.
[515] Schmitt, *Crisis*, p. 26.
[516] Schmitt, *Crisis*, p. 28.

the issue of identity.[517] Indeed, in *Crisis* Schmitt views the issue of identity as being the dominant problem of the politics of his time.[518] By severing the links between liberal-parliamentarianism and democracy, Schmitt also severs the links between the reassuring assumption that there can be an indefinite extension of the legitimacy conferred by democracy and the protection offered by the democratic state. For in Schmitt's thought identity can be said to be paired with difference. Democratic identity creates an inside and outside; and equality for some means inequality for others.[519] To fail to recognise this is likely to lead to the weakening of identity and with it the foundations of legitimacy for the state and law. Identity thus speaks to groups who share something in common.

For Schmitt, the basis for the friend-enemy distinction is thus the shared identity of a people who recognise themselves to be acting politically. The recognition of this shared identity gives rise to three important consequences. First, it is this identity which takes priority over all others.[520] Such an identity is recognition of the friendship group, and the making of this manifest in the constitution and state. It commands loyalty and obedience. Second, it is this group which is the carrier of both will and decision. Such a group underwrites the constitution and provides the basis for the identification of friends and enemies in both the inter-state and domestic arena. As such an identity can never be fully represented, the people remain unrestrained by the constitution, states, and laws to which their identification gives rise.[521] Third, such a group must achieve both homogeneity and equality if its bonds are to last.[522] Such a self-identifying group must therefore take the measures necessary to ensure that its commonality is enhanced and protected. Here, then, Schmitt draws out explicitly the nature and location of the bonds that are left implicit in *Concept*. It is a people (realised as a nation) which is the primary instance and model for the friendship group. In order to see why this view of the identity and unity of a people standing before politics is so significant, Schmitt's thought can be usefully contrasted to that of Hobbes. As we shall see, for Schmitt (and unlike Hobbes) there *is* a primary form of bonding that in some sense stands before the state. It is the primary form of bonding which provides the material for his edifice.

---

[517] Schmitt, *Crisis*, p. 26. See also Schmitt, *Constitutional*, pp. 239-242.
[518] Schmitt, *Crisis*, p. 29.
[519] Schmitt, *Constitutional*, p. 258.
[520] Schmitt, *Constitutional*, pp. 125, 128, 140. For Schmitt's discussion of identity (and representation) see pp. 239-242, 302.
[521] Schmitt, *Constitutional*, p. 240.
[522] Schmitt, *Constitutional*, pp. 248, see also 107, 127, 159.

Individuals and peoples

Schmitt is sometimes viewed as a kind of heir to Hobbes, and Schmitt's focus on the state and order encourage this. Indeed, Schmitt concurred with Hobbes' insight that there was a connection between obedience and protection.[523] Furthermore, both Hobbes and Schmitt recognise the possibility of death as being a limit and structuring force of the political. However, whilst the theories of Hobbes and Schmitt share certain similarities, they also have deep structural differences. Famously, in Hobbes' theory the pre-political situation is one of warring individuals. Politics is cast as the transcendence of conflict and the association of persons. In contrast, for Schmitt the political presupposes and institutionalises the life of not individuals but groups.[524] Thus for Schmitt there is already some form of bond between person and person. In addition, two further contrasts should be noted. First, in Hobbes' account the rights of the *individual* and the possibility of discerning the Laws of Nature in the pre-political 'state of nature' lay the foundations for the liberal state. In Schmitt's account the *group* takes precedence over both the individual and higher obligations, thus setting the stage for authoritarianism. Second, whereas in Hobbes' thought individual wills are brought together to make something *new* (the Commonwealth), in Schmitt's thought the institution of the constitution and state is *not* something *entirely* new. Instead it is perhaps best described as a kind of confirmation and intensification of an existing unity.

In order to better focus on these contrasts (and thus define the role and nature of the bonds theorised in Schmitt's thought, bonds that it is claimed have stood behind his view of friendship) it is desirable to say a little more about the points of similarity between Schmitt and Hobbes. For in some respects Schmitt's and Hobbes' thought appear to move along the same lines. Significantly, political order is a kind of normative goal for both thinkers, as is the distinction of the conformity required within the state compared to the anarchy and difference

---

[523] Thomas Hobbes, *Leviathan: Or the Matter, Forme, and Power of A Common-Wealth Ecclesiasticall and Civil* (Middlesex, England: Penguin Books, 1961 [1651]), p. 272; Carl Schmitt, *The Leviathan in the State Theory of Thomas Hobbes: Meaning and Failure of a Political Symbol*, George Schwab and Erna Hilfstein trans. (London: Greenwood Press, 1996 [1938]), pp. 53, 83. Note too George Schwab, *The Challenge of the Exception: An Introduction to the Political Ideas of Carl Schmitt between 1921 and 1936* (New York: Greenwood Press, 1989), p. 52; Gary Ulmen, 'Between the Weimar Republic and the Third Reich: Continuity in Carl Schmitt's Thought', *Telos* 119(Spring), 2000, p. 31.

[524] Arditi, 'On the Political', p. 26; Slomp, *Carl Schmitt and the Politics of Hostility*, p. 48.

which remains external to it.[525] Both thinkers also agree on two further points. First, that political institutions arise as the result of a decision or the will of those governed; and second, that the identification and establishment of a political system is also the establishment of law and justice.[526] For Hobbes, the consequence of this is that individuals contracting to authorise another to govern them cannot place limitations on the will or ability of the sovereign to make law.[527] Indeed, the very idea of restricting the sovereign *by law* becomes contradictory.[528]

Schmitt's thought echoes this idea. Just as Hobbes' sovereign remains semi-detached from law (and thus able to underwrite it), for Schmitt law derives its legitimacy and force from something external to it: the will of the people. Furthermore, Schmitt agrees with Hobbes that the will that creates and underpins law cannot be limited by it. Thus, in his discussion of constitutional theory (and the constitution of the Weimar Republic in particular) Schmitt writes that:

> A constitution is not based on a norm, whose justness would be the foundation of its validity. It is based on a political decision concerning the type and from of its own being, which stems from its political *being*.[529]

A little later Schmitt goes on to observe that the political will determining such a decision 'remains alongside and above the constitution'. Hobbes' and Schmitt's positions appear to be similar here. Yet this similarity is somewhat superficial. For whilst both Hobbes and Schmitt locate the basis of legitimacy as existing outside and prior to the constitution, their reasons for doing so are radically contrasted. Whilst Hobbes makes the concession that the laws that the sovereign commands *conform* to the precepts set out in the Laws of Nature as outlined in Chapters Fourteen and Fifteen of *Leviathan*,[530]

---

[525] Slomp, *Carl Schmitt and the Politics of Hostility*, p. 54; Paul Hirst, 'Carl Schmitt's Decisionism', in Chantal Mouffe (ed.), *The Challenge of Carl Schmitt*, p. 14; Hans Sluga, 'The Pluralism of the Political: From Carl Schmitt to Hannah Arendt', *Telos* 142(Spring), 2008.
[526] Hobbes, *Leviathan*, p. 188. Cf. Schmitt, *Constitutional*, p. 76.
[527] Hobbes, *Leviathan*, pp. 232, 264-265.
[528] Hobbes, *Leviathan*, p. 313.
[529] Schmitt, *Constitutional*, p. 125. See too p. 128 where Schmitt claims 'The people, the nation, remains the origin of all political action, the source of all power, which expresses itself continually in new forms… It does so, however, without ever subordinating itself, its political existence, to a conclusive formation.'
[530] Hobbes, *Leviathan*, pp. 314-315, 318-319, 376. These Laws of Nature are properly pre-fixed with the adjective 'so-called' as Hobbes concedes that they are not actually laws in the strict use of that term (as he has defined it) *unless* they are considered the commands of God. See *Leviathan*, pp. 216-217.

Schmitt recognises no such limitations.[531] For Schmitt the sovereign is not identified primarily by its law-issuing power, but by its power to both suspend the law and to make judgments in cases which fall between the gaps of the established law and to protect the constitution as a whole. Schmitt agrees with Hobbes that 'Law in the sense of the political concept of law is the concrete *will* and *command* and an act of sovereignty'.[532] However, there is no Law of Nature to which this must conform. Furthermore, sovereignty is seen not in the framing of specific or even general laws, but in the ability to identify the exception. Such a concept of sovereignty and law rests not on mere legalism or neutrality, or the appeal to a higher law or norm, but a political decision. In practical terms, this decision is *declared* by an individual or elite, although it is 'assented to' by the nation.[533] Thus, for Schmitt there is no contradiction between the will of the people and the decision of a dictator — at least in principle. Relating his discussion to the instance of the 'German people' Schmitt writes:

> Prior to the establishment of any norm, there is a fundamental *political decision by the bearer of the constitution-making power*. In a democracy, more specifically, this is a decision by the people...[534]

Subsequently certain clauses and articles in the Weimar Constitution are identified by Schmitt in the following terms:

---

[531] Curiously Schmitt doesn't seem to emphasise his own contrasts with Hobbes in terms of the issue of the right to protect and sacrifice of life. Instead, in *Leviathan in Thomas Hobbes* Schmitt argues for Hobbes the need for the sovereign is to overcome individual claims to truth in order to end strife, pp. 45,47. This sees the sovereign deciding 'whether something is to be considered a miracle', p. 55. Nevertheless, Hobbes also recognises that there is a difference between 'inner faith and outter confession', p. 56. The sovereign demands outer confession only. Here, two sources of authority, and two kinds of demands, are enshrined in *Leviathan*. The individual was outwardly commanded to obey, but inwardly left free. Thus Schmitt concludes that this *religious* freedom was the 'seed of death that destroyed the mighty leviathan from within and brought about the end of the mortal god', p. 57. On this issue (and Schmitt's relationship with Hobbes more generally) see Gottfried, *Carl Schmitt: Politics and Theory*; Slomp, *Carl Schmitt and the Politics of Hostility*; Ellen Kennedy, *Constitutional Failure: Carl Schmitt in Weimar* (Durham and London: Duke University Press, 2004), pp. 86-91.

[532] Schmitt, *Constitutional*, p. 187.

[533] Schmitt, *Constitutional*, pp. 77-80. See too Schmitt, 'Ethic of State and Pluralistic State', pp. 200-201. Here there is a troubling distance between the people and their leaders. This is intensified by Schmitt's preference for authoritarianism and dictatorship. See Jeffrey Seitzer and Christopher Thornhill in their Introduction to Schmitt, *Constitutional*, pp. 39-40.

[534] Schmitt, *Constitutional*, p. 77. A similair point is made in a way which connects it to the concrete reality of 'kith and kin' in Schmitt, *State, Movement, People*, p. 51.

They are *more* than statutes and sets of norms. They are, specifically, the concrete political decisions providing the German people's form of political existence and this constitutes the fundamental prerequisite for all subsequent norms, even those involving constitutional laws.[535]

What Schmitt has in mind is not a *neutral* constitution, but a constitution which reflects the pre-existing features and will of the bonds between person and person in the nation. As we have now seen, there are significant differences concerning the limits that Hobbes and Schmitt place on the decision-making entity. Partly this arises from the features that the theorists identify as existing before the establishment of commonwealth and constitution. Hobbes' account sees individuals who are obligated to protect their own life enter into the social state. For Schmitt no such prior obligations exist and 'individuals' (such as they are) are already bound together as peoples. This leads to the second major difference between Hobbes and Schmitt: the issue of the sacrifice of life. For Hobbes, the sovereign can justly command a subject to endanger their own life, although the subject is obliged by right to disobey.[536] For Schmitt no such tension can exist. In addition, although Schmitt recognises the link between obedience and protection, he counterbalances this with a commitment to membership of a group. Switching allegiances just isn't possible: individuals are bound to the group to which they belong and share the history and culture of that group. Moreover, the issue of fighting others for the sake of a people is central to Schmitt's thought. This manifests both externally (i.e. fighting other states) but also internally (for Schmitt there is the possibility of a domestic enemy of the people).[537] This situation and demand for sacrifice follows not only from the individual's subordination to the group (as an ontological and practical fact), but also from the group's transcendence of any limitation or norm. In any event, such a demand represents a moment of absolute unity with the group and the closest—and deadliest—of human bonds. Here we see a connection between the way that the intensity of the unity of the group is presented in *Constitutional* and *Concept*.

We the people

Running through Schmitt's account of the unity of a people understood as a nation is the idea of a primary form of friendship. The nation twice displays the hallmarks of friendship. First, it can decide on the friend and enemy, but second, its members are bound together in the closest

---

[535] Schmitt, *Constitutional*, p. 78.
[536] Hobbes, *Leviathan*.
[537] Cf. Schmitt, *Concept*, pp. 46-47.

degree of association the intensity which can motivate combat and killing. The nation infuses the state and law with *normative* content: the will and way of life of the nation. For Schmitt, the nation creates an Us and Them. For it is this sense of unity and identity (and the creation of an Us and Them) which enables Schmitt to suggest in *Constitutional* that the basic political form is democratic. In a democratic system the will of the people 'legitimates' political arrangements and the decisions of officials. In a sense, even in monarchical regimes, the monarch is ultimately dependent on this foundation. Monarchs rule with the support of their people. However, we should bear in mind that for Schmitt democracy can take varying forms including dictatorship. It is democracy in the sense of dictatorship rather than multi-party elections and parliamentarianism which pervades his thinking.

For Schmitt democracy also entails equality. An attempt might be made to see this equality played out formally (in terms of a basic equality before the law, or the recognition of a category such as humanity). However, for Schmitt equality has to be more substantial. Although equality can be thought of abstractly, unless there is a real sense of identity between members of the polity it is likely to lose legitimacy. Indeed, recognising others as political equals is the very source of equality.[538] This sense of identity might be fostered and reinforced by law, but it finds its foundation in history and culture. For Schmitt, the friendship manifest in the unity of a nation is not simply legal but actual. It is found in the members of the nation sharing common qualities; thus it is the very opposite of enmity and heterogeneity. As Schmitt writes in *Constitutional*:

> ...the nation concept means a people individualized through a politically distinct consciousness. Different elements can contribute to the unity of the nation and to the consciousness of this unity, such as common language, common historical destiny, traditions and remembrances, and common political goals and hopes... What is definitive is the commonality of historical life, conscious willing of this commonality, great events and goals.[539]

Thus, for Schmitt the group that pre-exists the state is a people. However, although there is a basic bond here, this bond is realised (as a *political* bond) when a people is constituted as a *nation*. As a nation, a people has a will and an identity. Such a nation (as a political entity) will 'have the capacity to distinguish friend from enemy' but it is the government which assumes this right through representing the

---

[538] Schmitt, *Constitutional*, p. 268ff.
[539] Schmitt, *Constitutional*, pp. 261-262.

political unity.[540] Thus Schmitt threads together the line of people-nation-state-friend-enemy weaving them into a seamless whole. When this is played-out in historical examples, Schmitt is able to present this logic with an air of inevitability. Schmitt returns repeatedly in *Constitution* and elsewhere to portraying peoples as having national traits.[541] The German, French, and English people are prime amongst his examples. This is played out again, under the shadow of National Socialism, in *State, Movement, People*. Although a development of an earlier position, here Schmitt's tone is far less compromising:

> The political unity of the German People does not rest upon the German lands or the German tribes, but upon the self contained unity of the German People and of the National-Socialist Movement, carrier of State and People.[542]

However, Schmitt goes on to couch this in ethnic terms. He writes that:

> The *ethnic identity* of the German People, united in itself, is thus the most unavoidable premise and foundation of the political leadership of the German People.[543]

This need for homogeneity results in Schmitt being clear that heterogeneous elements face either assimilation or exile.[544] This also has a bearing on Schmitt's view of the possible pluralism to be found in a state. In contrast to the pluralism of the liberals which reduces the state to one competing interest group amongst many (and thus strips it of its political character, i.e. the state as a representation of the decision of a people) Schmitt argues that some pluralism is inevitable and even tolerable.[545] It could be that different interests even exist within the same state.[546] In the quote highlighted above from *Constitutional* Schmitt goes on to say that whilst language is important it is not determinate. Revolutions and wars can be successful if they justify the sense of national belonging. This opens up the possibility of different peoples sharing friendship and political unity. However, for Schmitt in the final analysis the political nature of the state has to be recognised. Sub-state groups partake in this insofar as they share in the decisions of state.[547] A people, then, may admit some pluralism, but there is much

---

[540] Schmitt, *Constitutional*, pp. 247-248.
[541] Seitzer and Thornhill, 'Introduction', in Schmitt, *Constitutional*, pp. 33-35.
[542] Schmitt, *State, Movement, People*, p. 20.
[543] Schmitt, *State, Movement, People*, p. 48.
[544] Schmitt, *Constitutional*, p. 262. This is seen all too uncomfortably in rhetorical form in Schmitt, *State, Movement, People*.
[545] Schmitt, 'Ethic of State and Pluralistic State', p. 201.
[546] Schmitt, 'Ethic of State and Pluralistic State', p. 203.
[547] Schmitt, 'Ethic of State and Pluralistic State', p. 203.

more that binds them than differentiates. This form of friendship is one of sameness rather than the accommodation of difference.

Thus, Schmitt's account of 'the people' in *Constitutional* fills in the gaps that the account in *Concept* leaves empty. For in *Constitutional* Schmitt confirms that the political begins with a people. The political subject is always spoken of with the pronoun 'we'. Friendship is not so much the relationship between individuals, but the identification of an existing group. However, as in *Concept*, Schmitt's account in *Constitutional* runs up against the same problem: how is action motivated? In *Constitutional* too Schmitt does not opt for pure decisionism (although he talks at times as if his account is a decisionist one). Instead he links the notions of unity, equality, and homogeneity in friendship to tangible, historical and cultural features. In the end, *Constitutional* and *Concept* share the same basic framework. Schmitt cannot conceive of friendship and unity in any other terms than of an inside and an outside, of sameness and difference, of sacrifice and hostility. *Concept* shows one face of this—*Constitutional* the other.

Schmitt: The Siren call of Friendship

Schmitt's association with friendship has raised the profile of the idea. However, this association may not be entirely welcome or predominantly beneficial. The Schmittian coupling of friendship to his intervention in politics has had at least two restrictive effects. First, Schmitt's association with the Third Reich (and Right-wing authoritarianism more generally) has cast suspicion on the notion of friendship. Does the idea of friendship somehow belong to the Right? If not wholly belonging to the Right, is the idea inherently conservative nonetheless? Second, Schmitt's framing of friendship makes it a tool of his polemical and statist politics. This seems to link friendship not only with authoritarianism, but to mix it with violence. Despite these difficulties, it could still be contended that no serious contemporary theorist of friendship can avoid engaging with Schmitt's thought, at least minimally. His influence on contemporary debates on the issue of friendship cannot be entirely evaded, and for some contributors his bearing is as necessary and as unavoidable as that of Aristotle's. Thus, notwithstanding the dangers, the attraction is evident enough. Three points are salient.

First, whereas many theorists remain silent on friendship or simply neglect the idea, Schmitt has something to say. Moreover, his thought is firmly rooted in a world that is comparable to our own. Schmitt's world is one which is closer to us in both structure and time than many other thinkers who have engaged with friendship—and especially the Ancients. Indeed, Schmitt's refusal to recognise any higher norm in a world characterised by plurality and power might suggest that he is particularly well suited to aid the theorisation of friendship in contemporary times. Those looking to re-theorise friendship are thus drawn to Schmitt as a thinker who provides an especially contemporary model. Second, Schmitt makes friendship a public category. This is crucial. He moves away from treating friendship as a personal relation based on emotions, and boldly conceives of the idea as something which relates to groups. In so doing Schmitt appears to offer a route out of the modern tendency to personalise friendship, and to restore it to its pre-modern status as a location and term of analysis. Importantly Schmitt attaches the idea of friendship to the recognisably modern ideas of nation and state. Thus it might be thought that Schmitt overcomes the restrictions placed on friendship in contemporary parlance, and relocates its subject in entities more immediately recognisable as being 'political'. Finally (and related to the second attraction), Schmitt reconnects friendship with the political. This is perhaps the most alluring feature of Schmitt's thought. For Schmitt's connection of friendship and the political is no mere compromise or apology. That is to say, friendship is not presented as simply one more theme alongside others, or as an extension or supplement to other ways of thinking. Instead, Schmitt boldly declares that the friend-enemy distinction is *the* defining feature of the political. In so doing he challenges all those who would marginalise and even eclipse the link between friendship and the political with other concerns. Seen from this perspective it is perhaps all too obvious that those concerned with friendship — and even those who simply notice but do not actively pursue the concern — tend towards Schmitt.

Much of what has been said in this chapter has been a warning against this attraction. It has also been a demonstration as to why such a warning is proffered. The view developed here has been very much that Schmitt's thought on friendship cannot be easily extracted from the assumptions and politics in which it is situated and which condition it. Thus, Schmitt persists as an interesting but negative example. His thought presents an illustration of friendship askew. As we have seen, Schmitt constructs and deploys friendship as a polemical device. It is for this reason that if we approach Schmitt in order to learn what friendship is, then he will prove to be either a disappointing or deceptive teacher. For Schmitt's value to the theorist of friendship lies not so much in what he writes, but in the use that he makes of friendship. In allowing friendship to reside as a kind of empty category on to which the reader is encouraged to project their own assumptions, Schmitt's thought is illustrative of the statist discourse that conditions thought about friendship and the political in modernity. Whilst this focus on the public, nation, and state makes Schmitt's account initially attractive to the contemporary theorist, it is precisely this discourse that makes thinking about friendship and the political so difficult in modernity. Schmitt's account highlights some of the underlying difficulties of theorising friendship in modernity precisely because it exaggerates these difficulties in the manner of its presentation and the extremity of its assumptions. For far from reconciling friendship and the state by producing a truly political account of friendship free from statist assumptions, Schmitt subsumes friendship under a bellicose statist framework. In doing so his thought is merely an exaggeration of the dominant trend of modernity. In particular it amplifies the statist discourse which favours a separation of inside and outside, an Us and Them, a stress on sameness as identity, and a conception of top-down power. All of this makes the production of a plural friendship characterised by difference difficult.

Schmitt amplifies all of these problematic features of the state and its politics, and weaves them into his account of friendship. There is no real elaboration on what friendship might mean independently of the state. First, characterised by Schmitt almost exclusively by the intensity of its association, friendship is seen as the opposite of enmity. It tends to be thought of as simply those whom one will not kill, those with whom one is similar, and those of whom one can demand sacrifices. As such, friendship becomes linked with the notion of the exclusion of difference and violence to others. It also becomes linked to the loss and subordination of the individual to the group. The friends become locked-in together and opposed to those outside who are seen in terms of a threat. Schmitt leaves no neutral or liminal space either within friendship groups or between states. Nor does he attempt to 'problematise' friendship in any way. Friendship is simply the binary opposite of enmity.

Second (and following from this), it can be observed that the details of such a group are to be found within the features of the nation. In many ways the nation becomes the basic building block of History and Politics for Schmitt — at least in modern times where it is connected to the state. Again, Schmitt draws on modern assumptions about this form of bonding, and again he amplifies these conclusions. Thus nationals are assumed to hold something in common and to share qualities and features not attributed to non-nationals. Moreover, Schmitt tends to stress the homogeneity of those bonded as both a descriptive and a normative fact. As a result, the state is seen to have both the ability and the right to defend such a friendship group from its enemies (both externally and internally). In addition, the equality which characterises those who are a part of the nation (expressed by

Schmitt in the substantive terms of sharing a common way of life and will) is contrasted to the inequality of those excluded.

It is for these reasons that if the theorist of friendship merely follows Schmitt's voice then their enterprise is likely to run aground. It will be wrecked on his statist shores. What can be learned from Schmitt must be ascertained from a distance, and not so much by listening to his voice in the hope of elucidation, but by careful observation. As has been suggested, the crucial lesson that can be learned from Schmitt is that in his hands friendship becomes a tool of polemicisation, and that his construction of friendship exaggerates the terrain which has proved so harsh for the theorisation of friendship in modernity. As has been seen, far from being derived from evidence and analysis, Schmitt presupposes the construction of the connection between the friend-enemy distinction and the political. Moreover, he builds the notions of both division and conflict into his notion of friendship, and then projects this into not only his account of the political, but the other 'non-political' realms too. As a result, Schmitt is able to present the political as inherently conflictual and divisive. The friend-enemy distinction is therefore seen to be both an identification of the political (at the theoretical level) and also a device to identify and politicise issues at the level of practice. As soon as the friend-enemy criteria is applied to any issue that issue thereby enters into a new stage of intensification. We should be extremely wary of simply accepting Schmitt's binary and conflictual logic here. For in theorising in this way Schmitt also casts friendship as a vitalist event—such a view undermines and ignores the potential of friendship to operate as a shared form of identification and bonding which can accommodate both reason, empathy, and difference.

Schmitt's influence will no doubt persist. However, those who are drawn to Schmitt's thought on the issue of friendship should take care. For in following Schmitt's voice we are likely to be drawn towards the rocks on which he sings: homogeneity, violence, and the sovereign nation-state. Ultimately Schmitt's call is the siren call of both statism and nationalism. Taken to the extreme, both are dangers to developing friendship. To be sure, those who would sail towards friendship must chart the location of this island. All who wish to navigate friendship must know that this island is there—it is a part of the greater archipelago of the state and modernity itself. However, to be drawn towards it is to head towards disaster. Schmitt's voice lures us to an island where friendship meets its undoing, and Schmitt himself must be considered no friend of friendship.

Chapter Seven

Friendship and the Political

If the mutual love of friends were to be removed from the world, there is no single house, no single state that would go on existing.

Cicero, *De Amicitia*

FRIENDSHIP is coterminous with the political. The one inhabits the space of the other: they are aspects of the same concern. The political draws its shape, content and vitality from the friendships that permeate it. In turn friendship is variegated or monochrome, multiplied or diminished, and emboldened or enervated by the particular *form* that the political takes. Here there is a difference between the political (as a general object of ontology) and its expression in form (as a particular instance of politics). There is also a corresponding difference between friendship (understood as the general notion of human bonding) and its expression as manifest norms and practices in the forms of politics. The form that the political takes also reflects the nature of the kind of friendship which permeates it. Both friendship and the political take concrete shape in the forms of politics. Thus friendship and the political *become* politics.

Friendship and the political entail each other. Yet not all friendships are directly or immediately a part of the manifest processes of politics. Nor ought they to be. The question as to whether the forms of friendship in politics must be seen to register overtly as politics is here taken to be a matter of evaluative concern and judgement. All forms of politics are dependent on friendship — both formal and informal, both public and private — but the best forms of politics do not confuse the two. The best forms of the political do not fear the personal, private or particular — perhaps even the peculiar. In the best forms of the political room is left for such varieties of friendship. Friendships such as these bear fruit away from attention and publicity. They benefit best from politics when cultivated only by the approach of laissez-faire. Simultaneously, politics benefits from avoiding mixing these kinds of friendship with its overt concerns. However, friendship always registers within the political, and all forms of friendship have the *potential* to register within the forms of politics. All forms of politics are found to have their friendships: tribes, clans, dynasties, families, fraternities, citizens, patriots, unions, associations, comrades. All forms of politics have allegiances, loyalties, attachments, obligations, commitments, connections, and solidarities of multiple and varying kinds. The richest forms of politics are able to sustain a plurality of such bonds. In these forms political life is infused and sustained by these bonds. For all forms of politics are dependent on the bonds between person and person, and their shared world of order and value. Friendship both facilitates and shows the limit of politics and the political.

Thus to conceptualise the political is to conceptualise friendship. These endeavours are resolved concurrently. For the political is something greater and more complex than what can be understood using the language of power and the individual alone. If this is all that the political is taken to be, then it reflects a poverty of understanding. Yet curtailed though this view is it necessarily reaches beyond its own limits. For even these terms quickly touch upon wider concerns and so cannot remain isolated. No one seriously suggests that the political is a solitary pursuit. The political concerns a world where there are others, and that those others must be encountered. Moreover, the political concerns a world that must be *shared* with others. Such a world sees a structure held together and animated by the bonds between person and person.

To propose a 'political solipsism' is to entertain a conceptual contradiction. The idea of a truly atomistic individual pursuing politics through treating all others as thoroughly discrete individuals is almost unthinkable. If it can be imagined it is surreal: it is at once both comic and disturbing. Of course, such a picture is sometimes composed. Such compositions are assembled only for effect. Such pictures do not to offer a serious alternative to the view that the political involves what we share with others, but to serve to highlight some hitherto unnoticed or underappreciated aspect of politics. Such pictures are composed to bring attention to some *detail* of the political. Usually the purpose is one of advocacy and promotion. These pictures retain the air of the surreal precisely because they juxtapose elements in an incongruous and impossible way. This surrealism cannot be sustained. Eventually what is distorted must reassert itself, and proportion is restored. Here it is suggested that part of this readjustment involves the perspective established by a framing that views the political as the shared world of order and value. It always involves others, and involving others means recognising their irreducibility and our connectedness to them. In others we find both value and the source of new values. This can never be completely or irreversibly expunged or suppressed. The recognition of others provides the political with a starting point which represents a kind of foundation. This political foundation recognises too that the world is created and shared by self and others. Thus the start of the political is also the start of friendship. To fail to recognise this shared world with others is to cut the political off from its source. It is to deny our connectedness to each other and the origins of order and value. It is the end of the political and the end of friendship.

[1]

TYRANNY

Tyranny and despotism represent the very limits of the political. The Ancients knew this, and tended to warn against it. For them tyranny represented a danger both for the polis and for the person. It was a seriously impoverished and limited condition, harming both the polis and tyrant in equal measure. It is true that for the Ancients tyranny was preferable to no order at all. Tyranny preserved some hope of a human life — but not much of one. It was the last resort. Still, the Ancients were by no means only ones to posses this knowledge concerning tyranny as a limit. This is an evaluation acknowledged and endorsed throughout the history of political thought. The warning is refreshed with every new reinvention of the tyrant's tools, and with whatever incarnation the tyranny takes.

Tyranny is the least political of all the forms of politics. It is also the form of politics which is most devoid of friendship. This is no accident. For in a tyranny friendship is always under suspicion. This suspicion stretches between all the nodal points of politics, and to all forms of bonding sponsored by the tyranny. Tyrants themselves can have no friends as a matter of necessity. They cannot trust others and they elicit no trust. Such orders seek no greater good than that of the interest of tyrant, and even this is confused with an isolated aggrandisement. Such orders create a hostile soil for the benefits that friendship can bring. In a tyranny all things become possessions, and the greatest possession of all becomes power which is horded selfishly and at the expense, and to the exclusion, of others. The tyrant's obsession with power undermines their capacity for friendship. Friendship manifests only in its weakest forms in the self-serving instrumentality of flattery and collusion.

Occasionally it can oscillate the other way and erupt in the madness of a self-sacrificing devotion. Either way the forms of friendship are weak and the structures of politics are brittle. This is not a *shared* world, but a world where things use and dominate other things. Politically, virtually all recognition and bonding is lost. It is no surprise that tyrannies are dependent on the minority who spy their own advantage in the employment of extortion, force and violence.

Tyranny is thus a limit. From Ancient times to the advent of totalitarianism, tyranny is almost invariably considered to be at the very edge of friendship and the political. Of course, no tyranny has ever been realised in its pure form. Nor will it be. Its failure to achieve full incarnation reflects something deeper about the meaning and features of the political. No one can achieve complete mastery over others. Human beings are never reducible to objects — however degrading and inhumane their treatment or conditions. Some cinder of possibility always remains, and the tyrant always needs others to make sense of their accumulation of power. Power only makes sense (i.e. it only retains value) when others recognise it too. Perhaps perversely — perhaps inevitably — tyrannies end up strengthening the very thing that they seek to control and destroy. The machinery of tyrannies might well attempt to poison and scatter the earth in order to disrupt and displace friendship. Such tyrannies may well introduce their own constricting and thorny forms of friendship with which they hope to control others. Tyrannies are thus inclined to sponsor favouritism, nepotism, the party card, and state-administered religions. They attempt to spread their own insidious form of friendship throughout personal and family life. Yet all of these attempts merely push the friendships they seek to destroy elsewhere. They are cultivated and grow in secluded places. They germinate underground. New strains are apt to adapt and evolve. Eventually their shoots can be ignored no longer, and what was suppressed returns. Thus a new view of the political emerges, and one order is replaced by another — new values are brought to life.

In another time, and to another audience, Machiavelli suggested that given the choice of whether to be loved or feared, the Prince should choose fear. We must note that such a decision leads us away from the political. It is not clear that fear is more reliable than love. It is probably self-defeating, and it is certainly less worthy of human beings as a basis for politics. Yet Machiavelli remains an astute reader of the political. He recognises and cautions against one thing which is always to be avoided if the Prince is to maintain power — a Prince is to avoid becoming *hated*. For when it is directed against the tyrant hatred is an eruption of the political. It is a bubbling up and energising of the bonds between person and person and a declaration of their shared conceptions of order and value. Despite his advice on this issue, Machiavelli too realised that a Prince's regime depended on the friendship of the people. That is to say, there has to be a *shared* sense of order and value in a polity after all. People are not the mere tools of power, they are complicit in its work, or they resist it. In the final analysis, non-compliance and resistance both demonstrate an alternative and work towards it. Tyrants know this only too well. Tyranny is thus a limit to the political, and a limit to friendship. Yet even here friendship must operate, both officially and unofficially, both above and below ground. Without the minimal amount of friendship tyranny falls apart. In trying to restrict and control that very minimal amount, tyranny finds that the outcome of its policy is to multiply and then to free.

[2]

IDENTITY

Friendship and the political denote a concern with identity. Identity is a recognition of, and connection with, value in self and others. It can develop over time and intensify or weaken. Ultimately identity can never be singular, it is something shared in construction and acknowledgement. Understood in this way, identity does not so much belong to a person as belonging to set of relations between persons. As an aspect of friendship and the political, identity helps to locate the substance of bonding and to structure the relations of politics. Identity thus has a connection to, and consequences for, the living structures of order.

Identity can be said to operate across two planes. Care is needed to differentiate them. The first is concerned with similarity and difference. This plane takes up the questions of attraction and affinity aired in discussions such as *Lysis* and the *Nicomachean Ethics*. The second plane focuses on the question of equality and inequality. Here this plane is constructed so as to be conceptually distinct from the first. Whereas similarity and dissimilarity denote *qualities*, equality and inequality denote aspects of *treatment*. Thus, equality and inequality *are not* to be understood as mere synonyms for similarity and difference. Nor are equality and inequality to be understood to run in serial order with similarity and difference. On the contrary, whereas similarity *tends* to denote equality, it is not the case that it must. Furthermore, it should be recognised that difference does not entail inequality. This has important implications for our understanding of friendship and the political. Specifically, friendship can see both the conjoining of difference and equality (on the one hand), or the production of inequality through a focus on sameness (on the other). Similarity and difference tell us nothing about significance in themselves. In this respect, the first plane is to be considered strictly analytic. It is the plane of equality and inequality that gives such observations significance. This second plane takes the observation of the first plane and draws out *consequence*. The second plane manifests arrangements in positions held in the form of politics.

'Difference' is here used to denote a focus on similar and dissimilar things. Of course, there could be all manner of features and attributes which we find to be similar or dissimilar. Ultimately what is seen depends on where the eye is directed to look. The focus here is with persons, and the bonds between persons. In terms of difference as an aspect of friendship, the concern is with the descriptors that similarity and dissimilarity locate and use for binding persons together. From the perspective of friendship, it is important to note that similarity and dissimilarity do not necessarily map directly on to the notions of self and other. For similar and dissimilar elements can be found in both self and other. Dissimilar elements can exist within self; and similar elements can exist across or between self and other. The propensity to talk of self and other at the conceptual level (especially when this is linked to the notion of discrete persons) overlooks the composite nature of both self and other. It also inclines us to discount the idea that selves can be shared or exist in relation. What should be emphasised is that others are never wholly dissimilar. Even on the more restrictive view all others are other selves. Classically friendship tends to this with the paradoxical formula of an-*other* self. Friends are *both* self *and* other. The political must also calibrate this relation. The kind of friendship manifest in, and recognised by, the form of politics often rests somewhere on the scale between the extremes of similarity and dissimilarity. However, insofar as others have selfhood they are both creators of value and valuable, and are thus demanding of our attention. In this respect friendship is important as it recognises that the basis of this attention is found in both similarity and dissimilarity. This is the case as both separate moments of bonding (i.e. similarity or dissimilarity could form the basis of the bond) *and* in bonds existing over time (which tend to harmonise elements of both similarity and dissimilarity).

Taken as a concern with sameness, friendship is a uniting of what is common. This is to say, bonds can be forged between like elements as an aspect of identity. This might be based around common features, common attitudes, or common ground. Here friendship uses likeness to cultivate bonds based on sharing. This may be diverse and heterogeneous (there could be many such points of likeness), and these points could overlap. Persons have many attributes, characteristics, qualities and experiences, and they can connect in many ways. In such a scenario the bonds of friendship unify the political in a nexus or web-like structure. Such a heterogeneous nexus speaks to pluralism (where 'pluralism' is understood to indicate the existence of multiple values rather than competing powers). Taken to its opposite extreme, political form might exhibit a focus on a very narrow set of features. For example, the only friendship that is promoted or recognised politically might be said to be nationality, religious belief, ethnicity, or even allegiance to a location. Such a friendship might be based upon the subscription to certain doctrines or ideals. It might be a subscription to certain practices. In each instance there is a form of bonding based around some value or feature which is perceived to be the same for those thus bonded. Whether this bond is extended or limited, widespread or rare, is a consequence of the distribution of what is considered the same or like. There is nothing to suggest that the adherents to a specific religion, or those of a certain ethnicity, or the subscribers to a doctrine need to be either numerous or sparse. Practically, if sameness is to become the principle form of bonding in the age of the mass then its features probably do need to be widespread which would incline one to generality. Be this as it may, however it is located, however it is distributed, sameness remains *a* basis of identity and bonding. Whether this gives rise to a positive or a negative evaluation depends on the second plane: equality and inequality.

Taken in its opposite direction bonds can also be said to be created by difference. Here the emphasis is on finding what is supplementary and supportive. Recognising that difference can be attractive, complementary, and cooperative and without antagonism and exclusivity is to notice an important basis of human bonding. It is the evaluation of difference (i.e. the construction of equality and inequality) which foretells potential strife. Taken merely as a feature of bonding, difference is to some degree necessitated. Significantly, here others can play an important role as bearers of difference. No person is entirely self-sufficient. The self-sufficient life (where this is taken to be a complete independence from all others and an imperviousness to all difference) is theoretically impossible and humanly undesirable. Such a life would be static. It is far removed from the most fulfilling forms of human life. Such lives involve development and creativity. In these forms difference is required not only to supply the materials for survival, but also to supply what is needed for our emotional, intellectual, religious and moral lives too. Without *some* difference there is no possibility of movement or development. Without difference there is no alternative. Without difference we could not sustain the possibility of contrasting values. Difference, then, attracts and bonds as surely as similarity. In so doing, it speaks both to human dependency and interconnectedness, and to human possibility and freedom.

Difference and similarity are therefore only opposed in the abstract—and there only as a kind of exotic rarity. Considered concretely, human bonding is composed of a mixture of the two. Nothing is ever wholly the same, and nothing is ever wholly other. Indeed, sameness is needed to locate difference, and difference points to what is the same. Sameness and difference provide us with the basis for an observation. This observation locates a foundation, tendency, or *form* of bonding. It is the second plane that provides us with comment on *evaluation*: equality and inequality. Equality and inequality do not mean sameness and difference, they relate to our *responses* to sameness and difference and the effects of those responses. When we say that things are equal we do not simply mean that they are the same. What we have in mind is a comparison of value or significance, and a relationality which follows from this. Equality and inequality are judgements about sameness and difference. They are a way of identifying *what* is to count and *how* it is to count. It is an evaluation which results in a recommendation for *action*.

Friendship tends towards a kind of equality. Perhaps the best friendships are the most equal as it is in equality that the greatest degree of sharing can be realised. Something perfectly shared is something perfectly equal. It is also something that belongs to neither but to both (or, in more complex friendships, all). It should be noted that 'equally shared' doesn't simply mean 'equally shared *out*' but 'equally shared *in*'. Friendship and the political are primarily about sharing *in*, not sharing *out*. This common endeavour and ground between the friends, and the sense that they hold something together to which they are both mutually committed and mutually care for, is a crucial feature of this form of bonding. It leads to joint responsibility. This kind of friendship is something which can grow and diversify. In politics it is the shared values and a shared sense of order that sees the friends committed in this way. This is not imposed from outside (or from above), but cultivated by and between the friends themselves.

As such there is a contrast between the best forms of politics and those which fall short of the challenge to realise human potential. A politics might be based around a form of bonding that links sameness with equality. Here some salient feature acts as the focus for the bond between person and person *and* this feature also serves to mark such persons out as having special purchase on, or consideration in, the political process. As it heads towards the extreme the intensity of such sameness and equality is likely to become a kind of enclosing circle. Within the circle we see those bonded through a link of sameness and treated equally. Outside of this circle we see difference which is here characterised by inequality. Thus we have a politics of inclusion and exclusion. Such a politics is apt to see inequality grow as sameness seeks to regulate and protect itself and its privilege. Such a politics is also apt to see the bonds between those inside and outside such a circle weaken. A weakening of these bonds leads to domination and fragmentation. Ultimately inequality indicates a failure to share (and especially to share *in*). As such, it is antithetical to a conception of the political which views this experience and endeavour as that of the shared world of self and other, order and value.

In contrast, the best forms of politics see the combination of sameness and difference. These forms of politics are structured by diversity and heterogeneity. They are held together by a variety of points of sameness and difference. Paradoxically, it is this nexus of diversity with its multiple ties between person and person, which makes political form stronger and more comprehensive. A form bonded in this way can also accommodate change. These forms of politics tend towards extending equality. The process of politics is characterised by widespread inclusion, participation, and is sensitive to multiple interests and concerns. This does not mean that all persons must enter the political process at the same point and in the same way. What it does mean is that persons have a stake in politics, and seek to achieve their ends in conjunction and collaboration with others. Such a politics recognises the diversity of persons and values, and works to accommodate pluralism. Here difference is not understood to be the end of equality, nor is difference understood as a source of exclusion or antagonism. Friendship itself presupposes a bonding of sameness and difference where a basic equality of worth and commitment is maintained. The best forms of politics see this replicated within their own structures and relations, not as a uniform standard, but in variation in both location and form.

Identity is thus intrinsic to both friendship and the political. It rests (in part) on an observation about bonding based on sameness and difference. However, the consequences of this are revealed to be constructed between persons. Insofar as it is concerned not merely with observation but consequences, and insofar as it is constructed relationally, all identity is focused — however minimally — with the issue of value. Identity is weakest when it is developed as inequality. Inequality closes down the possibilities of alternative values and fails to recognise others are the source of values. Where this occurs the potential of friendship and the political are undermined. Identity is strongest where it is shared. Of course, sharing does not mean that things must be the same. Both friendship and the political presuppose this possibility. Indeed, friendship itself forms a template of a shared identity where sameness and difference are negotiated in a forum of equality. Thus identity is not merely the identification *of*, but an identification *with*. This is the *beginning* of friendship and the political.

[3]

HOLDING

Friendship and the political denote a nexus of holding. Holding is the theorisation of the dynamics of structure. Its thematic is both the overall shape of the links and bonds which form the political, and the processes and dynamics which cultivate and maintain them. Holding is thus a theorisation of the relationship and interactions of persons in location, position, and place. As such it is an aspect of the concern with orders and values. Holding is to be considered analytic, descriptive, and evaluative. Two approaches are possible. Approached in its capacity as *recommendation*, holding is a theorisation of modes of belonging and inclusively understood in terms of sharing, acknowledgement, and respect. This is simultaneously a theorisation of the dynamics of cooperation, support, and help. Here holding is understood as mutuality and combination. Conversely, approached as *disapprobation*, holding is censured as inflexibility, ossification and objectification. Here the dynamics are those of cajolery, threat and force. Mutuality is usurped by pressure and struggle. Thus, whilst the thematic of holding overlaps with that of identity, the primary foci are differentiated. Identity is primarily a theorisation of issues relating to how bonds and structure are formed and with the recognition of value in self and others. Holding is primarily a theorisation of the shape and structure of bonds as a whole, and the dynamics that it reproduces. Nevertheless, they can be constructed to share concerns, and both are an aspect of friendship and the political. Persons are thus related structurally through identity and holding.

As an aspect of friendship and the political, holding connects the analytical with the evaluative. Both friendship and the political suggest structures where persons can find a place. In this way, friendship and the political are to be considered different aspects of the same concern. As indicated, holding suggests potentially divergent evaluations. Holding can be supportive or restrictive, an aid to freedom or its curtailment. Crucially, this hinges on the issue of respect for persons. If the form of politics is to be something more than the most minimal form of order, then more complex and diverse forms of friendship are needed to support and animate its structure. It is in part for this reason that tyranny must be considered a limit of the political. It lacks substantial friendship. Yet such a limit can still be instructive to the norm—albeit as a contrasting negative lesson. For tyranny also represents one extreme of holding. Here holding is seen as restriction, fastening, and control. Through bonds sustained by fear or collusion, holding becomes holding-*in-place* and holding-*down*. In such forms of politics, friendship sees holding become a conduit of power, and holding-in-place becomes an expedient of this desire. Friendship becomes a tool of manipulation and control. As has been suggested, such forms of friendship are ultimately self-defeating. The strongest grip merely squeezes and displaces friendship elsewhere.

Where friendship manifests only as a form of holding-in-place we enter the domain of tyranny; and tyranny is the limiting case. Before tyranny is reached there are a whole variety of other cases and mixed forms. These cases are more complex and harder to analyse and evaluate. A 'closed' community or grouping which restricts its membership, forms an enclave, or possesses and practices a distinct culture and norms (perhaps within a more dominant culture), is a case in point. Such a community might assign specific roles for specific persons. This might be seen in terms of hierarchy (where hierarchy is considered to be a top-down structure of power), but there is nothing to *necessarily* suggest that such as community must be characterised by subordination. Such a community might be the most egalitarian commune or collective. The important factor is that the structure of such a community is in some way to be considered *rigid*. Perhaps such a community might be religious, cultural, militaristic, or bound by some common purpose or code of honour. It should be noted that not all closed communities are permanently closed. It is likely that none exist in total isolation. Indeed, such communities can exist beside and within others. Furthermore, we should not assume that the membership of such communities is static. Membership of such communities could be voluntary, and here closed does not necessarily mean segregated—merely subscription to, or compliance with, the purposes, norms, and rules of the community in question.

How can we evaluate this variety of holding? Much depends on the specifics of the case in question, but in general closed communities are a different case to that of tyranny. Whilst there is a clear sense in which persons must occupy their place, and whilst power will be in operation, such communities are not simply or even primarily concerned with power. Such communities see bonds of holding form as a recognition of the value of others (especially as other selves), and there is authentic concern for them and the community to which they belong. Of course, whilst such concern may be genuine and well-intentioned, how it is perceived and evaluated (both within and from outside such communities) is an open and contentious question. Nevertheless, it is possible to see how such communities could be supportive, formed around bonds of mutual recognition, assistance and aid, and focused on the values implicit in self and others. Here holding is mutual—it is a holding-*onto* and a holding-*with*.

Seen from this perspective, closed community is something other than tyranny or domination. Indeed, it could present an instance of genuine concern for others, and a positive and productive form of holding. Nevertheless, it is also recognised that not all such communities may be so normatively appealing. However, caution is advised. In objecting to *some* instances of such closed communities on the grounds that holding-*with* morphs into holding-*down*, we must be careful not to loosen the bonds too far. In a society where the bonds of holding are allowed or encouraged to become too lax, friendship and the political are undermined in another way. In a society where friendship is weak and fragmented (shallowly assumed and easily shed) we are likely to see persons withdrawing to maintaining only a minimal concern with others. That concern is not likely to be especially deep, nourishing, or sustained; nor is it likely to be especially extensive and encompassing. Such a withdrawing is also indicative of a thinning of the political—value becomes vaporous and then evaporated. In such a scenario persons struggle to find a place; and they struggle to maintain it if they do. The minimal foundations of belonging which underpin attempts to realise our potential are replaced by giddying flux. Alienation and despondency are one response to such a fragmentation. So, too, is flight into the kinds of closed and insular communities which will provide such a sense of holding. In a fragmented society such communities act as fortresses, hostile to outsiders. Thus, freedom and potential are damaged not only by bonds of holding which are too tight and restrictive, but also by bonds which are too weak or insubstantial. In the later scenario we head towards solipsism; solipsism cancels the political.

As previously observed, there is a perspective which considers the political to be understood almost exclusively as being concerned with order. This is often played-out in terms of the individual and power. Even so, it must be conceded that some minimal form of friendship is also required. Just as something is needed to form the bonds between person and person (identity), something too is needed to structure and animate even the most impoverished sense of order. Thus friendship and the political must attend to the issue of holding: how do persons relate and interact with each other in location? Negatively this might be seen as restriction and curtailment. Holding-*down* and holding-*in-place* are thus a signs of an objectionable politics. It is a view which tends to impose identity and gestures towards inequality. A view focused on the individual and power might well be inclined to quickly recognise such a picture. A subscriber to such a view might be torn between accepting this as a necessary state of affairs and trying to find ways to escape it. Holding-down is also objectionable from the current perspective which moves away from a focus on the individual and power and towards a view of a necessarily relational and social self. As such, this view does not accept the holding-down view as inevitable (even though its practice might be widespread). If it *is* inevitable, its inevitability is not total. It is not the only thing which can be practised, and alternatives should be promoted. In contrast, seen positively, holding can be practised as a holding-*onto* and a holding-*with*. Such holding recognises the value of (and values in) others. It is supportive but not restrictive. It strikes a balance between the freedom necessary to move and develop (for which we must have confidence in foundations), and the extremes of ossification and flux. The best forms of politics achieve this by multiplying the bonds between person and person, thus shoring-up the mechanisms of support, cooperation, and concern. In multiplying the sources of holding the best forms of politics lessen dependence on any one source of friendship. Thus persons can feel that they can belong without having to feel that they are possessed. In the best forms of politics such holding-*onto* and holding-*with* is a shared and mutual enterprise that builds and rebuilds a complex structure of relations and possibilities that is shared-*in* by all. Such a picture is the very image and work of friendship.

[4]

POSSIBILITY

Friendship and the political represent a domain of possibility. Possibility gestures towards a politics of hope—although it does not guarantee it. Hope is dependent on the actions of human beings. Here possibility is considered in its capacity as such a normative endeavour. Taken as a feature of a form of politics, possibility is the recognition *within that form of politics* of its own impermanence and mutability. It is also a recognition by that form of politics of its own relativity. In terms of mutability, possibility indicates that alternatives are open to us, and that things may change: things could be different to how they are now. This change might be thought to be positive and desirable (it might be something to *aim* for); it might be seen as negative and to be avoided or prevented (it might be something considered *undesirable*). Possibility also reminds us of the relativity of our practices and institutions. Our own politics is only one of many possible politics. This relativity should not be taken to mean that practices and institutions are thereby equalised, devalued or undermined. It is not a nihilism of anything goes where justification and reason are futile. Instead, possibility draws our attention to the features and purposes of our own form of politics and the bonds that constitute its fabric. It is a locating of value. As such it is also a recognition of the value that may be found in other forms of politics, and that other forms of human bonding may have value too. Thus, here relativity is understood to indicate a form of pluralism. Pluralism recognises contrasting values not all of which can be pursued at once. Thus, it holds open the possibility of alternatives.

In recognising and promoting pluralism, possibility opens the path for the comparison, contrast and critique of our own forms of politics — and that of others. Such a comparison is also a re-evaluation of our values and ways of bonding. However, possibility also suggests that the purpose of such comparison is not to assert superiority or certainty, to but to assess and preserve what is valuable *wherever* it is found. It also suggests a way of approaching both self and other which preserves difference but which also poses questions about the role of difference. Thus, possibility is to be considered both liberating and limiting. Liberating because it leads to an engagement with others and offers a dynamic for change. Limiting because it proposes an approach to others which is characterised by restraint and self-questioning, and because it throws us back to a recognition that our form of politics is only one amongst many.

The best forms of politics embrace the liberation and limitations offered by possibility. In doing so, these forms of politics continuously entertain and make a space for the questions raised by the terrain identified by friendship and the political. In terms of the form of politics, this space recognises that the existing relations can always be re-forged. Values and bonding are a part of this form; but they might take other forms, or change over time. They will almost certainly exist amongst other values and ways of bonding. This is an aspect of an open and plural politics. Taken in terms of friendship and the political, possibility points to something deeper. Here possibility takes us to the question of the *grounding* of friendship and the political. If something concrete, unchanging, or original is intended by 'grounding' — if what is intended is a break with what went before in the sense of a primary foundational moment of establishing — then the role of possibility in friendship and the political is to deny the completeness of a foundation so conceived or sought. What is suggested instead is a different sense of foundation and grounding. Such a grounding is to be considered a kind of starting-point, but a starting-point which is an immanent feature of our condition. It is not a starting-point that happens once and for all time, but is constantly renewed. It is also a starting-point which leaves things open. This starting-point is the factuality of other people, and our connection with them. It is the fact of a shared world. Such a starting-point also recognises that persons and their world are never complete, nor could they be.

Seen in this way, the grounds of friendship and the political generate living structures characterised by creation and recreation. There is a continuous interplay between possible orders, values and bonds. Yet, although such a view opens a vista of freedom, it is also characterised by necessity. For persons cannot simply change their worlds as they wish. Nor can they do so without recognising the very starting-point of friendship and the political: the factuality of others. This grounding acknowledges the irreducibility of persons. It also views persons as being connected not only in terms of material and social interdependency, but also as relational selves. Thus the bonds between person and person remain fundamental to any understanding and construction of the political. Yet necessary though these bonds are, what possibility makes room for is the realisation that there is no fundamental or primary mode of bonding. Possibility points to the openness of this scenario. There is no one model or template for human bonding. Thus, friendship and the political are not static endpoints, but are to be understood as a domain characterised by change and transformation. Such change and transformation is engendered by the bonds formed by person and person as they create and re-create value in a shared world. Friendship and the political are thus a living structure which speaks to the necessity and potential of human beings as relational and social selves.

A politics which remains true to these foundations is a politics of hope. A politics of hope focuses not only on the irreducibility of others, but also on our relational and social condition. A politics of hope is a politics which is concerned with value. In remaining true to the foundations of the political, a politics of hope appears as a paradoxical tension. It is a politics which focuses on the potential of this condition, instead of attempting to close it down. It is also a politics which recognises the limits of this condition rather than aiming at transgression. Such a politics is based on the recognition of the shared world of self and other, and focuses on the possibilities for mutuality that this engenders. Thus, persons are seen as sharing a fate—a fate which involves not only some concern for each other, but also a joint responsibility to improve our shared condition. This sees persons develop a commitment to justice and ethics, and to take increasing responsibility and concern for others. It seeks to distribute power widely, but is sensitive to the link between power and human bonding. It is a politics which is based on affinity, concern, and mutual support. It is also a politics which allows a space for forms of bonding which are not brought directly into the public realm. A politics of hope seeks to build-up and multiply these bonds. In so doing it seeks to hold open the possibility of an alternative and better future, and to provide the connections and concern for others to make this desirable.

There are, of course, limits to the shape of such a politics, yet it is not structurally doctrinal. It admits variety both in the way that it could take shape, and within its various forms. Ultimately the shape of such a politics depends upon the values and bonds which structure it—and the manner in which persons develop and transform these bonds. A politics of hope seeks ways to develop these bonds for the good of all. That good is pursued in the form of politics. Order, value, and human bonding are all interwoven. Friendship and the political are thus two aspects of the same concern. Without order and value there is no bonding—without bonding there is no order and value. Considered as a part of the best form of politics, they are here argued to be generative of an *ethos* and way of pursuing politics. Friendship and the political are best realised as a sharing-*in* rather than a sharing-*out*, and a holding-*with* rather than a holding-*down*. Friendship and the political are not merely projects pursued in common, but the shared endeavours of persons understood as relational and social selves. Such a view rests on the foundation of the possibility of shared values, shared worlds, and shared selves. It recommends a pluralism in the political—a pluralism which rests on diverse and multiple bonds lived and theorised as the concern with the diverse and multifaceted bonds between person and person. Such a concern is a concern with friendship.

Bibliography

Abbey, Ruth. 'Circles, Ladders and Stars: Nietzsche on Friendship', *Critical Review of International Social and Political Philosophy* 2(4), 1999, pp. 50-73.
— — —. *Nietzsche's Middle Period*. Oxford: Oxford University Press, 2000.
Ackermann, Robert John. *Nietzsche: A Frenzied Look*. Amherst: The University of Massachusetts Press, 1990.
Adkins, AWH. 'The Connection between Aristotle's *Ethics* and *Politics*', *Political Theory* 12(1), 1984, pp. 29-49.
Aguilar, Mario I. 'Localized Kin and Globalized Friends: Religious Modernity and the 'Educated Self' in East Africa', in Sandra Bell and Simon Coleman (eds.), *The Anthropology of Friendship*. Oxford and New York: Berg, 1999, pp. 169-184.
Andic, M. 'Is Love of Neighbour Love of and Individual?' in George Pattison and Steven Shakespeare (eds.), *Kierkegaard: The Self in Society*. London: Macmillan, 1998,
Ansell-Pearson, Keith. *An Introduction to Nietzsche as Political Thinker*. Cambridge: Cambridge University Press, 1994.
Appel, Fredrick. *Nietzsche Contra Democracy*. Ithica and London: Cornell University Press, 1999.
Arditi, Benjamin. 'On the Political: Schmitt contra Schmitt', *Telos* 142(Spring), 2008, pp. 7-28.
Aristotle. *The Politics*. Translated by TA Sinclair. Penguin Books: London, 1981.
— — —. *Nicomachean Ethics*. Translated by Terence Irwin. Hackett Publishing: Indianapolis, 1985.
Avramenko, Richard. 'Zarathustra and His Asinine Friends: Nietzsche and Taste as the Groundless Ground of Friendship', in Richard Avramenko and John von Heyking (eds.), *Friendship and Politics: Essays in Political Thought*. Notre Dame, Indiana: University of Notre Dame Press, 2008, pp. 287-314.
Axtmann, Roland. 'Humanity or Enmity? Carl Schmitt on International Politics', *International Politics* 44(5), 2007, pp. 531-551.

Bell, Robert R. *Worlds of Friendship*. London: Sage Publications, 1981.
Bell, Sandra, and Simon Coleman. 'The Anthropology of Friendship: Enduring Themes and Future Possibilities', in Sandra Bell and Simon Coleman (eds.), *The Anthropology of Friendship*. Oxford and New York: Berg, 1999, pp. 1-19.
Bendersky, Joseph W. *Carl Schmitt: Theorist for the Reich*. Princeton, New Jersey: Princeton University Press, 1983.
Berkowitz, Peter. *Nietzsche: The Ethics of an Immoralist*. Cambridge, Massachusetts: Harvard University Press, 1995.
Bickford, Susan. 'Beyond Friendship: Aristotle on Conflict, Deliberation, and Attention', *The Journal of Politics* 58(2), 1996, pp. 398-421.
Blosser, Philip, and Marshell Carl Bradley, (eds.). *Friendship: Philosophic Reflections on a Perennial Concern*. Lantham, New York, and Oxford: University Press of America, 1997.
Blum, Lawrence. *Friendship, Altruism and Morality*. London and New York: Routledge, 1980.
Blundell, Mary Whitlock. *Helping Friends and Harming Enemies: A Study in Sophocles and Greek Ethics*. Cambridge: Cambridge University Press, 1989.
Boas, George. *The History of Ideas: An Introduction*. New York: Charles Scribner's Sons, 1969.
Böckenförde, Ernst-Wolfgang. 'The Concept of the Political: A Key to Understanding Carl Schmitt's Constitutional Theory', *Canadian Journal of Law and Jurisprudence* 10(1), 1997, pp. 5-19.
Booth, David. 'Nietzsche on "The Subject as Multiplicity"', *Man and World* 18(2), 1985, pp. 121-146.
Botwinick, Aryeh. 'Same/Other verses Friend/Enemy: Levinas contra Schmitt', *Telos* 132(Fall), 2005, pp. 46-63.
Boys-Stones, Geroge. 'Eros in Government: Zeno and the Virtuous City', *The Classical Quarterly* 48(1), 1998, pp. 168-174.
Brogan, Walter A. 'The Decentred Self: Nietzsche's Transgression of Metaphysical Subjectivity', *The Southern Journal of Philosophy* 29(4), 1991, pp. 419-430.
Bruckner, Elke, and Karin Knaup. 'Women's and Men's Friendships in Comparative Perspective', *European Sociological Review* 9(3), 1993, pp. 249-266.
Cady, Linell E. 'Alternative Interpretations of Love in Kierkegaard and Royce', *The Journal of Religious Ethics* 10(2), 1982, pp. 238-263.
Caldwell, Peter. 'National Socialism and Constitutional Law: Carl Schmitt, Otto Koellreutter, and the Debate Over the Nature of the Nazi State, 1933-1937', *Cardozo Law Review* 16(December), 1994-1995, pp. 399-427.

Carrier, James G. 'People Who Can Be Friends: Selves and Social Relationships', in Sandra Bell and Simon Coleman (eds.), *The Anthropology of Friendship*. Oxford and New York: Berg, 1999, pp. 21-38.
Cauchi, Francesca. *Zarathustra Contra Zarathustra*. Aldershot: Ashgate, 1998.
Collingwood, R.G. *An Autobiography*. Middlesex, England: Penguin Books, 1939.
Collins, James. *The Mind of Kierkegaard*. Chicago: Henry Regenry Company, 1953.
Conway, Daniel W. *Nietzsche and the Political*. London and New York: Routledge, 1997.
Cook, Ian. 'Theorising Schmitt's Friend-Enemy Through Deleuzian Folding and First-Person Shooters', *Symploke* 17(1/2), 2010, pp. 215-230.
Cooper, John M. 'Aristotle on the Forms of Friendship', *Review of Metaphysics* 30(4), 1977a, pp. 619-648.
― ― ―. 'Friendship and the Good in Aristotle', *The Philosophical Review* 86(3), 1977b, pp. 290-315.
― ― ―. 'Political Animals and Civic Friendship', in Günther Patzig (ed.), *Aristoteles' "Politik"*. Gottingen: Vandenhoeck Ruprecht, 1987, pp. 220-241.
Cristi, Renato. *Carl Schmitt and Authoritarian Liberalism: Strong State, Free Economy*. Cardiff: University of Wales Press, 1998.
Crites, Stephen D. 'The Author and the Authorship: Recent Kierkegaardian Literature', *Journal of the American Academy of Religion* 38(1), 1970, pp. 35-54.
Danto, Arthur C. *Nietzsche as Philosopher*. New York: Columbia University Press, 1980.
Devere, Heather. 'Reviving Greco-Roman Friendship: A Bibliographical Review', in Preston King and Heather Devere eds.), *The Challenge to Friendship in Modernity*. London: Frank Cass, 2000, pp. 149-187.
Devere, Heather, and Graham M. Smith. 'Friendship and Politics', *Political Studies Review* 8(3), 2010, pp. 341-356.
Donnellan, Brendan. 'Friedrich Nietzsche and Paul Rée: Cooperation and Conflict', *Journal of the History of Ideas* 43(4), 1982, pp. 595-612.
Edelstein, Ludwig. 'The Role of Eryximachus in Plato's *Symposium*', *Transactions and Proceedings of the American Philological Association* 76(1), 1945, pp. 85-103.
Elrod, John W. *Kierkegaard and Christendom*. New Jersey: Princeton University Press, 1981.

Ferguson, Harvie. *Melancholy and the Critique of Modernity*. London and New York: Routledge, 1995.
Ferreira, M. Jamie. *Love's Grateful Striving*. Oxford: Oxford University Press, 2001.
Fortenbaugh, WW. 'Aristotle's Analysis of Friendship: Function and Analogy, Resemblance, and Focal Meaning', *Phronesis* 20(1), 1975, pp. 51-62.
Freund, Julien. 'Schmitt's Political Thought', *Telos* 102(Winter), 1995, pp. 11-42.
Friedländer, Paul. *Plato: The Dialogues 2*. Translated by Hans Meyerhoff. London: Routledge and Kegan Paul, 1965.
— — —. *Plato: The Dialogues 3*. Translated by Hans Meyerhoff. London: Routledge and Kegan Paul, 1969.
Frye, Charles E. 'Carl Schmitt's Concept of the Political', *The Journal of Politics* 28(4), 1966, pp. 818-830.
Fuss, Peter, and Henry Shapiro, (eds.). *Nietzsche: A Self-Portrait from His Letters*. Cambridge, Massachusetts: Harvard University Press, 1971.
Garrett, Stephaine. 'Friendship and the Social Order', in Roy Porter and Sylvana Tomaselli (eds.), *The Dialectics of Friendship*. London and New York: Routledge, 1989, pp. 130-142.
George, Peter. 'Something Anti-Social About *Works of Love*', in George Pattison and Steven Shakespeare (eds.), *Kierkegaard: The Self in Society*. Basingstoke: Macmillan Press Ltd., 1998, pp. 70-81.
Gottfried, Paul. *Carl Schmitt: Politics and Theory*. London: Greenwood Press, 1990.
Grube, GMA. *Plato's Thought*. London: Hackett, 1935.
Halévy, Daniel. *The Life of Friedrich Nietzsche*. Translated by J.M. Hone. London: Unwin, 1917.
Hall, Amy Laura. *Kierkegaard and the Treachery of Love*. Cambridge: Cambridge University Press, 2002.
Hannay, Alastair. *Kierkegaard*. London and New York: Routledge, 1982.
Hartshorne, M. Holmes. *Kierkegaard Godly Deceiver*. New York: Columbia University Press, 1990.
Hayman, R. *Nietzsche: A Critical Life*. London: Weidenfeld and Nicolson, 1980.
Higgins, Kathleen M. 'Reading *Zarathustra*', in Robert C. Solomon and Kathleen M Higgins (eds.), *Reading Nietzsche*. Oxford: Oxford University Press, 1988, pp. 132-151.
— — —. *Nietzsche's Zarathustra*. New York: Lexington Books, 2010.
Hirst, Paul. 'Carl Schmitt's Decisionism', *Telos* 72(Summer), 1987, pp. 15-26.

―――. 'Carl Schmitt's Decisionism', in Chantal Mouffe (ed.), *The Challenge of Carl Schmitt*. London: Verso, 1999, pp. 7-17.
Hobbes, Thomas. *Leviathan: Or the Matter, Forme, and Power of A Common-Wealth Ecclesiasticall and Civil*. Middlesex, England: Penguin Books, 1961 [1651].
Hollingdale, RJ. *Nietzsche: The Man and his Philosophy*. London: Routledge and Kegan Paul, 1965.
―――. *Nietzsche*. London and Boston: Routledge and Kegan Paul, 1973.
Hough, Sheridan. *Nietzsche's Noontide Friend: The Self as Metaphoric Double*. Pennsylvania: The Pennsylvania State University Press, 1997.
Hunt, Lester H. *Nietzsche and the Origin of Virtue*. London and New York: Routledge, 1991.
Hutter, Horst. *Politics as Friendship: The Origins of Classical Notions of Politics in the Theory and Practice of Friendship*. Ontario: Wilfrid Laurier University Press, 1978.
Irigaray, Luce. 'Sorcerer Love: A Reading of Plato's *Symposium*, Diotima's Speech', *Hypatia* 3(3), 1989, pp. 32-61.
Irwin, Terence. 'The Good of Political Activity', in Günther Patzig (ed.), *Aristoteles' Politik*. Göttingen: Vandenhoeck & Ruprecht, 1987, pp. 73-98.
Jaeger, Werner. *Paideia: The Ideals of Greek Culture*. Translated by Gilbert Highet. 3 vols. Vol. 2. Oxford: Basil Blackwell, 1957.
Jaspers, Karl. *Nietzsche: An Introduction to the Understanding of His Philosophical Activity*. Translated by Charles F. Walldaff and Frederick J. Schmitz. Baltimore, Maryland: The Johns Hopkins University Press, 1997 [1936].
Kaufmann, Walter. *Nietzsche: Philosopher, Psychologist, Antichrist*. Fourth ed. Princeton: Princeton University Press, 1974.
Keeley, LC. 'Subjectivity and World in *Works of Love*', in George B. Connell and C. Stephen Evans (eds.), *Foundations of Kierkegaard's Vision of Community: Religion, Ethics and Politics in Kierkegaard*. London: Humanities Press International, 1992.
Kennedy, Ellen. '*Hostis* not *Inimicus*: Toward a Theory of the Public in the Work of Carl Schmitt', *Canadian Journal of Law and Jurisprudence* 10(1), 1997, pp. 35-47.
―――. *Constitutional Failure: Carl Schmitt in Weimar*. Durham and London: Duke University Press, 2004.
Kierkegaard, Søren. *Søren Kierkegaard's Journals and Papers*. Translated by Howard V. Hong and Edna H. Hong. Vol. 3. Bloomington and London: Indiana University Press, 1975.
―――. *Two Ages*. Translated by Howard V. Hong and Edna H. Hong. Princeton: Princeton University Press, 1978 [1846].

———. *The Sickness Unto Death*. Translated by Howard V. Hong and Edna H. Hong. New Jersey: Princeton University Press, 1980 [1849].
———. *Either/Or*. Translated by Howard V. Hong and Edna H. Hong. 2 vols. Vol. I. Princeton: Princeton University Press, 1987 [1843].
———. *Either/Or*. Translated by Howard V. Hong and Edna H. Hong. 2 vols. Vol. II. Princeton: Princeton University Press, 1987 [1843].
———. *Upbuilding Discourses in Various Spirits*. Translated by Howard V. Hong and Edna H. Hong. Princeton, New Jersey: Princeton University Press, 1993 [1847].
———. *Works of Love: Some Christian Deliberations in the Form of Discourses*. Translated by Howard V. Hong and Edna H. Hong. Princeton: Princeton University Press, 1995 [1847].
———. *The Point of View*. Translated by Howard V. Hong and Edna H. Hong. New Jersey: Princeton University Press, 1998.
King, Preston. *Thinking Past a Problem: Essays on the History of Ideas*. London: Frank Cass, 2000.
Kirmmse, Bruce H. 'Call Me Ishmael—Call Everybody Ishmael: Kierkegaard on the Coming-of-Age Crisis of Modern Times', in George B. Connell and C. Stephen Evans (eds.), *Foundations of Kierkegaard's Vision of Community: Religion, Ethics and Politics in Kierkegaard*. London: Humanities Press International, 1992.
———. '"But I am Almost Never Understood..." Or, Who Killed Søren Kierkegaard?' in George Pattison and Steven Shakespeare (eds.), *Kierkegaard: The Self in Society*. Great Britain: Macmillan, 1998.
Köhler, Joachim. *Nietzsche and Wagner: A Lesson in Subjugation*. Translated by Ronald Taylor. New Haven and London: Yale University Press, 1998.
———. *Zarathustra's Secret: The Interior Life of Friedrich Nietzsche*. Translated by Ronald Taylor. New Haven and London: Yale University Press, 2002.
Konstan, David. *Friendship in the Classical World*. Cambridge: Cambridge University Press, 1997.
Kraut, Richard. 'Egoism, Love, and Political Office in Plato', *The Philosophical Review* 82(3), 1973, pp. 330-344.
———. *Aristotle: Political Philosophy*. Oxford: Oxford University Press, 2002.
Lackey, Michael. 'Killing God, Liberating the "Subject": Nietzsche and Post-God Freedom', *The Journal of the History of Ideas* 60(4), 1999, pp. 737-754.
Lampert, Laurence. *Nietzsche's Teaching: An Interpretation of Thus Spoke Zarathustra*. New Haven and London: Yale University Press, 1986.

Lee, Seung-Goo. *Kierkegaard on Becoming and Being a Christian*. Meinema: Uitgeverij Meinema-Zoetermeer, 2006.

Lefebvre, Alexandre. 'The Political Given: Decisionism in Schmitt's Concept of the Political', *Telos* 132(Fall), 2005, pp. 83-98.

Lilla, Mark. *The Reckless Mind: Intellectuals in Politics*. New York: New York Review of Books, 2001.

Little, Graham. *Friendship: Being Ourselves with Others*. Melbourne: Scribe Publications, 1993.

Lovejoy, AO *Essays in the History of Ideas*. Baltimore: The Johns Hopkins Press, 1948.

———. 'The Study of the History of Ideas', in Preston King (ed.), *The History of Ideas: An Introduction to Method*. London and Canberra: Croom Helm, 1983 [1936], pp. 179-197.

Lowrie, Walter. *A Short Life of Kierkegaard*. New Jersey: Princeton University Press, 1970.

Lübcke, Poul. 'Kierkegaard and Indirect Communication', *History of European Ideas* 12(1), 1990, pp. 31-40.

Ludwig, Paul W. 'Politics and Eros in Aristophanes' Speech: *Symposium* 191E-192A and the Comedies', *The American Journal of Philology* 117(4), 1996, pp. 537-562.

Magnus, Bernd. 'Nietzsche's Philosophy in 1888: *The Will to Power* and the *Übermensch*', *Journal of the History of Philosophy* 24(1), 1986, pp. 79-98.

Magnus, Bernd, and Kathleen M Higgins. 'Nietzsche's Works and Their Themes', in Bernd Magnus and Kathleen M Higgins (eds.), *The Cambridge Companion to Nietzsche*. Cambridge: Cambridge University Press, 1996, pp. 21-68.

Mara, Gerald M. 'Politics and Action in Plato's *Republic*', *The Western Political Quarterly* 36(4), 1983, pp. 596-618.

Marcuse, Herbert. *Reason and Revolution*. London: Routledge and Kegan Paul, 1941.

McNeill, William. 'The Poverty of the Regent: Nietzsche's Critique of the "Subject"', *Epoché* 8(2), 2004, pp. 285-296.

Middleton, Christopher, (ed.). *Selected Letters of Friedrich Nietzsche*. Indianapolis: Hackett Publishing Company, Inc., 1969.

Miller, Hillis J. 'The Disarticulation of the Self in Nietzsche', *The Monist* 69(2), 1981, pp. 247-261.

Moore, Thomas. 'The Paradox of the Political: Carl Schmitt's Autonomous Account of Politics', *The European Legacy* 15(6), 2010, pp. 721-734.

Moravcsik, Julius. 'Inner Harmony and the Human Ideal in *Republic IV* and *IX*', *The Journal of Ethics* 5(1), 2001, pp. 35-56.

Mouffe, Chantal. 'Carl Schmitt and the Paradox of Liberal Democracy', in Chantal Mouffe (ed.), *The Challenge of Carl Schmitt*. London: Verso, 1999, pp. 38-53.

Mulgan, Richard. 'The Role of Friendship in Aristotle's Political Theory', *Critical Review of International Social and Political Philosophy* 2(4), 1999, pp. 15-32.

Müller, Paul. *Kierkegaard's "Works of Love" Christian Ethics and the Maieutic Ideal*. Translated by C. Stephen Evans and Jan Evans. Denmark: CA Reitzel, 1993.

Neal, Andrew W. *Exceptionalism and the Politics of Counter-Terrorism: Liberty, Security, and the War on Terror*. Abingdon: Routledge, 2010.

Nehamas, Alexander. *Nietzsche: Life as Literature*. Cambridge, Massachusetts: Harvard University Press, 1985.

Neumann, Harry. 'Diotima's Concept of Love', *The American Journal of Philology* 86(1), 1965, pp. 33-59.

Nicoletti, M. 'Politics and Religion in Kierkegaard's Thought: Secularisation and the Martyr', in George B. Connell and C. Stephen Evans (eds.), *Foundations of Kierkegaard's Vision of Community: Religion, Ethics, Politics*. London: Humanities Press, 1992,.

Nietzsche. *Ecce Homo*. Translated by RJ Hollingdale. Penguin: Harmondsworth, 1979 [1888].

Nietzsche, Friedrich. *Thus Spoke Zarathustra: A Book for Everyone and No One*. Translated by RJ Hollingdale. Penguin: Middlesex, England, 1969 [1883-1885].

– – –. *The Gay Science*. Translated by Walter Kaufmann. Vintage: New York, 1974 [1882].

– – –. *Daybreak*. Translated by RJ Hollingdale. Cambridge University Press: Cambridge, 1983 [1881].

– – –. *Beyond Good and Evil: Prelude to a Philosophy of the Future*. Translated by RJ Hollingdale. London: Penguin, 1990 [1886].

– – –. *Twilight of the Idols/ The Anti-Christ*. Translated by RJ Hollingdale. Penguin: Middlesex, England, 1990 [1888].

– – –. *The Birth of Tragedy and Other Writings*. Translated by Ronald Spiers. Cambridge: Cambridge University Press, 1999.

– – –. *Human, All Too Human: A Book for Free Spirits*. Translated by RJ Hollingdale. Cambridge University Press: Cambridge, 1999 [1878-1880].

– – –. *Human, All Too Human: Assorted Opinions and Maxims*. Translated by RJ Hollingdale. Cambridge University Press: Cambridge, 1999 [1878-1880].

–––. *Human, All Too Human: The Wanderer and His Shadow*. Translated by RJ Hollingdale. Cambridge University Press: Cambridge, 1999 [1878-1880].

Outka, Gene. 'Equality and Individuality: Thoughts on Two Themes in Kierkegaard', *The Journal of Religious Ethics* 10(2), 1982, pp. 171-203.

Owen, David. *Nietzsche, Politics and Modernity: A Critique of Liberal Reason*. London: Sage Publications, 1995.

Pahl, Ray. *On Friendship*. Oxford: Polity Press, 2000.

Paine, Robert. 'In Search of Friendship: An Exploratory Analysis in 'Middle-Class' Culture', *Man* 4(4), 1969, pp. 505-524.

–––. 'Friendship: The Hazards of an Ideal Relationship', in Sandra Bell and Simon Coleman (eds.), *The Anthropology of Friendship*. Oxford and New York: Berg, 1999, pp. 39-58.

Pakaluk, Michael, (ed.). *Other Selves: Philosophers on Friendship*. Indianapolis: Hackett, 1991.

Palaver, Wolfgang. 'Schmitt's Critique of Liberalism', *Telos* 102(Winter), 1995, pp. 43-71.

Parekh, Bhikhu. 'An Indian View of Friendship', in Leroy S Rouner (ed.), *The Changing Face of Friendship*. Notre Dame, Indianapolis: University of Notre Dame Press, 1994, pp. 95-114.

Pattison, George. *Kierkegaard: The Aesthetic and the Religious*. London: Macmillan, 1992.

Pattison, George, and Steven Shakespeare, (eds.). *Kierkegaard: The Self in Society*. Great Britain: Macmillan, 1998.

Perkins, Robert L. 'Climacan Politics: Polis and Person in Kierkegaard's *Postscript*', in George Pattison and Steven Shakespeare (eds.), *Kierkegaard: The Self in Society*. Great Britain: Macmillan, 1998, pp. 43-53.

Perkinson, Jim. 'A 'Socio-reading' of the Kierkegaardian Self: Or, the Space of Lowliness in the Time of the Disciple', in George Pattison and Steven Shakespeare (eds.), *Kierkegaard: The Self in Society*. Great Britain: Macmillan, 1998, pp. 156-172.

Petrovic, Predrag. 'Enemy as the Essence of the Political', *Western Balkans Security Observer* 13(April-June), 2009, pp. 3-8.

Piety, MG. 'The Place of the World in Kierkegaard's Ethics', in George Pattison and Steven Shakespeare (eds.), *Kierkegaard: The Self in Society*. Great Britain: Macmillan, 1998, pp. 24-42.

Pitt-Rivers, Julian. 'The Kith and the Kin', in Jack Goody (ed.), *The Character of Kinship*. Cambridge: Cambridge University Press, 1973, pp. 89-106.

Plato. *Phaedrus and Letters VII and VIII*. Translated by Walter Hamilton. London: Penguin Books, 1973.

———. *The Republic*. Translated by HDP Lee and Desmond Lee. London: Penguin Books, 1987.

———. *The Symposium*. Translated by Christopher Gill. London: Penguin Books, 1999.

———. *The Laws*. Translated by Trevor J. Sanders. London: Penguin Books, 2004.

———. *Early Socratic Dialogues*. Translated by Trevor Saunders. London, England: Penguin Books, 2005.

Poole, Roger. 'The Unknown Kierkegaard: Twentieth-Century Receptions', in Alastair Hannay and Gordon D Marino (eds.), *The Cambridge Companion to Kierkegaard*. Cambridge: Cambridge University Press, 1998, pp. 15-47.

Price, AW. *Love and Friendship in Plato and Aristotle*. Oxford: Clarendon Press, 1989.

Pyper, HS. 'Cities of the Dead: The Relation of Person and Polis in Kierkegaard's *Works of Love*', in George Pattison and Steven Shakespeare (eds.), *Kierkegaard: The Self in Society*. London: Macmillan, 1998,

Rasch, William. 'Conflict as a Vocation: Carl Schmitt and the Possibility of Politics', *Theory, Culture and Society* 17(6), 2000, pp. 1-32.

Rezende, Claudia Barcellos. 'Building Affinity through Friendship', in Sandra Bell and Simon Coleman (eds.), *The Anthropology of Friendship*. Oxford and New York: Berg, 1999, pp. 79-97.

Rhodes, James M. 'Platonic *Philia* and Political Order', in John von Heyking and Richard Avramenko (eds.), *Friendship and Politics: Essays in Political Thought*. Notre Dame, Indianapolis: University of Notre Dame Press, 2008, pp. 21-52.

Richardson, Cyril C. 'Love: Greek and Christian', *The Journal of Religion* 23(3), 1943, pp. 173-185.

Rorty, Richard. *Philosophy and the Mirror of Nature*. Princeton, New Jersey: Princeton University Press, 1979.

———. *Philosophy and Social Hope*. London: Penguin Books, 1999.

Rosen, Stanley. *The Mask of Enlightenment: Nietzsche's Zarathustra*. New Haven and London: Yale University Press, 2004.

Rudd, Anthony. *Kierkegaard and the Limits of the Ethical*. Oxford: Clarendon Press, 1993.

Safranski, Rüdiger. *Nietzsche: A Philosophical Biography*. Translated by Shelly Frisch. London: Granta Books, 2003.

Santaniello, Weaver. *Zarathsutra's Last Supper: Nietzsche's Higher Men in Thus Spoke Zarathustra*. Aldershot: Ashgate, 2005.

Santas, Gerasimos. 'Plato's Theory of Eros in the Symposium: Abstract', *Nous* 13(1), 1979, pp. 67-75.

———. *Plato and Freud: Two Theories of Love*. Oxford: Blackwell, 1988.

Saxonhouse, Arlene W. 'Eros and the Female in Greek Political Thought: An Interpretation of Plato's *Symposium*', *Political Theory* 12(1), 1984, pp. 5-27.

Schacht, Richard. *The Arguments of the Philosophers: Nietzsche*. London: Routledge and Kegan Paul, 1983.

– – –. 'Nietzsche's Kind of Philosophy', in Bernd Magnus and Kathleen M Higgins (eds.), *The Cambridge Companion to Nietzsche*. Cambridge: Cambridge University Press, 1996, pp. 151-179.

Schmitt, Carl. *The Crisis of Parliamentary Democracy*. Translated by Ellen Kennedy. Cambridge, Massachusetts, and London, England: The MIT Press, 1988 [1923, 1926].

– – –. *The Concept of the Political*. Translated by George Schwab. Chicago and London: The University of Chicago Press, 1996 [1927, 1932].

– – –. *The Leviathan in the State Theory of Thomas Hobbes: Meaning and Failure of a Political Symbol*. Translated by George Schwab and Erna Hilfstein. London: Greenwood Press, 1996 [1938].

– – –. 'Ethic of State and Pluralistic State', in Chantal Mouffe (ed.), *The Challenge of Carl Schmitt*. London: Verso, 1999 [1930], pp. 195-208.

– – –. *State, Movement, People: The Triadic Structure of the Political Unity*. Translated by Simona Draghici. Corvallis, Oragon: Plutarch Press, 2001 [1933].

– – –. *Constitutional Theory*. Translated by Jeffrey Seitzer. Durham and London: Duke University Press, 2008 [1928].

Schoeman, Ferdinand. 'Aristotle on the Good of Friendship', *Australasian Journal of Philosophy* 63(3), 1985, pp. 269-282.

Schofield, Malcolm. *Saving the City: Philosopher-Kings and Other Classical Paradigms*. London: Routledge, 1999.

Schwab, George. *The Challenge of the Exception: An Introduction to the Political Ideas of Carl Schmitt between 1921 and 1936*. New York: Greenwood Press, 1989.

Seneca. *Ad Lucilium Epiestulae Morals*. Translated by Richard M. Gummere. Vol. 1. Massachusetss: Harvard University Press, 1917.

Seung, T.K. *Plato Rediscovered: Human Value and Social Order*. Maryland, USA: Rowman and Littlefield, 1996.

Simmel, Georg. 'The Web of Group-Affilitations', in Everett C. Hughes (ed.), *Conflict and The Web of Group-Affiliations*. London: The Free Press of Glencoe, 1955 [1922], pp. 125-195.

Singer, Irving. *The Nature of Love: Plato to Luther*. 2 ed. 3 vols. Vol. 1. Chicago and London: The University of Chicago Press, 1984.

Slomp, Gabriella. 'Carl Schmitt on Friendship: Polemics and Diagnostics', *Critical Review of International Social and Political Philosophy* 10(2), 2007, pp. 199-214.

― ― ―. *Carl Schmitt and the Politics of Hostility, Violence and Terror*. Basingstoke, England: Palgrave Macmillan, 2009.

Sluga, Hans. 'The Pluralism of the Political: From Carl Schmitt to Hannah Arendt', *Telos*, 142(Spring), 2008, pp. 91-109.

Small, Robin. *Nietzsche and Rée: A Star Friendship*. Oxford: Clarendon Press, 2005.

Smart, Alan. 'Expressions of Interest: Friendship and *guanxi* in Chinese Societies', in Sandra Bell and Simon Coleman (eds.), *The Anthropology of Friendship*. Oxford and New York: Berg, 1999, pp. 119-136.

Smart, Ninian. 'Friendship and Enmity among Nations', in Leroy S Rouner (ed.), *The Changing Face of Friendship*. Notre Dame, Indiana: University of Notre Dame Press, 1994, pp. 155-168.

Smith, Graham M. 'Kierkegaard From the Point of View of the Political', *History of European Ideas* 31(1), 2005, pp. 35-60.

― ― ―. 'Through A Glass, Darkly: The Vision and Visions of Political Theory', *British Journal of Politics and International Relations* 11(2), 2009, pp. 360-375.

― ― ―. 'Friendship and the World of States', *International Politics* 48(1), 2011, pp. 10-27.

Smith, John E. 'Two Perspectives on Friendship: Aristotle and Nitezsche', in Leroy S Rouner (ed.), *The Changing Face of Friendship*. Notre Dame, Indiana: University of Notre Dame Press, 1994, pp. 57-76.

Smith Pangle, Lorraine. *Aristotle and the Philosophy of Friendship*. Cambridge: Cambridge University Press, 2003.

Stern-Gillet, Suzanne. *Aristotle's Philosophy of Friendship*. New York: State University of New York Press, 1995.

Taylor, Mark C. *Kierkegaard's Pseudonymous Authorship*. Princeton, New Jersey: Princeton University Press, 1975.

Teschke, Benno. 'Decision and Indecisions', *New Left Review* 67(January-February), 2011, pp. 61-95.

Theodore Tracy, SJ. 'Perfect Friendship in Aristotle's *Nicomachean Ethics*', *Illinois Classical Studies* 4, 1979, pp. 65-75.

Thiele, Leslie Paul. *Friedrich Nietzsche and the Politics of the Soul: A Study in Heroic Individualism*. Princeton: Princeton University Press, 1990.

Timmermann, Jens. 'Why We Cannot Want Our Friends to Be Gods. Some Notes on "NE" 1159a5-12', *Phronesis* 40(2), 1995, pp. 209-215.

Tönnies, Ferdinand. *Community and Civil Society [Gemeinschaft und Gesellschaft]*. Translated by Jose Harris and Margaret Hollis. Cambridge: Cambridge University Press, 2001 [1887].

Ulmen, Gary. 'Beyond Schmitt? Reply to Miglio', *Telos* 100(Summer), 1994, pp. 129-133.

– – –. 'Between the Weimar Republic and the Third Reich: Continuity in Carl Schmitt's Thought', *Telos* 119(Spring), 2000, pp. 18-31.

Valk, Francis Vander. 'Political Friendship and the Second Self in Aristotle's *Nicomachean Ethics*', *Innovations: A Journal of Politics* 5, 2004-2005, pp. 49-63.

Van der Zweerde, Evert. 'Friendship and the Political', in Preston King and Graham M Smith (eds.), *Friendship in Politics*. London and New York: Routledge, 2007, pp. 31-50.

van Tongeren, Paul JM. 'Politics, Friendship and Solitude in Nietzsche (Confronting Derrida's Reading of Nietzsche in 'Politics of Friendship')', *South African Journal of Philosophy* 19(3), 2000, pp. 209-222.

Vernon, Mark. *The Philosophy of Friendship*. Basingstoke and New York: Palgrave MacMillan, 2005.

Vlastos, Gregory. 'Justice and Psychic Harmony in the *Republic*', *The Journal of Philosophy* LXVI(16), 1969, pp. 505-521.

– – –. *Platonic Studies*. Princeton: Princeton University Press, 1973.

Walker, Karen. 'Men, Women, and Friendship: What They Say, What They Do', *Gender and Society* 8(2), 1994, pp. 246-265.

Watkin, Julia. *Historical Dictionary of Kierkegaard's Philosophy*. Maryland, Toronto, and Oxford: The Scarecrow Press, Inc., 2001.

Weigandt, Manfred H. 'The Alleged Unaccountability of the Academic: A Biographical Sketch of Carl Schmitt', *Cardozo Law Review* 16(5), 1994-1995, pp. 1569-1598.

Williams, Bernard. *Moral Luck*. Cambridge: Cambridge University Press, 1981.

Wittgenstein, Ludwig. *Philosophical Investigations*. Translated by GEM Anscombe. Oxford: Basil Blackwell, 1953.

Wolin, Richard. 'Carl Schmitt, Political Existentialism, and the Total State', *Theory and Society* 19(4), 1990, pp. 389-416.

– – –. 'Carl Schmitt: The Conservative Revolutionary Habitus and the Aesthetics of Horror', *Political Theory* 20(3), 1992, pp. 424-447.

Wolz, Henry G. 'Philosophy as Drama: An Approach to the Symposium', *Philosophy and Phenomenological Research* 30(3), 1970, pp. 323-353.

Yack, Bernard. 'Community and Conflict in Aristotle's Political Philosophy', *The Review of Politics* 47(1), 1985, pp. 92-112.

— — —. 'Political Friendship and the Second Self in Aristotle's *Nicomachean Ethics*', *Innovations: A Journal of Politics* 5, 2004-2005, pp. 49-63.

Zeitlin, Irving M. *Nietzsche: A Re-Examination*. Oxford: Polity Press, 1994.

Zelechow, Bernard. '*Fear and Trembling* and *Joyful Wisdom* — The Same Book; A Look at Metaphoric Communication', *History of European Ideas* 12(1), 1990, pp. 93-104.

Index

A
Abbey, R 130
action 1, 67, 191
admiration 110-111
aesthetics 199, 201, 206
agape 15
Agathon 26, 27, 31-25; 'doesn't know what he's talking about', 32
agonism 130, 147, 153, 156, 162, 173, 184
Alcibiades 25, 27, 33, 41
altruism 52, 100
amity 15
Arachne 79
aristocracy 68, 130, 144, 181
Aristophanes 27, 28-31
Aristotle vii, 24, 29, 45-75, 94, 100-102, 109, 111, 135, 220; aim of friendship is the loveable, 48; emotions, 73; equality as quantity and quality, 52, 56, 58; fourth species of friendship, 58-59; friendship and equality, 46, 50-60; friendship and justice, 46, 5-60, 56, 60; friendship as activity, 72; friendship more important than justice, 46; friendship of equal worth, 57, 60; friendship, justice and community, 46, 47, 61; friendships of superiority, 57, 59; general and special justice, 53, 56; generic type of friendship, 48, 53; hierarchy, 72; incomplete friendship, 48; justice in distribution, 54-55, 56; loving the virtue of friendship, 72; mixed friendships, 58; pleasure friendship, 48, 49, 50, 53, 57, 72; political friendship, 46, 60-63, 63-71, 73; for advantage, 62, 65, 69-70, 74; not specialised, 60; two forms of, 65; pragmatist, 71; purposes of friendship, 50; systematiser, 71; two-tier understanding of equality, 56; utility friendship, 48, 49, 50, 51, 53, 57, 72; more nuanced than exchange, 69; view of citizenship, 63, 64; virtue friendship, 48, 49, 50, 53, 57, 62, 69, 72, 102, 103, 104, 106, 107. **Works of:** *Eudemian Ethics*, 62; *Nicomachean Ethics*, 45-63, 106, 229; virtual standard, 45; *Politics*, 45, 46-47, 54, 63-71, 73
association 195
Athens 41
authoritarianism 220
authority 190

B
Bacon, F 184

beauty 21, 33, 35, 37
benefactor 59, 142-144
beneficence 51
betrayal 95, 99
Beyreuth 133, 149
Bonn 195
boredom 102
Brandes, G 133
brotherhood 35, 36
Burckhardt, J 131

C
calculation 51-52
children 56
Christ 119, 165, 169
Christendom 79, 88
Christian/ity 83, 86, 97, 108, 112, 113, 122, 133, 182-183, 184; reflection game, 87, 127
Cicero 24, 101, 225; *De Amicitia*, 101, 225
citizen/ship viii, 15, 21, 38, 43, 44, 46, 49, 60, 102; advantage pursued by, 70; equality 66
civil society 7, 8
civil war 207
closed community 235-236; not concerned with power, 235
Cold War 211
commonality 141
communication 159, 179
companionship 116-117, 156-158, 164, 178
concord viii, 15, 60, 63-71, 73, 74; agreement, 66-67; stability, 68
consciousness 91-92, 137
conservative 220
constitution 60, 63-71, 74, 217; agreement on, 66; correct and deviant, 64, 70
Copenhagen 79, 83
correspondence theory 11
Corsair 83

creativity 162, 168-172; replaces discovery, 177
Ctesippus 21

D
death/killing 122, 151, 214
defining 10-13, 14; too broad, 11; and infinite regress, 12; purposes of, 12, 14
Delphic injunction 137
democracy 64, 67, 68, 168, 218
Derrida, J xi
dictatorship 212, 218
difference/sameness 209, 220; defined, 230; only opposed in abstract, 232
Diotima 25-26, 27, 31-35, 42
disgust 175

E
economics 199, 201, 206, 211
education viii, 21, 24, 25, 35, 39, 68
empiricism 134
emotion 100, 106, 110, 126
empathy 208, 223
enemies/enmity 36-37, 122, 129, 130, 139, 162, 166, 167, 177, 179, 180; domestic, 217
Enlightenment 136
envy 81
episteme 28
equality/inequality x, 1, 2, 3, 8, 15, 21, 46-47, 48, 50, 65, 123, 126, 143, 144, 175, 179, 183, 211, 213, 220, 223; as evaluation, 232-233; inclusive, 118; justice in Aristotle, 50-60
equally shared out 232
equally shared in 232
Er 40
eros 15, 19, 21, 25, 31, 41, 42, 43, 94, 132, 145, 168; ethical character, 27-28; as a god, 26, 32; human

Index

desire, 32; social consequences of, 34; wholeness and harmony, 28-31
Eryximachus 27, 28-31
eternal 90, 91, 96, 99
Eternal Recurrence 159
ethical obligations/duties 93-94
ethnicity 192, 208
eudemonia 105-106
Europe 177, 181
exceptionalism 188
exclusivity 94-95, 97, 110

F

family viii, 15, 36, 40, 43, 49, 50, 59, 73, 81, 106, 207, 228
father/parent and son/child 50, 53, 57, 59, 124
fidelity 95, 98, 99, 110, 112, 119
fraternity 15, 43, 131
Freud, S 129
friendship 'best' kind, 135; bonds between person and person, vii, 1, 4, 10; civic, 41; closed politics, 2; commonsense/ordinary view, 4-10, 13-14; contemporary view, vii; coterminous with the political, 225-227; created by difference, 231-232; dependency, x; educative, viii, 20, 35; enmity, 168, 172-174; ethical friendship, ix, 100-108; failed idea, 99; friend-enemy distinction, 189-190, 195-196, 221, 223; generates living structures, 239; Greco-Roman view, 2-3; holding, 234-237; horizontal, vii, 1; idealised form, 99; identity beginning, 234; identity intrinsic to, 233; identity, 229; irreducibility of persons, 239; justice, viii, ix; minimal amount, 229; modernity, ix; moral task/duty, ix, 100-102, 104, 126; mutually other orientated, 108-109; need not undermine politics, 44; numerical limits, 50; one true form, viii, 42, 143, 179; overcoming, 153-156, 180, 185; personal, viii, 1, 9-10, 14; philosophical, x, 40, 81, 96; possibility, 237-240; problems defining, 10-13; public, x; rare and unstable, 98-99; spiritual, ix, 124; standard analysis, 2 standard problems, 6-8; structural, 57-59; template for shared identity, 234; the Good, 20, 35; too lax, 236; uniting what is common, 230-231; utility, viii; variety, viii. **See also:** *political*

G

Gast, P 131, 149
gaya scienza 158
gender xi, 7
German People 216-217, 219
Gersdorff, C 131
ghosts 150-152
God ix, 81, 91, 96, 107, 108, 109, 113, 117, 120, 122, 123, 124, 127, 128; love of, 115; middle term, 114
God-relationship 112
gods 59, 169
Good (Form of) 33, 35, 41, 42
'Good Samaritan' 119
goodwill 49, 51, 67, 69, 72, 111
gratitude 142-144, 146
group 194, 195, 205, 206, 213, 222; self-identity, 210

H

harmony 19-20, 27, 28-31, 35-39, 43, 147
Hartshorne, MH 121
hate 98
heterogeneity 195, 205, 209, 218
Higher Men 160, 161
higher types 178-179, 181
Hippothales 21, 24, 27
Hobbes, T 115, 196, 213, 214-217; Laws of Nature, 214-216; *Leviathan*, 115, 215
holding xi, 234-237
holding-down 235
holding-in-place 235
Homer 36
homogeneity x, 188, 192, 193, 194, 195, 205, 209, 210, 211, 213, 219, 220
Hume, D 115

I

identity xi, 31, 193, 205, 209, 211, 212-213, 218, 222, 229-234, 236; defined, 229; equality and inequality, 232-234; similarity and difference, 229-232
immortality 33, 34, 38
inclination 114
inclusion/exclusion 65, 192, 223
independence 179
individual/ality 3, 42, 125, 126, 130, 144-145, 178, 181-183, 184, 194, 207, 214-217, 220; responsibility, 117; subordinate to group, 217
inside/outside 209, 213, 220
intimacy 94, 111, 130, 140-141, 156, 158, 177,178-179, 181, 185

J

jealousy 110, 111
Jekyll and Hyde 7

John the Baptist 168
justice viii, ix, 1, 2, 3, 8, 32, 33, 36, 44, 46-47, 48, 69, 107, 142, 199, 215; and equality in Aristotle, 50-60; helping friends, 36

K

Kennedy, E 211
Kierkegaard, S ix, 4, 79-128; 'A', 85-86, 102-104; aesthetic, 81, 84, 85, 86, 88, 102, 104, 109; Anti-Climacus, 91; authorship and pseudonyms, 82-89; overall strategy, 82; parallel series, 84-85; pseudonyms non-aesthetic purpose, 86; authorship has Christian purpose, 81, 83, 84, 87; becoming a Christian, 86-88, 89; biography, 82-83; chatter, 79; communication, 80, 87-88, 121; Cordelia, 85; despair, 81, 82, 89-92, 93, 96, 108-112, 117, 118, 121; objective conditions of, 90; three kinds of, 91-92; double-mindedness, 89-92; ethical, 82, 88, 103-104, 107, 109, 125, 127; exclusion, 95; friends cannot secure against change, 96; friendship a failed ideal, 99; friendship as mis-relation, 107; friendship no moral task, 100; friendship not result of choice, 97; human friendship, 93, 114, 127-128; indirect communication, 84; Judge William, 85-86, 102-104, 112; friendship as a fog, 102; Kierkegaard contra, 104-108; life-view, 103; levelling, 79; Neighbour, 112-124; commanded, 113, 114-118; spiritual friendship, 113, 124; underpins other relations, 113;

pseudonyms, 79, 80, 90;
relationship with God, 80, 82,
90; religious, 86, 125; signed
works, 84; single individual, 84;
sociality, 81, 92, 111, 112, 114,
125-126, 127; spiritual equality,
81; test of friendship, 99-100;
Victor Eremita, 85. **Works of:**
'Purity of Heart is to Will One
Thing', 90-92; *Concluding
Unscientific Postscript*, 83;
Either/Or, 85-86, 105; 'Rotation
of the Crops', 103; 'Seducer's
Diary', 85; *Point of View*, 83;
Sickness Unto Death, 91, 92; *Two
Upbuilding Discourses*, 86;
*Upbuilding Discourses in Various
Spirits*, 90; *Works of Love*, 92-124;
as Christian deliberation, 92;
'Our Duty to Love the People
We See', 120-122; 'The Work of
Remembering One Who is
Dead', 114, 122-124
kingship 68
kinship 7, 182
knowledge 132, 135, 149, 146, 148

L

La Boétie 98, 182
Last Man 164, 165
law 70. 212, 215
liberty/liberal/ism 15, 182, 184,
188, 198, 199, 212, 214, 219
Locke, J 196
love ix, 7, 24, 39, 92, 110, 112, 114,
121, 127, 169; Christian, 123;
commandment, ix, 93, 108, 113,
114-118; egoism, 145; fact of,
116; freest, 124; God's, 93, 118;
human need for, 93, 116, 123;
laws, 40; right kind, 30, 30, 42,
117, 170, 180; romantic/erotic,
ix, 81, 94, 96, 98, 103, 110, 113,

117, 123; spontaneous, 98-99;
three causes of, 48-49
Lysis (person) 21, 22, 23, 29, 51

M

Machiavelli, N 228-229
Man of the future 170
marriage 7, 168
Matthew 166, 172
Marx, K 129
masks 140
Menexenos 21-23
merging 168, 174-177
Meysenbug, M 131, 157, 159
mirrors 153, 176
modernity ix, 2, 80, 115, 125, 168,
178, 180-186, 189, 190, 194, 220-
223
monarchy 218
Montaigne, M 98, 182
morality 196, 199, 201, 203, 206
moral task ix
Motley Cow 160, 163, 165

N

nation 188, 194, 195, 211, 217-220,
222; has will and identity, 218-
219
nation-sate ix, x, 190-191, 193, 209,
212, 223
Nazi/sm 208, 219
Neal, AW 189
neighbour ix, 15, 81, 93, 96, 97, 110,
112-124, 162, 170;
commandment, 169
nepotism 1
New Testament 165
Nietzsche, E 158
Nietzsche, F ix, 4, 83, 129-186;
circle friendship, 141, 147, 152-
156, 184; harmonic, 152, 155;
holds elements together, 152;
new aspects, 153; reordering of

the same, 154; cold on friendship, 182; 'crassly misunderstood', 158; dialogue with Greek culture, 134-135; divided self, 135-138; dynamite, 129; eclipse of friendship, 162; final years, 131, 177-180; former friends, 148, 150-152; free spirits, 129, 131, 178, 179, 181; friendship as ability, 146-156; friendship as danger, 140-145; friendship and enmity, 168, 172-174; friendship as shared striving, 145; friendship as thing given, 141-145; friendship and power, 144-145; future friends, 130, 185; genuine/true friendship, 143, 179; hermit, 157; initial entertainment of friendship, 129; ladder friendship, 141, 147-152, 153, 153-156, 162, 184; agonistic, 152; breaks, 150; unstable, 154; middle period, 130-134, 182; not monolithic, 129; overcoming friends, 153-156, 180, 185; perspectivism, 135-138, 141; technique, 136; not relativism, 137; internal and external, 137, 138; and self, 123; 'revalution of all values', 177; self-discovery, 138-141; sovereign solitude, 130; 'star friendship', 151; task as philosopher, 132; Wagner mania, 133. **Works of:** *Assorted Opinions and Maxims*, 150, 155; *Beyond Good and Evil*, 129, 177-180; *Daybreak*, 134; *Ecce Homo*, 134; *Human, All Too Human*, 129, 132, 134, 135, 136, 139, 141, 142, 144, 145, 147, 154, 155, 161, 162; *The Gay Science*, 135, 144, 145, 148, 150, 151, 161; *The Genealogy of Morality*, 140; *Thus Spoke Zarathustra*, x, 129, 130, 132, 135, 136, 155, 159-177, 178, 180, 182, 183; camp-bed, 173; creative eruption, 156; least representative, 159; 'many-too-many', 167, 175; 'Of Love of One's Neighbour', 169; 'Of Marriage and Children', 168; 'Of the Bestowing Virtue', 165-166; 'Of the Flies in the Market Place', 167; 'Of the Friend', 162, 167, 173, 176; 'Of the New Idol', 167; 'Of War and Warriors', 167, 173; 'On Chastity', 168; *Twilight of the Idols*, 180

O

oligarchy 64, 68
order vii, 1, 228, 235, 236
Overbeck, F 131, 158

P

parliamentarianism 198, 212, 218
Parsifal 134
partiality 93-96, 107, 108, 120
particularity 93-96, 107, 125
passion 39, 81, 97-100, 104, 120, 123, 125; intoxicating, 98
Pausanias 27-28
peace 209
people/s 193, 194, 196-198, 199, 210, 211, 212, 213, 214-220
perspective 13, 135-138, 141, 153, 183
Phaedrus 26, 27-28, 32
philia 15, 19, 43, 49, 94
phronesis 28
Piety, MG 120
pity 168, 174-177
Plato viii, 19-44, 45, 72, 100-102, 124, 125, 134, 145; beauty, 21;

education, 20, 21, 24, 25, 39; friendship and the harmonious polis, 19-21; the Good, 20, 21, 24; good men, 24. **Works of:** *Lysis* 20, 21-25, 27, 29, 34, 35, 39, 97, 229; central question of, 22; dialogue, 23; friendship impossible, 23: *Republic* 19, 21, 24, 29, 33, 34, 35-41, 43, 102; not a blueprint, 41; fulfilment of concern with friendship, 37; Guardians, 39-41, 43, 102; enquiry into justice, 36: *Symposium* 20, 21, 24, 25-35, 36, 37, 39, 41, 101, 131, 145; authority, 25-26; drama, 25; speeches of, 27-35. **See also**: *Socrates*

pleonexia 54

plural/ism xi, 43, 74-75, 125, 198, 219, 221

Plutarch 24, 101

Polemarchus 36

polis 3, 47, 48, 50, 60-71, 74; aims to secure good life, 61

political best forms, 225, 232-233, 237; coterminous with friendship, xi, 15; defined, vii; dependent on friendship, 225; embrace liberation and limitation, 238; extend equality, 233; form, 225; generate living structures, 239; has own language, 10; holding, 234-237; hope, 237-240; identify intrinsic to, 233; identity beginning, 234; identity, 229; impermanence, 237; instance, 225; irreducibility of persons, 239; locating of value, 238; more than power and individual, 226; multiply bonds, 237; not solitary pursuit, 226; ontology, 225; order and value, 227; others must be encountered, 226; others starting point, 227; possibility, 237-240; sameness and difference, 233; shared world, 227 solipsism, 226, 236; sustain plurality, 226; tyranny limit of, 227-229. **See also:** *friendship*

political science 47

polity 68

Poole, R 84

possibility xi

power 2; as possession, 227

preference 81, 93-96, 97, 104, 107, 110, 115, 120, 126

pre-modern 2, 125

public 207

public-private divide 2

pyrrhic victory 140

Pythagoras 24, 29

R

Reason/rationality 104-105, 106-107, 112, 125, 208, 225, 199, 212

recognition 121

Rée, P 131, 132, 157-158, 161

re/production 25, 33-34, 43, 168

reciprocity ix, 1, 5, 6, 23, 46, 49, 50-52, 58, 67, 69, 81, 95, 108-112, 115, 119, 123, 126, 142, 170

religious 200, 206, 211

resentment 143, 171, 175

revenge 143

revolution 207

Rohde, E 131, 157

Rousseau, J-J 115, 196

S

Salomé, L 131-132, 157-158, 161

Schmitt, C ix, 4, 187-223; as siren, 223; attraction of, 220-221; 'authoritarian landscape', 188; authoritarian Right, 188;

decisionism/vitalism, 205-209, 211; softened, 206-207, 208, 223; 'draws reader onto his terrain', 188; essence of the political, 196; existential threats, 192; fascism, 188; friend not merely opposite of enemy, 193; friend-enemy distinction, 189-190, 195-196, 221, 223; functional, 190, 191-192; 'human endeavour', 196, 199-200, 203; identified existentially, 204; intensity, 203-210, 211, 218-222; problem, 201-203; structuring device, 192; subject to change, 204, 206; tool of polemicisation, 209; friendship public, 221; imposes order, 202; killing, 195, 205, 209, 210, 222; nationalist, 188; negative example, 221-223; not a friend of friendship, 223; political autonomous, 196; political determines action, 203; political guises, 187; political has no subject, 203; prejudice for dichotomy, 199; question-begging, 199; reception, 187n; reconnects friendship and political, 221; rejects normativism, 205; role of friendship, 194; similarity with Hobbes, 215; state-centric, 188; 'symptomatic figure', 189; Us and Them, 222; 'ways of life', 192, 208, 211-212, 218. **Works of:** *Concept of the Political*, 189, 190, 193, 195-210, 217, 220; a polemic, 209; *Constitutional Theory*, 193, 194, 208, 210-220; *Crisis of Parliamentary Democracy*, 212; *State, Movement, People*, 208, 219; *Theory of the Partisan*, 194, 211

self becoming, 89-90; before God, 93, 116, 119; cancellation, 185; confidence, 171; constituted by action, 147; deception, 138; development, 151, 148; discipline, 173; discovery, x, 130, 138-141, 153, 156, 150, 178, 181, 184-185; disharmony, 168; forging/shaping, 130, 178, 181, 184; knowledge 135, 138, 140, 151, 154, 155; a struggle, 139; love 115-118, 120, 123, 125, 170; transformed, 116; merging, 153, 155-156; mis-relation, 89, 92; nature of, 137-138, 140, 141, 183; observation, 139, 155; overcoming, x, 162, 164, 167, 171, 172, 173, 176, 177; preservation, 195; realisation, 130; relational, 96, 120; sacrifice, 115, 228; selfishness, ix, 81, 93, 96, 98, 108-112, 123, 126; degrees of, 122; selfless, 100, 169; serving, 169; shared, 141, 183-184, 230; sufficiency, 178, 180; task of 87, 89, 126; understanding, 130
Seneca 24, 101
sexuality 7-8
Seydlitz, R 149, 157
shared-ideal 150
Simonides 36
Slomp, G 194
Smith, A 115
Socrates 19, 20, 21, 27, 45, 50, 97, 124, 132, 134, 137, 145, 170, 184; and Agathon, 31-35; questions Agathon, 32; and Diotima, 26; feigns defeat, 23; view of justice, 36-37; as lover, 34; as midwife, 25, 27; and myth, 39-41; pedagogical role of, 22. **See also:** *Plato*

solidarity 15, 43, 207
solitude 129, 156-158, 162, 168, 169, 174-177, 179, 182
Sophocles 145
soul 38, 43, 44, 137-138
sovereign/ty 188, 195, 209, 223
spiritual 112; equality, 114, 118-120, 123, 124, 127; freedom, 90, 108, 120; imperative/task, 114, 116; selfhood, 90, 91, 108, 121, 128
state 188, 196-198, 207, 208, 211; entity of the people 197; intensified, 199
statism 192, 209, 220
stranger 206, 209

T
talent (innate) 147
telos 3, 105, 107
territorial unit 197
territory 208
thing-in-itself 138
Third Reich 220
Thrasymachus 36, 41
totalitarianism 228
trust 69, 126, 156, 227
truth 8, 179
tyranny xi, 227-229, 236; most devoid of friendship, 227; least political, 227

U
Übermensch/Superman 130, 159, 162, 164, 168-172, 174, 176, 178, 184; friendship foretaste of, 169-172; goal of existing humans, 169, 171
unfaithfulness 139

unity x, 191, 192, 193, 210, 214, 217, 218, 220
unselfish 122-123
'upbuilding' 114, 116

V
value vii, xi, 1, 15, 181, 183

W
Wagner, R 132-134, 148, 150, 152, 158; Nietzsche exploited by, 132; nationalism, 133; confidence shared, 133; break with, 148-149
war 209, 219; gives meaning, 210
Watkin, J 89
Weimar 196, 198, 215
well-wishing 111
will 126, 193, 212; act of sovereignty, 216
wisdom 32, 163, 166
Wittgenstein, L 12, 14
World War Two 188, 190

Z
Zarathustra (person) x, 159-177; conception of community, 165; disciples, 163, 165-166, 167, 169; discourses, 166-177; friendship with animals, 163-164; happiness, 173; identified with Nietzsche, 161; mission failure, 160; quest to find audience/companions, 160, 162-166; rejects Higher Men, 161, 178; teacher of friendship, 162; tension in account of friendship, 176; tight-rope walker, 163, 164-165, 168
Zeus 30, 31